National Thought in Europe

National Thought in Europe

A Cultural History

Joep Leerssen

AMSTERDAM UNIVERSITY PRESS

Cover design Joseph Plateau, Amsterdam
Cover illustration *Panel of the Peoples* (*Völkertafel* c. 1730-1740), Austrian Ethnographic
Museum, Vienna
Layout JAPES, Amsterdam

ISBN   978 90 5356 956 6
NUR   694

— Persecution, says he, all the history of the world is full of it. Perpetuating national hatred among nations.

—But do you know what a nation is? says John Wyse.

— Yes, says Bloom.

— What is it? says John Wyse.

— A nation? says Bloom. A nation is the same people living in the same place.

— By God, then, says Ned, laughing, if that's so I'm a nation for I'm living in the same place for the past five years.

— Or also living in different places.

— That covers my case, says Joe.

James Joyce, *Ulysses*

Contents

Appendices

List of Illustrations

Note: in some cases, illustrations have been reproduced from banknotes so as to demonstrate their wide currency as part of a state-endorsed iconography.

Preface

This book is the revised and expanded English version of the Dutch-language *Nationaal denken in Europa: een cultuurhistorische schets* (Amsterdam University Press, 1999).
When it was decided to make that book available in English for a wider international
readership, I took the opportunity to expand what was originally a survey handbook
for students into an intervention in nationalism studies generally; an intervention
which I thought was timely (despite the great amount of excellent work being done in
that field, and the large number of existing publications) because I felt there was room
for a view that was culturally oriented without reifying the notion of 'culture' into
something static or primordial, and that was historically oriented without subordinat-
ing the cultural dimension of nationalism to its political one.

Portions of this book draw on previously published books and articles, referred to
under my name in the bibliography. Some issues addressed here for the early nineteenth century are more extensively thematized in an ongoing project on the role of
philologists and 'men of learning' in romantic and cultural nationalism; for that particular project, and its publications to date, I refer the reader to the website www.hum.
uva.nl/philology.

When I have provided my own translations/paraphrases from non-English source material (rather than quoting published translations), the original is given with the source
reference. Source references are given in the endnotes; the footnotes provide *obiter
dicta* and information on side issues and background.

The form that this book has taken owes much to the European Studies programme at
the Universiteit van Amsterdam, with its focus on the interaction between ideas and
events, culture and politics, and European cross-border exchanges. I wish to thank my
colleagues there, in particular the team with whom I teach the survey course on the
cultural formation of Europe.

On going over this book I realized, even more than when I was first writing it, how
deeply indebted my approach is to Hugo Dyserinck and his erstwhile Comparative
Literature programme at Aachen University, where I studied in the 1970s. The fundamental tenets of this book (the contingent nature of state formation, the need to
demythologize the discourse of national identity, the idea that nationalism is the political instrumentalization of ethnotypes, the link between romanticism and nationalism) all reflect the outlook of the Aachen comparatist school.

As always, I am deeply and happily indebted to the support and companionship (intellectual, moral and domestic) of Ann Rigney.

I dedicate this book to my mother, who remembers the war, and to my children.

Introduction

The aim of this book is to give a cultural history of national thought in Europe. What does that mean, and how does this hope to add anything new?

There is an overwhelming body of research on nationalism, much of which focuses primarily on social and political developments. Nationalism is, after all, a political ideology – one of the dominant ones of the last two centuries. The rise of nationalism is usually analysed as a factor in the development of states, or in the development of national consciousness and national cohesion as part of a society's development towards modernity. After initial work by intellectual historians such as Isaiah Berlin and Hans Kohn, the study of nationalism was given a more political and social orientation in the 1960s and 1970s, and received a huge upsurge following the work of Ernest Gellner, Eric Hobsbawm, Benedict Anderson and A.D. Smith in the 1980s. Most of these studies attempted, on the basis of various sample cases, to arrive at a model of nationalism as an ideology. For Gellner, nationalism was a side effect of modernization with its shifting patterns of education and economic scale enlargement, driven largely by intellectuals; in this 'modernist' view, a sense of national identity was fabricated by nineteenth-century nationalists. Hobsbawm, while also taking a modernist view, advocated a more 'bottom up' societal model, claiming that nationalism was an ideology born of the people rather than imposed by intellectuals; Anderson stressed the developing role of media and the growth of communication as a crucial factor. There were also anti-modernist voices, which insisted that national identity has been a long-standing ideological presence in Europe since long before the nineteenth century. A very prominent role in this debate was played by A.D. Smith, who sought to steer a middle course, opposing Gellner's modernism by tracing the pre-nineteenth century ethnic origins of nations, while at the same time arguing that these ethnic identities were largely subjective and underwent an ideological transformation and modern instrumentalization in the nineteenth century.[1]

These debates have brought to the foreground two main questions: How 'modern' or recent is nationalism as a historical phenomenon? Did the 'nation' (as a cultural and social community that people identify with and feel political loyalty towards) only emerge as a meaningful concept in the nineteenth century, along with the ideology that named itself after it, or does it, contrariwise, have a more long-standing presence in human affairs?* And so nationalism is usually studied as something that emanates either from modernization processes or else from a social category called 'nation' or 'ethnicity'.

---

* There have been other debates over the typology and various sub-types of nationalism, e.g. the distinction between the expansionist nationalism of established states and the emancipatory nationalism of minorities, between an 'Eastern European' and a 'Western European' variant, or between 'civic' and 'ethnic' nationalism; cf. below, p. 169-170.

In this book, I would like to take a different approach, and trace nationalism as something that emanates from the way people view and describe the world – in other words, as a cultural phenomenon, taking shape in the constant back-and-forth between material and political developments on the one hand, and intellectual and poetical reflection and articulation on the other. That way of viewing the world is itself an active part of historical processes, subject to changing conditions and with a dynamics and development of its own. Hence the subtitle of this book: a cultural history.

~

In order to explain what this cultural-historical approach stands for (and also in order to explain the terminology of this book itself), it will be useful to clarify, briefly, what is meant here by concepts like 'nationalism', 'nation' and 'ethnicity'.

People have used concepts like 'nations' and 'nationalism' in very contradictory and confused ways; that is one of the reasons why nationalism as an ideology has been so successful and so dangerous. The idea of nationalism slides without obvious change from mild virtues like 'loving one's country' and 'being a good citizen' to militant intolerance and genocide. In general parlance, the word 'nationalism' can be loosely used to denote a whole set of meanings, as listed by the Oxford English Dictionary: 'Devotion to one's nation; national aspiration; a policy of national independence'. Since we must gain a sharp focus on what is unavoidably a fuzzy topic, it is all the more necessary that in our analysis we keep our critical concepts and our own terminology as unambiguous as possible. 'Nationalism' is not just a sense of national identity, or an assertion of ethnic separateness, or a chauvinistic proclamation of one's superiority over one's neighbours. In this book, the word *nationalism* is used in a much more specific and restrictive meaning: as that political ideology which is based on the combination of the three assumptions:

a. that the 'nation' is the most natural, organic collective aggregate of humans, and the most natural and organic subdivision of humanity; and that, as such, the nation's claim to loyalty overrides all other allegiances;

b. that the state derives its mandate and sovereignty from its incorporation of a constituent nation, so that civic loyalty to the state is a natural extension of 'national' (cultural, linguistic, ethnic) solidarity;

c. that territorially and socio-politically, the most natural and organic division of humankind into states runs along 'national' (cultural, linguistic, ethnic) lines, so that ideally there is a seamless overlap between the outlines of the state and of its constituent nation.

In this definition, I follow the common ground established by the main authorities. Whatever their mutual differences, there is broad agreement between the likes of Hans Kohn, Elie Kedourie, Ernest Gellner, Anthony Smith and John Breuilly as to the defining characteristics of nationalism. Kohn (1946, 9) defines nationalism as 'a state of mind, in which the supreme loyalty of the individual is felt to be due the nation-state'. Kedourie defines nationalism as:

A doctrine invented in Europe at the beginning of the nineteenth century. It pretends to supply a criterion for the deter-
mination of the unit of population proper to enjoy a government exclusively its own, for the legitimate exercise of power
in the state, and for the right organization of states. Briefly,
the doctrine holds that humanity is naturally divided into
nations, that nations are known by certain characteristics
which can be ascertained, and that the only legitimate type of
government is national self-government (1960, 9).

Gellner (1983, 1) succinctly defines nationalism as 'primarily a political principle,
which holds that the political and the national unit should be congruent'. Anthony
Smith's definition is 'an ideological movement for attaining and maintaining autonomy, unity and identity on behalf of a population deemed by some of its members to
constitute an actual or potential nation' (Smith 1998, 187). Breuilly identifies nationalism as:

A political doctrine built upon three basic assertions: 1. There
exists a nation with an explicit and peculiar character. 2. The
interests and values of this nation take priority over all other
interests and values. 3. The nation must be as independent as
possible. This usually requires at least the attainment of political sovereignty (1993, 2).

This strict definition of nationalism used in this book explains why our historical
analysis 'zooms in' on the nineteenth century, from the French Revolution to the First
World War. It is in the nineteenth century that nationalism emerges as such, as a
specific and recognizable ideology with a specific and recognizable political and cultural agenda.

If, in the title of this book, I speak not of nationalism but of 'national thought', it is
because I want to include the wider pre-nineteenth-century source traditions and ramifications of the nationalist ideology, without confusing the source traditions with
the thing itself. 'National thought' is wider and less specific than 'nationalism'. Following the common sense of the definitions of nationalism cited above, by *national
thought* I mean a way of seeing human society primarily as consisting of discrete, different nations, each with an obvious right to exist and to command loyalty, each characterized and set apart unambiguously by its own separate identity and culture.

The ideology called nationalism did not emerge suddenly out of nowhere, but is the
nineteenth-century result of a long run-up. This is the reason that there is so much
debate about the modern or pre-modern origin of nationalism. For at the core and at
the root of the recent word 'nationalism' is the much older word 'nation'.

What is a nation? The concept is itself notoriously vague and contradictory; its
semantic shifts will receive ample attention in this book. For the purpose of providing
a starting point it is useful, rather than attempting an analytically watertight definition, to recall the general consensus that has been operative in people's minds over the

past century. In all its vagueness, this popular meaning is clearly set forth in the Oxford English Dictionary: 'An extensive aggregate of persons, so closely associated with each other by common descent, language or history, as to form a distinct race or people, usually organized as a separate political state and occupying a definite territory.' Readers will realize that the concept of 'nation' in these terms hovers between three poles: one is that of a *society* (people living together, communicating, and sharing the same socioeconomic and political conditions); another is that of *culture* (people sharing the same language, social habits and historical memories); the third is that of *race* (people sharing the same descent and having passed on a shared culture through a filiation of generations). Over time, we see that the concept of a nation can be used with emphasis either on the social, the cultural or the racial aspect; usage is particularly slippery from case to case.

That same slippage also applies to the related word 'people', which sometimes refers to a social layer ('power to the people') and sometimes to nations ('the self-determination of peoples'). The confusion is made worse by the fact that the adjective 'national' is often used to refer to *states*. (The debt that a state incurs is called 'the national debt'; the government that rules a state is called 'the national government'; a state's capital is called 'the national capital', a sports championship that covers the entire state is called 'a national championship'.) Indeed in terms like 'The United Nations' the words 'nation' and 'state' can be used interchangeably (although the former refers to a group of people, and the latter to a sovereign fiscal-legal-political institution with a territory). That interchangeability is also hinted at in the concept of the 'nation-state', by which we refer to a state as representing and incorporating a nation (or rather, as claiming to do so; cf. Roobol 1998).

The conclusion is unavoidable: the 'nation', that thing which is at the core and at the basis of the ideology of nationalism, is a slippery and elusive concept. This is one of the reasons why nationalism has taken on so many appearances and sub-types (civic, ethnic, modern, primordial, etc.).

In order to introduce a less threadbare and more focused term, the neologism of the *ethnie* has arisen as an alternative to 'nation'. Derived from the Greek *ethnos*, an *ethnie* is defined in modern scholarship as a group bonded intersubjectively by a chosen common self-identification, involving a common sense of culture and historical continuity (Poutignat & Streiff-Fenart 1999, Eriksen 2002). This notion of ethnicity emphasizes that what matters in group identity is not any objective presence of real physical or cultural similarities or differences, but rather a group's acknowledgement of perceived similarities or differences, and the willingness to consider these meaningful. *Ethnicity* here means nothing more or less than the collective acceptance of a shared self-image (cf. Dyserinck's suggestion, 2002, to speak of *ethno-imagology*). The French term was intended, then, to be as neutrally descriptive as possible, registering only ad-hoc identities arising from social attributions of meaning to cultural differences, and free from all preconceived notions as to which human aggregates were more 'natural' or 'organic' than others; and, as such, it was originally introduced into nationalism studies by A.D. Smith. Nonetheless, it must be pointed out that the terminology has become contaminated and that the word is now as contradictory and problematic as all the others. In English and other languages, terms like 'ethnic' and 'ethnicity' are widespread in a wholly different sense, quite different from the technical one. Ethnicity is by now a euphemism for 'race' (witness phrases like 'ethnic studies', 'ethnocentrism' and 'ethnic cleansing'), and 'ethnic nationalism' is usually understood to refer to that nationalism which sees the nation as a biological community sharing a common bloodline and descent.

In this book I want to clear the deck by taking as my starting point a return to the technical meaning of the *ethnie*, not as a biological race or bloodline but as a subjective community established by shared culture and historical memories; to this I add that such a subjective community is not in the first instance merely a sense of 'belonging together' as that it involves a sense of being *distinct from others*. In other words, a perceived collective identity, or a shared self-image, presupposes a perceived separation from others, a process of exclusion (Räthzel 1997). A community constitutes itself by distinguishing itself from the world at large, in the process also excluding from its constituent membership all those that do not belong to it. We order the world primarily by subdividing it, and the sense of collective togetherness involves unavoidably a sense of collective separateness.

This process of self-silhouetting against an Outside is in the deepest, dual sense of the word an *articulation* – meaning a realization that the world is not homogenous but 'hinged' between different parts, as well as a naming of that difference.

A collective sense of identity derives, then, not from a group's pre-existing cohesion, but from the perception and articulation of external differences. How this perception and articulation of differences results in a sense of identities has been identified by specialists in Comparative Literature and cultural studies as the interplay between Otherness and self-image.[2] It is in this sense that I want to trace the development of national thought and nationalism: as the articulation and instrumentalization of collective self-images, derived from an opposition against different, other nations.

Thus, whereas Smith sought the root system of nationalism in 'the ethnic origins of nations', I propose to locate it in a tradition of *ethnotypes* – commonplaces and stereotypes of how we identify, view and characterize others as opposed to ourselves. In tracing the development of national thought and nationalism, it is important to follow, alongside the socio-political 'nation-building' developments that take place in and between societies, also the discursive patterns of self-identification, exoticization and characterization that take place in the field of culture. It is on this basis that this book claims to be a cultural history of national thought and nationalism in Europe; and on this basis I hope to complement the existing, primarily politically-oriented body of research, by an approach that thematizes the constant interweaving of intellectual and discursive developments with social and political ones.

～

If groups such as nations are constituted not only by material realities but also by cultural patterns and choices of self-identification, then it follows that they are variable and changing. That, indeed, is what European history shows us. Small groups can vehemently distinguish themselves from each other, and oppose each other, yet at another moment they can coalesce into a shared whole. What at one moment is a category identifying itself as Yugoslav has coalesced from, and can fission back into, constituent groups: Croats, Serbs, Montenegrins, or older, now-forgotten categories such as Dalmatians or Morlacks (cf. Wachtel 1998, Kohn 1960, Wolff 1994 and 2001). At a single moment in history, different national aggregates can compete with each other: between 1850 and 1900, inhabitants of the Netherlands had the options of identifying themselves as narrowly 'Dutch' pure and simple; joining with Flemings in a Greater Netherlandic identity; or else joining with Germans in a Greater-Germanic whole, or even as part of a specific Greater Low German area between Dunkirk and Königsberg/Kaliningrad (Leerssen 2006a). The history of European nationalities may be described as the competition between different models of national aggregation. The result of that competition is often determined by hard, socio-economic and political power; but the terms in which the various competing models and scenarios are conceived emanates from the sphere of cultural reflection.

To a large extent, the outcome of that process, the state-system as we see it in Europe in the twentieth century, is a historical contingency. Alternatives to it were thinkable, and were circulating. In tracing the cultural history of these ideals and models, I hope to stress the contradictory, indeterminate, open-ended nature of how people envisaged their identity and their national aspirations. The history of nationalism is far more complex than merely a pre-history of the contemporary states.

Yet that ('a prehistory of contemporary states') is often how nationalism studies are conducted. In many cases, the modern state, as it emerged from history, is taken as a starting point and retrospectively it is traced how this state came about. But the historical landscape is far more complex than the trajectory we can see in the rearview mirror of modern state formation; in order to understand nationalism, we need to take into account the roads not taken, the ideals that were not realized (cf. Koselleck 1979).

~

There are many outstanding histories of aspects of national movements in the various European countries; I have made grateful use of them in preparing this book.[3] Even so, if we study national movements on a single-country basis, the study of national thought and nationalism will collapse into the history of a single country. In order to understand nationalism and national thought in their own right, and not just as factors playing into a country's history, we must work comparatively and study various countries and cases.

There are, to be sure, many studies of wider European trends and/or macro-regions, usually taking the form of collections. While the aim is to bring out transnational patterns in the history of nation- and state-formation, and the volumes in question usually have good synoptic introductions, they often consist of separate essays addressing separate countries. The individual essays, again, are usually illuminating and informative,[4] applying a shared perspective on the national movement in question. But it often remains unclear what connections there were between these cases. The overlaps, exchanges, influences, parallels or antagonisms often fall between the cracks. Juxtaposing national case-studies is not the same as transnational comparison. However, an inspiring example of how such European juxtapositions can yield important comparative insights is provided by the work of Miroslav Hroch (1968, 1986, 1996, – and see below, p. 164-165).

Many nationalism studies will aim for a broad data-sample by collating cases from historically unrelated areas, e.g. in Europe, Africa and South Asia. However, nationalism in its European development and profile cannot be easily compared to processes of state- and nation-formation elsewhere in the world (cf. below, p. 236-237). Nation-building and state-formation in areas as diverse as Chile, Ghana, Israel, Iran, Indonesia, Japan, Morocco, Senegal, the USA and Vanuatu differ so widely from case to case, by so many case-specific and historical variables, that any attempt at a generalized description raises more questions than it can answer.

Between the micro-level of nationalism in a single country and the global level of a total world-theory, the case of Europe presents a challenging and, I think, workable mid-size case, if we study it, not just as an accumulation of separate nation-states each with their own antecedent national movement, but comparatively, as a multinational whole to be analysed from a supranational point of view.[5] Particularly inspiring in this respect is Anne-Marie Thiesse's *La création des identités nationales* (1999), whose influence permeates this entire book.

From a culture-historical point of view, Europe presents itself as a zone of traffic and exchange. If our main focus is on the developing discourse of national identity, then we see the formative ideas and tropes move across the European map, in a catchment area that reaches from Iceland and Scandinavia to the Mediterranean, and from the Atlantic to the Volga. This is what so saliently emerges from a culture-historical perspective: national thought is *mobile*. It is not just a reaction, within a given country, to the socio-political conditions of that country, but it moves over the map like a weather system or an epidemic. Thoughts are formulated by an author in one country to be read an picked up by readers in wholly different places. The traffic of ideas does, indeed, resemble an *epidemiology*, as Dan Sperber put it, where anyone who is affected by (or 'infected' with) a certain idea may pass it on to others.[6] Nationalism and national thought proliferate internationally, spreading and ramifying across the European map; movements and debates in one country may spawn copycat movements and spin-off debates elsewhere. This book attempts to trace that mobility and contagiousness of ideas, the cultural traffic and exchange, the patterns that cannot be subsumed in the individual cases of separate countries. When one traces this traffic and exchange, it is striking and very suggestive that the area in which all this ideological contagion and migration took place coincides pretty precisely with the continent of Europe.[*] The developments

---

[*] Europe in this respect (as the historical catchment area of the epidemiology of nineteenth-century nationalism) forms a 'society' in Lévi-Strauss's definition of that term: 'A society consists of individuals and groups which communicate with one another. The existence of, or lack of, communication can never be defined in an absolute manner. Communication does not cease at society's borders. These borders, rather, constitute thresholds where the rate and forms of communication, without waning altogether, reach a much lower level. This condition is usually meaningful enough for the population, both inside and outside the borders, to become aware of it.' Lévi-Strauss 1963, 296.

traced here take place in an area stretching from Gibraltar to Murmansk and from Reykjavik to Istanbul and Odessa.*

This Europe shades into the wider world-at-large through a dual periphery: a geographical and a political-historical one, respectively. The geographically neighboring area that is peripherally involved in the developments traced here is formed by the Maghreb, the Levant, Turkish Anatolia, the Caucasus and the area between the Volga and the Urals. The other periphery consists of the European colonies in the rest of the world. (In the course of the nineteenth century, these were still under European domination, except for the United States and the areas liberated by Simon Bolívar in Latin America.)

This book attempts, then, to describe national thought and nationalism as they took form in Europe. The focus of attention will often shift, certainly for the period before 1800, from one country to another; I cannot claim to present pre-modern or early-modern Europe as a unified single whole, nor do I claim that the examples I highlight are representative of Europe as a whole. My topic is the spread of ideas, not the development of societies; and the ideas I trace were largely confined, for a long time, to a literate elite sphere in Western, or even North-Western Europe.

This changes after 1800, and that change is something that struck me, as I was preparing this book, as something remarkable in itself. In the course of the nineteenth century, we can see the development of nationalism affecting Europe as a whole. The emergence of nationalism in Iceland is linked to, and similar to, developments in Catalonia, Finland and Bulgaria. Indeed, in that development the outer corners of Europe (the Balkans, the Baltic, Ireland) are by no means lagging behind the centre. All these areas were spanned by a Europe-wide circulation of ideas and a Europe-wide network of intellectuals; they were jointly affected by the repercussions of the French Revolution, the upheavals of the Napoleonic times, and the end of the Enlightenment. All of Europe shared, albeit to varying degrees, the ambience of urban middle-class sociability, the increasing social spread and penetration of print and education, and the new organization of learning in universities, academies, libraries, archives and schools. These institutional and intellectual factors, in the climate of Romantic idealism, were to determine the type of nationalism that developed in Europe in the nineteenth century.

~

The structure of the book is as follows. I trace, from a variety of source traditions, the emergence of nationalism in the years following the French Revolution. Central to these source traditions (surveyed in part one), is an ongoing use of ethnotypes in European views on collective identity. This ethnotypical tradition starts as raw ethno-

---

* While the topic of this book is Europe, and its scope is therefore Europe-centred, this is not the same, I hope, as mere, smug Eurocentrism. For one thing, there is the unsettling realization that near its outer margins, Europe is often marked off by the legacy of political failure, and by bitterly contested cities and territories: Belfast, Gibraltar, Nicosia, Grozny.

centrism; from the end of the Middle Ages onwards it influences (and is in turn influenced by) the process of state centralization. Various post-medieval developments in political and cultural thought play into this ethnotypical tradition: the seventeenth-century development of the notion of 'character' and the emergence of modern anthropology; the modern and Enlightenment urge to systematize; new ways of viewing the relations between state and territory, state and people, people and culture. Part one leads up to an inventory of the various conceptualizations of what a 'nation' is, by the end of the eighteenth century. In Enlightenment democratic thought, the nation is seen as the locus of sovereign power, while at the same time, in pre-romantic cultural thought, the nation is seen as the communal unit in which the diversity of human culture expresses itself.

Part two traces how these various source traditions are fused together into the ideology called nationalism in the turbulent, tense decades of Napoleonic rule. Political upheavals and Romantic philosophy are traced in their impact upon the emerging nationalist ideology. This early nationalism (also described as political romanticism) sees nations as natural human categories, each defined in its individual identity by a transcendent essence, each self-perpetuating that identity transgenerationally through history, each deserving its own self-determination. Each nation has a natural or moral right to be incorporated in its own state, while conversely every state should incorporate the natural, organic solidarity of its proper constituent nation. The repercussions of this idea (the hyphenation of nation and state into the ideal of the nation-state) are traced. Nationalism as an ideal of a congruence between nation and state can take various forms: as state centralism (adapting the constituent nation to the identity of the state); as a national unification ideal (abolishing the divisions that keep a nation separated over different states); or as a separatist movement (the nation opting out of an uncongenial state). In each case, however, the ideology's backbone is still a belief in ethnotypes: essential individual dispositions giving each nation a separate character, identity or 'soul' and setting it apart from others.

Part three traces the further implications across the rest of the nineteenth century, in particular nationalism's more totalizing aspects, its implicit tendency to see the ideal state as a monocultural one, and its slide from the left-wing to the right-wing end of the political spectrum. The transition from cultural self-assertion to territorial demands is critically surveyed and analysed; so is the tendency that all culture is seen and cultivated as 'national' culture, a proclamation of collective rootedness and identity.[*] Finally, the impact of scientific thought is traced, with its tendency to see nations in racial-biological terms. This part ends with the ultimate translation of cultural activism into constitutional reality during the Paris Peace Conference: the 'Versailles' system emerging out of the First World War.

Part four, finally, is a concluding survey of the twentieth-century aftermath, and offers some more contemporary implications of the historical analysis.

---

[*] For a further analysis of nationalism's 'cultivation of culture', I refer the reader to my article Leerssen 2006b.

To some extent, unfolding this historical survey is in itself the point that I am trying to make: that a historical analysis of national thought and nationalism may be fruitfully conducted by studying the shifting interactions between countries, between ideas, between culture and politics, across the centuries. If an overall pattern emerges (besides the aforementioned facts that ethnotyping is the origin and core of national thought and nationalism, that it always takes place against an Outside, and that the development of European nations took place in a flux of shifting self-identifications amidst a widespread and intense exchange of ideas) it is perhaps the following.

Nationalism contains within itself two vectors, 'vertical' and 'horizontal', which it consistently conflates. The 'vertical' aspect concerns the rights of the nation (i.e. the people-at-large) within the state, vis-à-vis superiors and rulers; the 'horizontal' aspect concerns the identity and separateness of the nation (i.e. the cultural community based on a shared sense of descent and a shared set of historical memories) vis-à-vis outsiders and neighbours. In its 'vertical' concerns, the nation's self-vindication is essentially democratic; in its 'horizontal' concerns, it is essentially ethnocentric or xenophobic. One of the most problematic aspects of nationalism has been its Jekyll-and-Hyde ambivalence between these two poles, and the complex patterns of interaction between them. It is all the more important to gain a clear analytical focus on this feature of the ideology. In particular in language activism, so central to the nationalist agenda, we can recognize (and we are apt to confuse) the modality of monoculturalist ethnic chauvinism and the modality of civil rights.[*] To a large extent, also, the transition from Enlightenment patriotism to Romantic nationalism can be seen as a process in which civic ('vertically' oriented, intra-national) vindications of popular sovereignty acquired the added 'horizontal' component of inter-national and ethnic rivalry (cf. Koselleck 1992).

This is an attempt towards a cultural history, not an analysis of current affairs. Even so, this book was written in the hope that a cultural-historical perspective may be useful for understanding the contemporary cultural conflicts that are confronting Europe – hampered as it is in a shrinking multi-ethnic world by its self-imposed delusion that it is a modular aggregate of 'nation-states', each incorporating a separate national identity.

---

[*] This problem is addressed in an appendix, below, p. 262-267.

Source Traditions, 1200-1800

Wilderness, Exoticism and the State's Order: Medieval Views

Upon entering Edinburgh's Museum of Scotland (built in the 1990s), the visitor passes between two sentences, calligraphed on opposite walls, from the Declaration of Arbroath (1320) asserting Scottish independence and freedom; their heavily symbolic placement clearly lifts these phrases from the field of antiquarian anecdote and turns them into a motto for contemporary culture and politics. On one wall is written: 'As long as only one hundred of us remain alive, we will never on any condition be brought under English rule'; on the opposite wall: 'For we fight not for glory, nor riches, nor honours, but for freedom alone, which no good man gives up except with his life'. The explanatory notice gives the Latin original of the phrases, and emphasizes their modern resonance:

> These still resounding words appeal for freedom in the face
> of conquest by England. The 'Letter of the Barons of Scot-
> land' to Pope John XXII, dated at Arbroath on 6 April 1320,
> was a declaration in the name of the *whole community of the
> Realm* on their determination to maintain the independence
> of Scotland and to support King Robert Bruce.[7]

This recent Scottish example of anchoring a late-twentieth century national museum in a medieval bedrock is representative of the tendency of modern national thought to hark back to ancient or medieval roots and continuities. Nineteenth- and twentieth-century Flemish national thought is full of references to anti-French resistance in the Battle of Courtrai (1302); the Irish and Greek nations invoke the memory of resistance against Turkish and English rule over many centuries. But does a claim to ancestry really prove direct descent? Must we, on the basis of nationalist self-historicizations, accept that nineteenth- and twentieth-century nationalism is the direct continuation of a persistently asserted, unchanging Scottish, Flemish, Irish or Greek 'nationality' across all these centuries? If modern Scots, Flemish or Greek nationalists recognize their ideals in medieval precursors, does that mean that those medieval precursors would have recognized themselves in these self-proclaimed nineteenth- and twentieth-century successors? Would the Scottish Barons who so resoundingly asserted their inalienable liberty in 1320 have cheered the movie *Braveheart* as modern Scottish audiences did? Would they have endorsed a parliamentary democracy with voting rights for all, including workers and women? Did 'freedom' and 'English rule' mean the same thing in 1320 as in 2000, and can we equate the medieval notion of a feudal realm with the modern notion of a nation-state? To ask these questions, and to realize that they are unanswerable and even impossible, means confronting modern nationalism, and its rhetoric of national remembrance, with the danger of anachronism.

The history and pre-history of nationalism consists of changes as well as continuities, none of which are simple or straightforward. When confronted with the self-historicization of national movements, scholars should not repeat histories, but study history; we should study historicist claims critically, rather than accepting them as the basis for our own research. Cultural history in particular must always be aware of the historicity and variability of culture, and avoid anachronism. Most continuities in history are retrospectively imposed rather than spontaneously generated, imposed upon the past by latter-day needs and desires. There may be similarities between attitudes and rhetoric that we encounter in various centuries, but similarities do not constitute unchanging identity or persistent continuity; they should not blind us to all that changed over the course of time.

Medieval Europe was aware of distinctions between languages and regions, and these were often couched in the nomenclature of 'nations'. The nation was not, however, a rigorously thought-out concept. Sometimes it referred to the fellow-inhabitants of a shared region (*pays, paese*). Sometimes it referred to people sharing a notion of common descent. Thus, clans in medieval Ireland and Scotland were referred to, in medieval documents, as *nations*; Hessians, Suabians and Bavarians were considered nations, as were Picardians or Burgundians. Well before the development of reliable maps, the realms and territories of Europe, and the people who inhabited them, were demarcated in a far less systematic manner than what we are accustomed to nowadays. Everywhere in Europe there was an intense, but unsystematic proliferation of ancestry myths that attempted to link back the present population of the world to the figures and tribes known from Classical Antiquity or from the Old Testament. Thus the inhabitants of Britain believed that their island was named after a legendary Roman, Brutus; many genealogical filiations were drawn up tracing family roots back to ancient Greece or Troy, or to the Tribes of Israel.[8]

There was, to be sure, a tendency to ascribe to the different regions and populations a certain set of moral virtues and vices; these, however, were fairly unspecific. Virtues such as honesty, charity, filial piety, marital fidelity, chastity and hospitality, and vices such as lust, sloth, wrath and mendacity, had been listed by Aristotle, Cicero and the church fathers; they were universally human but could be predicated, as the case required, to any nation that one wished to praise or blame. The base modality of ethnographic characterology was, if any, the crude ethnocentrism of the cartoon character Obélix, who finds all non-Gauls, be they Roman or Goth, Briton or Hispanic, 'funny' and 'queer in the head'. Nationality and national character were certainly not the basis of a systematic division of mankind, let alone the basis for a territorial division of the world by nation-state.

If we want to trace the rise of national thought in pre-modern Europe, it is useful to look at other forms of societal grouping and stereotyping. Much more fundamental to the medieval world order, in terms of social organization and the regulation of human behaviour, was the opposition between civilized culture and wild nature. Humans who fail to live up to civil standards are prone to a savage inferiority which is proper to beasts and wild nature: mankind is poised between the higher, spiritual world and the lower, bestial world, and society, too, is divided vertically in the higher, refined orders and the lower, brutish underclass. As Jacques Le Goff put it:

In the Middle Ages the great contrast was not, as it had been in antiquity, between the city and the country (*urbs* and *rus*, as the Romans put it) but between nature and culture, expressed in terms of the opposition between what was built, cultivated and inhabited (city, castle, village) and what was essentially wild (the ocean and forest, the western equivalents of the eastern desert), that is, between men who lived in groups and those who lived in solitude.[9]

The place of the individual is always positioned in the vertical terms of the order or estate to which one belongs, the lord or liege whose servant or subject one is. In medieval society, the centre of civility is the noble court. Codes of chivalry are in force here, with their ritual and ceremonious self-discipline. Table manners, protocol, an elaborate hierarchy of dignities and titles, and courtly behaviour, indeed the very notion of *courtesy*: all this manifests a triumph over crude 'natural', savage behaviour. Its most powerful expression is sexual self-denial, either in the abstinence of clerical celibacy or in the reticence of 'courtly love'.

The courtier's opposite is the churl, bumpkin, low-class country dweller. The names given to him invariably become terms of insult: churl, *vilein*, boor, peasant; a 'heathen' was originally someone who inhabits the barren, savage heathlands (the *pagus* in Latin where lives the *paganus*). These rustics are denigrated by the same token that glorifies the courtly chivalric role model. Churls' eating habits and personal hygiene are animal-like, unrestrained, revolting, demonstrating their lower position in the social and natural order. The medieval Flemish *Kerelslied* or 'Song of the Churls' mocks and taunts their boorishness and lack of breeding, and their sloppy diet of 'curds and whey'.[10] A late example of such anti-churlish invective is the mid-seventeenth century Irish-Gaelic satire *Pairlement Chloinne Tomáis* ('The Parliament of Tom's Clan'), which with aristocratic scorn describes the bestial condition of upstart menials, who presume to hold a parliament; they feed on:

> The head-gristle and trotters of cattle, and the blood, gore
> and entrails of dumb animals; and furthermore these were to
> be their bread and condiment: coarse, half-baked barley
> bread, messy mish-mashes of gruel, skimmed milk, and the
> butter of goats and sheep, rancid, full of hairs and blue pock-
> marks.[11]

Outside the sphere of control of the civilized court (always conceived of, like the city or the cloister, as a walled-in or fenced-in place) lies also the wild countryside.[12] At its wildest, it can be a forest; the absolute counterpart of the ordered, refined world of the court with its regulated life, the forest is an unkempt wilderness with no rules but only savage nature. According to Emile Benveniste the very word 'forest' derives from the late-Latin *foris*, 'outside' indicating anything that is external and alien.[13] It is here that the courtly discipline and protocol can be relaxed in the sport of hunting; it is here that the wild things are. In many romances from the chivalric Middle Ages, the hero makes a sortie into this wild world of the Forest Perilous. A knight's quest will take him from banquets and refined conversation into the sombre haunt of dragons and damsels in distress. The forest is a labyrinth without charted roads, and knights invariably start their adventures by getting lost there.

Interestingly, the separate status of the forest had a special legal title. Medieval England knew two sets of law: Common Law for the civil part of the country, that is to say, for 'society' proper, and Forest Law for the wilderness.[14] This status provided a means to dominate the wild Outside, mainly by stipulating that human individuals had no rights or legal standing in the forest, except for the King to hunt there.[15]

By the sixteenth century, the forest becomes, then, the playground of the court; hunting parties become increasingly refined demonstrations of the King's prerogatives,[16] enacting time and again a symbolic victory of courtly nobility over wild nature. This attitude, that courtly knights and kings can demonstrate their power and heroism by having adventures in the wild countryside, still informs in later centuries a specific notion of colonial expansion. The heroes of Victorian adventure romances by Kipling (*The Man who Would be King*, 1888; *Kim*, 1901) and Rider Haggard (*King Solomon's Mines*, 1885; *She*, 1887) follow the patterns of medieval chivalric heroes like *Yvain*; in the American Western, with its cowboys, outlaws and Indians, a similar questing hero is to be encountered in a similar savage testing-ground. The humans who are native to this wildness/wilderness are likewise savage: the 'Wild Man' or *homo sylvestris* of the medieval imagination is succeeded in later representations by native Africans, Pashtuns and American Indians. Thus the expansion of the power of the state goes hand-in-hand with a denigration of the people who dwell at its uncultivated, uncontrolled frontier. One early case within European history involves the expansion of the Teutonic Order into the non-Christian, heathen areas of the Baltic, where native tribes like the Old Prussians were either enslaved and forcibly converted to Christianity, or else exterminated.[17] Another well-documented example is Ireland.

Exoticism and propaganda: Giraldus Cambrensis and the English conquest of Ireland

From the very beginnings of the English hegemonic presence in Ireland, all these attitudes were operative.[18] As early as the 1170s, when ambitious noblemen had begun to claim Ireland for the English crown, the intellectual courtier and cleric Giraldus de Barri (an Anglo-Norman better known as Giraldus Cambrensis, 'Gerald of Wales') justified this hegemonic claim with two tracts: *Topographia Hiberniae* ('The Topography of Ireland') and *Expugnatio Hibernica* ('The Irish Conquest'). Prince John, son of the English king Henry II, had been appointed Lord of Ireland, *Dominus Hiberniae* on the basis of a papal bull. Issued by the English-born pope Adrian IV, this bull (which Giraldus quotes at length) pointed out that Ireland was too savage to govern itself and that accordingly it had to be placed under the rule of the English crown.[*] Wildness and savagery thus signal an inferior, subordinate position in the order of things, and English hegemony is presented as a civilizing mission. Pope Adrian had empowered his 'beloved son in Christ', Henry, to:

> Enter that island for the purpose of enlarging the boundaries
> of the church, checking the descent into wickedness, correct-
> ing morals and implanting virtues, and encouraging the
> growth of the faith of Christ.

A subsequent papal confirmation even emphasized this motivation:

> Once the stains of this land have been cleansed, its savage
> people, Christian only in name, may through your efforts
> take on proper mores; and this nation may, once the disor-
> dered church of that land is brought into line, be worthy of
> the name of Christians.[19]

In fact, Ireland was not a savage wilderness, though that is what these sources suggest. It had a rich monastic life and had been known in previous centuries as *insula sanctorum et doctorum*, 'island of saints and scholars'. The papal donation, which elsewhere in the same bull states to meet an expressed desire on the part of the English king, may have been a political 'deal' between Henry II and Adrian IV, and the rhetoric of moral improvement only a propagandistic pretence. Even so, it is remarkable that political expansionism should choose to drape itself in this type of rhetoric.

Giraldus's descriptions move in two patterns. One is a description of the country's marvels and strange phenomena, the other a strenuous denigration of the Irish natives.

Giraldus follows standard patterns of the exotic imagination. From Roman to medieval authors (Solinus and Mandeville), we encounter a tendency to describe foreign lands in terms of their strangeness. They are doubly *strange*: unaccustomed to, and also weird. In strange lands, nature plays strange tricks; weird phenomena and monstrous creatures abound. A good example in case are the so-called 'Plinian races', named after the Roman geographer Pliny, who filled in the blanks on the world map with the help of his imagination and peopled them with fantastical creatures. Cyclops, phoenix, creatures without heads with their faces in their chest, creatures with one leg who can rest from their hopping by reclining in the shade of their parasol-sized foot; etcetera.[20]

---

* Ireland thus counted as a lordship that the English king held in fief from the pope. Only with the English Reformation did Henry VIII break with this arrangement: he declared himself, not *dominus Hiberniae*, but King of Ireland. From then on, Ireland was seen as a kingdom in personal union with the English Crown.

1. Plinian races

This reservoir of fabulous monsters and fantastical marvels (*mirabilia*) was used as a marker of exoticism. In order to describe foreign lands in terms of their strangeness, to emphasize their exotic nature, the description will use imagery that represents a distorted or topsy-turvy version of the world as we know it. It is this stock-in-trade of *mirabilia* that Giraldus activates, especially in the *Topographia*, in order to describe Ireland. He thereby signals that the country should be seen as a different country, an exotic land, an Elsewhere. Thus, under the heading *De mirabilibus Hiberniae* ('On the Marvels of Ireland') he tells of an offshore island where people do not die; of a fish with golden teeth, a speaking wolf, a bearded woman and a man who is half bull, half human; a cow shaped partly like a deer, unnatural carnal relations between a woman and a goat, a woman and a lion... Ireland, it is made obvious, is strange, weird, a perversely twisted outpost of the normal world. This leads into chapters on the Irish lack of Christian manners and Irish vices: descriptions of Irish strangeness shade into a denunciation of Ireland's barbaric uncouthness:

> This people is extraordinarily dirty and completely covered in sins. Of all peoples it is the least instructed in the rudiments of Christian doctrine. They pay no tithes or harvest sacrifices, they do not celebrate marriage, they shun no unchastity and neglect to visit God's church with the necessary respect.[21]

The accusation of sexual looseness is the gravest of all. The implication is that the Irish will have sex with any available partner, without any taboo, restriction or social rule whatsoever. This is behaviour that truly marks them as bestial, beneath the standards of humanity: they copulate as freely as animals.[*] In Giraldus's book, the savagery of the Irish is not just a sign of their lack of civility, but an abomination of the natural order of things, because it perversely breaks through the barrier between man and beast.

> This is a people of forest-dwellers, and inhospitable; a people living off beasts and like beasts; a people that still adheres to the most primitive way of pastoral living. For as humanity progresses from the forests to the arable fields, and towards village life and civil society, this people is too lazy for agriculture and is heedless of material comfort; and they positively dislike the rules and legalities of civil intercourse; thus they have been unable and unwilling to abandon their traditional life of forests and pasture.[22]

The conclusion: England will have to restore the natural order of things by 'taming' Ireland; English hegemony is a moral imperative. The *Expugnatio* accordingly concludes with practical tips on how to reduce the country to obedience, and how to administer it; the *Topographia* ends with a chapter in praise of the good king Henry, who in classicist terms is eulogized as a latter-day Alexander the Great, with references to Ovid, Caesar, Seneca and Horace: the representative of true civility in the face of Irish savagery.[23]

The classicism of this twelfth-century cleric is, in fact, remarkable. At some points, Giraldus's idea of civility is not merely courtly-chivalric, as one might expect from a feudal courtier, but even Roman-inspired, breathing the spirit of Cicero, and seeing

---

[*] The underlying principle has been pointed out by thinkers like Freud and Norbert Elias: human civility consists in the tabooing and social regulation of bodily functions (such as sex) and aggression. Accordingly, discourse that wants to stress the savagery of a given society will frequently do so by imputing the free performance of strongly tabooed acts of sex and violence: especially cannibalism, promiscuity and incest; cf. Arens 1979; Arens 1986.

progress (as we can gather from the quoted passage) in the transition of pastoral life to agriculture and the building of cities.

Order within, wilderness beyond

English policy in Ireland, from the days of Giraldus onwards, was aimed at demarcating and separating the areas of wildness and civility. The civil portion of Ireland was the part where royal power was duly acknowledged, where 'the king's writ ran'. *De facto* the area in question was a semicircle around Dublin, with a radius between 50 and 100 miles. It was known as 'The English Pale', from a Brabant loanword signifying 'border post' or 'frontier'; even now the phrase 'within/beyond the pale of civilization' recalls this state of affairs. There was also a legal distinction between the two worlds that confronted each other in Ireland: the ordered English-governed realm, and the savage Irish wilderness. The *Statutes of Kilkenny* of 1366 defined a constitutional distinction between 'the king's English subjects' and 'the king's Irish enemies'. The nomenclature may have been ethnic, but being English or Irish was a matter of choice, not of descent. Those who adopted a civil lifestyle in obedience to English law were *ipso facto* English (and this may have included a good deal of Irish natives who had submitted). Those who maintained native customs that had been outlawed (dress, hairstyle, beard/moustache, keeping bardic court-poets, etc.) were thereby declaring themselves savage Wild Men, 'Irish enemies' (and this included families of Norman-English descent). The laws made no proviso for anything like Irish subjects or English enemies.[24]

As long as Ireland remained a feudal dominion or lordship, the division between 'within' and 'beyond the Pale' echoed chivalric patterns. Ireland Beyond the Pale was like the Forest Perilous where the wild things are. In a way, it was also the natural back garden of any chivalric court: every Camelot needs its Forest Perilous. It represented that wildness which

> [...] implied everything that eluded Christian norms and the established framework of Christian society, referring to what was uncanny, unruly, raw, unpredictable, foreign, uncultured, and uncultivated. It included the unfamiliar as well as the unpredictable.[25]

The change from feudal-chivalric patterns towards a more modern state organization was to make itself felt in this Irish arrangement as well. Once Columbus had sailed to the far shores of the Atlantic, America took on the role, in the English imagination, that the Irish wilderness had had before: a New World beyond the sea, full of savage Wild Men, monsters and weird phenomena, a testing ground for the bravery and resourcefulness of heroic adventurers. By the same token, Ireland was now seen as belonging in its entirety to the king's realm; any lawless wilderness where the king's writ did not run was an intolerable defiance. The existence of a race of Wild Men in the forests and wildernesses of Ireland was as unacceptable as a tribe of rebellious Apaches would be nowadays in the suburbs of Phoenix, Arizona.

All this was reflected in Henry VIII's 1541 claim to the kingship of Ireland (as opposed to the lordship it had been before). It was not merely a side effect of his breach with the papacy, or a coup by his Dublin subjects; it also extended his centralization policy to Ireland. As a result of his becoming king of Ireland, all inhabitants of that realm became his subjects and the distinction between an Ireland within and beyond the Pale was abolished. Anyone who would under the old laws have been considered an 'Irish enemy' now became an Irish rebel: a internal traitor, rather than an external barbarian. Significantly, Henry's policy in Ireland was to rely less and less on feudal nobles like the earls of Ormonde, Desmond or Thomond, but rather on appointed officials and a bureaucratic administration, involving sheriffs and a Privy Council. Irish territory was no longer shared out as fiefs among noble courtiers, but as 'plantations' (colonial holdings) among English 'adventurers' or 'undertakers' (colonists).[26]

At the same time, cultural policies were sharpened. Whereas native Gaelic custom had been proscribed earlier as signifying a refusal to submit to the King's power, it now became an illegal act of rebellion. A policy of anglicization formed the cultural manifestation of this centralist agenda:

> A conquest draweth, or at the least wise ought to drawe to it,
> three things, to witte, law, apparayle, and languague. For
> where the countrye is subdued, there the inhabitants ought
> to be ruled by the same law that the conqueror is governed,
> to weare the same fashion of attyre, wherewith the victour is
> vested, & speake the same language, that the vanquisher par-
> leth. And if anye of them lacke, doubtlesse the conquest lim-
> peth.[27]

Uniformity of language and culture thus mirrored uniformity of law. From this more modern perspective, the Irish wilderness ought not to have been left to its own devices beyond the Pale; government ought to have been imposed, by Forest Law if need be. One of James I's foremost advisers, Sir John Davies, wrote in 1612:

> Againe, if King *Henry* the second, who is said to be the K.
> that Conquered this Land, had made Forrests in Ireland [...]
> or if those English Lordes, amongst whom the whole King-
> dome was devided, had beene good Hunters, and had re-
> duced the Mountaines, Boggs, and woods within the limits
> of Forrests, Chases, and Parkes; assuredly, the very Forrest
> Law, and the Law *De Malefactoribus in parcis*, would in time
> have driven them into the Plain & Countries inhabited and
> Mannured, and have made them yeeld uppe their fast places
> to those wild Beastes which were indeede less hurtfull and
> wilde, then they.[28]

*2. National types in the margin of an early-modern map of the world
(by Petrus Kaerius, 1611).*

Accordingly, a law was enacted around the same time (1612) formally abolishing the existence of an inimical Irishry:

> In that all the natives and inhabitants of this kingdome,
> without difference and distinction, are taken into his Majes-
> tie's gratious protection, and doe now live under one law as
> dutiful subjects of our sovereigne lord and monarch, by
> means whereof, a perfect agreement is and ought to be settled
> betwixt all his Majestie's subjects in this realm.[29]

Not only do we see in these developing English attitudes, from Giraldus to Davies, a foreshadowing of what was to become a European colonial policy in the world at large – Davies's views were also to result, within Ireland, in the 'plantation' of the rebellious Ulster counties with Scottish undertakers. And that, in turn, marks the beginning of the ethnic and religious tensions which have dominated political relations in the north of Ireland ever since. One of the most violent flashpoints of nationalist strife in late-twentieth-century Western Europe, Ulster represents also the impact and importance, even in modern state formation, of archaic imaginative patterns. Medieval notions of savagery and civility, wild nature and ordered society, are operative in European eth-notypes. These influence in turn the developing notion of a well-ordered, properly governed realm or state, the order which that state includes and the wild Otherness from which it is separated.

The Renaissance and Democratic Primitivism

The idea of 'the Renaissance' covers a whole cluster of great European transitions and revolutions in the fifteenth and early sixteenth centuries: the great advances of art and learning in Italy, the scientific revolutions from Copernicus to Galileo, the Turkish conquest of Byzantium, Columbus's successful crossing of the Atlantic, the invention of movable type printing, the various initiatives towards an anti-papal reformation of Western Christianity from Jan Hus to Martin Luther. All these are loosely grouped around the vague but indispensable concept of a European *Renaissance*. That term evokes not just progress or even revolutionary innovation but rediscovery: a rebirth, a reawakening, and more specifically a re-acquaintance with the learning and culture of classical antiquity. In the eyes of intellectuals from the period, they participated in a re-classicization of Europe after the previous chivalric-Gothic centuries.

However, the Renaissance involved not only a new ideal of 'the grandeur that was Rome'; it also brought into fresh circulation the misgivings that Rome had about itself, and the mixed feelings with which Rome regarded primitive tribes outside its frontiers. The Renaissance not only rediscovered classical civility, but also classical primitivism.[30] For the civilizations of Greece and Rome had their own 'discontents': misgivings about the decadent over-refinement found in the city, nostalgia for an arcadian existence in the countryside, close to nature, as expressed by in bucolic poetry or Virgil's Georgics. In certain Roman sources, such 'back-to-nature' primitivism could lead to a backhanded appreciation even of the barbaric tribes of the north. And this, in turn, when translated into the frame of reference of early-modern Europe, would lead to a new form of tribal nomenclature and self-identification in the emerging states of the period.

Gauls, Belgae and Goths at universities and councils

The Low Countries – a set of lordships including, among others, the duchy of Brabant and the counties of Flanders, Holland, Zeeland and Hainault, between them covering much of the present-day Benelux – were called 'Low' from the more elevated perspective of the heartland of Burgundy. The dukes of Burgundy acquired these *Pays-Bas* in the early fifteenth century, as part of their great expansion, which for a while looked as if it might lead to the establishment of an independent Middle Kingdom between France and Germany. The Dukes of Burgundy signalled their ambitions by many monarchical claims and gestures: they even founded a chivalric order, the Order of the Golden Fleece, which had as much prestige as the Order of the Garter in England. In another typically monarchical gesture, the dukes founded a university in their newly-acquired possessions: at Louvain, in 1425, five years before their Order of the Golden Fleece was founded at Bruges.

It was around Louvain that Latinate humanists found another, classical name for the Burgundian Netherlands. They called them the 'Provincia Belgica'. That name they gleaned from Caesar's *De bello gallico,* with its flattering description of the tribes of the appropriate regions of North-Eastern Gaul, between the Marne/Seine and the Rhine. Geographically, the name made for a good fit. Morally, it was an even happier choice, because Caesar had shown himself quite appreciative of the Belgae. Famously, Caesar opened his description of Gaul as follows:

> Gaul is a whole divided into three parts, one of which is in-
> habited by the Belgae, another by the Aquitani, and a third
> by a people called in their own tongue Celtae, in the Latin
> Galli. [...] Of all these peoples the Belgae are the most coura-
> geous, because they are farthest removed from the culture
> and the civilization of the Province, and least often visited by
> merchants introducing the commodities that make for ef-
> feminacy; and also because they are nearest to the Germans
> dwelling beyond the Rhine, with whom they are continually
> at war.[31]

We notice Caesar's implicit macho primitivism: Southern Gaul (the Gaulish 'Province' around Narbonne, nowadays still called the *Provence*) is mollified and effete because of its proximity to the comforts and luxuries of Roman civilization. Conversely, the Belgae, being farthest removed from Rome and its influence, are the doughtiest and most stalwart tribe. The 'Belgian' self-appellation accordingly was flattering and stayed in use from the early 1400s onwards; it was eventually to be applied to the still-existing kingdom, Belgium, which proclaimed its independence in 1830. (That new kingdom assiduously continued and cultivated the historical remembrance of the 'ancient Belgae' as tribal forerunners and godfathers of the nation.)[32]

During the period of the foundation of Louvain University, Europe was going through major upheavals, of which Burgundy's attempts to wedge itself as an independent realm between France and the Holy Roman Empire formed only a part. Owing to the Western Schism – the division of the Western church between competing popes and anti-popes – the unifying role of the Roman church had been severely handicapped. A centrifugal tendency, away from Rome, was in evidence everywhere. There was the Hussite religious reform movement in Bohemia, which took on national overtones: the claim to use Bohemian (Czech) as a language of administration and liturgy was part of it. And in the Council of Constance (1414-1438), bishops no longer deliberated and voted as a united body, but chose to cast 'block votes' organized by archdiocese – that is to say, nationally.[33] National-dynastic interests (that is to say, the separate interests of different kingdoms and their monarchical rulers) began to dominate the agenda. Against the older ideal of a European Christendom united beneath the twin aegis of emperor and pope (bickering though they may be), kings began to develop the ideology that they had total, imperial sovereignty within their own realms.

This was voiced particularly strongly by kings whose realms did not fall within the limits of the old Carolingian Empire.[34] The king of Scots affected the heraldic use, not of a royal crown but of an imperial-style 'open' crown: something still in evidence on many Scottish towers, such as that of the University of Aberdeen. The invocation of ancient tribal roots, as gleaned from classical authors, falls into this trend.

A particularly potent tribal name to be invoked was that of the Goths. These had originally emerged from Southern Sweden to settle, in late imperial times, at the lower course of the Danube, and from there had been instrumental in the break-up of the Roman Empire, founding sixth-century kingdoms both in Northern Italy (the Ostrogoths under Theodoric, around Ravenna[*]) and in Spain (the Visigoths). Like the associated tribe of the Vandals, the name of the 'Goths' lived on in memory as the destroyers of the Western Roman Empire;[†] but the Goths' early conversion to Christianity and their bravery had been praised by Latinate authors like Jordanes and Isidore of Seville. This Gothic prestige was invoked in the mid-fifteenth century from opposite ends of Europe. The Kingdoms of Sweden and of Spain both claimed status based on the fact that they had been founded, not under the aegis of Charlemagne, but by independent Gothic forebears. To be sure, both kingdoms were as yet in flux: the Spanish *reconquista* would not be completed until the fall of the Moorish Kingdom of Granada in 1492, and Spain was (feudally and dynastically speaking) a conglomerate of various separate royal realms; Leon, Aragon, Navarre and Castille. Even so, the dynastic memory of having originally been founded by Visigothic conquerors was alive, and strong enough to play a role in the seating arrangements and order of precedence at the Council of Basel in 1436. Such precedence, now a matter of national-dynastic honour (after the foregoing Council, at Constance), was heavily contested. Bishop Alfonso of Burgos claimed seniority on the basis that he represented a most ancient, Visigothically-founded monarchy. In so doing, he attempted to rebut a similar claim by bishop Nils Ragvaldsson of Uppsala to claim precedence on the basis of Sweden being the aboriginal homeland of the Goths.[35]

These examples, of Lowland-Burgundian Belgae and Spanish or Swedish Goths, show how the spreading influence of Latinate learning and humanism in the early fifteenth century would gradually replace older, biblically-derived models of ethnic descent. The most influential of these sources came to light even during these decades: Tacitus.

---

[*] The prestige of this Ostrogothic capital (later recaptured by the Byzantine Emperor Justinian) was such that the chapel built in Charlemagne's residence of Aachen was consciously modelled on Ravenna's main church of San Vitale, with its Byzantine octagonal ground plan.

[†] Thus Giorgio Vasari (1511-1574), the first great art historian and proponent of classical taste, made 'Gothic' a term of aesthetic abuse, and a byword of medieval tastelessness and wayward decoration-overload; cf. Panofsky 1930.

Tacitus

One of the first great effects of the new medium of printed books was not so much to facilitate the production of new types of text as to reissue and redistribute older canonical classics. The first printed book, Gutenberg's Bible, stands as an example, and the most meaningful early printed books are perhaps best characterized as 'reprints'.

One of the classical authors who was best served by the new medium of print was Publius Cornelius Tacitus. Whereas much of Horace, Virgil and Cicero, as well as other texts such as Caesar's *De bello gallico,* had been extensively circulated in manuscript throughout the Middle Ages, and Livy's history of Rome had been fairly widely known at least since the thirteenth century, Tacitus's work was coming to light on the very eve of the invention of print. Portions of the *Annales* (books 11-16) and the *Historiae* (books 1-5) had been sighted around 1360 in the monastic library of Monte Cassino by none other than Giovanni Boccaccio, and slightly less than a century later, around 1455, the sole surviving manuscript of his *Germania* surfaced in Rome. It may be said that Tacitus is the classical author who owes most to humanism.[36]

With Tacitus's texts, a number of Roman reflections on North-European societies came to the attention of contemporary intellectuals. He had written around the year 100 AD, that is to say, a full century and a half after Cicero and Caesar; he describes the vicissitudes of Roman rule in Gaul and Britain after Caesar, and his historical survey therefore covers, not only the march of conquest, but also its ultimate stalling, and the troubles of consolidation. Caesar in his Gaulish conquest had triumphantly described how he overcame the stalwart resistance of Gaulish and Belgian chiefs like Vercingetorix or Ambiorix; Tacitus's subsequent history also takes in the disastrous annihilation of Varus' army at the hands of Arminius the Cheruscan in 9 AD, the nobility of the defeated Britannic leader Caractacus in 51 AD, and the risings of the Iceni under Boadicea in 62 AD and of the Batavi under Civilis in 69 AD.

Tacitus echoes the implicit primitivism that we already encountered in Caesar, and adds to it a dose of cultural pessimism. Writing as he does after the Roman Republic had become an empire, he evinces a fundamental unease concerning the loss of primitive, republican *virtus.*[*] In particular his *Germania* is a mirror held up to Rome. While, on the one hand, the patrician Roman cannot but despise the rustic savagery of the Germanic tribes and their lifestyle, there is a continuous awareness that these savage tribes had in 9 AD destroyed two entire Roman legions in the Teutoburg Forest under their leader Arminius, and that what they lack in refinement they more than make up for in moral and political 'manliness'. They are frugal, chaste, and have a republican political system in that they elect or appoint their leaders on the basis of merit (as opposed to the dynastic empire, with its decadent court culture, that Rome was becoming).

---

[*] The notion of *virtus* contains far more machismo than a straightforward translation 'virtue' would suggest. The word indicates an ideal of masculinity (the first syllable is the same as in *virile*), and may best be translated as 'manliness': the strength of character, courage, resolve, self-abnegation and self-discipline that makes men superior to women, or children (cf. McDonnell 2007).

Tacitus's appreciative comments on the Germans' tribal republicanism are well known. Witness the following passage, with its heavy undertone of self-criticism:

> [...] the marriage tie with them is strict: you will find nothing in their character to praise more highly. They are almost the only barbarians who are content with a wife apiece [...] So their life is one of fenced-in chastity. There is no arena with its seductions, no dinner-tables with their provocations to corrupt them. Of the exchange of secret letters men and women alike are innocent; adulteries are very few for the number of the people. Punishment is prompt and is the husband's prerogative [...] No one laughs at vice there; no one calls seduction, suffered or wrought, the spirit of the age. [...] to limit the number of their children, to make away with any of the later children is held abominable, and good habits have more force with them than good laws elsewhere. There they are, the children, in every house, growing up amid nakedness and squalor into that girth of limb and frame which is to our people a marvel. Its own mother suckles each at her breast; they are not passed on to nursemaids and wetnurses.[37]

After almost every sentence one might tacitly add: 'unlike our own, depraved, Roman morals'. Tacitus's appreciative, primitivist ethnotypes contrast sharply with the denigrations of Giraldus; yet both follow the same rhetoric in juxtaposing uncouth otherness contrastively with an implied domestic standard. Both silhouette an implied self-image against the otherness of an opposing Outside.[38] Tacitus's praise for the combination of primitive, rustic frugality and unadulterated *virtus* is very close indeed to the withering satire that his contemporary Juvenal levelled against Roman vice. Juvenal's sixth satire, denouncing the decline of marital fidelity and the loose sexual mores of women in particular, opens with a wistful evocation of primitive virtue, as it had once existed in a bygone Golden Age. When the old father of the gods, Saturn, ruled, and his successor Jupiter was still young, mankind was in a natural state, without elegant clothing or comfortable housing – much like contemporary German tribes. It was before sentimental maidens could indulge their effete posturing, when manners were rough but chastity and virtue still dwelt among primitive mankind:

> I can believe that Chastity lingered on earth during Saturn's reign [...] when a chilly cave provided a tiny home, enclosing fire and hearth god and herd and its owners in communal gloom, when a mountain wife made her woodland bed with leaves and straw and the skins or her neighbours, the beasts. She was nothing like *you*, Cynthia [...]. Instead she offered her paps for her hefty babies to drain, and she was often more unkempt than her acorn-belching husband. You see, people lived differently then, when the world was new and the sky

3. Enea Silvio Piccolomini sets out for the Council of Basel as secretary to the papal legation. From a fresco in the Piccolomini Library, Siena.

was young – people who had no parents but were born from split oak or shaped from mud. It's possible that many or at least some traces of ancient Chastity survived under Jupiter too – but that was before Jupiter had got his beard [...] at a time when no one feared that his cabbages or apples would be stolen but people lived with their gardens unwalled.[39]

Like Juvenal's satire, Tacitus' *Germania* denounces Roman decadence. As such, it was to affect the course of history repeatedly, and to become the single most influential piece of Latin literature in post-medieval Europe. Anyone who believes that monarchies and royal courts are a congenial climate for intrigue and moral corruption; anyone who for that reason prefers republics to monarchies; anyone who extols the virtues of simple, solid citizens over immoral aristocrats; anyone who believes that Northern Europeans are more trustworthy than Southern Europeans – is indebted to Tacitus.

The first humanist intellectual to betray the influence of Tacitus was Enea Silvio Piccolomini, later Pope Pius II. At the Council of Basel, he already felt that from Austria to Scotland, the Germanic languages were perhaps more suited than Latin to unite Christendom in the struggle against the Turks; and in a later correspondence with the archbishop of Mainz's secretary (1457), he let slip some references to Tacitus's just-discovered *Germania*.[40] A few years later, in 1470, *Germania* hit the printing press, followed in 1515 by the *Annales*.

Tacitus's impact in Germany

By the time Tacitus's works appeared in print, they had acquired a whole new, but uncannily apposite, political urgency: because Germany and Rome were now embarking on a new war, that between Luther and the papacy.

The escalating Lutheran conflict marks the beginning of Europe's first successful anti-papal Reformation. To recapitulate briefly a few famous dates:

- 1517: Luther nails his 95 theses to the church door at Wittenberg, denouncing the trade in indulgences and their theological underpinning (that salvation can be 'bought' by good deeds);
- 1520: A papal bull threatens Luther with excommunication unless he recants; Luther burns it;
- 1521: Luther is excommunicated; he defends himself before emperor Charles V at Worms; after the lapse of his free conduct he is declared an outlaw and goes into hiding at the Wartburg, where he translates the New Testament into German (printed in 1522).

Politically speaking, the salient fact is that the emperor obviously could not afford to remove Luther as ruthlessly as an earlier reformer, Jan Hus, had been removed. Luther was protected by a groundswell of sympathy (or perhaps better, by a groundswell of anti-Roman feeling) among German princes, which tied Charles V's hands. This anti-Roman feeling was given a fortunate, powerful rhetoric by Tacitus's recently published *Germania*.[41]

As early as 1497, the Rhineland humanist Conrad Celtis had lectured on *Germania* at Vienna University, and two of Luther's most vociferous defenders, Ulrich von Hutten and Georg Spalatin, began to praise him as a veritable champion, not of private religious faith, but of the German nation. Luther was made a political as much as a moral champion. In his tract *Arminius, c.* 1520, Hutten made the obvious and very effective comparison: just as in Roman times the ancient German chief had defended the liberties of his country by defeating Varus's legions in the Teutoburg Forest, so the modern German theologian would defend the liberties of the country by defeating the Roman pontiff. One had blocked the Roman Empire as it attempted to expand beyond the Rhine, the other proved that the rule of the papal inquisition reached no further than that same river.

And so the printing of Tacitus's *Germania* in 1470 and of the *Annales* in 1515 facilitated the printing of Luther's New Testament in 1522. It proved an invaluable asset in politically justifying the Reformation by a recourse to anti-Roman patriotism. *Germania* and Arminius have maintained that role ever since in German history. The Cheruskan chief's name was even retrotranslated into its putative original form: the name must have been derived, so it was thought (for this was when scholars were fond of etymological speculation) from an original *Hermann*, most *Ur*-German of names. Did it not evoke martial virtue as a *Heer-Mann*, 'army-man'? Did it not, in fact, stand to reason that from *Hermann* had been derived, not only the Latin *Arminius*, but also the Latin *Germani*, and that therefore the very name of the nation, *Germani*, meant nothing else than 'the Hermanns', the army-men, the warriors?

Over the following centuries, the Tacitus-derived opposition of Germany against Rome, as exemplified by the names of Arminius and Luther, became one of the great commonplaces of European history. Within Germany, it was repeatedly activated whenever a 'national' cause was championed against enemies from beyond the Rhine. When the eighteenth-century poet Friedrich Klopstock attempted to develop a native German literature, based on its own sagas and history, he used Arminius repeatedly: in the ode *Hermann und Thusnelda* of 1752; in the tragedy 'Hermann's Battle' (*Hermanns Schlacht*, 1769); and its sequels 'Hermann and the Princes' (*Hermann und die Fürsten*, 1784) and 'Hermann's Death' (*Hermanns Tod*, 1787). Trying to gain favour with the enlightened-autocratic emperor Joseph II for his project of a German Republic of Letters, Klopstock glorifies Hermann as 'Patriot King', ruling an alliance of princes and relying on the advice of his bardic counsellors. Indeed, so bardically-enthusiastic is Klopstock's tragedy that he himself subtitled it *eine Bardiet für die Schaubühne* ('a bardite for the stage'), coining that word from Tacitus, who had used it in *Germania* to describe a chant used to inspire courage before battle.[42]

More explosive was Heinrich von Kleist's *Die Hermannsschlacht* of 1808, which updated the Teutoburg tale into an anti-Napoleonic political allegory. By 1808, Napoleon had Germany under control along the Rhine, with Bavaria and Prussia being reduced to the status of satellites. Among German intellectuals, anti-French feeling was beginning to ride very high indeed. Even Kleist, usually a refined and lyrical poet and playwright, threw himself into vitriolic propaganda. His anti-French verse we shall encounter further on; his play of 1808 represents the title-hero, Hermann, as a Cheruscan chief bracing himself to shoulder the task, as the play points out he must, of uniting the Germanic tribes under his leadership to face the Roman foe. Kleist obviously intended this as an incentive for the Prussian king (then still a French client) to take on the leadership of an anti-Napoleonic German coalition. In the event, that is what Prussia was to do: after Napoleon's disastrous failure in the Russian campaign of 1812, Prussia joined the British-Russian camp. The Battle of Leipzig (1813) was to defeat Napoleon and send him to Elba.

What strikes us in Kleist's piece is how neatly the classical story fits the contemporary situation. The imperial threat from beyond the Rhine is now Napoleonic, not Roman, but Germans can still effortlessly see themselves as simple-minded, frugal and virtuous sons of the soil, and thereby oppose themselves morally to the *ooh-la-la* culture of frivolous France, autocratically ruled by its Corsican warlord-emperor. Tacitus's democratic primitivism is effortlessly applied as a metaphor to later circumstances. Tacitus's ethnography is cited to establish a moral distribution between northern virtue-and-patriotism against southern decadence-and-imperialism.

That became once again manifest when, in the course of the 1870s, a huge statue was erected in honour of Arminius in the Teutoburg Forest, near Lippe. Not only does it honour the old German military chief and celebrate his struggle's final fulfilment in the creation of Bismarck's empire; it also is, once again, an anti-Roman statement. For in the 1870s, Bismarck's empire was locked in a bitter struggle with the papacy over the loyalty of Germany's Catholic citizens. Should German Catholics be first and foremost Germans, or Catholics? The so-called *Kulturkampf*, which ensued over this question, culminated in Bismarck more-or-less banning Roman Catholicism from the empire. We recognize this close link between German chauvinism and anti-Roman feeling in the Teutoburg memorial to Arminius. In a contemporary political cartoon the Cheruscan hero, as represented in the newly-unveiled monument, is placed side by side with Germany's other hero, Luther (represented in the pose of the monument unveiled at Worms a few years previously). What unites them? The cartoon's caption tells us: *Gegen Rom*, against Rome. In this shared resistance Arminius, the forefighter of Germany's political independence, states *'Ich habe gesiegt'* – 'I have prevailed'. Luther, forefighter of Germany's religious independence, replies: *'Ich werde siegen'* – 'I shall prevail'.[43]

4. *United against Rome: Arminius and Luther. After a reproduction in Thomas von der Dunk,* De schaduw van het Teutoburgerwoud *(2000), 69.*

Meanwhile, the Low Countries were undergoing various religious and political pressures; and here too, the availability of a cultural template from classical antiquity provided a scenario and a self-image to an emerging political conflict. The ducal house of Burgundy had merged, in the person of Charles V, with the Habsburg dynasty, and the territory of the Burgundian lands had ties with the Holy Roman Empire. As the Reformation affected Charles's German empire, so too did it affect his Low Countries.

When Charles abdicated in 1555, he left these Burgundian fiefs, now only nominally part of the Holy Roman Empire (where he was succeeded by his brother Ferdinand) under the rule of the Spanish crown (where he was succeeded by his son, Philip II). This decision had grave consequences. The Low Countries were now linked with a distant, centralist monarchy. Philip's autocratic, centralist rule differed much from the looser, more federal structure of the Empire. The Spanish connection also made it possible for a Spanish institution to be introduced into this religious conflict: the Inquisition.

Tensions quickly increased as a result. The inquisitorial repression of the Reformation was particularly harsh, and Philip rode roughshod over the localist autonomies of the various Netherlandic Provinces. Eventually the situation polarized into a full-fledged revolt. Philip II was forsworn as king, the throne was declared to be vacant, and the breakaway Provinces became in essence self-governing. Various European rulers (including Queen Elizabeth, who supported the Protestant Reformation against Philip's hegemonism) were approached to accept the sovereignty of the Low Countries; when none was found willing, the joint provincial assemblies (or Estates General) took on the country's government, and appointed an erstwhile favourite of Charles V (his placeholder, *stadhouder:* 'locum tenens', stadholder) to fill the absence of an actual monarch. This was the highly respected Protestant magnate William of Nassau, prince of Orange, known as William 'the Silent'.

Constitutionally, this development was of momentous historical importance. While there had been republics or republic-like confederations even in medieval Europe (city-states like Geneva, Lucca or Venice, the Swiss cantons, the Lombard or the Hanseatic leagues), the Dutch development was unprecedented. The act by which the Estates General forswore Philip as king was truly revolutionary: as if an anointed monarch was a mere official who could be dismissed from his post if he performed badly. That, in fact, is the argument of the 1581 'Act of Abjuration', by which the Estates General declared Philip of Spain to have forfeited his monarchical rights; it was to find an echo two centuries later in the American Declaration of Independence. Princes (so the argument ran) were placed over their subjects to protect them; if they failed in that duty, and especially if they tyrannically oppressed their subjects, they forfeited their royal mandate. The implicit thought was that even monarchs did not rule absolutely, by divine right or by virtue of their dynastic descent, but by virtue of principles of a higher constitutional justice.

To those who believed in the divine right of kings (like Philip II), this justification added insult to injury. The revolt, and the Protestant Reformation, were in fact suppressed in the Southern Netherlands (roughly the area of present-day Belgium), in a ferocious campaign deploying Philip's great military might. The Spanish armies found

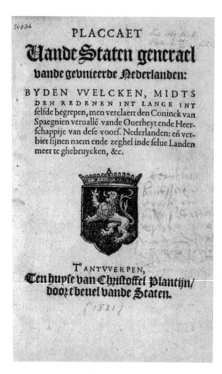

5. The Dutch Act of Abjuration

it more difficult, however, to campaign in the marshy terrain of the Northern Netherlands, and here the revolt, despite frequent setbacks, consolidated itself. Seven provinces in effect maintained their independence in the teeth of the Spanish crown. This independence was *de facto* accepted by 1610, and formally acknowledged (with that of Switzerland) in the Treaty of Westphalia, in 1648.

In the early days of the revolt, the stadholder, William of Orange (who became the victim of a political assassination in 1584) undertook a quasi-monarchical gesture by founding a Protestant university. The gesture echoed the foundation of the University of Louvain by the duke of Burgundy in 1425. Louvain remained firmly Catholic, in the Spanish-controlled Southern part of the Netherlands. To counterbalance this, William rewarded the Protestant town of Leyden, in Holland, for its stalwart resistance against a Spanish siege by founding a university there in 1575 – intended also as a counterbalancing, Protestant intellectual focus against Catholic Louvain.

The name that this Protestant, North-Netherlandic foundation chose for itself was as meaningful as the Louvain usage of *Provincia Belgica* had been 150 years previously. Holland and the other northern provinces were now opting out of the Burgundian, Spanish-dominated Netherlands, and also opting out of the name of *Belgia*. Latinate scholars were no longer referring to the language and the region as the *provincia* or *lingua Belgica* but as *Germania inferior* (Low-German, or *Nederduits*). And tribal ancestors were no longer sought among the Gaulish Belgae mentioned by Caesar, but among Germanic tribes as mentioned in Tacitus. The tribe which was selected to stand godfather over the fledgling Republic and its newly-founded university was, in fact, found mentioned in the *Annales*: the *Batavi*. Leyden accordingly latinized its name to *Lugdunum Batavorum*.

The Batavian narrative fitted the current political situation like a glove; Tacitus's story seemed tailor-made as a metaphor for the Dutch situation at the time. The Batavi are described by Tacitus as a tribe linked to Rome as confederates, who, however, under their leader Civilis, are driven to an anti-Roman insurrection. This could be read as an obvious parallel to the relationship between the modern Dutch and the Spanish monarchy. Much as Luther had been seen as a latter-day Arminius, so William the Silent became an obvious reincarnation of the Batavi's leader Civilis. The *Batavian myth*, as it has become known,[44] was assiduously cultivated by the Dutch republic in the seventeenth century: two of the country's most outstanding writers, Pieter Corneliszoon Hooft and Joost van den Vondel, wrote tragedies on Batavian themes, a painting by Rembrandt of the 'Oath of Civilis' was commissioned for the council hall of Amsterdam, when the Dutch East India Company captured the Javan royal city of Jakarta they renamed it 'Batavia', and when the renowned legal scholar Hugo Grotius pamphleteered to obtain international recognition for the new state, he presented it as a reincarnation of the ancient tribal commonwealth of the Batavi. Tacitus had not only provided modern Germany with a role model from classical antiquity, he had done the same for the Dutch Republic.

Further European repercussions: England and France

Roman history mentions some stalwart native defenders of their tribal liberty against the might of the Roman legions in Britain and France. In Britain, there are the figures of Caractacus and of Boudicca (or Boadicea). Both become popular literary and tragic themes in the late seventeenth and eighteenth century. Eventually the warrior queen Boadicea was to merge into the iconography of *Britannia*:* she is usually depicted in her war-chariot, personifying a combination of manly, courageous stalwartness and female (chaste) virtue – in that she was goaded into war because she wanted to avenge the outraged honour of her daughters, raped by Romans.

The dominant tribal origin-myth in early-modern English political thought, however, was not linked to the Roman conquest of Britain in the first century, but rather to the Norman-French conquest of the eleventh century, following the Battle of Hast-

---

* Many European countries have symbolized themselves in female allegorical form. In Holland there was the *Nederlandse maagd* or 'Dutch Maiden' (ill. 12); Germany came to cultivate the figure of *Germania*, to whom a huge statue was dedicated on the banks of the Rhine in 1877 (Mazón 2000); France came to see itself personified, after the 1789 revolution, in the figure of *Marianne*. The figure of *Britannia* had particular force because twice in the course of history the country had been led to glory under reigning queens: Elizabeth I and Victoria. It was towards the end of Victoria's reign that the monument of Boadicea was placed on the Thames Embankment, near the Houses of Parliament. On the female allegorization of nations, see Warner 1985.

6. Statue of Boadicea on Thames Embankment

ings of 1066. And the native tribes, whose love of liberty was taken as a shining example for contemporary politics, were not the Iron-Age Celts of Britain, but rather the Anglo-Saxons: tribes of Germanic origin, who had migrated to England in the fifth and sixth centuries, and whose reputation fitted, once again, the typology that Tacitus had given of the Germanic tribes in his *Germania*.

From the mid-seventeenth century onwards, British politics were dominated by a power struggle between Crown and Parliament. The Stuart dynasty developed a royal ideology of absolute monarchical power, while parliament insisted more and more urgently on its constitutional rights. This led to two constitutional crises in the course of the seventeenth century, indeed to civil war: in the 1640s, when Charles I was executed and Britain became a *Commonwealth* (republic) for a while, headed by Cromwell; and in the late 1680s, when James II was ousted from the throne and Parliament installed in his place his daughter and son-in-law, Mary and William III. Throughout these upheavals the constitutional conflict was schematized in ethnic terms. Royal powers and ambitions were seen as a 'French' type of government, introduced after 1066 by the medieval Norman-French kings starting with William the Conqueror; Parliament, in contrast, was seen as a native, 'Gothic' (i.e. Germanic) institution dating back to the tribal liberties as described by Tacitus, and recognized before 1066 by good Anglo-Saxon kings such as Alfred the Great.

This crystallized into a powerful national myth: that of the 'Gothic Liberty' versus the 'Norman yoke'.[45] The harsh feudalism of the Middle Ages, with its oppressive and extorting nobles and barons, was seen as a form of Norman-French occupation under which the aboriginal freedom of the Saxons languished, only to be reasserted by Parliament in the seventeenth century. The British class system was thus given an ethnic tinge: aristocratic names like De Vere, Montague etc. were obviously of French origin, and as such a foreign overlay over the demotic Saxon population.

As late as 1820, this democratic primitivism was given fresh expression in the hugely influential and popular historical novel *Ivanhoe* by Sir Walter Scott. Set in the times of the Crusades, it depicts an England dominated by corrupt, arrogant and cruel nobles of Norman-French extraction, with names like Reginald Front-de-Boeuf and Brian de Bois-Guilbert, who scorn the native Saxon population and see themselves more or less as colonists in an alien country. Against their harsh, oppressive rule, Saxon characters with Germanic names such as Cedric, Gurth and Athelstane pine for their lost liberty and engage in passive or active resistance. Even Robin Hood is introduced into the narrative: as a Saxon woodland guerrilla fighter driven to an outlaw existence because of Norman oppression. Scott eventually concludes *Ivanhoe* on a note of integration and reconciliation: the hero, Wilfred of Ivanhoe, is shown as a chivalric ideal where Saxon *virtus* is united with Norman aristocratic honour. The book looks forward to a merger between the Saxon and Norman traditions and languages to combine into a joint, mixed, *English* identity (see below, 205-6).

Even in France we can observe this national myth. That is remarkable, because France, from the days of Louis XIV onwards, was generally represented as the modern successor to ancient Rome: with its sumptuously elaborate court, its Catholic religion, its military power and its aggressive foreign policy. Nonetheless, even within France a national origin-myth was in force that celebrated a native, tribal-democratic tradition against the Roman-imported system of absolute monarchy. The ancestral tribe in question was, of course, the Gauls. Caesar's *De bello gallico* had described their resistance against his conquest, and this text was to do for French anti-absolutists what Tacitus had done in Germany. The rediscovery of the ancestral Gauls took place some time in the fifteenth century.[46] A particularly interesting example is that of the outstanding legal scholar François Hotman (or Hotomannus, 1524-1590), precursor of republican thought.[47] Already at the age of 23 (in 1547), Hotman was professor of law in Paris. In the same year he became a Protestant. After the infamous St. Bartholomew's Day massacre (an organized pogrom against Protestants, 1572), he fled to Geneva, and eventually obtained a university chair at Basel, where he died in 1590. His most famous work, with the remarkable title *Franco-Gallia* (1573) argued that royal absolutism (which he criticized because it led to religious intolerance) had no roots in the nation's history and stood at odds with the primal French tradition of Gaulish *virtus*. The manliness of the Gaulish ancestors needed to be revived so as to counteract popish corruption, which, as he saw it, manifested itself in the Machiavellian ruthlessness of the Medici dynasty, who had married into the French royal family and had instigated the Bartholomew's Day massacre. From Hotman onwards, the Gauls came to stand for the tribal-democratic bedrock of the French nation.[*] Class tensions in aristocratic France were to be translated into ethnic terms until well after the French Revolution, as we shall see: the plain people were seen as the continuation of the Gaulish population, while the aristocracy was either metaphorically linked to Rome or to the con-

---

[*] One particularly fanciful theory, which obviously twisted the facts of history to the needs of political allegory, argued that some Gaulish tribes had refused to submit to Rome's rule, had fled eastwards across the Rhine, to return, five centuries later, under the name of Franks.

quering Germanic Franks. This national myth has found its humorous modern embodiment in the cartoon figure of Astérix, who makes fools of officious Roman occupiers.[48]

From democratic primitivism to classical republicanism

Thus, everywhere in Northern Europe, national myths sprang up to glorify the manliness of primitive tribes such as Goths, Belgae, Germans, Batavi and Anglo-Saxons, who had inhabited the territories of the early-modern states – these, in the process, were metaphorically and morally adopted as the ancestors and role models of the modern nation. In particular their defence of independence and liberty was seen as a moral example. Frequently, the role of the villain was given to an imperial power from outside, which was represented as a reincarnation of the military imperialism of ancient Rome. The role division between 'manly, primitive natives' and 'corrupt, arrogant conquerors' can be schematized as follows:

country	manly, primitive natives	corrupt, arrogant conquerors
Spain, Sweden	Goths	—
Belgium / Low Countries	Belgae	—
Germany	Germanic tribes	Roman Empire Roman Catholic Church France (Napoleon)
Holland / United Provinces	Batavi	Spain
England	(British Celts) Anglo-Saxons	(Roman Empire) Norman French after 1066
France	Gauls	Romans (Catherine de Medici and Italian-imported absolutism) Franks

All these tribal ancestry myths, derived from Caesar and Tacitus, take shape, and obtain a fresh political function, in the early modern period – the time when, between the Council of Basel in 1436 and the Treaty of Westphalia in 1648, the state system of Europe began to emerge in its modern form. The myths had a triple function: to anchor the newly emerging state in history, by showing that the territory as it had been inhabited in Roman times already prefigured the modern situation; to profile the emerging state against possible hegemonic conquerors from outside, by showing that these had always been, and always would be, resisted; and thirdly, to show that the state embodied a moral collective, not merely united by the contingencies of feudal lordship, but organically linked by traditions, institutions, virtues and values.

This last function was momentous indeed. It meant that something called 'nations' could now be conceived of, and articulated, as a demotic collective, a type of extended family with its own family tree and ancestral roots, and its own inherited traits, customs and rights. The nation was, in other words, seen – not merely as a loose reference to regional-territorial background, or to a social layer (all the 'subjects' under the obedience of a given lord or overlord) – but as a *tribe*: precisely in the terms that Tacitus and Caesar had used. This had two enormously important implications. If the populations of the various states of modern Europe were 'nations', each with their own name and ancestry, then they could also be vested each with their own 'character' or collective culture. More importantly, there was (as will be outlined in the next chapter) a hugely subversive, implicitly democratic subtext to this historical myth: if the subjects of the various sovereigns of Europe were tribally linked as 'nations', then they could also be seen as the carriers of virtues, traditions and customs that made them an autonomous force in constitutional politics. The nation could become the counterpart of the king, even the king's adversary. That was spelled out in the Dutch Act of Abjuration; it manifested itself in the decapitation of Charles I in 1649, and in the ousting of James II in 1688; it was implicit in the Gaulish self-image of Hotman and his successors. What was picked up by all his adepts was Tacitus's original critique of the Roman Empire.

Germania, it will be recalled, was aimed at exposing the decadence that Rome had slipped into after it had turned from a Republic into an Empire. The message (also in Tacitus's contemporary Livy) was that *virtus* had driven the Republic and its conquests, while luxury and corruption had weakened the Empire. As we shall see in a subsequent chapter, all those political thinkers who, from Hotman to John Locke, Montesquieu and Rousseau, were to argue against the absolute power of kings, and who were forming the intellectual run-up to the democratic revolutions of America (1776) and France (1789), picked up on this Roman message: absolute monarchy means luxurious corruption, and only tribal democracy (in the form of parliaments) will maintain the nation's *virtus*. Thus the democratic primitivism of Tacitus was to inform the eighteenth-century tradition of classical republicanism;[49] its tribal nomenclature, grafted onto current ethnotypes, helped to schematize Europe's populations into a template of ethnic traditions.

Anthropology and the Nation: Character and Climate in the Seventeenth Century

The geopolitical state and the rise of systematics

In medieval statecraft, the realm was largely an abstract principle: the reach, or sphere of influence, as it were, of a ruler's power (*potestas, imperium*). Towards the end of the Middle Ages the monarch increasingly becomes the sole focus of a state's unity; a position he gains in a power struggle from his feudal nobles. Once the feudal disparateness of lordships under local noblemen has become centralized under an effective kingship with a growing bureaucratic state apparatus, the realization also takes hold that the *realm* is not just the reach of royal power and charisma, but a territorially discrete area cordoned off from its neighbours.

This process takes shape in different modes and at different times throughout Europe. The emergence of the Tudor dynasty establishes a centralized monarchical state in England and Wales; Philip II consolidates a Spanish centralist monarchy, and Louis XIV's surmounting of the *fronde* does the same for France. Compared to England, Spain or France, the German Empire remains diffracted. Emperor Maximilian I's attempt, as part of the 1495 *Reichsreform*, to establish a Perpetual Public Peace (*ewiger Landfriede*) throughout the empire, may be seen as a first, unsuccessful attempt to concentrate the right of using violence and of conducting warfare in the state rather than in the nobility. Kings and princes sometimes confront the self-government of cities, sometimes the ambitions of local noblemen; but disparate as the process is, in all cases the end result is that a king embodies his country and governs it through ministers and courtiers rather than through a feudal system of satellite lordships.

This process also signals the birth of geopolitics. The principle of a rounded-off territorial contiguity seems to assert itself. Whereas the map of Europe in the later Middle Ages resembles a game of Monopoly, with players trying to obtain titles and lands wherever these become available, a territorial rationalization takes places over the centuries.[50] The English crown abandons its claims on French territories, the various branches of the Habsburg dynasty withdraw to their own corners, and under Louis XIV France consolidates its hexagonal shape.

The French process is especially instructive. It was largely driven by the strategic thought of the great fortification engineer Sébastien de Vauban (1633-1707), one of Louis's ablest generals and one of the greatest fortification architects in European history. Whereas, under Richelieu, there had been an 'open' territorial policy, with Richelieu trying to stake claims for the French crowns at various points on the European map, Vauban wanted to turn all of France into one large fortress: a cordoned-off area which he called a *pré carré*. France had 'natural' frontiers along its sea coasts and the Pyrenees and Alps. The remaining, open frontier to the north-east would ideally

Vauban et les places fortes.

7. Outline of Vauban's fortifications. After Michèle Virol, Vauban: De la gloire du roi au service de l'état *(2003), 100.*

be closed off by gaining the Rhine as a border running from the Alps to the North Sea. Conquering and fortifying the cities of Metz, Strasbourg and Luxemburg was a first step in this direction:

> The old frontiers made up of 'provinces with their dependencies', and thereby complicated by irrational enclaves and feudal overlappings, had been satisfactory enough before the rise of the new armies and the new conceptions of political military power. A 'province with its capital city' could be a satisfactory 'gate' in Richelieu's parlance, but what was now needed was a frontier that could be defined and more easily defended by 'lines' to prevent marauding enemy detachments from collecting 'contributions' by invading the kingdom. Vauban had seen this in 1673 when he urged 'by treaty or by

a good war' that the irrational '*pêle mêlée*' of French and
Spanish fortresses scattered here and there on the frontier
should be made into a *pré carré*, a rational 'dueling field', that
could be defended without excessive costs. The Treaty of
Nymwegen did away with much of the irrationality on the
frontier with the Spanish Netherlands [...][51]

This process is partly made possible by a new look at the world: a cartographic one.
Rulers now study their territories from the bird's eye view from on high as the world
presents itself on a map; and following the development of perspective in Italian art
and architecture in the mid-fourteenth century, the art of map-making was likewise
much enhanced in the following centuries. As Jeremy Black points out, sovereignty,
which in the Middle Ages had been viewed in terms of feudal power, also came to be
perceived in geographical terms from the sixteenth century onwards, involving a greater and indeed cartographical sense of the extent and borders of a realm's territory:

There was a growing emphasis on what was seen as accuracy
[...] For both contemporary and historical maps this affected
a major subject, the depiction of frontiers. A firmer grasp of
the nature of a linear frontier developed, one that was possibly associated with improved mapping and a more definite
perception of the nature of political sovereignty [...][52]

The view of sovereignty also shifted morally. The Middle Ages had seen a flourishing
genre of writing known as the 'mirror of princes' – a moral looking-glass in which
kings were advised as to their proper behaviour, wisdom and attitude. The no-nonsense cynicism of Machiavelli's *The Prince* (1513) had dealt a death blow to these pious
moral mirrors. Instead, the new 'mirror of princes' was the map, where a king could
study the shape and lie of the land, the location and size of his dominions, enemies
and allies.

The new states cannot yet be called nation-states; they were, after all, centred
around the power of the king rather than based on the freedom of the people. But in
their rationalization and centralization they were moving away from the loose differentiation of the feudal Middle Ages.[53] The vernacular languages, for instance, were
everywhere becoming the official vehicle of state affairs and administration. Latin was
retreating into the institutions of the church and the university, while laws were now
enacted, and court cases were conducted, in the language of the land. At some point in
the late Middle Ages the English legal system abandoned the language of the conquering nobility of 1066, Norman French, and turned to 'The King's English' instead; and
in the course of the fourteenth century, the first lectures in English (rather than Latin)
were held at Oxford.[54] Dante's *De vulgari eloquentia* of 1303, though itself written in
Latin, stated the ambition of vernacular languages to be used for literary purposes – an
ambition that Dante himself was to make good with his *Divina Commedia*. The various vernacular dialects of Europe, as they were becoming languages of state affairs,
gained trans-local currency by means of the new state administrations and the printing

press, were beginning to crystallize into what was to become a system of European languages. In the Protestant countries, Bible translations into the vernacular (Luther's, the King James translation, the Dutch *Statenbijbel*) were to act as consolidating norms and provided a linguistic standard.

Europe, in other words, was becoming a modular system of separate states, each with a recognizable territory, language and profile. And by the same token, cultural thought on the diversity of the world was beginning to systematize. But what does that actually mean?

A good impression may be given by looking at a categorization that is *not* systematic. The most famous (but fictionally invented) example is a thought experiment conducted by the great Argentinian writer Jorge Luis Borges. He imagined a fictitious 'Chinese Encyclopedia', which in categorizing the animal kingdom lists the various types of animals in the following order:

> Animals are distinguished in: [a] those belonging to the Emperor; [b] embalmed ones; [c] tamed ones; [d] suckling pigs; [e] sirens; [f] fable animals; [g] dogs on the loose; [h] those included in this classification; [i] ones that move about madly; [j] countless ones; [k] those painted with a very fine camelhair brush; [l] etcetera; [m] those that have broken the jar; [n] those that from afar resemble flies.[55]

The reader gets a hilarious sense of unease when reading this quasi-taxonomy. We understand a proper taxonomy to provide a systematically ordered division of a complex system in its component parts (e.g. the Linnaean division of vertebrate animals in fishes, amphibians, reptiles, mammals and birds), to enumerate enough categories to cover the entire animal kingdom, while each category is in itself complete, neither overlapping with other categories nor leaving any lacunae between them. What Borges's list fails to provide, indeed what it provokes and irritates, is this sense of systematics, which is apparently conceived of as 'Western' – it is not for nothing that Borges presents his provocation of an unsystematic taxonomy in an Oriental, Chinese guise (though he goes on to draw attention to the no less bizarre categorizations in Western libraries). This fragment was also the starting point for Michel Foucault's inquiry into the beginnings of methodical and systematic thought in modern Western history: The preface to *Les mots et les choses* (1966) opens, precisely, with a self-analysis of Foucault's hilarity when reading Borges's 'Chinese Encyclopedia'.

The urge towards systematic, taxonomic ordering will lead, in the eighteenth and nineteenth centuries, to the great classifications of modern science. If we want to classify plants or animals, we do not do so by means of incidental, ad hoc qualities like colour or size, but by more fundamental characteristics, and this will lead to the systems of Linnaeus, Buffon and Darwin. Chemists will first distinguish elements from compounds, and eventually classify the elements in a 'Periodic Table'. Comparative linguistics following Sir William Jones, Grimm and Bopp will sort out, in a methodical and systematic manner, the relationships between languages and language families. Modern science is dominated by method, systematics and taxonomy. So too, cultures and 'nations' will be categorized in the course of the seventeenth and eighteenth centuries, on the basis of ethnotypes reconfigured into what comes to be called 'national temperaments' or 'national characters'.

The systematics of national character

The European taxonomy of national character is a perfect example of a process that also intrigued Foucault: methodical systematization as a hallmark of modern Western thought. The Middle Ages had, to be sure, known many commonplaces, stereotypes and prejudices about certain sets of people, but these were generally speaking neither stable nor systematic. Nobody was sure how the category 'French' related to the category 'Picardian', what was an Irishman and what a good subject of the King of England. The term 'Dutch' could apply specifically to the Low-German area at the estuary of the Meuse and Rhine, in Holland, or else, generally, to inhabitants of any part of the German Empire.

This unsystematic national mishmash crystallizes into recognizable, fixed patterns in the early modern period. Modern thought as it takes hold in the Renaissance and dominates the classically-oriented seventeenth century is obsessed with method and systematics and 'sorting things out'. A good example of this urge to systematize can be found in one of the foundational texts of early-modern European culture: Julius Caesar Scaliger's *Poetices libri VII* (1561). This encyclopedic work bespeaks an almost manic urge to list, order and sort. And among the many sorted lists with which this book classifies the world, there are also lists of national characteristics as attributed to certain nations:

> Luxury is the hallmark of the Asians, mendacity of Africans, cleverness (if you will allow) of Europeans. Mountain people are rough, people from the low-lying plains are demure and slow. [...] Germans are strong, simple, open, true in friendship and in enmity. The Swedes, Norse, Greenlanders and Goths are bestial, and so are the Scots and Irish. The English are perfidious, puffed-up, cross-tempered, arrogant, of a mocking and quarrelsome disposition, divided amongst themselves, warlike when united, stubborn, independent and pitiless. The French are attentive, mobile, nimble, humane, hospitable, spendthrift, respectable, martial; they scorn their enemies and are heedless of themselves; they are self-controlled, brave, not very tenacious, and by far the best horsemen of all. The Spanish have a dour life-style, they live it up when they sit at another man's table, they are fiery drinkers, talkative, busy, their arrogance is hellish, their disrespect infernal, their stinginess amazing; they are strong in poverty, their religious steadfastness is priceless, they are envious of all nations and all nations are envious of them. One nation sur-

passes them in wickedness and is even less magnanimous: the Italians.[56]

Although still a bit 'Borgesian' in its waywardness, this contrastive list shows an emerging comparative tendency to arrange moral praise and blame into patterns. This contrastive-comparative systematization was to become enormously influential all over Europe in the following century. Scaliger's work, and subsequent *Poetics*-style encyclopedias, loosely inspired by Aristotle, were to dominate the culture of seventeenth-century European classicism. In many poems and disquisitions, nations are collectively enumerated in contrastive lists, in which the spectrum of human dispositions, temperaments* and proclivities is sorted and distributed. Each nation has its defining traits, each human trait can be encountered in pronounced form in a specific nation.

This, then, is the most important side effect of Scaliger's listings: nations are now primarily ordered by temperaments, personality-attributes, *characters*. There is, I think, a specific (though unexpected) reason why this psychological ordering-by-temperament should have become so very influential: namely, the fact that it also dominated the literary imagination and suffused all of European literature.

Poetics and anthropology

It is not just a trivial coincidence that the context for Scaliger-style lists of national characteristics should have been made in a book that he himself called a *Poetics*. Indeed, the rich tradition of neo-Aristotelian poetical writings of the seventeenth century is precisely the genre where this type of characterization is most systematically set forth, and where it influences the many classicist dramas that dominated the European literary scene in this period. The *poetical* systematization of human types-by-character serves to program the European imagination, the way of looking at the world.

The numerous classicist poetical writings that appear in the course of the seventeenth century are all reworkings of the genre's prototype: Aristotle's *Poetics*. Aristotle, in this tract, attempted to define what precisely it was that made literature special: what literature's appeal consisted of, and why some literature, like Homer and the Attic tragedies, was so efficient in transporting us into fictional circumstances and moving us deeply. In the process, he defined a number of important literary proper-

---

* The idea of 'temperament' comes from the pre-scientific medical theories of Hippocrates and Galenus. People's physical-emotional disposition was considered to be determined by certain bodily fluids called 'humours': these included blood, bile, black bile or gall, and phlegm. These humours needed to be in a healthy balance (not unlike modern thinking about hormones); the mutual balance and 'tuning' of those humours was called a person's temperament. This theory has survived in informal phraseology. A state of emotional discomfort or disturbance is still called a 'bad temper' or *mauvaise humeur*. An excess of blood induced a passionate, 'sanguine' temperament; an excess of gall (*cholos* in Greek, 'bile' in English) made someone 'choleric' or 'bilious', and an excess of black gall 'melancholic'. The preponderance of phlegm (believed to be produced by the spleen) made someone 'phlegmatic' or 'splenetic'. Generally Zacharasiewicz 1977.

ties, techniques and strategies. One of these was the need to have a plausible connection between plotline and characters. A heroic action must be carried out by an admirable hero; an admirable hero cannot be deployed to carry out silly or despicable parts in the action. The things a given character does in a story must be in keeping with that character's personality. This link between personality (characterization) and plotline (plausibility), came to be known by its French term of *vraisemblance*, and was considered indispensable if a literary work was to convince its audience.[57]

Neo-Aristotelian poetics took Aristotle's descriptive analysis and turned it into a prescriptive set of rules. If a playwright wanted to construct a properly convincing tragedy, so the argument ran, a number of Aristotle's principles had to be observed: a structure in five acts, unified in time, space and plot, etcetera. Aristotle's descriptions were turned into prescriptions, and much of classicist drama went by the rules of neo-Aristotelian poetics, became drama-by-numbers, with the poetical handbook providing the recipe.

Part of the prescriptions of neo-Aristotelian poetics concerned, precisely, the plausible characterization of actors in the plot. And here, a marked tendency was to characterize by type: a male is like this, a female like that; a soldier, monk or princess comes with certain pre-programmed, stereotyped personality traits. These are the rules of plausibility that have to be observed. For a silly female personage, use the type of the servant girl; for a dignified woman, use a widowed queen; for a cheerful, energetic young man, use a student. And in many, many cases, the ready-made types that classified personality style were categorized by nationality. One may call this the poetics of predictability, and it reigned supreme throughout the classicist period.[58]

A good example is given by one among many of these works of poetics, the *Poétique* of Jules de la Mesnardière (1640). La Mesnardière urges playwrights again and again, not to shock *vraisemblance* and not to bewilder the audience: characters ought to be typified according to their function in the plot, and to be given matching social and ethnic attributes.[59] If, so La Mesnardière argues, Germans are proverbially dull and boorish, then a German character should always be shown as such. To introduce a clever, witty German would be a sin against *vraisemblance*. And so we get lists like these:

> Now, according to country: French will be courageous, indiscreet, generous, adroit, inconsiderate, impetuous, flighty, spendthrift, easy-going, polite, light-hearted in their love affairs, impatient and bold. Spaniards presumptuous, uncivil to strangers, knowledgeable in political intrigue, tyrannical, greedy, constant, capable of supporting great exertion, indifferent to climate, ambitious, scornful, stately (even extravagantly so), blindly passionate about their nation's glory, ridiculous in their love affairs and fanatical in their hatred. I have seen from visits that the English are faithless, lazy, valiant, cruel, attached to cleanliness, enemies to foreigners, proud and partial. If we can follow a great authority, excellent observer of the manners of each nation, the Italians are idle, impious, seditious, mistrustful, deceitful and stay-at-home,

fidelité, la parfaite connoiſſance de la Science
Politique; bref vn vtile meſlange de probité &
de lumiéres. Les Princes & les Princeſſes au-
ront les meſmes attributs que ie donne aux
Rois & aux Reines; auec quelque diminution,
non pas des grandeurs de l'Ame, mais des hau-
tes magnificences, qui doiuent eſtre reglées
par les degrez des fortunes.

Le Chancelier ſera ſçauant, graue, doux, iu-
dicieux, acceſſible, régulier, affable, mais incorruptible. Le Pontife, docte, éloquent, ce-
rémonieux, retenu, pudique, religieux, pa-
tient & venérable. Le Courtiſan ſera ciuil,
adroit, ſoigneux, agréable, propre, officieux,
cajolleur. Le Capitaine, vaillant, hardi, vigi-
lant, glorieux, amoureux de ſon meſtier, franc,
prudent & laborieux.

Voila ce qui eſt attaché, ou du moins ce qui
le doit eſtre, aux différentes conditions qui en-
trent dans la Tragédie, & s'y rendent conſidé-
rables.

Maintenant ſelon les Païs, les François ſeront
hardis, courtois, indiſcrets, genéreux, adroits,
inconſiderez, impetueux, inconſtâs, prodigues,
peu laborieux, polis, legers dans leurs amours,
impatiens & téméraires. Les Eſpagnols pré-
ſomptueux, inciuils aux étrangers, ſçauans dans
la Politique, tyrans, auares, conſtans, capables
de toutes fatigues, indifferens à tous climats,
ambitieux, mépriſans, graues iuſqu'à l'extraua-
gance, paſſionnez aueuglément pour la gloire

Margin notes: Qualitez des Princes & des Princeſſes. Qualitez des Chanceliers. Qualitez des Pontifes. Qualitez des Courtiſans. Qualitez des Capitaines. La Nation, 4. ſource des Mœurs. Qualitez des François. Des Eſpagnols.

de leur Nation, ridicules dans leurs amours, &
furieux dans leur haine. I'ay veu par la fre-
quentation, que les Anglois ſont infidelles,
parreſſeux, vaillans, cruels, amateurs de la pro-
preté, ennemis des étrangers, altiers & inte-
reſſez. Si nous en croyons vn Grand homme,
excellent obſeruateur des mœurs de chaque
Nation, les Italiens ſont oyſifs, impies, ſedi-
tieux, ſoupçonneux, fourbes, caſanniers, ſub-
tils, courtois, vindicatifs, amateurs de la poli-
teſſe, & paſſionnez pour le profit. Les Allemans ſeront ſincéres, groſſiers, fidelles, mode-
ſtes, banqueteurs, affables, vaillans, amoureux
de la liberté. Les Perſes religieux, ambitieux,
riches, adroits, doux, guerriers, & défians. Les
Grecs vains, menteurs, orgueilleux, adroits,
ſçauans, & raiſonnables. Les Egyptiens parreſſeux, timides, voluptueux, & addonnez à la
magie. Les Maures foux, deſeſperez, peu ſou-
cieux de la vie, opiniâtres, & infidelles. Les
Thraciens violens, iniurieux à leurs hoſtes, auares, farouſches, perfides. Les Scythes cruels,
miſerables, barbares & vagabons.

A cette heure ſelon les Sexes; les hommes
feront ſolides, rudes, hardis, genéreux, cha-
grins, réſolus, auares, prudens, ambitieux, tran-
quilles, fidelles & laborieux. Les Femmes ſont
diſſimulées, douces, foibles, delicates, mode-
ſtes, pudiques, courtoiſes, ſublimes en leurs
penſées, ſoudaines en leurs deſirs, violentes
dans leurs paſſions, ſoupçonneuſes dans leurs

Q ij

Margin notes: Des Anglois. Magnus Cæſar Sca-liger. Des Italiens. Des Allemans. Des Perſes. Des Grecs. Des Egyptiens. Des Maures. Des Thraciens. Des Scythes. Le Sexe, 6. ſource des Mœurs. Qualitez des hommes. Qualitez ordinaires des Femmes.

8. Page from *La Mesnardière's* La poétique.

subtle, courteous, vengeful, they love good manners and
adore profit. Germans will be sincere, stolid, faithful, mod-
est, big eaters, affable, stout and lovers of liberty.[60]

– and so on, down to Persians, Greeks, Egyptians, Moors, Thracian and Scyths...
Remarkably, these national characters are (as we can gather from La Mesnardière's
presentation) indiscriminately a matter of personal observation, hearsay, and empty
formula.

In this and the subsequent century, all treatises on cultural diversity use such classifications. It is not for nothing that literary criticism should have been in the vanguard
of this development: for it was in these poetics that people thought most specifically
about how to bring all the world together on a stage, and on the link between what
people *were* and what they *did*.[61] This logical 'hinge' between people's identity and
people's behaviour was acquiring a new relevance in modern times. In the moral perspective of medieval Christendom, humans had a free will and a *soul*, which was subject to temptations but also to the scrutiny of an all-knowing deity. The behaviour of
people was a constant set of ethical choices between the prescripts of religion and the
temptations of the Devil, between the urge to rise to salvation and the downward pull
of our animal nature.

In the context of seventeenth-century poetics, encyclopedias and anthropology, behaviour was also determined by mechanical factors such as humours and temperament (themselves influenced, as we shall see, by physical circumstances such as climate); and the agency that determined behaviour was conceived of less and less in terms of *conscience* or *soul*, and increasingly in the Aristotelian, poetic terms of personality, of how one's actions were motivated by one's station in life and one's type – or, to use a word that just came in vogue in these years: by one's *character*.

Early modern literature, and with it the imagination of early modern Europe, begins to acquire a habit of looking characterologically. Whereas, in medieval romance, the chivalric knights *were* exactly what they *did*, were mere functions of their plot activity (going on quests, rescuing maidens, fighting dragons, whatever), this one-on-one congruence between identity and behaviour is complicated in modern literature. The two great literary figures that stand at the opening of the modern period, Don Quixote and Hamlet, are marked precisely by this complex tension: between what they do and what they really are. The hero of Cervantes's 1605 novel marks a tragicomic dissociation between his role and his person, and this is precisely why *Don Quixote* is a modern novel (the first one, indeed) and not a medieval romance. Likewise, the introspective, wavering hero of Shakespeare's 1602 play keeps us guessing as to his motivation: is his slow course of action a sign of deliberate carefulness, repugnance at the task, or vacillating weakness? Has his moral dilemma (to kill his mother so as to avenge his father) driven him mad, or is he merely pretending to be mad in order to cloak his plans? The ambiguity is, again, one between action and identity, between what we do and what we are. Hamlet and Don Quixote (and a half-century later, the thematization of social role-playing and moral hypocrisy in Molière's *Tartuffe*) mark the beginning of psychological interest in post-medieval European literature.[62] As this new preoccupation with 'the fundamental part of our personality which motivates our behaviour' gains currency, a term is gaining currency to denote it: the notion of *character*.

Character: From behavioural reputation to psychological essence[63]

'That fundamental part of our personality that motivates our behaviour': that seems to be, simply and straightforwardly, the meaning of the word 'character' as we use it nowadays. It is not, however, the oldest, root meaning of the word. Originally the word referred, rather, to the *impression someone produced*. Old-fashioned English can still use the word in the sense of 'reputation': 'a man of good character' means that someone is positively seen among those who know him; 'character assassination' refers to ruining, not someone's personality, but someone's good name and reputation.

The oldest root of the word in fact referred to a *sketch* of the impression that someone made, the figure that you cut in society. It derives from a Greek word *grattein*, meaning to sketch, scribble or scratch on a wax tablet. (Hence one of the oldest meanings of the word 'character' refers to lettering: a book can be said to be printed in Greek, Cyrillic or Japanese *characters*.) The term was used as a title of a verbal 'sketch-book' by the Greek author Theophrastos, a pupil of Aristotle's. Theophrastos assembled, around 300 BC, a collection of *èthikoi charakteres* or 'behaviour-sketches', in which he outlined gently satirical descriptive portrayals of social types that one might encounter in the streets of Athens. That genre has remained popular ever since. We still enjoy the power of literature to 'typify' certain 'characters', often in humorous terms. We speak, almost unthinkingly, of a quixotic person, a Romeo or a Don Juan. In contemporary culture, Basil Fawlty, the choleric hotel owner in the television sit-com *Fawlty Towers*, stands in this Theophrastan tradition: he pinpoints, in height-ened, mocking form, a sort of human type that we may have encountered in various instances ourselves. Such stock types or characters are the boastful old soldier, the vain young dandy, the dumb blonde, the lusty widow, etcetera. Nowadays, character sketches are often incorporated into comedies or novels, or part of the repertoire of stand-up comedians (Dickens is full of them, Oscar Wilde has given us the 'type' of Lady Bracknell, and television serials have spawned an entire array of personality 'types'). The genre of the character sketch was popular throughout the seventeenth century, the most famous example being probably La Bruyère's collection *Les caractères ou les moeurs de ce siècle*. As the subtitle indicates, the idea of a 'character' is behaviour-al, social, referring to 'the manners of our times': modes of speaking, dressing, postur-ing.[64]

All this, to be sure, referred originally to someone's *outside*: the front they put up, the image they project, the pose they strike. A character dealt with how someone *came over* in his or her environment. As the seventeenth century, with its psychological interest, progresses, however, the notion of character becomes less and less one of social impressions and increasingly one of inner motivation: what makes that person tick? What makes them behave the way they do? From what inner disposition does this behaviour emanate?

Interestingly, an entire set of terms and words that originally refer to the social out-side of a personality, later come to refer to the inner mainspring of behaviour and identity. The word 'character' shifts from the semantic field of reputation and repre-sentation to that of psychology; likewise the words 'type' and 'style'.* Again, the word 'habit', now generally referring to fixed patterns of behaviour, originally referred to one's dress, and the word 'custom' referred to costume, or to the way one dressed one's hair. Terms like 'ethics' and 'morals', now primarily seen as reflecting inner eva-luations and standards on what should or should not be done, or what is right and wrong, originally derive from the neutrally-descriptive, non-valorizing Greek and La-tin words for behaviour and manners, social conventions: *mores, ethos*.

So, too, the notion of 'character' is psychologized, internalized, and shifts its mean-ing to the one still current today: 'The sum of the moral and mental qualities which distinguish an individual or a race [...] mental or moral constitution' (*Oxford English Dictionary*). In this shift, neo-Aristotelian poetics played a crucial role, in that it, more

---

* The word 'style' derives from the Greek *stylos*, the stylus or pen used for scribbling on wax tablets (cf. also Van Delft 1996 and, more generally, Amossy & Rosen 1982). This etymology adds an ironic extra dimension to the famous dictum by Buffon, in his *Discours sur le style* of 1753, that *Le style, c'est l'homme même* ('one's style is one's very personality').

than any other form of thought or writing, was concerned with the articulation of how the inner personality related to and motivated outward behaviour.

In the wake of this semantic shift, it comes as no surprise to see that the notion of character becomes the primary way of sorting out human and cultural differences. As the above-quoted definition in the *Oxford English Dictionary* has it, a character *distinguishes* an individual or a race. It is in fact tantamount to what gives us our identity as individuals. If modern thought is concerned with a systematic categorization of the world, as Scaliger already undertook; if one tries to replace the wayward ad hoc listings in the style of Borges's 'Chinese Encyclopedia' with something that can be called *methodical*; then the method consists of sorting out the diversity of the world by its fundamental, essential characteristics. As skin colour was used to classify the world's *races* (down to the nonsensical notion of calling Asiatics 'yellow' and Americans 'red'), so in the realm of human culture, character becomes a dominant criterion for sorting out Europe's *nations*. The seventeenth and eighteenth century sees the rise of a national anthropology in European cultural thought – a quasi-system lifted from the realm of stereotype and fictional characterization, of which we still, naively, uncritically and habitually, make use nowadays.

National identity – that is to say: national specificity within a European spectrum – will come to revolve largely around the idea of 'national character', but will incorporate under that heading other factors such as language, manners and customs. The margins of seventeenth-century maps are often embellished, not only with allegorical figures symbolizing the earth and the relations between countries and realms, but also with little vignettes depicting the various nationalities who inhabit the area in question – and marked out as such by the 'characteristic' dress and habit. In this manner, maps already take on to a small extent the notion of an ethnographically illustrated geography (cf. ill. 2).

Later in the seventeenth century, we see how the categorized listings in the style of Scaliger and La Mesnardière are systematized into a two-dimensional matrix. A number of attempts to give a summarized synopsis of knowledge (what will evolve into the genre of the encyclopedia) are cases in point. The earliest example of a national-characterological matrix I have been able to find comes from a book published in Nuremberg in 1696, by the Dominican priest Johann Zahn. In this encyclopedic volume, *Specula physico-mathematico-historica notabilium ac mirabilium sciendarum* or 'Physical-mathematical and historical mirrors of noteworthy and marvellous things to know',[*] the author – a very remote intellectual descendant of Giraldus Cambrensis, by way of Scaliger – also deals with the nations of Europe and lists their distinctive

---

[*] The title seems worthy of Borges's Chinese Encyclopedia. In full, it continues: 'In which the marvellous and amazingly ample world-system, obscure and complex as it is, is now brought into light, and a treasury of abridgements to learn the various sciences by a very easy method, is presented for inspection to all curious world-investigators' (*in qua mundi mirabilis oeconomia, necnon mirificè amplus, et magnificus ejusdem abditè reconditus, nunc autem ad lumen protractus ac ad varias perfacili methodo acquirendas scientias in epitomen collectus thesaurus curiosis omnibus cosmosophis inspectandus proponitur*). We see how the *mirabilia* of Giraldus Cambrensis's day have evolved by the end of the seventeenth century.

innumeræ aliæ splendore, divitiis, Incolarum multitudine, ac commerciis celeberrimæ.

§. Quemadmodùm diverſæ in Europâ regiones tùm Cœli, tùm Soli, tùm aquarum fluvialium, aliarumque ratione ſimiles non ſunt; ita nec Incolarum terreſtrium, hominumque mores ubivis conveniunt. Sic diu jam Thraces decantati ſunt pigri & iniqui; Itali laſcivi, avari, regalium dignitatum cupidi; Germani guloſi, bibuli, fortes, generoſi, ſimplices ac fideles; Hiſpani morum gravitate ampli, elata jactantiæ animoſitate præpoſiti, ambitioſi, ingenioſi & religioſi; Angli crudeles ac feroces, vafri & varii; Siculi acuti, Cretenſes ſemper mendaces &c. De quinque notiſſimis, valde tamen differentibus nationibus, Germanica ſcilicet, Hiſpanica, Italica, Gallica, & Anglica hæ vulgatæ ſunt obſervationes.

Differentiæ quinque præcipuarum in Europâ Nationum, ut Germanicæ, Hiſpanicæ, Italicæ, Gallicæ & Anglicæ.

	Germanus	Hiſpanus	Italus	Gallus	Anglus
Corpore	Robuſtus	horrendus	debilis	agilis	delicatus
Animo inſtar	Urſi	Elephantis	Vulpis	Aquilæ	Leonis
Veſtitu	finius	modeſtus	lugubris	protheus & vertumnus	ſuperbus
Moribus	ſerius	gravis	facilis	Oſtentator	ſuavis
Pulchritudine velut	Statua	Diabolus	Vir	Fœmina	Angelus
Victu	ebrius	faſtidioſus	ſobrius	delicatus	guloſus
Sermone	ululat	loquitur	delirat	cantat	flet
In arcanis	oblivioſus	mutus	taciturnus	garrulus	inſidiæ.
In ſcientiâ	Juriſta	Theologus	Architectus	ex omnibus aliquid	Philoſophus
In fide	fidelis	fallax	ſuſpectus	levis	perfidus
In conſiliis	tardus	cautus	ſubtilis	præceps	imprudens
In Religione	ſuperſtitioſus	conſtans	religioſus	zeloſus	mutabilis
Magnificentia	in munimentis	in armis	in templis	in aulis	in claſſibus bellicis
In Conjugio Maritus eſt	Dominus	Tyrannus	Carceris cuſtos	Socius	Servus
Fœmina	ſtudioſa ſupellectilis	Mancipium	Incarcerata	Domina	Regina
Famulus	Socius	ſubjectus	obſequioſus	Famulus	Mancipium
Morbi quibus affliguntur	Podagra	omnis generis morbis	Peſtis	Lue venerea	Lupus
In morte	paratus	generoſus	deſperatus	invitus	præſumptuoſus.

Fuit etiam Poëta, quimorum differentias in diverſis Europæ Nationibus artificioſè his verſibus expreſſit:

Hiſpanus, Gallus, Teuto, Italus atq Polonus
Conſtans, inconſtans, fidus, avarus inops
Splendorem, mores, promiſſum, lucra, ſuperbum
Quærit, commutat, ſervat, acervat, agit.

Qui verſus ſic legi debent: Hiſpanus conſtans ſplendorem quærit: Gallus inconſtans mores commutat & cæt.

9. Inſulæ

9. *Zahn's schematization of national characteristics, 1696*

characteristics under the heading 'The differences between the five most important nations in Europe, i.e. the German, Spanish, Italian, French and English ones'. These are, to be sure, lists in the style of Scaliger and La Mesnardière; but what is new is the grouping into a synoptic matrix. It tabulates how the nations in question differ in physical build, in the sort of animal they resemble, clothing, manners, style of beauty, eating habits, language, discretion, education, religion, etc. It is an anecdotal list that often appears satirical in intent: Germans resemble bears, Spaniards resemble elephants, the French resemble eagles; the speech of the Italians is raving, that of the English whiny; as husbands, the Spaniards are tyrants, the Italians are prison-keepers and the English servants.

The combination of categories is in itself remarkable. Nations are (and will for a long time continue to be) represented by the way they dress, and diet will also remains an important 'characteristic'. At the same time, observations will be added concerning the political and social system in which a given 'nation' lives. But all that will be summed up morally by references to character and disposition, as if the outward appearances are motivated by an inner essence.

This principle (outward appearances are taken to be motivated by an inner essence) we may properly call 'essentialism': and so the intriguing implication is that a comparative-systematic view of European nationalities arises conjointly with a new national essentialism.

Contrastive matrices like these became popular around 1700. The great Spanish Benedictine savant Benito Feijoo (1676-1764) borrowed the model from Zahn in his *Teatro crítico universal* (1726-1739);[65] but its most famous spin-off is doubtless the *Völkertafel* or 'Tableau of Nationalities' that was produced in a number of painted and printed copies in Southern Germany and Austria between 1690 and 1720, and which is reproduced on the cover of this book.[66] We see the various nationalities arranged left-to-right on a West-to-East axis, from Spaniard to Ottoman,[*] and represented by a figure in representative dress. Underneath, a matrix, distributing over the columns of these nationalities various characteristics – often whimsical or satirical – such as mode of dress, manners, intelligence, vices, love-life, prevailing illnesses, martial vigour, religion, political system, lifestyle etcetera. The *Völkertafel* obviously continues the pictorial tradition of map-making, the characterological lists of Scaliger and La Mesnardière, and the encyclopedistic approach of Zahn and Feijoo; but there is something new too.

The matrix imposes, as a form, the implicit rule that for each of the listed characteristics, a value must be filled in for each of the nationalities. It would not do to leave any of the squares blank. The comparative system imposes a discipline; not only does it make it easier to visualize things, it forces one to follow the system in all its steps and elements. Nor would it do to list similar values in different squares: each of the squares has to say something different. Zahn had already called his matrix a system of *differences*, and that is what it must be; a matrix listing similarities and saying the same things about different nations would be, by its own rules, stupid.

In other words: the comparative tabulation of European nationalities is oppositional in nature and leads to particularism; by which I mean that from the mid-seventeenth century onwards, the nations of Europe begin to locate their identities in their mutual differences. Common factors, common vices and manners, cease to be of importance in this taxonomy. Nations will come to see their character, their individuality, in those aspects in which they differ most from others.

---

[*] Curiously, the Ottoman is indiscriminately labelled Turkish or Greek, *Türk oder Griech* – a reflection perhaps of the fact that the Ottoman Empire was governed in an administrative division by religious groups (*millets*) rather than by ethnicity, and that its Christian *millet* in the European territory was largely administered at the time by an ethnically Greek elite, the Phanariots. Even so, it does startle the modern viewer to see such categories, nowadays so polarized, conflated. It reminds us how changeable national identities are over time.

Climate and temperament[67]

One of the great rationalizations for the new characterological anthropology of Europe's nations is by way of climate. The climatological explanation of national character has, again, long historical roots. In his medical treatises such as 'On conditions of air, water and location', Hippocrates had already made a link between the prevalence of certain sicknesses, and certain temperaments, with physical ambience (marshy and wet, or rocky and windy; hot or cold). Hippocrates's link between climate and temperament was easily enough transmuted into a link between climate and character. The legal thinker and historian Jean Bodin (1530-1596, a fellow-traveller of Hotman[68]) assigned, in his *Methodus ad facilem historiarum cognitionem* (1566) phlegmatics to cold and humid places, sanguinics to hot and humid ones, cholerics to hot and dry ones, and melancholics to cold and dry ones. In Du Bartas's epic on the history of the world, *La sepmaine, ou création du monde* (1578-1584, translated into many European languages), the link was already proverbial, a matter of commonplace. Hot climates will lead to a 'hot' temperament and a sanguine national character, as in Italy; cold, wet living conditions, e.g. in Holland, will lead to a phlegmatic, damp character. Generally, the world is seen to be divided into hot, moderate and cold climatezones. Every nation has a tendency to place itself in the central, moderate zone, with chilly neighbours to the north and fiery neighbours to the south. How this commonplace works its way through literary texts may be gathered from Daniel Defoe's satire *The True-Born Englishman* of 1700, where the sensual, untrustworthy character of the Italians is metaphorically likened to, and explained from, the hot climate of the place and the volcanic nature of the land. Etna, Stromboli and Vesuvius form, as it were, the geological underpinning of a Latin Lover:

> Lust chose the torrid zone of Italy,
> Where blood ferments in rapes and sodomy;
> Where swelling veins o'erflow with livid streams,
> With heat impregnate from Vesuvian flames:
> Whose flowing sulphur forms infernal lakes,
> And human body of the soil partakes
> There nature ever burns with hot desires,
> Fanned with luxuriant air from subterranean fires:
> Here undisturbed in floods of scalding lust
> Th'infernal king reigns with infernal gust.[69]

All this is the stuff of literary commonplace and stereotype, something which in literary criticism is called the objective fallacy (the generally current, but in fact untenable idea that there is a natural correspondence between the emotional, inner state of human subjects and the external situation). This climatological underpinning of temperaments and characters becomes more politically important if it is correlated with political systems. In eighteenth-century political thought, we see an increasing tendency to link the cool climates and characters of the North with a democratic, republican state system and with the protestant religion, while the hot south is linked to absolute monarchy and Catholicism.

The argument runs as follows: in cool, northern climes, the people are more pensive and less sensual than in the south. They are more retiring, less gregarious, and hence more individualistic (as opposed to the greater sociability of warm, southern climes). Correspondingly, northerners will rely more on individual judgment than on collective agreement; they will value personal responsibility more than popular consent. It is no surprise, then, to see Protestantism, which relies more on individual morality, more widely established in the north, whereas the ritual, ceremony and pageantry of Catholicism strikes a more responsive chord in the south. Also, northern government will be based more on the deliberation of individuals than on the obedience of a collective; hence, the north will incline towards parliaments and republics, the south more to monarchical systems (much as in church matters, Catholicism is more like a monarchy and Protestantism more like a federal republic).

The reader will recognize in this model the distant echoes of Tacitus's democratic primitivism; and indeed, it was formulated in its strongest form by none other than Tacitus's great modern adept, Montesquieu (1689-1755). Even in present-day politics, one can encounter such North-South stereotypes. Stereotypes they are, of course: they owe more to the commonplaces and formulas of La Mesnardière's poetics than to real-world observation, and on reflection this North-South model turns out to be a drastic, misleading simplification. Catholicism is not just the *Semana Santa* at Seville, or a papal ceremony in the Vatican: it also thrives in the rainy northern climes of Poland, Ireland and the Scottish Highlands. Prussia, despite its northern location, is a prime example of an absolute monarchy, while the strongest republican traditions of early modern Europe we find, not just in the Netherlands, but also in city-states like Venice, San Marino, Lucca and Dubrovnik; and Protestantism is not just the religion of Upsala, but also that of Geneva. 'North' and 'South' are, in characterological terms, vague and evocative metaphors, not real points on the compass.

Even so, climate theory became a massively important template in schematizing the temperaments and characters of the European nations, maybe because it formed such a natural extension of the implicit north-south contrast that was already inscribed into foundational texts like Tacitus's *Germania*. Thus the classical republicanism of the Enlightenment relied uncritically on the idea that history was partly driven by the different character-stereotypes of the European nations.

'National character' in Enlightenment philosophy

'The proper study of mankind is Man', as the poet Alexander Pope put it in his *Essay on Criticism* (1713). The fundamental preoccupation of the Enlightenment was the proper understanding of what it meant to be human. Aided by the faculty of critical reason, aloof from traditional nostrums, inherited dogmas and arguments-by-authority, a new notion was developed of humanity, the human understanding and human relations. It is no coincidence that the great Enlightenment spirits, such as Hume, Montesquieu, Voltaire and Rousseau, were at the same time historians and psychologists, philosophers and cultural critics. All these methods were centred around a large, ambitious agenda of *the proper study of mankind*: to understand the nature of Man, with Man's achievements, history and relations.

Following this anthropological* agenda, the Enlightenment seeks to gain knowledge, not only through abstract, philosophical cogitation (on the origin and function of language, or on the origin and development of an individual's intelligence and understanding), but also from empirical data, taken either from history or else from different societies and countries. These data illustrate the patterns, variants and variations of human affairs. A thinker like David Hume (1711-1776) not only studies the psychological development of human intelligence in the abstract (*Enquiry Concerning Human Understanding*, 1748), but also by investigating history. Indeed, Hume (now considered one of the greatest Western philosophers) was famous in his own lifetime mainly as a historian, with his *magnum opus* the *History of England from the Invasion of Julius Caesar to the Revolution of 1688* (1754).[70] This is one of the key texts in what is often called 'philosophical history'. For someone like Hume, history-writing was a branch of philosophy, analysing the historical record as if it were a long, diachronic database of human personalities, actions and choices, strengths and follies. History, as Hume's contemporary Bolingbroke put it, was 'philosophy teaching by example'.

But if history provided a diachronic database of human manners and personalities, then a synchronic database was turned to as well: the human variations as represented in different societies, different nations, different national characters. Hume is not averse to drawing on commonplace information on national characteristics; nor are his contemporaries. In the process, the Enlightenment's anthropological 'study of mankind' gives a 'philosophical' endorsement to racial and national stereotypes as these had been categorized and systematized in the previous century. Thus, there is only a small step from the *Völkertafel's* contrastive commonplaces to the philosophy of Montesquieu.

Montesquieu was deeply interested in the relativity of cultural standards, in the fact that there is no absolute, universal morality but rather different moral codes in differ-

---

* The term 'anthropology' originally refers to the philosophical investigation of what it means to be human. As such, it fits the undifferentiated universalism of the Enlightenment, which tends to deal in general categories (Man, Freedom, Understanding, Culture, Literature, Language). Obviously, this universalism egocentrically generalized the specific identity of Enlightenment thinkers (white, male, wealthy, European) into a universal type, thereby marginalizing all humans and all forms of human culture that do not fit this particular profile. By the end of the eighteenth century, these universals were broken up, and the generalities of Enlightenment thought were abandoned in favour of comparative reflections on diversity (the plurality of cultures, languages, literatures, various forms/races/types of humanity). In anthropology, we can see the shift between Kant, who still uses the term *Anthropologie* in its philosophical, universalist sense, and the Humboldt brothers, who already use it in the new, comparative-ethnographical sense familiar to us nowadays: anthropology as the ethnographical study of the distinctive cultural features of different societies. The Enlightenment has been heavily criticized by recent critics for its tendency to cloak a white, male, European supremacy in the discourse of universal values. Historically speaking, however, these blind spots in Enlightenment were exacerbated rather than resolved by the various forms of anti-Enlightenment chauvinism that became dominant in the following century.

10. Charles de Secondat, Baron de Montesquieu

ent societies. His satirical epistolary novel *Lettres persanes* (1721) illustrates this by mockingly describing French society from the foreign perspective of two Persian visitors; France is thus, ironically, seen through a foreign, exotic mirror, as a very odd country indeed.[71] One generation later, Rousseau's celebration of the *sauvage noble* was to go one step further, urging decadent, hyper-civilized Europeans to follow the example of the innocence, simplicity and moral purity of Noble Savages.

Montesquieu's cultural relativism was most forcefully expressed by his major treatise *De l'esprit des lois* (1748); the political context and repercussions of that influential work will be discussed in the next chapter. For our present argument, which concerns the anthropological view of the European landscape, it is important to realize that for Montesquieu (echoing to some extent also the thought of his near-contemporary, Giambattista Vico) a country's legal system emanates from its manners, climate, religion and economy. *De l'esprit des lois* specifies in its subtitle that it addresses 'the relations which laws must have with the constitution [i.e. the fundamental organization] of each government, with manners, climate, religion, commerce etc.' (*du rapport que les loix doivent avoir avec la constitution de chaque gouvernement, les mœurs, le climat, la religion, le commerce, etc.*). In other words: political and constitutional organization reflects a nation's specific character; and that character, in turn, is determined by a nation's physical environment, most importantly its climate. The climatological determinism which relates temperaments and characters to 'hot' or 'cold' climates gets a direct political and constitutional extension. Monarchy and authoritarian government are considered natural to hot climates; democracy, republicanism and parliamentarianism seem to fit the character of cool, northern nations.[72] And the implication is that France, with its intermediate climate, will need something called a mixed government: a parliamentary monarchy...

Montesquieu's strict physical determinism went too far for the taste of contemporaries like David Hume, who had a keen interest in the topic of 'national characters'.[73] (He repeatedly placed it on the agenda of the Edinburgh Select Society, a club of educated gentlemen that formed the A-team of the Scottish Enlightenment.) In his own essay on the topic (1748), Hume argues that national characters are not determined by climate, but that they arise from social intercourse. For him, national psychology (though that term did not yet exist as such) was not so much a matter of 'natural philosophy' as of 'moral philosophy' – sociological rather than ethnological. In the differing opinions of Montesquieu and Hume, we already see the opposition which in the twentieth century became known as the 'nature vs. nurture' debate.

Other Enlightenment philosophers also used nationality as the template for their inquiries; Montesquieu was aware of the then still-obscure Giambattista Vico's *Principi di una scienza nuova d'intorno alla natura delle nazioni* (1725); one can also think of Voltaire's *Essai sur les moeurs et l'esprit des nations et sur les principaux faits de l'histoire depuis Charlemagne jusqu'à Louis XIII* (1756). By the end of the century, the commonplaces of nationally-arranged knowledge are summed up in the famous *Encyclopédie* of Diderot and D'Alembert, which, under the entries *Nation* and *Caractère des nations*, gives the following end-point of a tradition which we have traced from the days of Scaliger:

> National characters are a certain habitual predisposition of the soul, which is more prevalent in one nation than in others (even though that predisposition need not be encountered in all the members of such a nation).

And:

> Thus the character of the French is their airiness, gaiety, sociability, their love of their kings and of the monarchy as such, etc. Each nation has its particular character; it is a sort of proverb to say: airy as a Frenchman, jealous as an Italian, serious as a Spaniard, wicked as an Englishman, proud as a Scot, drunk as a German, lazy as an Irishman, deceitful as a Greek.[74]

In the nineteenth and twentieth centuries, encyclopedias would continue to organize knowledge of the world around us by 'countries'. This category includes geographical, socio-political and cultural data indistinctly under the same single name, as if they naturally belong together, and lists, pell mell, matters of landscape, climate, geology, natural resources; along with state frontiers, institutions, mode of government, economy; and history, language, art, literature and the physical and moral character of the inhabitants. Such encyclopedic conflations are a closer echo of Borges's bizarre 'Chinese' quasi-systematics than we might realize at first sight. We have come to think of nation-states as an ideally systematic taxonomy of Europe, where the French live in France and speak the French language, and the Germans live in Germany and speak the German language, and each country has its own French or German cuisine, fashions, national anthem, and lifestyle. But this simplistic ideal-type of the nation-state is ultimately the inheritance of the encyclopedic and Enlightenment-anthropological systematization of stereotypes, hearsay and cross-cultural caricatures.

Politics and the Nation: Patriotism and Democracy in Enlightenment Thought

One of the by-products of the Enlightenment was the invention of modern democracy. The critical second-guessing of received authorities and traditional wisdom also involved a critique of the God-given dynastic power of kings. Montesquieu's *De l'esprit des lois* not only outlined a legal-anthropological idea of the types of law and government that went with various societies in different climates and cultures; it also formulated, famously, the ideal of the *trias politica* or tripartite separation of powers (the requirement that power in the state should ideally remain in separate institutions, each independent of the other).* Montesquieu was, of course, writing against the absolutist monarchy that reigned in France since the rise of Louis XIV; but his ideas have a far wider importance and bring a number of source traditions together into a highly influential and important form. Montesquieu's critique of the authoritarian state can be seen against a contemporary and against a classical background. One is his intellectual debt to Locke, the other his preoccupation with Tacitus.

John Locke (1632-1704) may count as one of the Enlightenment's great early protagonists. What is especially remarkable for our purpose is his characteristic combination of philosophical anthropology and constitutional thought. In his attempts to understand human understanding he pondered the growing mental capacity in the human individual, making him a precursor of Hume and one of the founders of modern psychology (*Essay concerning Human Understanding*, 1690); at the same time, he analysed political relations in two *Treatises of Government* (also 1690) – works which, published anonymously, were to prepare the democratic revolutions of 1776 and 1789 by way of the intermediary stages of Montesquieu and Rousseau.

The *Treatises of Government* were themselves written under the shadow of the parliamentarian *coup d'état* of 1688, when the English Parliament had foresworn king James II and in his stead had sponsored the rule of his daughter and his son-in-law, Mary and her husband William III. Much as this 'Glorious Revolution' had been foreshadowed by the Dutch Act of Abjuration of 1581, so too its political justification could fall back on political philosophers like Grotius, who argued that the relationship between king and people was essentially a contract. The English philosopher Thomas Hobbes had argued that the contract was an absolute and binding, non-negotiable one: in order to escape from a primitive, bestial dog-eat-dog existence, so Hobbes had argued, humanity had evolved a fundamental pact called society, where individual liberty was sacrificed for the sake of protection, security and civility. To be human

---

* Montesquieu's division of power was implemented almost to the letter in the United States of America, which drafted its constitution less than fifty years after *De l'esprit des lois*. We see the division between legislative, executive and judiciary powers neatly reflected in the 'checks and balances' between the powers of Congress, the President, and the Supreme Court.

meant to take one's part in that society, and to submit to higher authorities. Not so, Locke argued: the social contract was only binding inasmuch as it served the purpose and interests of the contracting parties; and in order to monitor this, the king's authority was constantly under the proviso that the people had to assent to it. This was achieved by means of having parliaments. Therefore, if parliaments were instrumental in authorizing the king's laws by giving their consent, they must also have the theoretical power of withholding that consent.[75]

In stipulating that all social power is subject to the 'consent of the governed' Locke famously laid down some fundamental civil rights: the fact that power can never be absolute power, and must allow for the possibility of civil disobedience. Otherwise, power shades into despotism, which can only be maintained oppressively and cannot claim to be lawful. The implications of Locke's thought are, then, more radical than their 'philosophical' presentation might suggest, and it is no wonder that the author should have chosen to remain anonymous.

Within Britain, the thought of Locke was to inspire the Enlightenment 'Commonwealthmen' and other proto-democrats,[76] including the leaders of the American revolution. Lockean thought was, however, incorporated within the existing political system (at the extreme left), since there was a functioning parliament which in 1688 had flexed its muscle. In France, however, where Louis XIV had destroyed all forms of parliamentarian power and had established an unchallenged royal supremacy in all spheres of the affairs of state, the impact of Locke was to prove far more subversive – revolutionary even.

Montesquieu was receptive to Locke's thought since he was facing a major quandary: Louis XIV's inability to realize his aggressive expansion towards the Rhine.[*] As we have seen, the rounding-off of the French territory was a fundamental goal of foreign policy. Louis himself, who thought of affairs of state in highly personal, dynastic and almost mystical terms, would not have phrased it in those words; but the end result was the same. For Louis, kingship was a mystically sacred thing; as king, he was, quite literally, the living embodiment of France. He may not have used the actual phrase *l'état, c'est moi*, but it does sum up his outlook quite well. Louis did not see himself as a private individual who had a task of government to carry out – he *was* that task. He had no private life. His getting up in the morning, his meals, his going to bed in the evening: all of these were affairs of state, elaborately ritualized. The thing which we nowadays would call the French 'national interest' was, for him, a personal matter, something which he considered his *gloire*. An insult to the king was an affair of state; a foreign war was waged for his personal dignity. A victory was useful because it added to the *gloire* of Louis, which was another way of saying that it added to the power of

---

[*] Louis took Strasbourg in 1681, and thereby managed a first implementation of the great Vauban scheme of turning the Rhine into France's north-east frontier (Ayçoberry & Ferro 1981). The city became henceforth an object of German Romantic nostalgia; Goethe celebrated its cathedral as a prime example of 'German architecture' in 1772, thereby triggering the European taste for the Gothic. At the same time, the French drive towards the Rhine seems to have remained constant in French history regardless of the *régime* in power; it was also espoused by Danton and by Napoleon, and even, in 1915, by the young lieutenant Charles De Gaulle (Lacouture 1984-1986, 1, 66).

11. Louis XIV in his gloire: *Portrait by Hyacinthe Rigaud, 1701.*
Extant in two copies, one in the Louvre, the other at Versailles.

France. Foreign policy, if it was not directed at placing relatives on foreign thrones (e.g. in the War of the Spanish Succession), aimed to expand French power by teaching neighbours a lesson or two about the king's *gloire*. In this total identification between the king and his realm, all other institutions of state (such as the regional parliaments, who had traditionally also acted as regional law courts) had been brought to Louis's heel.

One theatre where this was singularly unsuccessful was, precisely, the Low Countries between France and the Rhine. The recalcitrance of the Dutch Republic, with its mercantile-egalitarian Calvinist ruling class, was doubly repugnant to Louis because it resisted both his dynastic self-importance and his expansionist aims (he felt that the Duchy of Brabant should have devolved, by inheritance, to the French throne), and tarnished his *gloire* both by insult and by injury. Time and again he hurled his armies at his north-east; in the process, he turned the stadholder of the Dutch Republic, William III of Orange (a great-grandson of William the Silent) into his most inveterate opponent. Louis met his nemesis when this selfsame William III, now on the British throne as the son-in-law of the ousted James II, brought together a Europe-wide anti-French coalition and effectively bridled Louis.[77] The successive treaties that concluded Louis's various European wars (the treaties of Nijmegen, 1678; Rijswijk,

1697; and Utrecht, 1713, all named after the Dutch cities where they were signed) between them spell out the successive stages of a European containment policy regarding the Sun King, and also formulate in their preambles the rising notion that Europe should be a stable state system based on a balance of power.

The end of Louis's long, long reign, for all his *gloire*, was ruinous. France had been humiliated and, at one point, almost destroyed in its foreign wars. The building and running of Versailles, home to an elaborate choreographed protocol about the king's every movement, with a supporting entourage of nobility reduced to minions in Louis' daily rituals, was a huge drain on the country's wealth; and philosophers like Montesquieu faced a mystery. How was it possible for France's most powerful monarch to have been stymied by the Dutch Republic? How could Louis, having beaten the rebellious nobility into submission, having reduced the *parlements* to empty folklore, having smashed the power of the Palatinate, having established a power base on the Rhine in Strasbourg – how could this Sun King have failed to overrun a small mercantile republic on its north-eastern frontier?

In facing this dilemma, Montesquieu showed the influence of Tacitus, whom he had read deeply and attentively. His historical treatise *Considérations sur les causes de la grandeur des Romains et de leur décadence* (1734) betrays a Tacitus-inspired view: the Republic, manly, frugal and virtuous, was capable of greatness; the Empire, enervated, corrupt and decadent, proved weak. The parallel with France was unstated but obvious, and the implications were spelled out when, under the influence of Locke, Montesquieu formulated his constitutional ideas in *De l'esprit des lois*. That book is not just a legal-anthropological disquisition of the relations between laws, mores and societies, but also, importantly, an argument proving that concentrated authority does not necessarily make a state strong. Louis's France must be kept at the back of one's mind when reading *De l'esprit des lois*: Louis is the king who has ridden roughshod over the institutions that were needed to register the necessary 'consent of the governed' (in the Lockean phrase); Louis had suborned the state's legislative, executive and judicial powers into one single hand – his own; and while this may superficially seem like a concentration of power and a heightening of strength, it does in fact add up to the same weakness that befell ancient Rome between Julius Caesar and Nero.

The analysis itself is of the very highest importance. It means that the rule of law stands on an equal footing with the head of state, and cannot be made subordinate to the executive powers of the king. This meant that the law becomes almost a sovereign institution within the state; and with that principle, Montesquieu may truly count as the founder of the democratic state. For it is not merely the existence of an elected parliament, or the publicity campaigns of elections, or the rituals of the ballot box, that constitute a democracy; the most important protection of the citizen against arbitrary power may, in practice, lie in the hands of judges rather than politicians. It is the even-handed, autonomous rule of law that forms the most important basis of what we call a democracy. In the great nineteenth-century European struggle for democratic governance, German thinkers often opposed against the *Fürstenstaat* or 'monarch-ruled state' the notion of a *Rechtsstaat* or 'law-governed state'; they followed in Montesquieu's footsteps and laid down a principle on the rule of law which continues to be of undiminished importance.

Still, historically speaking, what needs to be emphasized here is that the separation of powers is a lesson for which Montesquieu invoked the legacy of democratic primitivism: Tacitus works his way, not only into Enlightenment anthropology, but also into Enlightenment politics. The eighteenth century will remain preoccupied with the decadence that befalls authoritarian states with absolute monarchy – the greatest example of this preoccupation being, no doubt, the great history of the *Decline and Fall of the Roman Empire* (1776-1788) by Edward Gibbon; the Enlightenment will glorify frugal republics like Rome in its early days, or ancient Sparta; it will celebrate, in historical and literary texts, heroic freedom fighters like William the Silent, William Tell, Gustav Vasa.* And all this because history demonstrates that absolute power corrupts the moral fibre of the state. Democracy thus becomes the politics of virtue, against the depravity that goes with an aristocratic court culture.

Virtue, love of country, Patriotism[78]

The point needs to be stressed: 'Patriot', throughout the eighteenth century, meant something quite different from the sense in which it is used nowadays. Nowadays, patriotism and love of the fatherland count as forms of national pride, as benevolent forms of nationalism, as 'banal nationalism'. Often invoked at the right-wing, conservative and national-chauvinistic end of the political spectrum, patriotism nowadays is a form of 'wrapping oneself in the flag'. This was quite different in eighteenth-century parlance.†

The root sense of 'patriot' seems to have been merely that of 'inhabitant of a *patria*', fellow-citizen, com-patriot. Much as the term 'citizen' derives from membership of the free and politically emancipated population of a city, so too the notion of 'patriot' seems to be, analogously, intended originally as signifying the citizenship, not of a city, but of a country at large.

The notion thus reflects an attempt to express someone's political status, not in the usual 'vertical' or feudal terms of the lord whose subject one was, but rather in the 'horizontal' terms of a society of equals, freemen, to which, or to whose geographic area, one belonged. In the root sense of the term, then, patriot seems to have meant, either 'compatriot', or else 'citizen of a country' (as opposed to 'subject of a sovereign').

The term was already used in the Dutch Revolt against Spain to denote those who opposed Philip II (e.g. by William of Orange in his *Apologia* of 1580); it was frequently combined with adjectives such as 'good', 'true,' 'worthy,' and as such came to refer to one who would function well as a citizen, who would perform his civic duties and live up to his responsibilities towards his compatriots. Indeed, in the 1680s, the decade

---

* When John Toland, a freethinker, edited James Harrington's *Oceana* in 1700 (itself, written in the 1650s, one of the seminal works on power control), the portraits on the frontispiece of this edition show Brutus, William III, Moses, Solon, Confucius, Lycurgus and Numa. (Venturi 1971, 59-60).

† In order to highlight the difference between eighteenth-century usage and the word's current meaning, I spell it, it the following pages, with a capital P whenever I refer historically to the Enlightenment doctrine.

leading up to the Glorious Revolution, the term Patriot was 'often applied to one who supported the rights of the country against the King and court.'

It is in this direction that the word's meaning developed in the century between the British revolution of 1688 and the French Revolution of 1789. Dryden, that staunch royalist, wrote in 'Absalom and Achitophel' that in the 'modern sense' a Patriot 'is one that wou'd by Law supplant his Prince.' In fact, that was an apt enough description of what John Locke was all about in his *Treatise of Government* of 1690, concerned as it was with the containment of arbitrary power by law.

The more generalized meaning of the word concentrated on the notion of 'selfless service to one's country' and which began to equate the notion of the Patriot with that of the 'good citizen', the loyal, responsible member of society. Patriotism as an ideology of social responsibility and selfless devotion to the common good was characterized aptly by the Enlightenment philosopher George Berkeley, who defined 'a Patriot' as 'one who heartily wisheth the public prosperity, and doth not only wish, but also study and endeavour to promote it.'

Characteristically, Patriots want to make themselves useful, in a kind of political philanthropy.* To that end, many charitable foundations and improving societies sprang up. In Ireland, the Dublin Society (to name but one example), was founded in 1731 for the promotion of agriculture, industry, the economy as well as the arts and letters. This essentially civic-philanthropic nature of Patriotism was encapsulated in a passage in Jonathan Swift's *Gulliver's Travels* (1726), where the wise King of Brobdingnag exclaims:

> That whoever could make two Ears of Corn, or two Blades of
> Grass grow upon a Spot of Ground, where only one grew
> before; would deserve better of Mankind, and do more es-
> sential Service to his Country, than the whole Race of Politi-
> cians put together.[79]

By the later eighteenth century, Patriotism will be a stand-in term for Republicanism, or radical democracy. The influential critic Shaftesbury (1671-1713) opposed national chauvinism or any instinctive sense of love and attachment to one's native land. As Franco Venturi sums up his views:

---

* The root meaning of the Greek word 'philanthropy' is theological, referring to God's love of mankind. This divine sense falls out of use after 1711 and is replaced by a secular one still current today. The word 'philanthropist' makes its first appearance in 1730. By the end of the century, a Hamburg-based Jacobin club was known, ominously, as the 'Philanthropic Society', 'devoted to the spreading of republican principles throughout Europe'. We should also take into account the Enlightenment overtones of a word like 'philadelphia', the 'brotherly love' which gave its name to an American city and foreshadowed the *fraternité* that came second only to *liberté* in the Revolutionary Trinity, and well ahead of the later-added *égalité*. Jane Austen's grand-aunt, by the way, had the Christian name of Philadelphia.

This [love of the fatherland, JL] was a passion of 'narrow minds', 'of a mere fungus or common excrescence to its parent-mould or nursing dunghill'. The new patriotism is cosmopolitan and indissolubly linked with freedom. It cannot be conceived, or at least would be absurd, without it. It cannot be felt except by those 'who really have a country and are the number of those who may be called a people, as enjoying the happiness of a real constitution and policy by which they are free and independent'. All kinds of absolute power deny and destroy the very base of true love of one's country. 'Absolute power annuls the publick, and where there is no publick, or constitution, there is in reality no mother country or nation [...] A multitude held together by force, tho' under one and the same head, is not properly united, nor does such a body make a people. 'Tis the social league, confederacy and mutual consent, founded in some common good or interest, which joins the members of a community, and makes a people one.' As we see, the word patriotism itself conveys, in terms of enthusiasm, passion and ethics, exactly the sense of equality and freedom of those who considered themselves the people and the nation in the ancient republics.[80]

We see similar sentiments elsewhere in Europe. The anti-Orangist party in the Dutch Republic, who wanted to see the almost hereditary grip of the Orange dynasty on the stadholdership abolished, called themselves 'Patriots' and Jan Wagenaar in his pamphlet *De Patriot of Politike bedenkingen over den Staat der Verenigde Nederlanden* (1747) stated:

A Patriot has such a strong and upright feeling for the welfare of his fatherland, that, in order to advance the interest of this, he puts not merely his own interest in the balance, but, if needs be, dares to put it entirely on one side. He considers his fellow countrymen and himself as members of one body. His highest wish is that he himself and all the individual members of the Civil State be happy and work together for each other's good. [...] He never presses his own interest to the disadvantage of the common cause. [...] A Patriot doesn't grumble about the present government, as long as it maintains the Law, and leaves Liberties and Privileges unrumpled.[81]

Similarly, a *Maetschappy tot nut van 't Algemeen* or 'Society for Public Improvement' was established in 1784; and odes to 'The fatherland' were the order of the day. But

12. William the Silent leads the Dutch Maiden to the throne of sovereignty. Allegorical frontispiece to J. Nomsz Willem den Eersten, of de grondlegging der Nederlandsche vryheid *(Amsterdam, 1779).*

then again, 'the fatherland' was a topic which could be invoked both by Orangist and by Patriot authors.[*]

Later on, the idea of Patriotism became firmly situated at the radical Republican end of the political spectrum, as a result of the American and French Revolutions. The principle invoked by opponents to absolute royal power had always been *la nation*.[†] The early years of the French Revolution opposed, in an interesting terminological polarity, the 'aristocratic' party and the 'patriotic party', and slowly but surely a

---

[*] A Patriot example: the poetry of Jacobus Bellamy (1757-86), e.g. his *Vaderlandsche Gezangen* ('Fatherlandish Cantos'), influenced by Rousseau. An Orangist example: Onno Zwier van Haren and his epic *Aan het Vaderland* ('To the Fatherland' 1769).

[†] Palmer 1959, I:88, quotes private remarks to this effect by the Marquis d'Argenson, and generally (88 ff. and 449) describes the opposition of the various *parlements* against court policy: anti-court opposition of the mid-century *parlements* put a good deal of incipient revolutionary language into wide circulation – *citoyen, loi, patrie, constitution, nation, droit de la nation,* and *cri de la nation.*

'Patriot', during the last decades of the century, could come to mean, quite simply, a revolutionary – a supporter either of the American Revolution or of the French one, more or less ardent, more or less radical or extreme, but – a revolutionary. This must be recognized behind Dr Johnson's manifest dislike of Patriotism, which he memorably denounced as 'the last refuge of a scoundrel'. English Jacobins of the 1790s frequently gave themselves, or their pamphlets, 'Patriotic' names. Thus, a Sheffield radical newspaper of around 1792 was called *The Patriot*; an important radical club around 1795 was the 'Norwich Patriotic Society'. Such nomenclature must have grated on the Doctor's ears with a cynical ring.

We shall see in the following chapter how the course of events after 1789 was to influence attitudes towards 'nation', 'patriotism' and 'love of country'. Until the early 1790s, the invocation of 'love of the fatherland' or 'patriotic pride' was couched in terms of civic duty and political philanthropy. The Swiss author Johann Georg Zimmermann, in his essay *Von dem Nationalstolze* (1758), pointed out that national pride should be a form of altruism towards one's fellow-citizens, never a form of chauvinism against foreigners. Likewise, the sermon given in 1788 by Richard Price, entitled *A Discourse on the Love of Our Country*, stressed the idea that 'love of our country' should not be equalled to 'any conviction of the superior value of it to other countries, or any particular preference of its laws and constitution of government.' Again, the same Richard Price (who worked with a club called the 'London Revolution Society[*])' worded an address of congratulation to the French National Assembly (the self-chosen name of which will be discussed in the next chapter), which began with 'disdaining national partialities, and rejoicing in every triumph of liberty and justice over arbitrary power'.[82]

Neither the idea of the 'nation', nor that of 'love of the fatherland' were, then, the specifically nationalist slogans they could later come to be. The bronze was there, and it rang; but nationalism had not yet arrived on the scene, like an occupying army, to commandeer those bells and recast them into cannons.

Virtue vs. nobility

The leading political ideal was not ethnic solidarity, but civic virtue. And all this virtue was opposed, consistently, to the selfish, arrogant corruption which was imputed to courtiers and aristocrats. As Patriot politics began to vindicate the rights of the nation ('the governed') within the state, Patriot moralists began to wage a very widespread and all-pervasive ethical campaign against the class system of the *ancien régime*. In

---

[*] The revolution in the club's name referred to the British 'Glorious Revolution' of 1688, whose centenary Price's *Discourse* commemorated. Price was, of course, a radical democrat. His sympathy for the French Revolution was viewed with suspicion and anger by the anti-revolutionary, conservative statesman Edmund Burke. In fact, Burke's *Reflections upon the Revolution in France*, the first and most forceful denunciation of the revolution in Europe, was written as an attack on Price.

order to understand the intensity, the persistence and the very wide appeal of this campaign, it must be stressed how far-reaching the class system was.

The nobility saw itself, quite literally, as a race apart. The notion of nobility was wholly linked to descent and to the 'blue blood' that flowed in one's veins. While it was possible for a commoner to be ennobled, this was a rare occurrence and restricted to the very rich landowning gentry or to very influential magistrates and politicians. The nobility kept its demography under control by elaborate registers of ancestry and descent. Its outward shows of privilege were not mere follies and vanities, as they might appear nowadays, although vanity undoubtedly played into it. Who was called *monseigneur*, who *excellence*; who had a right to four, or six, horses before their coach; whether one's coat of arms might, or might not, be flanked by allegorical side-figures called 'supporters': that is no more trivial than Louis XIV's sense of *gloire*, which was in fact a way of phrasing state interest in personal-dynastic terms. The 'right to bear arms' was not merely the heraldic vanity of displaying a shield, or coat of arms, but reflected also the very real privilege that one was allowed to wear a sword, or other weapons; any commoner caught armed would be punished. The right to self-defence, to rapid transport (riding a horse), to immunity from the law, to certain careers: all that was aristocratic prerogative. Noblemen could not be imprisoned for debt (and could therefore run up far greater bills than commoners); in order to become an officer in the army, one had to prove that all eight great-grandparents, or all sixteen great-great-grandparents were of noble birth; and in everyday life, a nobleman had an unquestioned right to boss around all commoners in sight. It took a nobleman's seal to make a contract legally binding (having a seal was a noble prerogative). A nobleman was exempt from many taxes, duties and punishments. His position, in other words, was not unlike that of a white colonial official in a nineteenth-century colony like India or South Africa, or a slave-owning planter in the southern states of the USA prior to the Civil War.

Long before the power of the nobility was challenged in political terms, its privileges were challenged in moral terms. The nobility was driven by a code of honour, with its roots in the chivalric courts of the Middle Ages. The worst thing a nobleman could fear was dishonour: shame incurred by cowardice or treason. (To allow insults to pass without revenge was a sign of cowardice and thus a form of dishonour.)

It was against this all-pervasive noble code of honour that the Enlightenment was to formulate, and bring into currency, the moral code of *virtue*. And as we might have guessed from the Tacitan context, virtue was seen in classicist (rather than Christian) terms: in terms of a nostalgically remembered Roman republic. Against the arrogantly asserted honour of the nobleman came dignity, against outward bravado came inner courage. Against elegance and pomp came simplicity and modesty; against pride in one's descent came the merit of one's deeds. And where the main aristocratic virtue lay in a duty to one's class (the liege lord and one's own *noblesse oblige*), the new morality of virtue stressed a sense of responsibility towards one's fellow-men. *Amor patriae*, or 'love of the fatherland' must be seen, then, as yet another virtue (not the only one) wherein a good Patriot differs from a depraved aristocrat.

The vilification of the nobility, in the Enlightenment, is remarkably sustained and all-pervasive. In all the sentimental and moralistic writings of the century, there is a stereotypical role division in which middle-class characters are virtuous, upright, whereas noble characters, while they may be forceful and heroic, have a tendency to be immoral, overweening, arrogant and depraved. In the works of Samuel Richardson (*Pamela* of 1740 and *Clarissa Harlowe* of 1747), young women from the middle classes must defend their chastity against lecherous aristocrats. Clarissa will ultimately be raped and driven to death; Pamela manages to withstand the schemes of 'Lord B.' and her virtue ultimately impresses him to the point of a decent marriage proposal. All this in long, drawn-out, sentimental novels-in-letters, full of anguished sighs and moral reflections; and tremendously popular and influential all over Europe. The role-division of arrogant noblemen and virtuous commoners was taken over in the hugely successful genre of the 'sentimental comedy', which dominated the London stage throughout the century. In Germany, it inspired the significantly-named *bürgerliches Trauerspiel*. France itself gives us the most telling example: Beaumarchais' comedy *Le mariage de Figaro* of 1784. It led to great controversies because of its anti-aristocratic tendency; showing, as it does, a Count as villain. Count Almaviva invokes the ancient aristocratic prerogative of the *ius primae noctis* and harasses the virtuous heroine, Figaro's bride-to-be. Things turn out alright once the wily Figaro (already a popular character from Beaumarchais' earlier play *Le barbier de Séville*, 1773) comes up with a cunning plan.* The later pornographic writings of the Marquis de Sade, a perverse Richardson, will still depict middle-class girls as virtuous victims, helplessly raped and tortured by noblemen and clergy. These various trends are all focussed in the work of one remarkable writer: Jean-Jacques Rousseau. Notions of virtue, primitivism, sentiment, civil rights and social contract all come together in a crucial combination.

---

* This *ius primae noctis* or 'right of the first night' (probably a myth more than a current praxis, cf. Boureau 1995) was widely loathed as the incorporation of all that was depraved and vile in feudal-aristocratic privilege. It represented in graphic symbolism the rape of society by the lecherous corruption and unrestrained power of the nobility. Beaumarchais could only get away with representing a nobleman as such a depraved villain by making him foreign; even so, the play was condemned by Louis XVI, briefly banned as a result, and triggered one of the more outstanding scandals in European literary history.

The Nation Empowered: Popular Sovereignty and National Unity in the French Revolution

Rousseau and the Geneva model

Jean-Jacques Rousseau (1712-1778) was one of the cardinally important eighteenth-century-thinkers.[83] Less original than Vico, less erudite than Montesquieu, less penetrating than Locke or Hume, less profound than Herder or Goethe, and less acute than Voltaire, he was more versatile and many-sided than any of these, and brings together a number of revolutionary strands in the Enlightenment. His novels *Julie, ou la nouvelle Héloïse* (1761) and *Emile, ou de l'éducation* (1762) became figureheads for sentiment as an affect equal in value to rational cogitation, and fixed for centuries the sentimental image of childhood as a period of innocence and openness. His proclamation to turn 'back to nature', and his glorification of the 'Noble Savage', gave voice, in the very heart of the Enlightenment, to a discontent with the rigidity of over-refined civility, and prepared the Romantics' opposition between human society and divine nature. His *Confessions* (1782-1788) re-launched the genre of the moral autobiography; widely admired as a benchmark in self-honesty, they prepared the way for the Romantic cult of the self: the preoccupation with one's own personality and personal growth. There was no cultural endeavour that he did not pursue: he speculated on the origins of language and human inequality along with the greatest philosophers of the century; he even wrote an opera.

But the Rousseau whose importance is to be traced here is the author of a book which was entitled *Du contrat social* and which he signed as a *Citoyen de Genève*. *Du contrat social* was written in 1754 and appeared in 1762; as the title indicates, it goes over the familiar ground, already trodden by Grotius, Hobbes, Locke and Montesquieu, of the mutual obligations of the partners, monarch and people, whose contract forms the root of human society and the basis of power distribution. But Rousseau's *Contrat social* was more than a mere rehash of familiar arguments; it was a radical and even revolutionary extension of democratic thought. Earlier thinkers had all started with an *a priori* top-down distribution of power: power comes from On High, and works its way downwards. Locke had argued for a control mechanism in the downward distribution of power, involving the 'consent of the governed'; Montesquieu had argued for an institutional separation and 'checks and balances' system, regulated by a rule of law that was itself not subject to the king's authority. Both had continued to accept, however, the top-down vector of constitutional power as a given. Rousseau turned it on its head, in what was in the most fundamental sense a 'revolution'. For Rousseau, power emanated from the collectivity of the people who together formed a society. The establishment of a collective volition or *volonté générale* is what constitutes

13. *Jean-Jacques Rousseau*

the primal social contract; and therefore the fundamental, sovereign authority of any state is the collectivity of the people expressing its volition. It is only in the second instance that the power to exercise and implement this collective volition is placed in the hands of individuals. They, the executive, even in a monarchy, are in fact just that: mere executives.

Constitutional power is then, in Rousseau's scheme of a social contract, bottom-up: it is entrusted by the people to officials. Governments rule as trustees of the will of the people; if they claim to rule in their own right they are tyrannical.

Rousseau, in short, formulated the tenets of 'popular sovereignty', and he did so in a most efficient and influential manner. Twenty years after the appearance of the *Contrat social*, the constitution of the newly independent United States of America was drawn up as the expression of a Rousseauesque *volonté générale*: it opens with the portentous opening phrase 'We the People of the United States...'; and by 1792, Rousseau was to be the guiding light of the French Republic. His body was the first to be placed, together with that of Voltaire, in the *Panthéon*, the hallowed shrine of a new religion of the fatherland where great men were to be buried or commemorated under the inscription *Aux grands hommes la Patrie reconnaissante* (a very Roman, Tacitus-style

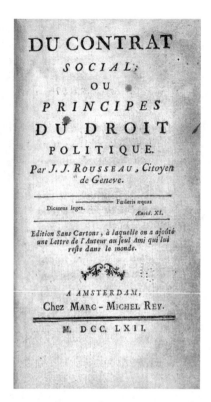

14. Title page of Du contrat social

phrase and sentiment).[84] And Robespierre, the leader of the radical Republican wing of the new Republic, was always seen with the *Contrat social* under his arm, a devotee of popular sovereignty.

From where did Rousseau get his ideal of popular sovereignty? For one thing, there had been a tenacious 'underground' of radical republican philosophy, drawing on seventeenth-century representatives like Algernon Sydney and John Harrington. The politicians who had rebelled against their kings, like the Dutch Estates General in 1581 or the British Parliament under Cromwell, had had their constitutional thinkers. But the most important influence is probably given away by that epithet which always appears under Rousseau's name on the *Contrat Social*'s title page, whatever the edition: *Citoyen de Genève.*

For that was Rousseau's political status. Geneva at the time, not yet fully part of Switzerland, was an independent and sovereign city-republic, one of a handful to have survived as such since the Middle Ages; like Ragusa (present-day Dubrovnik), San Marino, or Lucca, or some Free Imperial Cities in Germany such as Hamburg or Frankfurt. Other erstwhile city-republics, like Milan or Florence, had come under the rule of a dynastic aristocracy; or they had lost their privileges and self-governance in a power struggle with monarchs; only in rare instances had they maintained themselves.

Venice had maintained an independent republican constitution until the arrival of Napoleon, but had acquired such large territories that it was far more than a mere 'city'-republic. In practice the rule of such independent cities was in the hands of a small oligarchy of patrician families; but even so, the fact that members of these families were appointed to office rather than gaining power by inheritance, stood out from the dynasticism of aristocratic rule in most of Europe. Such city-republics were constitutional oddities, islands of civic self-rule in a continent wholly consisting of monarchies and feudal states.

Geneva was one such case. It had made the city one of the great European sanctuaries for Reformation thought; and indeed, Rousseau had briefly forfeited his Geneva citizenship when he had married a catholic. But by the time he published *Du contrat social* he was once again a Genevan citizen in good standing, and did not omit to mention that on the title page of his book. This was partly to stress that he was no subject of the French king, and enjoyed some form of constitutional immunity. Partly it also betrays the mainspring of his ideas of popular sovereignty: they are taken from the self-governance of a city.

Although in the climate of classical republicanism, many cities saw themselves as offshoots of the Mother of All Cities, Rome,[*] they had in fact sprung up as joint enterprises of people living and working together and acquiring wealth and privileges in the process. The city as a joint enterprise meant that to be a citizen (that is to say: a resident and financially solvent town-dweller) was tantamount to being a shareholder in the city, one of the participants in the city's common affairs. 'Joint enterprise', 'common affairs': the Latin phrase to express all that was *res publica*, the public endeavour. The notion of a republic therefore refers to a shared concern of co-owners, shareholders, participants. It is these that are the citizens.

Crucially (and, to a feudal mind, anomalously), a citizen is not a subject. In a world where all social relations were seen in the vertical terms of 'who obeys whom', citizenship in a city implied the horizontal relationship of being a fellow-participant in the city's public endeavour. That *res publica* turned the city into something that was variously called a *Gemeinde*, *gemeente* or *commune* (as in the English 'Commons' or 'commoner'), or a corporation. Cities had what they called the *freedom of the city*, and a citizen (burgess, *burger*, *Bürger*) was also called *freeman*. The Dutch saying had it that 'city air makes free': anyone in servile condition would become free once he was admitted a citizen of a city.

The *commune* is then the corporate totality of free equals. In order to administer their affairs they appoint a city council, which in turn appoints aldermen (*échevins*, *Schöffen*, *schepenen*) and mayors (*burgomasters*, *Bürgermeister*) as well as law enforcement officials. These are entrusted with power by way of an appointment, which is limited in time and subject to scrutiny and approval from the city council. In other words: a city functions exactly as a modern republic; or we should rather say that the

---

* The old public buildings of Dutch and Frisian cities such as Alkmaar, Franeker and Haarlem can still be seen to sport the abbreviations SPQA, SPQF and SPQH, calqued on the Roman SPQR, and indicating that the city was ruled by *senatus populusque*.

modern republic is a large-scale application of a model of governance which was practised originally only at city level. It took a Citizen of Geneva to draw up a model for the state which in fact mirrored in its organization the constitution of a city. A body politic that consists, not of a lord's subjects, but of a community of equal, free citizens, who exercise their corporate volition through councils and appointed officials: all that is Rousseau's model of a social contract based on popular sovereignty; all that is inspired by his native city of Geneva.

There is a deep symbolism, then, in the fact that the term *citoyen* – 'citizen' – became the only title of courtesy which was allowed in France when the French Republic had abolished all noble privileges and titles and forms of address such as *monseigneur* and *excellence*. Citizenship, the thing proclaimed almost as a Geneva singularity on the title page of the *Contrat Social*, became the hallmark of republican, democratic emancipation after 1789. And until well into the twentieth century, the carrier of a British passport would be called a 'British *Subject*', whereas the holder of an American passport would be called a '*Citizen* of the United States'.

The nation in power: Rousseau to Sieyès

By the mid-century, Patriot-minded politicians began with increasing frequency to use the term 'nation'. Usually, the meaning of the word was generally 'the great mass of the population' or ' the body politic'. That body politic had no specific, designed name of its own; although concepts like *Volk, people, narod, pueblo* or *popolo* were widely current in their respective languages, the French term *peuple* was almost derogatory (as German and Dutch loanwords such as *Pöbel* and *gepeupel* indicate), and was often used in the combination *menu peuple* (the 'people under command'), indicating a total lack of political rights or social standing. Another term was that of the *tiers état* or 'third estate' (after the clergy and the nobility, that is). This non-noble, non-church estate has its inner stratification: at the bottom of the scale was the *menu peuple*, somewhere in the middle the *roturiers* and at the top the worthy *bourgeois* who, if his family had a lengthy track record in the magistrature or in local administration, could be allowed into a minor nobility.* A term for the politically active part of the population, excluding the poor peasantry and servant class but including the minor nobility, did not exist; and it was in this meaning that the word 'nation' came to be used from ca. 1750 onwards. Rousseau does not use the *nation* to describe his *volonté générale*, but the word was to burst into political usage in a crucial episode of the French Revolution, in 1789. The person who launched it was the priest Emmanuel Sieyès (1748-1836).[85]

---

* This was the so-called *noblesse de robe* or 'nobility of the gown', to distinguish them from the older, more exclusive *noblesse d'épée* or 'nobility of the sword'. The old sword-nobility did much, in the course of the eighteenth century, to keep aloof from the rising tide of newly appointed *noblesse de robe*. Commissions in the army, or certain army regiments, became the jealously guarded preserve of the 'old' nobility with feudal roots. Similar trends can be noticed in other European monarchies.

15. Emmanuel Sieyès

Though as an ordained cleric Sieyès formed part of the first estate, the true power of that rank was reserved for higher dignitaries such as abbots and bishops – who, almost invariably, were from noble families. A low-ranking priest, Sieyès's real sympathies were with the Third Estate, the non-noble part of the population. By the 1780s, this segment of the population had not had any real say in the running of the state for a century and a half. Its original constitutional platform, the *États généraux* (an ancient type of parliament of the three estates together), had not been assembled since 1614. Another political platform where the Third Estate was represented was in the regional *parlements* (that of Paris, of Aix, of Bretagne, and other places) which had likewise been bulldozed by the absolutism of Louis XIV and XV. All the Third Estate could do was pay their taxes and obey their superiors. By the late 1780s, however, France was brought to the verge of absolute bankruptcy as a result of decades of profligate social exploitations. The king, Louis XVI, was reluctantly forced to admit that an economic *perestroika* was needed: the tax system was decrepit and askew, state expenditures were too bloated and out-of-control to be supported by the country as it stood. In the attempt to float the state financially, it was decided to convene the *États généraux*, the full three-estates parliament that would also include the productive part of society: the Third Estate. For the first time in more than a century and a half, the non-nobility could participate in the running of the state. It was to trigger an avalanche of long pent-up grievances, and the end result was, famously, a revolution rather than a reform.

The prospect of an *États généraux* assembly put the Third Estate across France into a ferment. Pamphlets and public registers prepared the public opinion for this chance to get a foot in the constitutional door. How should the Third Estate make use of the proffered opportunity?

In this ferment, the young priest Sieyès brought out a small pamphlet with the deceptively neutral title: *Qu'est-ce que le Tiers État?* – 'The Third Estate, What is That'? The answer he gave in this essay was perhaps as influential as Rousseau's *Contrat social*. For Sieyès, the Third Estate was not just the bottom rung of the social ladder, the 'number three' underneath the clergy and the nobility; on the contrary: the third estate was *all of society*. In Sieyès's argument, the clergy and the nobility did not form part of the French population; they were, rather, external parasites who had fastened themselves onto the Body Politic, feeding upon it, sucking it dry, but not participating in it. The First and Second Estate lived off the people but not with the people, were not a productive part of society but only a drain upon it. Hence, if one wanted to see the true representatives of France, then the Third Estate, and *nothing but the Third Estate*, was what counted.

This attitude was to prove of crucial importance in the events that unfolded in 1789. Once the *États généraux* were convened in Versailles, Sieyès was among them as an elected representative of the Third Estate of the Paris *Commune* – always the most disaffected, the most radical part of the French population. The representatives soon found, however, that the deliberations were meant to keep the lower orders firmly in their place. Palace protocol subjected the Third Estate to numerous petty humiliations, and certain parties at court obviously meant to keep a tight rein on the Third's political agenda. Indeed, the deliberations soon derailed, and Louis XVI went as far as calling off the entire assembly, in effect telling the Third Estate to return home.

It was at this point that world history stood on a knife's edge. The course of events was tipped towards a democratic revolution by the bullishness of Mirabeau (a nobleman by birth, the black sheep of his family, who was a delegate for the Third Estate), who cowed down a palace official and refused to accept the King's dissolution of the assembly. All the same, the Third Estate was now at a loose end. The First and Second Estates had obeyed the dissolution order, the palace at Versailles was no longer available as a venue, and there was in fact no constitutional precedent giving anything like a mandate to a separate assembly of representatives of the Third Estate. The delegates reconvened in a sports hall not unlike a squash court, the *Jeu de Paume*, and there vowed they would continue their session until they had achieved the programme that they had been entrusted with by their electorate: to reform the constitutional system of France and to replace the arbitrary government of the absolute monarchy with a written constitution.

Meanwhile, one of the first things that had had to be decided was the question how the Third Estate delegation should define its position; indeed, what it should call itself. It was at this point that Sieyès had taken the lead. On the basis of the argument already unfolded in his *Qu'est-ce que le Tiers État?*, he chose a name indicating that the representatives of the Third Estate represented all that mattered in the entire country. On his proposal, the assembly of the Third Estate, remainder of the dissolved *États généraux*, took the name of *Assemblée nationale*. The word 'nation' had suddenly become a galvanizing point for the unfolding battle between the people and the Court.

Henceforth, the word 'nation' comes to refer to the corporate identity of all political subjects of a given country. The realization that these people form, not a servile estate or a subaltern layer in society, but the general body politic, with a will and a mandate of its own, will call into play the concept of the nation. In the political thought and vocabulary of 1789 and after, a nation consists, not of subjects, but of citizens. Political clashes in 1789 saw the slogans *Vive la nation* (or *Vive la patrie*) used against the counter-revolutionaries' *Vive le roi* or *Vive l'aristocratie*. The birth of democracy vests power, not in the dynastic rights of kings, but in the united will of the people; and that people, following 1789, will proclaim its inclusiveness and emancipation by calling itself a *nation*.

Once the great organs of state (the ministeries, libraries, armed forces etc.) are no longer under the aegis of the king or the court, they will be called 'national', indicating that they are there on behalf of the entire population and for the benefit of the entire population. It is indeed the inclusiveness of the term 'nation' that dominates in the 1790s. If nationality excludes anything, it is the nobility or the church: national education will mean: education that is no longer under church control, and a national army is no longer a war instrument for the king's *gloire* run by the *noblesse d'épée*. Habitually, the French *nation* will consider any friend of democracy a fellow-national, and there is hardly any distinction between the Rights of Man (the philosophical declaration of fundamental human rights proclaimed in 1789), and the Rights of a Citizen.

Republicanism, Spartan style

As will be shown in more detail in a later chapter, the inclusiveness of the empowered nation hardened in the later, Republican phase of the revolution. The crisis of 1792 saw the definitive failure of the attempt at a constitutional monarchy. Louis XVI, suspected of making common cause with France's external counter-revolutionaries, was imprisoned, indicted and executed; France was declared a republic at a time of grave military threats on its borders. In that climate, the hardline republican factions became dominant, and their interpretation of popular sovereignty, inspired by Rousseau, stressed heavily that the sovereign people had to be a single whole: any internal differentiation of the nation, by region, class or otherwise, would be a fatal faultline in its supreme sovereignty. *Liberté*, fully thought through, presupposes a complete *égalité* between the citizens and a total concord of purpose (*fraternité*). Accordingly, the new republic carries the programmatic name of *République française, une et indivisible*.

It is curious to see how the idea of absolute democracy, total egalitarianism, seems to entail a state policy that is intolerant of diversity. The paradox is that out of the ideal of democracy, a dictatorship can arise. The case of Robespierre is exemplary in this respect.[86] Always on his guard against corruption from power-hungry elites, he saw himself as the watchdog of the people and the high priest of a Rousseauesque cult of *vertu* – the last and most chilling transformation of Tacitus's old ideal of *virtus*. He gloried in his nickname of 'the incorruptible', *l'incorruptible*, and established a watch-dog committee to ensure that the public good would not be threatened by creeping tendencies to old-style corruption. This *Comité de salut public* became an instrument of terror. Fanatically self-righteous, it denounced all dissent as a form of corruption. The guillotine became the prime instrument of a 'rationalized' turnover of denuncia-tions, show trials and executions. Robespierre's sinister sidekick, the angel-faced 24-year-old Saint-Just, formulated a policy whereby, chillingly, all human virtues were redefined as revolutionary virtues:

> A Revolution man is inflexible, but sensible; he is frugal,
> down-to-earth, without indulging in the luxury of false mod-
> esty. He does not brook lies, waste, or affectation; since his
> aim is to see the Revolution triumph, he will never criticize
> it, but he condemns its enemies without confusing it with
> them. He does not insult it but will improve it, and, mindful
> of its purity, he will, when speaking of it, take care to be
> respectful. He does not pretend to be the co-equal of author-
> ity, the law, but rather of people, especially unfortunate ones.
> A Revolution man is filled with honour; he is polished with-
> out being insipid, but frank, because he is at peace with him-
> self. Grossness for him is a sign of dishonesty and guile which
> disguises falsehood by being intemperate. Aristocrats speak
> and act tyrannically, but the Revolution man is intransigent
> only towards villains while remaining sensitive. He is so con-
> cerned for the glory of his fatherland and for liberty that he
> undertakes nothing lightly. He rushes into battle, he perse-
> cutes the guilty and defends the innocents before the courts.
> He speaks the truth so that it may instruct rather than out-
> rage. He realizes that the Revolution, in order to consolidate
> itself, needs people to be as good now as they used to be
> wicked in the past. His probity is not a spiritual refinement
> but a self-evident heart-felt quality. Marat was sweet-tem-
> pered within his own household, and terrified only traitors;
> and Rousseau, a revolutionary, was certainly not an insolent
> man. I infer that the Revolution man is a hero of good sense
> and integrity.[87]

The totalitarian politics of virtue, as practised during the reign of the Jacobins, form the more sombre outgrowth of classical republicanism. It took, for its guiding princi-ple in classical antiquity, not so much the ancient Roman Republic (though that is what furnished the themes of the paintings of David, and much of the official art and symbolism of the time) but also the myth of an older, much more harshly 'virtuous' city-republic: Sparta. That ancient Greek city-state had for centuries maintained itself as a totalitarian warrior society. It was based on a ruthless oppression of slaves and helots, a total disregard for suffering and sentiment in others and in oneself, and in a total subordination of the individual to the common interest. Sparta had had a sinister reputation in ancient Greece, had been the great dark rival of Athens, but had grudgingly won respect for its unflinching courage in the face of overpowering enemies: Persia, Alexander the Great. As such, it had been praised by Rousseau: as a society based on restraint rather than luxury, on loyalty rather than pleasure; on discipline rather than selfishness. As Paul Cartledge has pointed out, Rousseau formed his view of Sparta in the course of a polemic on luxury during the years 1749-1753. In his *Discours sur les sciences et les arts* (1749-1750), he described Sparta's *heureuse ignorance* and the *sagesse de ses lois*. Although projects for a regular treatise on Spartan history came to nothing, Rousseau continued to give favourable references throughout his later works, especially to its fabled legislator, Lycurgus. These virtues, Rousseau felt, had made Sparta strong enough to withstand the overwhelming power of great neighbouring monarchs; they also held out an ideal that was the very opposite of the dissipated, idle and vain aristocracy of latter days.[88]

It was this myth of Sparta which, after Rousseau, came to inspire the more totalitarian discipline-minded politicians of 'virtue'. The fact that so many sports clubs should have chosen to name themselves after the most gruesomely oppressive, inhuman warrior society of classical antiquity is one of the great, chilling ironies of European history. It was certainly the Spartan myth of dour, relentless and grim uprightness, which inspired Jacobin France and all totalitarian societies after it.

Indeed, if France in 1789 is the dawn of democracy for all of Europe, France in 1794 can be seen as the blueprint for all later totalitarian regimes of Europe, be they fascist or communist.

And Robespierre himself may be the very prototype of the modern dictator, in that he felt himself under an almost mystical mission to rule the people, all of the people. Stalin, Ceaușescu, Mussolini, Franco or Hitler: they all share with Robespierre the idea that they have an immediate, non-mediated responsibility for the nation-at-large, and they share with Robespierre a distrust of 'representative' government. Government should not *represent* the people, it should be a single, indivisible incorporation of the people-at-large. Such dictators claim to feel and embody, in an immediate and mystical directness within their own soul, what is good for the people. They are the instruments of history and of the people's destiny. Any bureaucracy, any career official, any other type of politician, will have to face their mistrust as selfish impostors, plotters, corrupt schemers. Again, Robespierre may himself have taken this idea of the transcendent 'lawgiver' – opposed to the wishy-washy 'law-makers' of modern states – from a Rousseauesque celebration of Spartan antiquity. In Lycurgus, Rousseau had seen

> an almost divinely inspired and authoritative legislator, so in
> tune with the temper and spirit of his people that he laid
> down laws which they could unswervingly abide by for cen-
> turies to come. Rousseau wrote, approvingly, that Lycurgus

fixed 'an iron yoke' and tied the Spartans to it by filling up every moment of their lives. This ceaseless constraint was, to Rousseau, ennobled by the purpose it served, that of patriotism, the ideal of which was constantly presented to the Spartans not only in their public laws, but also in their marital and reproductive customs, and in their festivals, feasts and games. In short, Rousseau saw in Lycurgus's Sparta a society devoted to implementing the general will in a collective, self-effacing, law-abiding, thoroughly virtuous way.[89]

Thus the sovereignty of the people, at first conceived as an inclusive all-embracing fraternization and solidarity, can turn into a recipe for stifling totalitarian unity. The luminous rise of modern democracy throws for its shadow the emergence of modern totalitarianism. But in one fundamental respect it all changed from the power of *ancien régime* monarchs: nothing was legitimate anymore except in the name of the *nation.*

Culture and the Nation: Literature, the Public Sphere and Anti-French Relativism

In previous pages we have seen that a good deal of attention was given to the idea that nations differed culturally and in their 'national character';[*] it remains to be traced how this cultural-ethnographical sense of nationality gained programmatic importance and eventually became instrumentalized into a cultural-political agenda.

So what, finally, is a nation, and where does it begin or end? The French Republic saw, at least in its high-minded beginnings, no obvious demarcation between 'the' nation and humanity at large: political usage at the time used the word 'nation' mainly in a societal sense, as the mass of the body politic. 'Nation' meant much the same thing that 'society' means nowadays – thus in Adam Smith's economic classic *An Inquiry into the Nature and Cause of the Wealth of Nations* (1776) – and the more particularly ethnic-anthropological meaning, referring to the cultures, manners and customs by which societies mutually differ, was more current in the realms of philosophy and cultural criticism than in the world of politics.

Literature and the emerging public sphere[90]

A general trend in Europe was to denounce the vices of the nobility and to praise the 'civic virtues' of the middle classes. Among these virtues was the patriotic 'love of the fatherland': the Patriotic citizen saw himself, ideally, as a useful member of society and of his nation. To this virtue belonged the rejection of 'foreign' vanities. It was a privilege of the upper classes and the nobility to have international contacts and to engage in foreign travel; and it was a matter of conspicuous wealth display to buy foreign produce and affect foreign manners. Command of a foreign language, the display of exotic plants or imported antiques, all that was considered a part of aristocratic showing-off, and was disdained by the solid citizen. In England (to name but one example), fashionable young gentlemen who had returned from the 'Grand Tour' (an educational journey to the Continent) formed the 'macaroni club', in honour of that exotic dish they had tasted in Italy; the word *macaroni*, still used sarcastically in the Patriot song 'Yankee Doodle Dandy', referred to pretentious showing-off. This exoticism was denounced countless times as profligate, irresponsible, in patriotically minded texts

---

* It should be stressed that the term 'national character' was not yet completely used in a national-psychological sense, but still largely also in a Theophrastan sense: as the way in which a nation presented itself to the world, as the set of remarkable, distinguishing external features (in manners and social conventions) that made a nation look different from others.

from verse to pamphlets to spectatorial essays,[*] and above all in the theatres and play-houses. If we can witness the emergence of something like a 'public sphere' in eight-eenth-century north-western Europe, then this is linked not only to the rise of venues like associations, clubs and coffee houses, or the rise of the spectatorial and periodical press, but also to the immense public function of the theatre. Indeed the very word 'public', and the specific term 'public opinion', were largely used in the context of playhouses: the audience of a theatre was its *public*, and their taste and preferences were, as early as the 1670s, called *l'opinion du public*. Neo-Aristotelian poeticists from the mid-seventeenth century onwards had stressed time and again that the playwright was bound by *tout ce qui est conforme à l'opinion du public* (that phrase was used by Rapin in his *La Poétique* of 1673), and as Gérard Genette has emphasized:

> This *opinion*, real or imputed, is fairly precisely what nowa-days would be called an ideology, that is to say: a body of rules and prejudices which forms both a world-view and a value-system.[91]

'Public opinion' begins, then, as the general rules of seemliness and plausibility (*bien-séance* and *vraisemblance*) which collectively govern an audience's reaction to theatrical representations, and will branch out from there into a general ideology whereby the public-at-large, i.e. the informed part of society, judges the world as it is presented to them. That is the sense in which Shaftesbury, in the above-quoted fragment (p. 77) distinguishes the sentient 'publick' from a mere governed 'multitude'. And much of what gave this public its moral cohesion happened in the 'virtual' sphere of the press and the printed media, much of it in the immediate public spaces of the coffee houses, associations and, indeed and still, the theatre. Thus, in the playhouses of mid-century London, a veritable ideology took place in the genre of the 'sentimental comedy', as popular and all-pervasive then as television chatshows are nowadays, where, in literally hundreds of plays, all forms of aristocratic profligacy were denounced in favour of solid middle-class virtues such as female chastity and innocence, filial piety, marital fidelity, and honesty. These were, increasingly, presented as *national* virtues, English virtues, against the aristocratic vices of gambling and duelling, and increasingly also against the aristocratic-cum-foreign vices of employing French servants, spending

---

[*] The eighteenth-century press saw the birth and great rise of a type of periodical, named after its prototype the *Spectator* (1711), combining moral essays, social satire and cultural criticism. The spec-tatorial press was, as Jürgen Habermas (1990) has pointed out, a 'virtual' media extension of the type of talk and gossip that would have gone on in the clubs and coffee houses that were so much in vogue in London from c. 1700 onwards. Like the social talk and gossip that went on in the public spaces of the European capitals, the spectatorial press contributed much to the emergence of a reg-ular 'public opinion', linking individual citizens into a sense of social cohesion and a 'civil society'. All this forms part, then, of the informal opinion-making and mobilization of the public that even-tually culminated in the democratic revolutions of the late eighteenth century. Benedict Anderson (1983), too, has emphasized the important role of the media in nation-formation, by their establish-ment of a public opinion and an 'imagined community'.

one's money abroad, and importing foreign life-styles out of brainless and spineless pretentiousness.

In other words: the critique of aristocratic immorality became also a critique of aristocratic cosmopolitanism; Patriotism and the ideology of civic virtue did, in its emphasis on *amor patriae*, begin to acquire some xenophobic elements. If an aristocrat was marked by his lack of involvement in his own country, then Patriotism would denounce the ethos of nobility and honour, not only for its immorality, but also for this lack of national rootedness.

In England, Holland and Germany, this anti-aristocratic anti-cosmopolitanism fastened, specifically, on the *Frenchness* of aristocratic culture. The France of Louis XIV and Louis XV was seen as the very home of all that was foreign, pretentious, hyper-refined and corrupt. France had been a dominant culture in Europe from the late seventeenth century onwards. The language of refinement was French; the technical vocabulary of refined pursuits such as fencing, etiquette, dance, ballet, fashion and *haute cuisine* was French. The language of international diplomacy was French. The court at Versailles was the point of orientation for all European monarchs, and so was its architecture. In Germany and Holland, palaces were built in the French-imported style of classicism, and given French names such as *Sanssouci*. The languages of the various courts of Europe were also increasingly shot through with French: famously, Frederick of Prussia used French for polite conversation and reserved German for his horses and his servants.

The international dominance of French high culture in aristocratic circles implied, logically enough, that the denunciation of aristocratic pretension and vanity also implied a denunciation of everything French. England took the lead in this, understandably, because throughout the century it was embroiled in wars with France. One of these conflicts, over the colony of Quebec, saw the presentation (significantly, in a playhouse, at the end of a theatrical performance!) of an anthem in support of George III: 'God Save the King' – the first modern 'national anthem' to emerge in the incipient formation of modern states in Europe.[*] The very genre of the 'sentimental comedy' was meant as a reaction against the dominant form of the classicist tragedy, as it had been prescribed by the likes of La Mesnardière and benchmarked by authors like Corneille and Racine. The sentimental comedy accordingly highlighted middle-class virtue rather than noble honour, and lost no opportunity to 'play to the gallery' by invoking anti-French and anti-foreign sentiments.[92] A revival of the works of Shakespeare almost gloried in the fact that *Macbeth* and *Hamlet* were written in ignorance of the rules of neo-Aristotelian classicism (something which still led an author like Voltaire to dismiss Shakespeare as uncouth).[93]

This message was soon picked up in Germany. 'Germany' did not exist at the time, of course; in the many principalities and petty monarchies which together formed the

---

[*] Strictly speaking, 'God Save the King' is not the oldest national anthem in Europe; the Dutch *Wilhelmus* is a good deal older, and formed part of an institutionalized canon of songs asserting Dutch independence. It was not until the nineteenth century, however, that the *Wilhelmus* obtained the status of national anthem.

loose and almost fictitious German Empire, French taste and French culture were the order of the day. The German public was dispersed over many different petty states, and a German literature was weak and disparate in the face of the overwhelming French hegemony at the many different courts in all the different German capitals: Munich, Dresden, Berlin, etcetera. Patriotically minded writers, in taking offence at this French-derived and court-dominated self-alienation, began to look to English taste and English literature as an alternative. Significantly, the obvious starting point appeared to be the mobilization of homegrown taste and a homegrown public sphere by means of creating a German *public*, that is to say, by creating a German theatre. A theatre venture was started in Hamburg, significantly an independent city-republic, which failed after a few years, but which sparked off a body of critical writing by one of the leading German intellectuals of the mid-eighteenth century. Gotthold Ephraim Lessing's *Hamburg Dramaturgy* resoundingly stated the need for German literature to abandon its formulaic classicism-by-numbers and its slavish imitation of the high French style.

Lessing sarcastically stated in 1768 that the idea 'of giving to the Germans a national theatre' had been quixotic 'because we Germans are not yet a nation';[94] but in invoking the notion of nationality he discussed a moral, social and literary problem as much as a 'national' one. In his view, Germany *does* need a theatre for the main mass of the population at large, in the cities, outside the aristocratic courts; but that population is as yet inchoate, unconnected and disparate, and can only follow foreign (French) taste. Following Lessing, early calls for a national theatre or a national literature seem to imply that what German society needs is, again, a *public sphere*, in Habermas's sense of the term: a forum for social concourse and opinion-forming, an intellectual space for egalitarian exchange and communal reflection of matters of common importance. Thus, the need for a German national theatre, as expressed by intellectuals like Lessing, can be read as a desire to have something like a German public sphere, a public opinion, a common bonding agent for society apart from the suzerainty of lords and princes. This, at least, is how Friedrich Schiller's 1784 essay on 'The stage as a moral institution' can be read:

> I cannot overlook the great influence which a good firmly-
> established theatre would have on the nation's spirit. That
> national spirit I define as the similarity and concord of its
> opinions and proclivities in matters where other nations
> think and feel differently. Only through a theatre is it possi-
> ble to effect such concord to a high degree, because theatre
> moves through the entire field of human knowledge, takes in
> all situations of life and shines into all corners of the heart: it
> unites all ranks and classes of society and has free access to
> the mind and to the heart. [...] if we would see the day when
> we have a national theatre, then we would become a nation.
> What else was it that forged Greece into a unity? What was it
> that pulled the Greeks to its theatre? Nothing other than the
> public-mindedness of their plays, their Greek spirit, the

great, overwhelming interest of the state and of the better
part of humanity.[95]

Theatrical practice followed this call. Lessing himself, whose main claim to fame nowadays is his philosophical play *Nathan der Weise,* adapted the English sentimental comedy into something he called, significantly, the 'bourgeois tragedy' (*bürgerliches Trauerspiel*). His followers, Goethe and Schiller, were to use the theatre as the prime launching pad for a revival of German culture, with plays like Goethe's *Götz von Berlichingen* (1773), *Egmont* (1788) and *Faust I* (1808), and Schiller's *The Brigands* (1781), *Don Carlos* (1787), *Wallenstein* (1798) and *Wilhelm Tell* (1804) – plays with an obvious historical, Shakespearian and (certainly in Schiller's case) Patriot character.

Thus, the great flowering of German literature is propelled by a consciousness-raising effort to reject French models and French classicism (and to turn to English models instead). A similar trend is noticeable in other Northern European countries: in Holland, the novels of Richardson are praised as both realistic and morally uplifting, and as such diametrically opposed to the artificial and decadent material that comes out of France. One of the 'classics' of late-eighteenth-century Dutch literature, an epistolary novel on the life and adventures of *Miss Sara Burgerhart* (1782),[*] sets itself up as a Dutch novel for young Dutch women, not only by casting all French characters and French influences either as silly or as villainous, but also with a preface stressing that a homegrown literature should turn to Richardson and turn away from French frivolity. The authors, Elizabeth Wolff and Agatha Deken were, significantly, part of the liberal-Patriot end of the Dutch political spectrum; after a failed *coup d'état* against the stadholder, William V of Orange, they had to take refuge abroad with other members of the Patriot faction.

Herder and cultural relativism

There was, then, a widely expressed resistance against the hegemony of a French-oriented cultural elitism in Europe. This was systematized most influentially in the philosophy of Johann Georg Herder (1744-1803), who formulated a notion of cultural relativism of truly seminal importance. Most of the 'national awakenings' that took place in Central and Eastern Europe, from Germany to Bulgaria and from Slovenia to Finland, can be more or less directly traced back to the philosophy and influence of Herder; and all of the Romantic (and later) preoccupation with popular culture, from the Grimms' collection of fairytales to the birth of folklore studies, is due to him. To this day, all folk-inspired artists, though they may not realize it, are still indebted to Herder's thought.

---

[*] The name is overtly programmatic: the heroine has a burgher's heart, i.e. she is clear-sighted, level-headed and independently minded. The name had been used in earlier drama by P.C. Hooft on the Batavian topic: in Hooft's *Baeto oft oorsprong der Hollanderen* ('Bato, or the origin of the Hollanders', 1626), the hero's most trustworthy companion is called Burgerhart. The name may play on the Latin 'Civilis'.

16. Johann Gottfried Herder

Like Lessing's, Herder's ambience was urban, and removed from the aristocratic court; but whereas Lessing worked in a mercantile-urban context, that of Herder was the Protestant church. He was for many years a pastor in Riga, that Baltic city that was so multicultural *par excellence*: a crossroads for Jewish, Finnish/Estonian, Latvian/Lithuanian, German, Polish and Russian influences. In keeping with the Enlightenment Protestantism of his time, Herder felt that all humans shared a fundamental dignity as God's creatures; this made him adverse to the idea that some human types should be superior to others. The status of being 'God's creatures' also implied a radical equality for all humans. And so Herder's thought gravitated to the problem of human diversity as opposed to human equality.[*]

---

[*] We can notice a similar trend in the person of Johann Caspar Lavater, a Swiss pastor of Patriot leanings who wrote on physiognomy. He classified, in typical encyclopaedic Enlightenment style, all variations and 'characteristics' of the human face; at the same time, he did so as a contribution to 'anthropology and philanthropy' (*Menschenkenntnis und Menschenliebe*, as the subtitle of his work has it), in that he saw in all facial variations still the underlying Biblical principle that humanity (and that included all humans) had been created in God's likeness; cf. Leerssen 1998, and see below, p. 209.

We may perhaps single out, as the core of Herder's manifold writings and trains of thought, a central insight regarding a question that much preoccupied Enlightenment thinkers: the origin of language. Language, it was universally agreed, was one of the prime distinctions between humans and animals, one of the main properties that make us human. What, precisely, lies at its root? How did language evolve? How does it take hold in the development of a young child? These questions, which are still equally important (and unresolved) nowadays, led to a number of exchanges of thought. Herder's contribution was characteristic and revolutionary in that he turned the question 'inside out', as it were. In asking whether language was a natural instinct or a cultural development, he pointed out that natural instincts (e.g. birds building nests, bees building honeycombs) are invariant and follow strict patterns. All bees stick to honeycombs with hexagonal cells, never triangular or square ones; no woodpecker will attempt to build a stork-style nest. Opposed to this invariance, human language dazzles because of its diversity. Humans do not speak a single language, but a great many, all of them adapted to their various living conditions and expressive of their identity and mentality. The great thing that makes language into a uniquely and characteristically human feature is, then, not its existence, but its potential for diversity.

With this mode of reasoning, Herder almost single-handedly turned Enlightenment notions of culture on their head.[96] The Enlightenment, though it had been aware of variations in humanity, culture, and language, had still studied these topics in the abstract. Man, Culture, Literature, Language: universal words in the singular, with a capital letter as it were. Variations were registered as secondary, as exceptions, as anomalies. In Herder's style of thinking, variation became the central essence of what made humanity human. Not humankind, but the diversity between societies and nations, each with their own language, their own outlook, their own literature, their own unique place in creation. And, what is even more important: it is this variation *as such* that is valuable: not any particular culture or language in its own right, but the existence of alternatives, of differences. Herder's view of human culture may, in short, be characterized as *ecological* – the richness of a given cultural landscape was, in his view, determined by the amount of variation and diversity to be encountered within it. The corn was not necessarily more valuable than the cornflower, the rose not necessarily more beautiful that the moss or the fern, the eagle not necessarily more highly valued than the lizard.

Herder propounded this view in many historical and philosophical treatises, but also in influential collections of folk songs from all the corners of Europe and indeed the world. Later known under the title 'The nations' voices in their songs' (*Stimmen der Völker in Liedern*), his collections of *Volkslieder* (1778-1779) marked a true turning point in European literature. Truly inclusive, they presented Finnish, South-Slavic and other materials in German translations. The simplicity of their form and the artless spontaneity of their style were very far removed from the official 'high' literature of the time, and readers were delighted by it; it must have been like hearing an Irish reel after a year of Wagner. The *Lied* or 'song' became the form of choice for German romanticism, both in poetry (Goethe) and in poetry-put-to-music (Schubert); simplicity of diction and spontaneity of sentiment became a Romantic ideal all over Europe, witness Wordsworth's contributions to the 1798 *Lyrical Ballads*.[97] What is more, it alerted all nations that were as yet without established 'high literature', that their cultural output, even if it took the (hitherto despised) form of oral folksong, was nonetheless a thing to be proud of, a manifestation of the nation's presence in the cultural landscape.

The huge impact and wide ramifications of this cultural ecology in the nineteenth century will be traced further on. In the eighteenth-century context, it will be obvious that Herder's thought necessarily led into a cogently argued denunciation of the hegemony of French-classical culture. In Herder's view, this amounted to an impoverishment of the cultural landscape and to a fatal self-estrangement of nations under French influence. Such self-estrangement amounted almost to a moral failure to live up to the divine dignity of human diversity. At times he vehemently denounced the flattening of characteristic cultural identities into a French-dominated one-size-fits-all. The Enlightenment's optimistic and cosmopolitan 'improvement-through-assimilation' is sarcastically mocked:

> How miserable were the days when there were still nations
> with different characters! What mutual hatred, xenophobia,
> stick-in-the-mud stolidity, patriarchal prejudices, attachment
> to the sod on which we were born and in which we will rot!
> Nativist thought, narrowly confined ideas, eternal barbarism!
> Now, thank God, all national characters have been obliter-
> ated, we all love each other, or rather: no one needs to love
> anyone else. We converse, we are wholly equalized: well-
> mannered, civil, happy. We do not have a fatherland, no
> sense of our own that we live for, but we are philanthropists
> and cosmopolitan citizens of the world. All rulers of Europe
> already speak the French language, soon we shall all speak it!
> And then, Oh bliss! we shall return to the Golden Age, when
> all the world had a single language and was one flock under
> one shepherd! Oh national characters, where have you
> gone?[98]

Herder attacks the central values of the Enlightenment as utopian, sinister and spiritually deadening. This makes him one of the greatest 'critics of the Enlightenment', one who paved the way for the intellectual and cultural fashions (like Romanticism) that were to take over one generation later. Unlike the eighteenth century, the nineteenth will always define national identity on the basis of international difference. National differentiation after Herder obtains a fundamental, categorical status in cultural and political thought. Following Herder, a nation's sense of identity will crucially, fundamentally, be based on the way in which that nation stands out from humanity at large. The abstract universalism of the earlier generation is overturned and made wholly impossible as a result of Herder's intervention. A nation's culture is no longer seen as its civility, or its artistic achievements, or anything imposed or cultivated from above; rather, a nation's culture is seen as the manifestation of its true, fundamental identity, something that comes from below, from the lower classes, from folklore, rustic traditions and popular customs. This is the basis, the root system, that culture must tap into.

The repercussions are manifold. Goethe will celebrate German popular literature – texts like 'Reynard the Fox' and 'Faustus', topics and themes which at the time were known only as the denigrated 'pulp' for the consumption of the lower classes. Poets will emulate the diction and simplicity of folksongs in their poems, which turn to the ballad form and the simple four-line stanza. The romantic return to the roots of popular culture was not just a parallel to a Rousseauesque call for a return to nature and innocence, its was given an urgent agenda of national identity politics as a result of Herder's philosophy. Indeed, the rise of romantic nationalism in Europe may be seen, to a very large extent, as the outcome of a fusion between the influences of Rousseau and Herder. Rousseau had proclaimed the sovereignty of the nation against the power of princes; Herder had proclaimed the categorical separateness of nations mutually; both exalted natural authenticity above civilized artificiality. As we shall see in the next chapter, the combined influence of Rousseau and Herder was to result in the idea that each nation, categorically separate from others as a result of its cultural rootedness and authenticity, deserved its own separate sovereignty. Which is the very definition and starting-point of modern nationalism in Europe.

Summing up

The survey of the source traditions of European nationalism started with ancient notions of ethnocentrism and exoticism, the separation between self and other, between ordered society and wilderness. Into these ancient attitudes play circulating 'ethnotypes': conventional commonplaces regarding the mores and manners of foreign peoples. In the sixteenth and seventeenth centuries, these ethnotypes, at first free-floating and ad hoc, crystallize into contrastive systematics of different characters and temperaments; these in turn are ordered by national names taken from the state system which begins to stabilize in Europe at the same period, and whose component states begin to formulate historical self-images linking present-day political ideals back to classical and primitive antiquity. Thus, the discourse of ethnic stereotype becomes 'national': arranged under the names of countries, referring to the character and purported identity of populations.

The relationship between country, population and character is further spelled out as a result of the rise of republican and democratic thought (resulting in the idea that the population (known increasingly as the 'nation') is welded into a whole (a 'public') by a communal solidarity and by shared civic virtues such as love of the fatherland, and on that basis deserves to exercise a constitutional mandate. At the same time, the notion of culture turns 'inside out' from a general one (culture opposing nature) into a comparative-contrastive one (mutually opposing cultures). The concept of nationality gains a political-constitutional importance as well as a defining function in establishing why and how countries and societies differ from each other.

These developments and source traditions between them form the root system, the ingredients as it were, of the ideology of nationalism. Over the period 1795-1815, these will be welded together in the pressurized atmosphere of the Napoleonic Wars, and coalesce into that ideology which sees humanity as naturally divided into nations, each with their different culture and character, each deserving a separate nation-based sovereignty, each commanding the overriding allegiance of their members.

The Politics of
National Identity

Napoleon and the Rise of Political Romanticism

In Germany, the French Revolution had initially been greeted with awe and enthusiasm. Goethe recognized the beginning of a new era when he witnessed, at the Battle of Valmy (1792), how a ragtag army of volunteers defeated the well-trained war machine of the monarchical allies, carried to victory by the inspirational force of their battle song, the *Marseillaise*.

In the wars that followed, the Republic's main trump card was a small wiry Corsican artillery officer, Napoleon Bonaparte. He conquered the Italian peninsula for France in a 1796-1797 campaign, and after a less successful campaign in Egypt overthrew the Republic's leading Directorate in a military *coup d'état*. Named 'first consul' (with Sieyès as second consul) Bonaparte resumed the French series of victories after 1800. In battle after battle he defeated variously aligned opponents: Marengo (1800), Ulm and Austerlitz (1805), Jena and Auerstädt (1806), Wagram (1809). And at each turn, the French territory was expanded until it covered all of Western Europe, with Prussia and Austria as helpless client states.

Important French gains had taken place as early as 1797. In a peace treaty with Austria, France traded in some of its Italian conquests (like Venice) for the Vienna-ruled Southern Netherlands. Indeed, France came to control practically all of the left bank of the Rhine, and Vauban's old dream, to have French territory bordered in the North-East by that natural frontier, came true at last. This was, however, to prove a fatal destabilization for the ancient Holy Roman Empire. Many lordships and fiefs west of the Rhine formed part of the old Empire; they were held by local nobles who constitutionally were vassals of the Emperor at Vienna. That emperor had now, almost literally, sold them down the river, and an arrangement had to be found to compensate them for their losses. When attempts failed to recapture the Rhineland territories, a formal imperial decision was taken (the dishearteningly named *Reichsdeputations-hauptschluss*) in 1803 to reshuffle the fiefs and lordships in the Empire. A number of territories in the imperial heartland (east of the Rhine), which previously had been free lordships immediate under the Imperial crown, were now placed as fiefs and lordships under the dispossessed nobles from the left bank; they lost their immediate status and were, as the terminology had it, 'mediatized' – a severe loss of something close to autonomous sovereignty. Many of these erstwhile free imperial fiefs had been church establishments (monasteries, free bishoprics); these also lost their legal independence and immunity and were placed under secular rule or 'secularized'.[99]

The reshuffle of 1803 had a momentous side effect. The old Empire – the Holy Roman Empire of the German Nation, to give it its full name – was by now fully a thousand years old* and as a state it was very decrepit indeed. The various princes who ruled under the auspices of the Emperor were largely autonomous. Indeed, in the course of the eighteenth century, the empire had had to look on almost powerlessly as the Electors of Brandenburg had first assumed the title of King in Prussia, and then King of Prussia (cf. below, p. 127), in a process that had even led to war between Berlin and Vienna. The Empire was largely a legal fiction, with all the charisma and the impressive ceremonial dignity that a thousand-year-old history can bestow, but with almost no political muscle. Whatever power the Empire had was restricted to the actual heartland of the ruling Habsburg dynasty† (i.e. Austria with the conquered kingdoms of Bohemia and Hungary, and a few other adjoining provinces); outside the Habsburg crown lands, the imperial power rested almost exclusively on its symbolic prestige, its venerable traditions, the idea that it had always been there, ever since Charlemagne had been crowned the first modern emperor in 800 AD.

The 1803 reshuffle broke down even this façade of unchanging traditional fixity. It demonstrated that the Empire, for all its venerable antiquity, lacked the force to withstand the tide of modern geopolitics. The 1803 reshuffle was not a sign of a flexible arrangement, but the first cracks and totterings of a rigid superannuated edifice about to come tumbling down. One year later, in 1804, Napoleon crowned himself Emperor of the French. Emperor Francis II, last successor to Charlemagne, abdicated in 1806 as Holy Roman Emperor and instead contented himself with the (decidedly less impressive) title of 'Emperor of Austria'.

This development may be the first sign of Napoleon's 'imperial overstretch'. Ten years earlier, German intellectuals had been willing enough to greet the French Revolution as a great new era of universal liberation; a marvellous irony was felt to lie in the fact that France, of all countries, previously the homeland of Louis XIV's expansionist warmongering and Louis XV's corruption, should now become the cradle of human rights and of Liberty, Equality and Brotherhood. This fond willingness to see France reborn as the home of freedom was most bitterly disenchanted when Napoleon proved to be Louis XIV's equal in arrogance and territorial greed. By the time Napoleon crowned himself Emperor, he had reduced all of Germany to French provinces or French puppet regimes, and had assigned even that most venerable institution, the Holy Roman Empire, to the dustbin of history.

The period 1800-1810 saw, then, the transmogrification of Napoleon, in German eyes, from a heroic titan of a new age towards a monstrous re-enactment of all that was fearsome in the French. Beethoven, who had still dedicated his third 'heroic'

---

* When Hitler's 'Third Reich' raised its claim to last for a thousand years, it was evoking the duration of this first Reich. (The intervening second Reich was the one under Prussian control, established in 1871 and ending in 1918.)

† The imperial crown was theoretically an elective monarchy: a college of Electors (consisting, with some changes over the centuries, of the archbishops of the ancient Roman-founded sees of Cologne, Mainz and Trier, and of important magnates such as the King of Bohemia and the Margrave/Elector of Brandenburg) appointed each new emperor. In practice, the imperial title had been contested property between the great dynastic houses of Luxemburg, Wittelsbach and Habsburg since 1273, with the Habsburgs in almost continuous control since 1438.

17. Ernst Moritz Arndt

symphony to Napoleon in 1804, tore up the dedication in disgust in 1806. From 1806 onwards, German intellectuals of the Romantic generation, like Görres, Friedrich Schlegel or Wilhelm von Humboldt, and the philosopher Fichte, many of whom had been quite positively predisposed towards the ideas of the Revolution originally, turned into fervent France-haters and anti-revolutionaries.[100]

Arndt, Jahn and nationhood

One of the most enduringly influential representatives of this new anti-French intelligentsia was Ernst Moritz Arndt (1769-1860).[101] He had been born as the son of a liberated serf on the island of Rügen, had been trained for the Lutheran ministry, and had made, in the style of the Romantic *Wanderjahre*, a journey through Europe.[102] A true Romantic, he was inspired by ideals of human equality, denounced the notion of aristocratic prerogative and the servitude of the rural poor; a true Romantic, he was also touched by the sight of the many ruins of medieval castles on the banks of the Rhine and Moselle. Arndt's vision of the Rhine, however, was also an intensely political one: at the time of his journey, that river formed the border of the French

Republic, and the ruins he saw had not been caused by the slow decay of centuries, but by French explosives. Most of the Rhineland castles had been laid to waste in the ferocious campaign of Louis XIV in the Palatinate War of 1689.

The Rhine became, for Arndt, the symbol of a Germany raped and ruined by its aggressive neighbour; and the canonization of the Rhine as the picturesque, but torn and tattered frontline of Germany's history was to remain central in the next generation;[103] it was not for nothing that Görres called his anti-French newspaper the *Rheinische Merkur*. More importantly, the experience goaded Arndt into an increasingly vehement denunciation of France and France's hegemony over Germany. His sarcastic lines addressed to the French nation on Napoleon's rise to power may give an idea:

> You, then, are that worthy people, which has swindled
> Europe out of its fairest hopes – and you claim to be the
> benefactors and lords of others, while you have yourselves
> again become crouching and miserable slaves?[104]

From a teaching post at the University of Greifswald, Arndt began a one-man pamphleteering war against French domination; this took some courage, since Napoleon's rule was in fact a dictatorship, and dissent was not treated mildly under French rule. Nonetheless, Arndt excoriated French rule in prose and in verse, in a series of pamphlets entitled *The Spirit of the Age (Geist der Zeit)*, and going as far as claiming, in dead earnest, that hatred of the French nation was a moral duty for each virtuous German.

Eventually, Arndt's position became too precarious, and he briefly went into exile in Sweden. Later, in St. Petersburg (one of the great European centres for fugitives from Napoleonic rule), he met the then-disgraced Prussian minister Karl vom Stein, who had been declared a public enemy by Napoleon, and he was employed by that statesman as a private secretary. From that moment onwards, Arndt's influence in political circles was to increase dramatically. Among the people-at-large, his standing was very high owing to political verse like 'What is the German's fatherland' (*'Was ist des Deutschen Vaterland'*), which enjoyed enormous popularity. Throughout the first half of the nineteenth century, this song was practically the unofficial national anthem of a 'Germany' that existed, not as an actual state, but as a cultural and political ideal.

Another populist activist stirring up anti-French opinion in these years was Friedrich Jahn (1778-1852). His formula was to be copied by many later nationalist movements: he founded a sports association. In Jahn's view, Germany's humiliation under French dominance was to be countered by a physical and moral regeneration. Germany's young men were to work hard in body and spirit to regain the stalwart manliness (traces of Roman-primitivist *virtus*, once again) that could alone form the basis of a German resurgence. As a result he began open-air training sessions of what was innocuously called a *Turnverein*, or Gymnastics Club, but which in reality was a hothouse of anti-French consciousness-raising, and a thinly veiled training camp for a future popular militia. Jahn, too, operated on the very fringes of what was permissible under law. His *Turnvereine* (which sprang up in many German cities, and were to form a radical-populist wing of German nationalism for decades to come) were repeatedly outlawed as seditious paramilitary organizations. But with his book *Deutsches*

Volkstum of 1806, Jahn was to create an important popular bible of national regenera-tion. Forty years later, both Arndt and *Turnvater* Jahn were elected to the 1848 National Assembly at Frankfurt, as revered godfathers of the German national movement.

Idealism and transcendence

It is instructive to look a little more closely at the titles of two activist publications just mentioned: *Geist der Zeit* and *Deutsches Volkstum* – 'Spirit of the Age' and 'German nationality'. Both formulate a new way of dealing with identity and politics. In both titles, the topics of contemporary politics are reduced to an abstract principle, an es-sence: a 'spirit', 'nation-ness' or nationhood. This vocabulary bespeaks a new type of thought which is particular to the period, and which we would not have encountered twenty years previously. It is a mode of thought that is peculiar to Romanticism and which we may call 'idealistic'.

I do not use the term 'idealism' in its standard, contemporary sense (holding a set of high moral standards and goals, and being willing to work for them). In the more technical sense as used here, the word derives from *idea* rather than *ideal*, and refers to a mode of thinking which believes that the true meaning of the world is to be found in abstract underlying principles rather than in concrete phenomena (in this sense, idealism is often opposed to materialism). It is a line of reasoning that originated with Plato, and which underwent a revival in post-Kantian philosophy; the most well-known philosophers of the generation after Kant being Schelling, Fichte and Hegel. However, it should be stressed that in the German intellectual climate of the 1790s and early 1800s, philosophical trends were set by men who nowadays are more famous as creative authors, but who in their day and age exerted great influence on the devel-opment of philosophy: e.g. Goethe, Schiller and Hölderlin. Conversely, philosophical developments were not restricted to the professional circles of dedicated, academic philosophy scholars, but had a wide participation among the intelligentsia at large.[105]

What distinguishes the intellectual patterns of the post-Kantian generation from its forerunners is, precisely, its idealistic bent. The phenomena of the world are not ana-lysed in their structural workings or in their historical roots, but are often seen as manifestations of an essential spiritual principle. The famous example of 'the horse' is hackneyed but still serviceable to make the line of reasoning clear: horses can be of many types, breeds and colours; yet, despite all these differentiations, we almost never confuse a horse with a donkey, or with a dog. That is because all different concrete, material horses that present themselves to our senses, are immediately understood by us to belong to the category 'horse', i.e. to incorporate some essential quality or idea of 'horseness'. That is precisely the drift of Jahn's title: instead of the German nation, his topic is German nation-ness, nationhood, *Volkstum*.[106]

Human intelligence means, then, to see through the incidental details of material reality and to grasp the underlying essences and principles. In other words: human intelligence is a continuous effort to transcend the level of the single details, to move from the concrete to the abstract, from the material to the spiritual, from the individual phenomenon to the more general truth.

The thought of the most influential philosopher of the period, Hegel, is also based on such a principle; in his case, he focuses on the principle of the human *Geist* as something which (like creation itself, and like all of world history) constantly strives towards transcendence. *Geist* will strive to embrace superficial contradictions into ever deeper and wider understandings of the underlying truth.[*] But this restless questing urge towards a transcendent understanding is not only the topic of abstract philosophical reasoning, it also expressed by non-academic minds, e.g. in Goethe's *Faust* (1808).

Indeed, all of Romantic poetry seems to reflect a tendency towards the transcendent. The actual topic of a given poem is often taken as something which the poet addresses in its more spiritual essence. A singing bird, for instance, is not just a specific feathered animal, but becomes instead the eternal, timeless principle of creativity. It is instructive, for a single example, to look at the way a lark is described by Shakespeare and by Shelley:

> Lo, here the gentle lark, weary of rest,
> From his moist cabinet mounts up on high,
> And wakes the morning, from whose silver breast
> The sun ariseth in his majesty;
> Who doth the world so gloriously behold
> That cedar-tops and hills seem burnish'd gold.
> (Shakespeare, *Venus and Adonis*, 1593)

> Hail to thee, blithe spirit!
> Bird thou never wert-
> That from heaven or near it
> Pourest thy full heart
> In profuse strains of unpremeditated art.
> (Shelley, 'To a Skylark', 1820)

Both poems express the beauty of the scene: Shakespeare by way of a sensuous and visual evocation of the radiant early morning and its splendour, Shelley by lifting the bird to the realm of the spiritual, more than a mere bird, the very symbol of divine musical rapture and poetical inspiration. Romanticism, and with it the entire climate

---

[*] The idea that understanding is reached, not through linear cause-and-effect reasoning but by way of getting to know both sides of a conflict, involves a sense of 'dialectics'. The notion that human history progresses dialectically, i.e. as a constant succession and resolution of conflicts, is typical of the nineteenth century (it also lies at the basis of Marx's thought); it may reflect the experience of the mother of all conflicts, the French Revolution and its many aftershocks. In contrast, the Enlightenment thinkers we have encountered (Locke, Montesquieu, even Rousseau) had a much more gradualist understanding of historical progress: as something taking place in a linear development from cause to effect.

of the early nineteenth century, participates in this trend towards grasping the true meaning of the world in terms of its deeper spiritual essences.

While this may be one of the core preoccupations of the Romantic school of literature[*] (the urge towards transcendence is as characteristic of Romanticism, as the belief in human progress and the power of the critical mind was of the Enlightenment), it also affects the type of political thought that we see in the titles of Arndt and Jahn. The issue is not just a political crisis, a distribution of power and hegemony, a conflict of monarchs and their armies and territories: at a more transcendent level, those conflicts are the manifestation of a deeper, more spiritual clash. For Arndt, History itself is facing a Crisis between the Powers of Morality and of Immorality (I capitalize all these nouns to draw attention to the Romantic habit of dealing with abstractions when 'explaining' current affairs); for Jahn, the point of concern is the essence of German Nationhood or National Identity (for that is how we may translate *Volkstum*, a word that he coined for the first time and introduced into the German language).

This is not just a rarefied point of philosophical nit-picking; it marks a crucial turning-point in European history. Against the pragmatic machinery of the French Revolution and of Napoleon's empire is opposed a Romantic, idealistic argument that invokes abstract spiritual essences; a 'philosophical' overlay on top of the old opposition between the Germanic (Arminius/Luther) and Latinate halves of Europe. On the one hand, it sets up Germany and France, not just as rivalling countries, but as two almost metaphysically opposing principles: France as the embodiment of pragmatic and systematic reasoning, Germany as the embodiment of moral and meditative

---

* This is not a literary history, and it is far beyond the scope of this book to give extensive coverage of the notion and periodization of Romanticism; I may refer to standard handbooks and studies such as Béguin 1946; de Deugd 1966; Gusdorf 1993; Praz 1930; Van Tieghem 1969. The following sketchy digest may, however, be useful by way of background: The notion of 'Romanticism' spreads in European literature from the 1790s onwards. It refers initially to whatever is thrilling, unusual and out-of-the-ordinary (the term 'romantic' originally meant 'as in a romance', much as 'picturesque' meant 'as in a painting' or the earliest 'grotesque' meant 'as in a cave-drawing'). Growing out of earlier trends of the 1760s and 1770s (such as the Rousseauesque cult of nature and sentimentalism, and the literature of passion and sentiment), Romanticism as a label is attached to specific groups of authors who work under Goethe's shadow in Germany in the 1790s through the 1820s. In English literature, the term applies to the 'Lake School' of poets (Wordsworth, Coleridge, Southey, De Quincey) and their successor generation (Byron, Shelley, Keats), flanked by the long-lived figure of Walter Scott; likewise active mainly in the period 1795-1825. In France, Romanticism is delayed until after Waterloo (1815), as a result of the dominant climate of classicism under the *directoire* and the *empire*. By the 1830s, Romanticism is more or less played out in German and English literature, but still important elsewhere in Europe, from Portugal (Almeida Garrett) to Russia (Pushkin). It has left traces and echoes in subsequent periods, down to the present day.

The poetics of Romanticism involve: a tendency towards idealistic abstraction (i.e. seeing the sublime and transcendent in the mundane and the small-scale); a tendency towards situational irony (the cleavage between human ambitions and the chaotic realities of the world); a tendency to thematize the topic of artistic inspiration and subjective alienation from society; a tendency towards exoticism in space (the Orient, other distant places; wanderlust) and in time (the past, the future, the Middle Ages). The Romantic artist has a strong sense of being different from (and misunderstood by) others, owing to his/her capacity for artistic inspiration.

contemplation; France as the social engineer, Germany as the moral philosopher. This perceived opposition (which of course is an over-simplification that does not do justice to the reality of European relations) became a dominant stereotype in the next century: Germany as the sphere of *Kultur* and *Geist*, France as the sphere of *civilisation* and *esprit*.[*] The Romantic resistance against Napoleon thus articulates and brings into being one of the deepest cleavages in Europe's cultural self-image.

The other result of this Romantic tendency towards abstraction was that the notion of national character was to undergo yet another shift in meaning, and this time a fateful one. The notion of 'character' had, we have seen, been moving in meaning: from someone's 'type' or outward appearance towards someone's inner predisposition. This internalization process was taken one step further as a result of Romantic idealism. A nation's 'character' from Arndt and Jahn onwards was no longer, as Diderot's *Encyclopédie* had phrased it, a *disposition habituelle de l'âme* or 'habitual disposition of the soul' – it became the nation's soul itself. Every nation owed its identity, the very fact that it existed as something separate from other nations, to its own essence, its own *Volkstum*, its own *Geist*. The notion of 'national character' obtained an almost metaphysical meaning: it became the underlying moral blueprint, the DNA as it were, that determined a nation's personality, its way of positioning itself in the world, its way of viewing the world. Roughly around this period, we see the emergence (the precise point is hard to pin down) of important new concepts like *Volksgeist*. Lessing and Herder had paved the way for this line of thought: they had credited different nations with a different *Denkungsart*, or mentality, or outlook. With the Romantics, this 'outlook' is canonized into the very core, indeed the soul or *Geist*, of a nation's identity. To lose one's national identity was to lose one's soul; to be true to one's national identity became, more than ever before, a moral, ethical duty.

Fichte's 'Reden an die deutsche Nation'

I do not merely extrapolate this from the thin evidence of two exemplary publications with catchy titles; the argument paraphrased here was set forth, at length and with the full firepower of heavy-duty philosophy, in the foundational text of modern nationalism: Johann Gottlob Fichte's *Reden an die deutsche Nation* (1808). In Fichte's view, the nation is more than just the 'social contract' of the democrats; it is a moral and transgenerational community. Moral, in that it is based on the deepest feelings and affections that make us human: love of our children, piety towards our parents, attachment to our native soil.[†] Transgenerational, in that the nation gives us a sense of rootedness

---

[*] The opposition between *esprit* and *Geist* was formulated as such by Eduard Wechssler in his book of that title, 1927 (cf. Dyserinck 1991, 141). The subtitle of the book is telling: *Versuch einer Wesenskunde des Deutschen und des Französischen*, where *Wesenskunde* would mean something like 'the study/understanding of identity/essence'. For the opposition *Kultur/civilisation* cf. Labrie 1994 and Karuth 1967.

[†] 'Attachment to our native soil' is something different from the Patriotic notion of 'love of the fatherland'. In the Enlightenment, the 'fatherland' is above all a society of those with whom we feel

in the past, and a sense of responsibility for the future generations. The nation is presented as a kind of extended family, and loyalty to the nation becomes almost like 'family values'.

We see in Fichte's lectures the merger of Herder's and Rousseau's thought, and the first blueprint for European ethnic nationalism. The term *Nation* is far-reaching in its implications. At first sight one might expect that Fichte would avoid that term, which is so redolent of the political jargon of the French Revolution; Ernst Moritz Arndt and Friedrich Jahn, after all, prefer the nomenclature of *Stamm* or *Volk*. Yet on closer scrutiny Fichte's term is deliberate, and apt. He gives his *Reden* under the shadow of the millennial trauma of the abolition of the Holy Roman Empire, *Das Heilige Römische Reich deutscher Nation*. Fichte's implication is that, although the empire no longer exists, its constituent *Nation* still does, bereft of its sovereign incorporation but alive in its substance. In the process, he takes the term *nation* back from the democratic-revolutionary register where it had been placed by Sieyès, and, while maintaining all its claims to sovereignty, equates it with the German-ness of the old Empire. What is more, Fichte proclaims the moral superiority of the *German* nation over *other* nations – an ethnic specification of the notion of nationality that comes straight from Herder, but which is now given political as well as cultural value. The superiority of the German nation, for Fichte, lies in its unbroken maintenance of its traditions and language. The customs and language of the Germans, so his argument runs, can be traced back for centuries, indeed millennia; and this bespeaks a loyalty and integrity that other, more fickle and changeable nations, lack.

To some extent this was merely an anti-Revolutionary argument, and aimed against the French who had thrown the *ancien régime* overboard. In their own style, the British political thinker Edmund Burke and the French anti-Revolutionary Joseph de Maistre formulated similar arguments.[*] The core of these was that it was amoral or immoral to see society purely as a contract of individuals, and the state merely as a regulating arbiter overseeing social intercourse and the distribution of power and finance. The nation was, in the anti-Revolutionary view, a community, across time and generations, and the state was therefore also an incorporation and protector of that continuity, with its traditions and its institutions. As we shall discuss in greater detail

---

solidarity; in the Romantic, nineteenth-century meaning of the term, it has to do with the emotional attachment we feel with the scenes and places of our youth, our emotional rootedness. The most powerful expression of 'attachment to the native soil' is the pain we feel when we are in exile – homesickness, or *Heimweh*. Jacob Grimm addressed this emotional/moral foundation for political loyalty in his inaugural lecture as professor at the University of Göttingen, *De desiderio patriae*. Cf below, p. 146-147.

[*] Burke's anti-revolutionary writings were known in Romantic Germany. Anti-revolutionary conservatism and Romantic idealism are linked in that both invoke a mode of apprehending the world that is not based on rational understanding and analysis, but on emotional response and an intuitive 'sensing'; cf. Jolles 1936 (a book that needs to be used with extreme caution, given its own historical and ideological background). On De Maistre, see Isaiah Berlin's classic essay 'Joseph de Maistre and the Origins of Fascism', in Berlin 1990, 91-174.

below, the reflex of 'historicism', crucial to the intellectual climate of the early 1800s and to the development of nationalism, was born as an anti-Revolutionary reaction.

Fichte went further, however, than mere historicism. For him the continuity and permanence of tradition involved, crucially, a maintenance of ethnic and cultural particularities, such as language and customs. Later that century, scholars like Grimm were to spell out the implications of Fichte's thought. Germany still consisted of the ancient tribes already known in antiquity: Catti, Bajuwari, Boii, Borussi, Suebi, Franci, Saxones; indeed, many of the modern states in the German lands still continued, in their nomenclature, those ancient tribal divisions: Hessia, Bavaria, Bohemia, Prussia, Suabia, Franconia, Saxony. The language was still that of the ancient tribes. The manners and customs, and some legal institutions, could be traced back to these Germanic-tribal days. The *Volk* or *Nation* was so deeply rooted historically as an ethnic community that no modern sociological theorist was needed to teach *them* solidarity: it was an implicit German virtue from times immemorial, and could flourish under royal rule as easily as in some new-fangled contrivance like a 'republic' or Napoleonic empire. Whereas all over Europe, nations had changed their languages and their systems, Germany had maintained its own; and therein lay a moral superiority, and also a moral imperative *not* to cave in under French hegemony.

Fichte's nationality-concept changes the Enlightenment-Patriotic invocation of civic virtue into a Romantic rhetoric of moral virtue. Fichte was also bringing together, in the superheated, pressurized climate of the Napoleonic domination, elements from Herder, Tacitus, and Montesquieu; he links the Rousseauesque principle that the people are sovereign to the Herderian principle that the nation should be true to its own culture, heightens this with a portion of his own idealistic philosophy (according to which the nation is characterized in its identity by an abstract, transcendent *essence*), and gives all this an anti-French, anti-Napoleonic political urgency. It marks one of the fundamental differences between the pragmatic, socially-based 'love of the fatherland' of Enlightenment Patriotism and the nascent ideology of nationalism.

Literary activism: Kleist, Schlegel, Körner

Most of this centred around Berlin and culminated in the period 1810-1813. The way Napoleon had carved up Germany into vassal states, and brought Berlin down to the status of a minor ally, rankled among the assembled intellectuals there. Even in the churches of Prussia, Protestant clergymen, in the spirit of Arndt, began to preach sermons on the moral duties of a true lover of one's native land – for instance, the great theologian Schleiermacher.[107] Heinrich von Kleist, until then a sensitive lyrical poet of human affection and tender feelings, participated in an anti-French newspaper entitled (portentously) *Germania*, and echoing in essays and verse all the anti-French hatred of Arndt and Jahn. Kleist himself contributed bloody-minded propaganda verse, exhorting people to kill all French found east of the Rhine:

> Only the Frenchman still shows his face
> In the German realm.

Brother, take up the cudgel
To make him, too, retreat.

And again:

All that their foot had trod on
Must be bleached by the dust of their bones;
Such carrion as is left by raven and fox
You may give to the fishes.
Use their corpses to dam the Rhine;
Let their skeletons divert its course
Around Trier and the Palatinate
And let that then become our frontier!
The lust of the hunt is like marksmen
On the trail of a wolf!
Slay them! The court of world history
Does not inquire into your motives.[108]

It was Kleist who dusted off the old theme of Arminius the Cheruscan, he who had annihilated the Roman legions in the Teutoburg Forest, and wrote a political allegory under the title 'Arminius's Battle' (*Die Hermannsschlacht*, 1808), urging the Prussian king to place himself at the head of Germany's princes and to re-enact the heroic deed of yore.[109]

Further south, Vienna, capital of the humbled Habsburgs, was another focus of anti-French intellectual resistance. Friedrich Schlegel (1772-1829), one of the leading intellectuals of his day and one of the leaders of the post-Goethe generation of Romantics, had obtained a position there; and in the year 1812 held a series of public lectures, a counterbalance to Fichte's earlier ones in Berlin, on 'ancient and modern literature'. An innocuous topic on the surface, it was a momentous intervention indeed. It addressed 'literature' in the broadest of terms, as all learned and written forms of a nation's culture, and instilled into it Herder's message as to the categorical specificity of all human cultures. Schlegel's view of the role of literature added to Herder's cultural relativism, precisely, a *historicist* impulse: cultural difference, for Schlegel, involves not just (as in Herder's view) different patterns of articulating the world and one's position in the world, but also a different historical identity, a different set of collective memories kept alive by a continuous discursive tradition:

From this historical standpoint, comparing peoples according
to their achievements, it appears above all important for the
entire development and even for the spiritual existence of a
nation that it should have great national [i.e., collective, JL]
memories, which often recede back into the dark periods of
its first beginning, and which it is the great task of literature
to maintain and to celebrate. Such national-collective memories, the finest inheritance a people can have, are a blessing

Grj. von Emma Körner.

Theodor Körner

18. Theodor Körner

> which nothing else can replace; and when a people can find
> itself elevated and ennobled in its awareness by the fact that it
> has a great past, that it has such memories from primitive,
> ancient times, and that in other words it has its own poetry,
> then we must acknowledge that it is thereby promoted to a
> higher rank [than savages, JL].[110]

This line of reasoning is not just antiquarian and anthropological, describing the primitive development of literary culture. There is also a topical-political and programmatic undertone, in that Schlegel's comments reverberate against the idea, current since Lessing, that Germany was not yet a proper 'nation' (cf. above, p. 96). Collective memory and rootedness in tradition are proclaimed as the very first requirement of a national literature and culture. Among the many young Romantics following Schlegel's lectures was a budding author, Theodor Körner, who, inspired by the intellectual and political climate of his time, was to become the first example of what we might call the type of the 'national poet' – the romantic young poet who, often in a

19. The philosopher Fichte volunteers for the anti-Napoleonic militia; contemporary sketch.

tragically brief life, will draw his main inspiration from his love of the fatherland and his desire to see it free. The type is represented all over nineteenth-century Europe, and forms the prime example of what we may call 'political Romanticism' – not just a politics inspired by Romantic concepts and attitudes, but also a Romantic literature inspired by national politics. After earlier representatives of the type such as Thomas Moore in Ireland, we encounter Dionysos Solomós in Greece, Sandor Petőfi in Hungary, Mickiewicz in Poland (and in exile), Runeberg and Arwidsson in Swedish-speaking Finland, Taras Shevchenko in Ukraine, Thomas Davis in (again) Ireland. Béranger was to have a similar status in France after 1815, and the fact that Byron died fighting for Greek independence in 1824 turned him into a mythical Che Guevara-style hero.

Of all these 'national poets', Theodor Körner may be considered the prototype.[111] His posthumous collection of poetry, with the symbolical title 'The lyre and the sword' (*Leier und Schwert*), is replete with poems extolling battle against the foreign tyrant. What is more, Körner lived (and even died) according to his poetical programme. After Napoleon's failed Russian campaign of 1812, a broad mobilization took place in Prussia. This not only involved the regular Prussian army, but also a whole host of volunteers, who organized themselves into 'free-corps' irregular units (the most famous of these being the 'Lützow Free Corps'). Students, poets and intellectuals took up arms in these irregular regiments, even the portly philosopher Fichte. To the enthusiastic Romantic of the time, it seemed an ideal convergence of the power of the king and the solidarity of the people: a national unity that could root in the constitutional tradition and need not attempt a new experimental regime as in France. In this Romantic view (supported by widely read pamphlets written by Arndt) the free corps seemed the flowering of earlier moral mobilization movements like Jahn's Gymnastics Clubs. The Battle of Leipzig (1813) and the eventual liberation of German soil from French hegemony was aided materially by these irregular regiments. Among them was Theodor Körner. His patriotic plays had begun to meet with success in the Vienna theatres, but he had preferred to enlist in the Lützow Free Corps and died on the battlefield in August 1813. His ardently patriotic verse was collected and posthumously edited, and became a symbol of political Romanticism – for the German reader, in its rhetoric, and for budding young poets elsewhere, as a heroic role model.

Under Napoleonic pressure, intellectuals and princes, poets and generals entered into a common cause. The message of this 'political Romanticism' reached into the very highest echelons of the state. It can be seen in operation in the fateful year 1813, when the King of Prussia mobilized his entire people by an edict ordering the establishment of a popular militia. At that point, his Chief of Staff Gneisenau – a typical representative of the Prussian *Junker* class of military nobility, in what was proverbially a no-nonsense, bureaucratic state – tendered a memo to the King 'on the preparation of a popular insurrection', stressing the opportunities offered by the fervent popular opinion of the day. The King, a prosaic old-school monarch who believed in diplomacy, armed forces and a tight and thorough organization of his realm, dismissed Gneisenau's memo as 'fit for poetry'. In his reply, Gneisenau showed that the rhetoric of the Romantic intellectuals (Schleiermacher, Fichte, Arndt, Schlegel, Körner and Kleist) had reached its political goal:

> Religion, prayer, love of the ruler, of the fatherland, of virtue:
> all that is nothing but poetry. There is no enthusiasm with-
> out a poetic disposition. If we act only from cold calculation,
> we become rigid egoists. The security of the throne is
> founded on poetry.[112]

Napoleon and the Rise of National Historicism[113]

Hankering after continuity

Anti-Napoleonic feeling suffused all of Germany, from north to south, from high to low. Even the Brothers Grimm, who at the time were just emerging as fairytale collectors, contributed their bit: they brought out an edition of the ancient German tale *Poor Heinrich* (1813) with a preface stating that the proceeds of the sales would go to the support of the irregular regiments. And within the Brothers' collection of folk- and fairytales, there was a tale that was generally interpreted as a political allegory: the story of the poor fisherman, who (thanks to his capture of a magic fish) can wish for greater and greater riches and splendour – until he finally overreaches himself and is reduced to his original destitution. Many contemporaries read it as a parable on the rise and fall of Napoleon.

The cult of the native German past was a natural reaction to the innovations that had been sweeping across Europe in the wake of Napoleon's armies. Everywhere in Germany, a nostalgic cultivation of traditions sprang up in the teeth of historical change. The dissolution of the Holy Roman Empire in particular was felt as a traumatic self-estrangement, and the historicist impulse that we have noted in the reactions of Fichte and Schlegel made itself felt in the field of letters and learning everywhere. Three reactions to the fatal year 1806 can be noted by way of an example.

The first of these involved the Bavarian Crown Prince Ludwig. He conceived, in 1807 – that is to say: at the height of Napoleon's power and at the nadir of Germany's subjection – a plan to enshrine the great German past in nothing less than a national Pantheon. The original Pantheon, at Paris, had already been reconstituted into a shrine of heroes of the French nation, such as Rousseau and Voltaire.[114] Ludwig wanted to establish a great temple, to be filled with busts and plaques honouring the great representatives of the German nation. Once he mounted the Bavarian throne, he was in a position to put his ideas into practice. National architecture flourished under his rule. Not only did he order a massive *loggia*, the 'Generals' Hall' or *Feldherrnhalle* to honour the generals of the *Befreiungskriege* (built 1841-1844 in Munich), there was also a 'Liberation Hall' or *Befreiungshalle* (built near the village of Kelheim in 1842), with eighteen colossal statues allegorizing the German tribes. Most importantly, Ludwig implemented his idea of a German Pantheon with the *Walhalla*, built on the banks of the Danube near Regensburg in the shape of the Parthenon; it housed a collection of busts and commemorative plaques to the great German representatives of statesmanship, arts and sciences. All of this cult of the great national past was, it must be stressed, triggered by a sense that in 1807 this past was receding into a bygone, lost distance and needed recalling and remembrance.[115]

20. Walhalla temple near Regensburg

Secondly, also in Bavaria, the gentleman-scholar Johann Christoph von Aretin – who was in charge of the cataloguing of ancient monastic libraries which (following the secularization of the monasteries as ordered by the *Reichsdeputationshauptschluss* of 1803) were now being relocated to the Munich Court Library – edited an ancient manuscript which he had found in the old abbey of Weihenstephan, near Munich, on the life of Charlemagne. The edition came out in 1803, when the Holy Roman Empire was just beginning to creak under the weight of Napoleon-imposed modernity; and Aretin opened the preface as follows:

> It is now just a thousand years ago that Charlemagne
> founded the German Empire. I draw the reader's attention to
> this fact, not only to point out how amazingly things are
> changing at the present day; nor to bring to mind the recent
> events which threaten to destroy this same empire after its
> thousand-year existence; such reflections I leave to politics.
> My intention is rather to offer a literary jubilee celebration of
> this great anniversary, and a suitable occasion to do so pre-
> sented itself when I consulted a remarkable old-German
> manuscript in the very ancient abbey of Weihenstephan near
> Freising.[116]

In other words: the political crisis of the present is remedied with a cultural reflection on the enduring past. The empire is tottering and collapsing, but its traditions remain to inspire us. The very same feeling was offered in another text edition that came out a few years later, when the threatened overthrow of the Holy Roman Empire had in fact run its course.

For once again in the fateful year 1807, a young scholar, Friedrich Heinrich von der Hagen, published a modernized version of another old-German text, and did so in order to boost his country's morale at the lowest ebb of its political fortunes:

> In the days of Tacitus people tried to recall the ancient Roman language; so too, in the middle of the most destructive storms, an attachment is making itself felt to the language and the works of our stalwart ancestors, and it seems as if in the past and in poetry we seek what is so painfully declining in the present.[117]

The work that Von der Hagen offered to his bereft countrymen was the *Nibelungenlied* – that poem of honour and revenge which was to echo through the nineteenth century to culminate in the operas of Wagner, which was to inspire the notion of *Nibelungentreue* between the German and Austrian empires in the First World War, and which was to drive Hitler's destructive vision of a *Götterdämmerung* towards 1945.[118]

In 1807, the story of Siegfried the dragon-slayer and of the vengeful Chriemhilde was largely forgotten, remembered only in distant echoes. Fragments of a medieval manuscript had been brought to light, however, in 1775 and 1779 and Von der Hagen revived this fateful tradition in German literature with his 1807 rendition. His firebrand preface refers to 'the indestructible German character' (*unvertilgbaren Deutschen Charakter*), which 'sooner or later would break free from all foreign fetters'; in expectation of which, the heroic poem was offered to readers as 'a comfort and veritable support for any German soul'. Later, Von der Hagen himself would look back on the edition as ' a true encouragement, during the fatherland's most shameful episode, and a high promise for the return of German sovereignty'.[119]

This, then, is one possible manifestation of Romantic historicism: the tendency to counter a modern sense of self-alienation by taking recourse to tradition and to one's rootedness in the past. We see it in the Romantic vogue for the Middle Ages; we see it in the nineteenth-century cult of monuments and historical buildings; we see it in the antiquarianism of Romantic philologists who begin to re-edit medieval texts. On the surface, this historicist impulse is a manifestation of political Romanticism, and belongs to the general spectrum of resistance against a Napoleon-imposed loss of nationhood – Aretin belongs with Friedrich Schlegel, Von der Hagen's edition fed the same sensibilities as Fichte's *Reden an die Deutsche Nation*, Ludwig's memorials have the same commemorative-inspiring function as the posthumous editions of Körner's poetry.

At a more fundamental level, however, the historicist impulse can celebrate any notion of authenticity and connectedness with the past. It is remarkable, for instance, how Napoleon-dominated Germany develops a sympathy for Spain. Spain had long enjoyed a rather bleak reputation, as a country full of morose arrogance, cruelty, and rigid Catholic fundamentalism. As Spain showed, in the years 1808-1812, that it was among the fiercest rebels against Napoleonic rule, waging insurrection after insurrec-

tion even while Prussia was still under France's thumb, the reputation of Spain ame-
liorated dramatically, especially among German Romantics. Spain began to count as
one of those truly authentic countries that had developed without self-estrangement
from the Middle Ages into the present. Tellingly, one of the first serious philological
works that was brought out by the budding Jacob Grimm was not a German, but
Spanish collection: *Silva de romances viejos* or 'collection of ancient romances'
(1815).[120] And the great authority August Wilhelm Schlegel (brother of Friedrich) had
in his 1809 lectures on Drama and Literature held up Calderón alongside Shakespeare
as a truly 'national' poet. Schlegel had already translated plays by Calderón in 1803.

It is to be stressed, therefore, that the development of a historicist view did not
restrict itself to the German context. Germans looked further afield, and as we shall
see, an important historicist impulse came from another corner of Europe altogether:
Walter Scott's Scotland. Even so, the link between anti-Revolutionary 'political Romanticism' and historicism seems a predominantly German conjunction.

The special position of German intellectuals in this development is exemplified by
two names: Jacob Grimm, and his teacher Friedrich Carl von Savigny. Grimm's name
has already been mentioned a few times; the years between 1810 and 1820 mark his rise
from German provincial life to Europe-wide fame.

Grimm and Savigny[121]

Today, the name of Jacob Grimm (1785-1863) is linked especially to the collection of
folk- and fairytales that he edited together with his brother Wilhelm, and which appeared in the years 1811-1814. At this time the two brothers were sub-librarians at Kassel, in the Napoleon-created kingdom of Westphalia, and were training in law under
the Göttingen professor Savigny. Their collection of folk- and fairytales was an extension of a literary taste for oral tradition, which had already led to an important collection of folk verse brought out by their associates Arnim and Brentano, inspired by
Herderian appreciation of the artless naiveté of popular culture. Following the great
success of this collection (Arnim and Brentano's *Des Knaben Wunderhorn*), the register
shifted from balladry and verse to fairytales and folk beliefs. At the same time, however, the Grimms were being trained by their mentor Savigny in the skill of reading
ancient manuscripts and ancient forms of the language.

Friedrich Carl von Savigny (1779-1861) was, before all, a legal historian, and his
main speciality was the comparison of customary German law and formal Roman law
– two types of law which had co-existed in the Empire. Now, however, the new *Code
Napoléon* had been imposed as the legal blueprint for Europe, on the rigid systematics
of a written constitution with two main branches, civil law and criminal law. Savigny
loathed the new Napoleonic system, for precisely the type of nostalgic-historicist impulse that we have seen with Von der Hagen, Aretin and Fichte. Against the theory-
driven French model, which saw the role of law only as an instrument for social conflict management, he believed that the German system had been the expression of a
national character, that German law had organically developed with the German nation through history and had with the generations been the expression and instrument

of their morals, their outlook, their culture and indeed their identity. Savigny's organicism (which is in turn ultimately rooted in the thought of Montesquieu and Vico, see above p. 68) led him to anchor law in the nation's traditions, and it is this tendency to see an entire country's culture as the end product of a long, organic growth process which can be properly termed 'historicist'.[122]

Historicism began, then, as a reaction among constitutional legal scholars against the anti-historicism, the innovative modernity, of the Napoleonic system. It had, of course, profound political repercussions in the development of an ideology which can be variously called 'anti-Jacobin', 'anti-Revolutionary' or, as the most common term is nowadays, 'conservative'. Edmund Burke, the great ideological founder of anti-Revolutionary conservatism, had famously defended the slowly-accumulated prestige and age-old charisma of the traditional state against the notion that a perfect social order could be devised and fabricated in contentious deliberations by a group of ad hoc legislators.

When Jacob Grimm aided his master's legal-historical work (among other things, by accompanying him to the great libraries of Paris and copying out old manuscripts for him), this legal historicism fused with his Herderian interest in popular culture. Grimm came to the insight that a nation's entire outlook, including its myths, poems, language and laws, all constituted a long, slow commentary on its historical experiences. Herder had still seen culture and identity in almost timeless terms, as an anthropological system of primitive differentiation. For Grimm, all of culture became a nation's historical track record. He learned from Savigny that 'whatever *is*, should be seen in terms of *how it had grown*'.[123]

The most important effect of this insight was, at first, linguistic. In studying the various differences between the European languages, Grimm systematized them and aligned them as a set of historically grown divergences. Thus, the Germanic languages had split away from the common Indo-European family by shifting certain consonants in patterns; the identification of these consonantal shifts later became known as 'Grimm's laws' (see below, p. 260).

The comparative-historical method turned Grimm-style philology into the nineteenth century's cutting-edge discipline. Grimm was to apply the method to his research of literary imagination, comparing mythologies, saga material and themes like the animal fable. Philology, in short, became something that embraced linguistics, literary history and cultural anthropology.

Savigny's historicism was not only applied to the realm of philology by Grimm, it also affected the field of history writing. In literature, Grimm had become a great defender of 'reading historically'. He felt that texts should not be adapted to the reader's contemporary frame of reference, but that, on the contrary, the reader should reach out to them, reconnect with their pastness:

> For lyrical poetry, arising as it does out of the human heart
> itself, turns directly to our feelings and is understood from all
> periods in all periods; and dramatic poetry attempts to trans-
> late the past into the frame of reference, the language almost,
> of the present, and cannot fail to impress us when it suc-

ceeds. But the case is far different with epic poetry. Born in
the past, it reaches over to us from this past, without aban-
doning its proper nature; and if we want to savour it, we
must project ourselves into wholly vanished conditions.[124]

In a similar vein, Grimm's co-worker Leopold von Ranke felt that the historical past
should be studied *as it had been within its own terms*, not as it appeared in a latter-day
judgement. The trend was then (and this is perhaps how we can summarize the impact of historicism in cultural thought) that it does not befit us to judge the past and
to adapt it to our standards, but to reconnect to it and to accept it on its own terms.
Historicism is – to adapt the later phrase of T.S. Eliot regarding the historical sense –
an awareness, both of the pastness of the past and of its presence.[125]

Reconnecting with the past will henceforth dominate nineteenth-century taste. We
shall encounter the restoration of ancient buildings, the editing of ancient texts, the
rise of something called 'the historical novel', the spread of neo-Gothic architecture.
Most of this will be in the service of the ideal of the nation-state: in order to proclaim
its ancient roots and its enduring permanence.

The close link between historicism and political Romanticism is perhaps peculiarly
a result of German circumstances and certain individual German intellectuals –
though, like the figure of the 'national poet', it was soon to spread far and wide across
Europe. This does not mean that historicism was a uniquely German monopoly. Elsewhere under Napoleon's shadow, European poets were beginning to celebrate the national past as a great medicine against present-day dishonour. In the Netherlands, Jan
Frederik Helmers wrote a long epic poem on the great deeds of *The Dutch Nation*
(1812). In Sweden, Tegnér's *Svea* (1811) tried to come to terms with the loss of Finnish
territories, and in Denmark, Oehlenschläger had by then already begun the historical
verse and drama that turned him into Denmark's national poet. No one's influence
was as important, however, as that of Sir Walter Scott.[126] By the time Scott published
his first historical novel, *Waverley* (1814), he was already one of the leading poets of
Britain, with a track record of themes taken from history. He had also edited older
minstrelsy and balladry and was one of the leading antiquarians* of his day. In his
hands, the genre of the historical romance (less than prestigious until then) became
based on interesting, factual-historical *couleur locale* and a way for readers to identify
with the past through an engrossing narrative. The historical novel often engaged with
a past constructed as 'national' and therefore of particular, immediate interest to modern readers who were asked to reconnect with their 'own' roots; indeed, the historical
novel frequently centred on crisis moments in the nation's past as seen through the

---

* Antiquarians were those whose interest in the past did not take the form of regular history-
writing: collectors of informal texts, artefacts and other informal sources, they had an interest in 'life
in the past' rather than in diachronic developments. Antiquarianism was a pursuit for learned gentlemen of leisure and became slightly outdated in the nineteenth century; it was overtaken by other
forms of cultural and literary history, and by archaeology. Scott himself gave an ironic but affection-
ate portrait of his own source tradition in his novel *The Antiquary* (1816). Cf. Momigliano 1955;
Sweet 2004.

21. Sir Walter Scott

eyes of characters with whom modern readers could identify. As such, they constituted a powerful identification with the nation's roots and crises, and provided something akin to an epic origin-story. That was the function of Scott's Scottish novels for Scotland, or of Scott-inspired spinoffs like Conscience's *De Leeuw van Vlaenderen* in Belgium, or Manzoni's *I promessi sposi* in Italy, or Rangavis' and Pushkin's historical novels in Greece and Russia. (Cf. also below, p. 202-203)[127]

To sum up: nationalism emerges in the nineteenth century from eighteenth-century roots: Herder's belief in the individuality of nations, Rousseau's belief in the sovereignty of the nation, a general discourse of national peculiarities and 'characters'. What changes from the eighteenth century to the nineteenth is this:

1. an unprecedented imperial campaign mounted by Napoleon and fiercely resented outside France; this turns the eighteenth-century notions of tyranny and liberty from a power imbalance within the state (between rulers and governed) into one of power imbalance between states (between occupier and occupied);

2. the rise of Romantic idealism which sees national character as a spiritual principle, a 'soul', rather than as a set of peculiarities;
3. the Romantic belief that a nation's culture, and in particular its language, are the manifestation of its soul and essence;
4. the historicist belief that all culture must be seen as an organic tradition linking generations across centuries.

By the time Napoleon's empire was definitively removed from the European map, the great powers assembled at the Congress of Vienna attempted to return to the pre-revolution situation of monarchical states. The intellectual trends outlined here, however, could not be undone as easily as Napoleon's state systems; they maintained their currency and were to manifest themselves as the nineteenth century's leading ideology: nationalism.

Restoration and the Nation-State

1815 saw the old monarchies of Europe restored. In France, the series of Louis resumed, when Louis XVIII ascended the throne (1815-1824; the hiatus in the numbering between Louis XVI and XVIII was due to a crown prince who had died in captivity). Louis 'restored' the *ancien régime* in more ways than one. Not only was the dynasty restored to the throne, and the King restored to his old position and prerogatives – the ravages of the intervening period were patched up, brought back to an old condition: in one word – restored. Public spaces were stripped of their revolutionary names, statues removed or reinstated, and on the spot where Louis XVI and Marie-Antoinette's guillotined corpses had been thrown into a common mass grave, a *chapelle expiatoire* or 'penance chapel' was built. The abbey church of St. Denis, which for centuries had been the burial place for French Royals, had been turned into a stable during the revolution – under Louis XVIII, it was brought back to its former state, with handsome new grave monuments for Louis XVI and Marie-Antoinette. Restoration was a return to the past, an attempt to remedy the ravages of time and to undo the damages of the intervening years. Louis XVIII's brother and successor, Charles X (1824-1830), went so far as to re-instate royal rituals of medieval vintage such as bestowing a magically healing touch on scrofula patients.[128] Yet in this very urge towards conservation and restoration, the newly reinstated monarchy showed its historicism – that is to say: the fact that its dynastic sense of family history had itself entered into the nineteenth-century climate.

In Prussia, too, the Romantics continued their historicist influence even now that Napoleon was gone, and the tide of revolution and innovation had turned. The cult of medieval castles, chivalric heroes etc. had been in fashion in romances from the 1770s onwards both in English and in German letters (indeed, this was the tradition from which Walter Scott had emerged); as a result, ruins and historical sites now gained a 'romantic', symbolic interest which they had not had heretofore.

So it was, in Prussia, with the Marienburg. This had been the headquarters of the Teutonic Order, and the centre of that order's rule over the conquered Prussian territories east of the Mark Brandenburg. The margrave-electors of Brandenburg had, in the eighteenth century, been able to assume a royal title mainly as a result of their succession to these lands of the Teutonic order: they had first styled themselves 'king in Prussia' and finally 'King of Prussia'.[*] The Marienburg had, then, special dynastic

---

* The rise of the Hohenzollern dynasty from the rank of margrave (later elector) of Brandenburg to that of king of Prussia is almost unique in the *ancien régime*. Not even the Wittelsbachs of Bavaria had moved beyond the rank of duke, prince or elector until Napoleon came and kingdoms and royal titles were created in great numbers. Technically, ranks of nobility within the Holy Roman Empire were bestowed by the emperor, who could also create kings; in practice, however, this had not happened since Naples/Sicily and Bohemia had become kingdoms in the thirteenth century. All other royal titles in Europe derived from tribal kingships outside the borders of Charlemagne's empire (the Iberian Peninsula, the British Isles, Scandinavia, Central Europe), and in fact so did the Prussian

importance for them; but by 1800 it had fallen into disrepair. Calls for its restoration were first made by antiquarians and men of letters, and subsequently taken over by the Berlin Court. In the course of the years 1810-1840, the Marienburg was restored (as the St. Denis abbey church was restored), not only as a dynastic prestige object for the Hohenzollerns, but also as a historical landmark for all of Prussia. The romantic poet Joseph von Eichendorff, employed as an official in a Berlin ministry, wrote a heroic history play, *Der letzte Held von Marienburg*, which was performed in its actual setting; in the course of the century, the Marienburg became a prime locus of Prussian historical consciousness.[129]

What is interesting in this, and in similar restorations, is that they show a transition from the familial, dynastic consciousness of ruling families towards a national-collective one. The St. Denis Chapel and the Marienburg are rooted in a Bourbon and Hohenzollern lineage, a private affair (or private-dynastic, in that for such monarchs, family affairs and affairs of state were synonymous). In the course of the century, we see how the cult of remembrance becomes a more collective property and investment: historical sites are important for the nation at large, have a symbolism which collectively affects all of the public, become tourist destinations, open to all visitors, funded by taxpayers' money; joint property, as it were. Correspondingly, we see that monuments (which throughout the eighteenth century had been erected for monarchs, as part of dynastic self-glorifications) are still focussed on the ruling heads of state and their *gloire* after the Restoration, but soon shift to more collective symbolism, personifying and remembrancing the nation-at-large. An interesting case can be seen in The Hague, where two statues were erected to the memory of Prince William 'The Silent' of Orange in the space of three years. The first, put up in 1845, is obviously dynastic in nature: an equestrian statue, it shows William as a prince, and is erected in front of the Royal Palace by his descendant, King William II. Three years later, in 1848, the bicentenary of the Treaty of Westphalia was marked by putting up a statue of the same William the Silent, but this time as a contemplative patriarch, in a standing pose without regalia, placed on the square behind the Parliament buildings. The 'national' (as opposed to dynastic) nature of this monument is borne out by the inscription on its plinth: 'To William the First, Prince of Orange, Father of the fatherland: His grateful people'.[130]

Although the monarchs of Europe might have wanted to turn the clock back to pre-1789 days, it is obvious that states are no longer seen as the realms of princes inhabited by the prince's subjects; on the contrary, the presence of something like a nation, and the idea that history is the nation's common possession, has taken root. In 1815, however, the climate was very much one of royal restoration: the anti-Revolutionary reaction, linked to the name of Metternich, attempted in the system of international congresses to create a stable, power-balanced Europe based firmly on royal prerogative.

---

one, which referred to lands conquered by the Teutonic Order outside the original Holy Roman Empire. The Hohenzollerns arrogated this title and forced the Vienna court to acquiesce.

22. Two statues of William the Silent in The Hague

The disgust of romantic-historicist intellectuals – a disgust with democratic revolutions, dictatorial republics and Napoleonic inventions, all in one go – was such that at first this royalist restoration was greeted with enthusiasm. Dynastic princes were hailed as the embodiment of their nation's unity, and their will was idealized as such an organic, and organically rooted, expression of what was best for the people, that obedience to the royal will was considered a fulfilling form of self-expression. Conversely, it was implicitly expected of the post-revolution monarchs that they were to rule, not by whimsy and egoism, but as father-figures, as benevolent patrons of their subjects' welfare. The monarchs, for their part, rejected the revolutionary notions of the natural Rights of Man, and were even reluctant to have their rule fettered by a constitution. In most cases, constitutions as they were issued after 1815 were only procedural regulations on how the king's power should be channelled (not limited); and in a number of cases, constitutions were abrogated in the 1820s and 1830s. The Metternich ideology was that people should obey their rulers – even in the case of religious differences, e.g. in the Ottoman Empire – and that stability was the overriding principle on which to found international relations.

National resistance against the Restoration regime

The 1815 honeymoon did not last long. The first sign of popular dissatisfaction with autocratic monarchical rule came in 1817, when students celebrated the anniversary of the Battle of Leipzig, along with the tercentenary of the Lutheran Reformation. A combined festive commemoration took place at the Wartburg, the refuge where Luther had accomplished his Bible translation. By this time, student bodies known as *Burschenschaften* were among the few associations that made a trans-local popular organization possible, and like the Gymnastics Clubs founded by Jahn kept alive a populist view of national mobilization. Tellingly, the colours chosen by many of the Burschenschaften, and by the Wartburg crowd, were the gold, red and black of the old Lützow Free Corps; they were in the course of the century to become the flag (still used in the present-day German Federal Republic) of those who wished the German state to be rooted in the nation, rather than dependent upon the princes.

The Wartburg festivities became a flashpoint of anti-reactionary radicalism. Bonfires were lit, and symbols of hatred were burned. These included books, a wig and a corset, symbols of error, artificiality, constraint and decadence, and themselves an echo of the standard anti-French rhetoric of earlier years. In the present climate, however, they had gained a new and more subversive significance, hinting that the German princes, rather than being the champions of their nation's liberty, were backsliding into a French-style autocratic court culture. The Wartburg manifestation was widely perceived as a fist shaken in the face of Metternich's new order. When one of the participants committed a political murder less than a year later (the victim was the playwright Friedrich von Kotzebue, widely believed to be a hack in the service of monarchical autocrats), the climate soured further. The 1819 Carlsbad Decrees imposed limitations on press freedom, dissolved all student associations and tightened the constitutional clampdown. The very figurehead of German national regeneration, Ernst Moritz Arndt, was dismissed from his post at the newly founded Prussian University of Bonn – one of the first of the new generation of Romantic professors to fall out of favour with the German princes. Twenty years later, in 1837, the dismissal of seven professors from the University of Göttingen – among them such highly respected men of letters as Dahlmann, Gervinus and the Grimm Brothers – continued this trend, and the poet-philologist Hoffmann von Fallersleben was dismissed from Breslau University in 1841 over a satirical collection of political verse.[131]

The period 1815-1830 was dominated by Metternich's restoration policy; but murmurs were heard. In Ireland, Napoleon was remembered in folk songs as the harbinger of civil liberties, the one who was to free the country's Catholic majority from Protestant oppression; an abortive uprising took place in 1803; the young, radical poet Shelley attempted to stir up revolutionary feelings in Dublin in 1810; and the light verse of Tom Moore, respected friend and biographer of Byron and caustic satirist, began to celebrate Irish resistance in deceptively sweet musical settings and cloaked in elegant phrases. Another song and verse poet, Béranger, kept the memory of the glory of the empire alive in France, at a time when Napoleonic sympathies were considered a crime against the state;[132] after Napoleon's death on St. Helena, the memoirs of his physician Las Cases were published in 1824, triggering a revival of the Emperor's mythical stature. Secret societies like the *Carbonari* in Italy plotted against the restored rulers, in the name of a constitutional regime remembered from Napoleonic days; and especially in Habsburg Central Europe, e.g. in Hungary and Slovenia, Napoleon was remembered, not as the 'Corsican Ogre' or usurping warlord, but as the liberator who had spread constitutional rule for a brief, happy period.

LE VIEUX DRAPEAU

23. Illustration from Béranger's patriotic chansons

Metternich's system was to show its first cracks in Ottoman Europe. It was here that the nostrum of stability and obedience proved untenable, owing to the manifest decadence of the Ottoman government. An uprising in Serbia in 1810 was the first sign – at first nothing more, perhaps, than a sign of armed unrest from mountain outlaws, but soon to take on a more far-reaching impact. More importantly, an uprising plotted for years by a Greek secret society, in 1821, and affecting both Romania and Greece, signalled the rise of a new nationalism in the Balkans.

All these terms are anachronistic and distortive, of course. 'Romania' did not exist as such at the time. In the Danubian principalities of Wallachia and Moldavia, as in all of Ottoman Europe, Greek was the language of all educated classes, who were more aware of their religious than of their ethnic identity; the Greek language was by no means linked specifically to what is now Greece. It was spoken in the form of demotic dialects by the mountain population of the southern tip of the Balkans and the adjacent islands, but also by the ruling class of Christian officials within the Ottoman Empire. But in the perception of the secessionist Greeks themselves (organized in associations like the *Filiki Eteria*, and often with important centres of congregation in Vienna or Odessa), the rising was linked to a notion of Hellenic traditions and nation-

24. Swearing a member (Kolokotronis?) into the filiki eteria, *a secret society devoted to the liberation of Greece from Turkish rule. Painting in the National Museum of Greece, Athens.*

hood, organized around Orthodoxy and dimly remembering the great days of Byzantium.

More importantly, this Greek insurrection attracted waves of sympathy in Western Europe.[133] Known as 'philhellenism', sympathy for the Greek cause was based on two deep-rooted and widespread European attitudes: dislike of the Ottoman Turks and admiration for ancient Greece. The Islamic Turks, since their capture of Byzantium in 1453 and their power expansion in South-Eastern Europe, counted as the proverbial arch-enemy of European Christendom; they were seen as wicked, immoral and cruel tyrants. This hate-image was to some extent based on religious xenophobia and centuries of war propaganda; and the harshness of Ottoman rule, such as it had been, had abated somewhat in the course of the eighteenth century. Still, to expect Christian nations such as the Serbs or Greeks to submit to their status as second-rate citizens in a decadent Sultanate, and this in the name of obedience and stability (as Metternich would have it) was, to say the least, counter-intuitive. What is more, the image of the Greeks in Western Europe was highly positive. Although Greeks were proverbially seen as untrustworthy and wily, their ancestors were revered as the originators of all that was best in Europe. Arts and sciences, literature and learning, philosophy, democracy: Europe owed it all to the Greeks. What, then, could be more natural than to support the oppressed Christian descendants of Socrates and Euclid against the sadistic Janissaries and Bashi-Bazouks of the depraved Sultan in his Topkapi palace? Not only did this philhellenism inspire great figureheads like the poet Byron and the painter Eugène Delacroix, it also provided a coded rallying-cry for all those who believed in the self-determination of peoples to resist the Metternich system of obedience and stability. In 1824, Byron, who had already written hugely popular poems about Ottoman Greece, such as 'The Giaour', travelled to Greece in support of the insurrection.

25. Eugène Delacroix: 'The Chios Massacre' (1824). Painting in the Louvre.

He died in Missolonghi that year. In the same year, Eugène Delacroix exhibited his 'Massacre of Chios' in the Salon, taking for his subject the killing of 20,000 Greeks by Ottoman troops. Six years later, Delacroix was to testify to the revival of democratic ideas in his famous 'Liberty leading the people' of 1830 (see below, p. 214).

Nationalism in Europe affects, then, not only the centre (Germany), but also the periphery: in Ireland and in the Balkans.[134] Greece and Serbia were able to gain an amount of autonomy within, or even independence from, the Ottoman Empire – the first to break through the Congress of Vienna's map of Europe. That this should be so is largely a result of the way in which the European powers were trying to exploit Turkey's weakness in the Balkans for their own geopolitical interests. The European powers had reasons to support the insurrections in spite of the priorities of the Metternich system. But for the public-at-large, those insurrections counted as inspiring examples of how the people can gain their liberty against an oppressor. What was new, compared to similar revolutionary ideals in the 1780s and 1790s, was that by now the nation's freedom was not just the emancipation of one social layer from under the rule of its superiors, but the liberation of an ethnic community from under the hegemony of alien conquerors. Romantic nationalism revives the 'vertical' notion of freedom as the assertion of popular rights, but adds to this a 'horizontal' aspect, namely the separateness of the nation amidst its neighbours. In short, the ideals that had moved Germans to resist Napoleon's rule were still alive and operative ten years after Waterloo. The new ideology had obviously survived the Restoration.

The crowned heads of Western Europe were realizing this as well. As we have seen, the cult of commemoration, in shifting from dynastic to a collective-national register, meant that the royals were already buying into their new role as figureheads of

26. George IV in Highland dress: Portrait by Sir David Wilkie, 1829. Painting in Holyrood House. The Royal Collection © 2005 Her Majesty Queen Elizabeth II.

national identity and national continuity.[135] Ludwig of Bavaria, in commissioning the *Walhalla* and the various other monuments, had, Romantic as he was, shown that he was in touch with the climate of the time, and his example was followed in the other monarchies, from St. Denis to the Marienburg. Nowhere more efficiently so than in Great Britain. Here, anti-French patriotism had been stirred up to fever pitch by the threat of a French invasion in 1803, and the great general and admiral who finally brought Napoleon down (Wellington and Nelson) were heroes of a popular stature unmatched until the days of Churchill. But George IV entrusted himself to writers and painters even more than to army and navy. When he was finally crowned in 1822 he visited his Scottish capital of Edinburgh in an event carefully stage-managed by none other than the novelist, poet and antiquarian Walter Scott (whom he had raised to the title of baronet as 'Sir' Walter Scott).[136] Scott, one of the exponents of Romantic historicism, was a true anti-Revolutionary in that he firmly believed in tradition and in loyalty to one's king. The crux was, however, that the dynasty to which George IV belonged had never been popular in Scotland and that violent insurrections against George IV's great-grandfather had taken place as recently as 1745. George IV, indeed, was the first of his dynasty (that of Hanover) who dared to set foot north of the Scottish border. In Scott's stage-management, the visit became a triumph of public relations, precisely by playing the trump card of nationality, culture and tradition.

George IV showed up wearing a kilt, a dress so outlandish that until recently it had been outlawed (George still needed to wear flesh-coloured tights under the kilt for decency's sake, so little were people used to it). Scott artfully prepared public opinion in Edinburgh for a festival of Highland local colour, with clans, kilts, bagpipes and exotic pageantry, which were considered typical of the remote moors and valleys of Scotland – and known to the public largely from the local colour in Scott's own novels. George IV played the tartan trump, and the result was a huge success for his popularity in Scotland. Ever since, Scotland and Scottish culture have been loyally integrated participants within a British imperial system; and that may be due in no small measure to the influence of Walter Scott. Royalty could obviously benefit from playing to the gallery and posing as incorporations of the nation's identity, culture and traditions.

Even in France, where the monarchs refused to curry popular favour except by touching scrofula patients, we see that the grounding of dynastic rule in the nation's historical continuity becomes a leading principle. Louis XVIII himself, a scholarly, bookish man, oversaw the foundation of a school for the study and conservation of ancient manuscripts, the famous *Ecole des Chartes*, which still exists today. Tellingly, archival science was represented as 'a branch of French letters in which Your Majesty is particularly interested, concerning the history of the fatherland'.[137]

The appeal of nationality

Everywhere in Europe, then, the national ideal subsisted and endured after Waterloo and the Congress of Vienna. Disaffected regions of the multi-ethnic empires remembered the ideals of popular sovereignty and constitutional rule, and ancient kingdoms realized that national identity and historical consciousness provided the firmest foundation for royal power. The joint influence of Rousseau, Herder, and the Romantic historicists merged into a template that ideally equated the state with the nation, and the nation with culture and tradition.

It is in the repercussions of this guiding principle that we can register nineteenth-century nationalism: the ideal of a congruence between nationality (understood in cultural-historical terms) and the state. Almost nowhere in Europe was this ideal-typical situation actually realized, and everywhere we see attempts to bring the two into line. Depending on the actual lay of the land, three basic manifestations of nationalism can be distinguished (though sometimes they operate simultaneously):

– In the case of 'old states', cultural divisions within the state are seen as problematic and potentially weakening fault lines; the state may respond with a centralizing policy, aimed at culturally homogenizing all the inhabitants into a joint whole. This form of state-driven cultivation of a national ideal will be described below under the header 'Centralist nationalism';

– In the case of cultural communities dispersed over different states, an urge towards unification may make itself felt, the need to group together into a common state. This will be described below as 'Unification nationalism';

– In the case of multi-ethnic states or empires, cultural and ethnic differentiations may become so important as rallying factors for political disaffection, that the state cannot hold its various minorities together. These may develop autonomist demands ranging from mild regionalism to outright separatism. This will be described below as 'Separatist nationalism'.

Various crossovers and interactions between these various forms of nationalism are (as will be described) possible. Hungarian nationalism as represented by Lajos Kossuth (1802-1894) exhibits both a separatist aspect (vis-à-vis Vienna) and a centralist aspect (Magyar hegemonism vis-à-vis Slovak and Croatian minorities). Adjoining minorities in neighbouring states can each develop a separatist form of nationalism, which subsequently join forces and become a type of unification nationalism: thus with 'hyphenated' nationalisms such as the Czecho-Slovak or the Serbo-Croat case (uniting separatist Czechs under Austrian rule with separatist Slovaks under Hungarian rule; or uniting separatist Croats under Habsburg rule with separatist Serbs under Ottoman rule). Pan-movements like Pan-Celticism and Pan-Slavism are typically of this nature.

Again, what begins as separatist or unification nationalism may, after an initial independent territory has been established, try to expand that territory to include 'outlying' fellow-nationals. Such irredentism is well documented in the cases of Italy and Greece.

Still, I think it is possible to broadly group all manifestations of nationalism along the parameters of Separatist, Centralist and Unification nationalism. This typology has the advantage that it allows us to take great states as well as small minorities into our analysis, Eastern as well as Western Europe, old (long-established) states with newly established ones, and to trace the development of the nationalist ideology through all these variables.

Nationalism as State Centralism

I have in a previous chapter drawn attention to the fact that the doctrine of popular sovereignty involved a totalizing tendency. The people, once it has been proclaimed sovereign, cannot be at odds with itself; the *volonté générale* is not conceived of as a confused mass of conflicts but as something whole, unified, lapidary. The slogan *liberté, égalité, fraternité* can be read as a logical progression: Liberty cannot truly exist without equality, and equality requires a unity and solidarity of purpose; which means that dissent is easily interpreted as disaffection or disloyalty.

The course of events in France from the proclamation of the Republic onwards (in 1792) bears this out. To be sure, the course of events was also under severe external pressure: the *ancien régime* monarchies of Europe were armed against France, and the Revolution's survival stood on a knife's edge. The *levée en masse* or general military draft for all able-bodied men was part of the climate that saw the birth of the new Republic; the lines of the '*Marseillaise*' (written in April of that fateful year 1792) likewise testify to an apprehension that an armed foreign invasion might restore the centuries-long oppression of the Bourbons:

> Come, children of the fatherland, the day of glory has come.
> Against us, tyranny's blood-stained flag has been raised.
> In our lands you hear those fell soldiers howl;
> They come to cut the throats, even in our embrace, of our
> children and our women.
> To arms, citizens! Form your battalions! March, march
> And let their foul blood soak our fields.
>
> What does that gang of slaves, of traitors and of conspiring
> kings want?
> For whom are those ignoble shackles, those long-prepared
> iron fetters?
> Frenchmen, that's meant for us; oh what rage and fury must
> this provoke!
> They dare to plan reducing *us* to our ancient slavery!
> To arms, citizens! Form your battalions! March, march
> And let their foul blood soak our fields.[138]

The call for unity was, then, a military necessity as much as a piece of ideology. The Republic that was eventually proclaimed bore the title, logically enough, of the *République française une et indivisible*: the Republic was stipulated as being French, one whole, and indivisible. This formula allowed for no inner distinctions. Frenchness became the only loyal qualification for a citizen of the Republic. Much as ancient titles of nobility, and forms of address such as *monseigneur* and *excellence* had been abolished in favour of the single, Rousseauesque appellation *citoyen*, so too the ancient feudal-regional divisions of France were swept aside, and a deliberately artificial, rational new system of *départements* replaced it; this created more than eighty administrative districts, each with a central city, and each drawn up in such a way as to have that city within one day's journey from anywhere in the district. Not only did this rationalize the accessibility of regional and local government, it also cut the ground from under older regional loyalties, which could threaten the monopoly position of the Republic as the sole focus of the Frenchman's *amor patriae*. The civil wars then raging in the Vendée illustrated, after all, the extent to which regionalism could feed into anti-Revolutionary resistance.

The notion that the new France, one and indivisible, allowed no subsidiary or 'hyphenated' identities, is also manifested in the legislation prepared by the leading politician Henri Grégoire – like Sieyès a radical priest, who had been elected departmental bishop under the new system. It was none other than this Grégoire who had formally proposed the abolition of the kingship in the National Convention in 1792. It was on his initiative that the Jews of France had, as early as 1789, been given the unrestricted status of citizens (a radical emancipation unprecedented in Europe) and that first moves were made to give civil rights to coloured ex-slaves from the colonies. In 1794, Grégoire was also one of the movers behind a law formally banning all forms of slavery. All this was largely a humane application of the Enlightenment doctrine of human rights and human equality; but it also fed into a policy to buttress the Republic against outside threats by strengthening inner homogeneity. The Republic was French, it was One, and it was Undivided. Accordingly, anyone who was a citizen was French, and vice versa. The gesture of giving the Jews of France unrestricted civil rights and full citizenship was at the same time egalitarian (in that it removed their earlier second-rate status) and assimilationist (in that it wanted to see France's Jews as French, wholly French and nothing but French). Tellingly, Grégoire was as intolerant of regional diversity as he was of slavery and anti-semitism: the man who ensured the emancipation of the Jews also stressed the need to outlaw all non-French dialects as being by definition suspect and counterrevolutionary.

In 1794 Grégoire presented to the national Assembly a report 'On the necessity and the means of destroying regional dialects and to render the usage of standard French universal' (*Sur la nécessité et les moyens d'anéantir les patois et d'universaliser l'usage de la langue française*). That report painted a shrill picture of the republic's linguistic situation: standard French was the language of only 15 out of 83 *départements*; there were no less than 30 different regional languages in France; of 28 million inhabitants, only 3 million habitually used standard French as their everyday language, 6 million were ignorant of French and another 6 million spoke it with difficulty.

For Grégoire, this linguistic diversity resulted from ancient feudal divisions; also, the continued existence of regional dialects kept alive the heritage of those ancient feudal regions. 'We have abolished the Provinces but we still have some thirty dialects that recall their names'. Non-French was thereby inherently anti-Revolutionary. Barère, of the *Comité de Salut Public*, had already denounced this in his *Rapport sur les idiomes*:

Federalism and superstition speak Breton; the nobles in exile
who hate the Republic speak German; the counter-revolu-
tionary speaks Italian, and religious fanaticism speaks Basque.
It is time to break these instruments of damage and terror.

Grégoire, too, wishes to eradicate dialects so as to facilitate an ideological unity between all Frenchmen. He too (like Barère) refers to the evil effects of linguistic particularism for the Basque region:

Our commissioners in the Western Pyrenees have reported in
October 1792 that among the Basques, a mild and good people, a great number was susceptible to fanaticism because
their language is an obstacle to the spread of the Enlightenment. The same thing has happened in other *départements*,
where villains could successfully base their counter-revolu-
tionary machinations on the ignorance of our language.[*]

But Grégoire's report shows more than just heavy-handed strategic and tactical prag-
matism: it is based on more general notions of progress and the new type of state
which France represents. He recalls the old ideal of establishing a universal language,
and dismisses it as a pipe dream. However:

At least we can homogenize the language of a great nation, so
that all its citizens can communicate their thoughts without
obstacle. This undertaking, never wholly put into practice in
any nation, is worthy of the French people, which is centralizing all the branches of its social organization and which
must be watchful to enshrine as soon as possible, in a *République une et indivisible*, the unitary and unchanging usage of
the language of liberty.[139]

There had been attempts at linguistic unification before; an early one dates from
Henry VIII's reign in Ireland. But that had been part of an ideal of 'total conquest',
without any concerted policy to carry it into practice.[†] Here, the eradication of dialects and the standardization of the nation's language is advanced for two new types of
reason: progress and state centralization.

The notion of progress fills Grégoire's report. The use of *patois* hampers education,
limits the mental horizon of the countryman. Progress must also mean: improvement

---

* The reference is to Brittany, a region firmly dedicated to the monarchy and to the church, which
participated in the Vendée wars and had anti-revolutionary insurrections known as the *Chouannerie*.

† Loyal Tudorites in Dublin had urged that Gaelic-Irish recalcitrance had to be put down on all
fronts, including the linguistic one; as a result of this agitation Henry's Irish parliament had passed a
law banning the use of Gaelic as a treasonable act. See above, p. 33 and Leerssen 1996b, 39-49.

of the language as a tool of understanding and communication. In this respect, Gré-goire joins the ranks of eighteenth-century linguistic improvers who, as part of a gen-eral Enlightenment climate of improving society, had also undertaken language-refor-mist programmes: Leibniz in Germany, Sneedorf in Denmark, Swedberg in Sweden, Verlooy in the Austrian Netherlands.* In this light, indeed, the purification, consolida-tion and propagation of a standard language (undertaken for the Patriotic reasons of social improvement and public rationalization) can be seen as a nationally subsidiary, smaller-scale parallel to the utopian ideal of a universal language.

Grégoire goes further, however, in that he places the entire mechanism of the cen-tralizing state at the disposal of this language reform; or (to say the same thing the other way round) that he places this language reform in the context of state centraliza-tion. The improvement and rationalization of the public sphere is no longer a matter for concerned individuals or associations, but a state responsibility. The state has a mandate to improve society and its living conditions, and that mandate involves the areas previously left to the church, or to associations and individuals: health care, education, culture.

Thus the French Republic's basis in popular sovereignty is translated, first, into an ideal of undivided one-ness, and then into a programme for creating a single, undiffer-entiated culture for all citizens. Grégoire's programme, democratic and humane as it was, is also motivated by mistrust of cultural difference; much as his emancipation of the Jews is also an assimilationist move.

The French Republic did in fact develop ambitions to become a 'total' state, order-ing and arranging all public aspects of its citizens' lives. Education was one of the main frontlines: no longer a responsibility for parishes or church orders, the formation of young minds is taken in hand by the state.† But even in matters like dress, the new Republic wishes to abolishes regional traditions. Thus, the geographers Lavallée and Breton wrote, in a geographical survey of the 1790s:

> It is to be hoped that the Revolution will sooner or later lead
> to the blessing of a national costume, and that the traveller

---

* Such language improvers should not be confused with later, nationalistically motivated language activists: to those they relate as Enlightenment Patriots relate to Romantic nationalists. This does not mean, however, that there is no continuity between the two. Nineteenth-century language activists could, and did, fall back on their eighteenth-century forerunners, cite them by way of example, and in some cases recontextualize their publications in a new, nationally flavoured way. Thus, Jan-Baptist Verlooy's treatise on the neglect of the native language (*Verhandeling op d'onacht der moederlyke tael,* 1788) was cited as an inspiration by Flemish language activists like Jan Frans Willems and Philip Blommaert in the 1830s. For Grimm's invocation of a seventeenth-century language improver, see below, p. 181-182.

† Ever since, education has been the most hotly contested borderland between the public respon-sibilities of the state and the private responsibilities of parents (including their religious beliefs). The nineteenth-century battle over secular or religious education raged in many countries, and has found later continuations in the debates about the teaching of Darwinism (especially in America) or of Islamic values in educational facilities (in various European countries). For the mid-nineteenth-cen-tury French case, see van der Heijden 2004.

who passes from one *département* to another will no longer have the sensation of meeting different peoples. Who would believe that we are dealing with one single nation if one places the inhabitants of the *département des Bouches-du-Rhône* next to those of the *département du Nord*, or those of Finistère next to those of the Lower Rhine, or those of the Lower Seine next to those of the Var?[140]

Interestingly enough, this urge towards national homogenization survived its revolutionary origins.[141] Even in the states that emerged from the Restoration and the Congress of Vienna, a fresh habit is making itself felt towards the national collectivization of culture. Perhaps this is partly the ongoing effect of a reformist 'rationalization' urge that had been widespread in Europe and not only linked to the French Republic – thus, Emperor Joseph II in Austria, and the kings of Prussia, had undertaken measures which were aimed at abolishing traditional differentiations within their territories: Joseph II had, ineffectively, attempted to impose German as the language of government even on his Hungarian and Croatian realms, and Prussia had issued an *Allgemeines Landrecht* in 1794 that had placed all schools under state control. In that respect, the centralization efforts of the French republic fitted a wider European pattern, although they were conducted with greater fanaticism.

To some extent, however, the later European trend towards state centralization in cultural matters must count as an influence of French attitudes even among their enemies – a bit like the decimal system of weights and measures, or the *Code Napoléon*-style legal system with its fundamental binate structure of civil law and criminal law based on a written constitution.[142] These French-Revolutionary innovations were exported across Europe together with the French army,* and remained influential even after Waterloo.

A good case in point is that of the Netherlands. It had until the 1790s been a loose association of provinces, the northern half of which was united in a federal republic, the southern half being part of the Habsburg dominions (Spanish until 1714, Austrian from 1714 onwards). After the French and Napoleonic years, they were given a new status as a 'Kingdom of the Netherlands'; and a vigorous centralization campaign immediately followed. A school system was instituted, canals were commissioned, the Dutch language and a common 'Burgundian' heritage were propagated. Although the unification drive overshot its mark in the South (which split away to form, in 1830, the independent kingdom of Belgium), the remaining Netherlands underwent a process that gradually obliterated all regional differences and established a central, unified state. Regional differences had been considerable (the various traditional costumes, differing farmhouse-styles etc.). But national institutions, first introduced by the

---

* It is for that reason that, while most West-European currencies and weights/measures systems went decimal and adopted a roughly Napoleonic legal system, the United Kingdom, unconquered, maintained its unwritten constitution and its system of Common Law, along with its non-decimal pence, shillings and pounds, or feet, yards and miles.

French government in the years 1806-1815, and adapted by the restored Prince of Orange after 1813, turned the erstwhile confederate archipelago of independent coastlands, islands, estuaries, cities and provinces into one of the most tightly integrated countries in Europe.[143]

Even in the United Kingdom, which had resisted the threat of a Napoleonic invasion, we see a new cultural Anglocentrism rising in the course of the nineteenth century. The case of Wales bears this out. Wales had been a subordinate English principality since the late Middle Ages, and although the Welsh appointments of bishops or judges sometimes raised issues, given the distinct difference of the Welsh language, this had not generally been an unmanageable problem. In the course of the nineteenth century, however, linguistic difference began to constitute itself as a political flashpoint. The great rise of Methodism in Wales was partly abetted by the widespread indifference to Welsh among the Anglican clergy; and in England, conversely, the separate existence of something like Welsh began to be seen as a worrisome faultline in the national system. A parliamentary enquiry in 1847 linked the existence of Welsh to a general backwardness and lack of social cohesion in Wales, and resulted in recommendations to have the Welsh language discountenanced and to hasten rather than hinder its extinction; a policy strongly reminiscent of what Grégoire had proposed in Paris half a century previously.[144]

We can see echoes of the 'unity and indivisibility' ideal of 1792 throughout Europe and throughout the century. In the newly independent state of Italy, in 1861, the politician and novelist Massimo D'Azeglio spoke the prophetic words 'Now that we have made Italy, we need to make the Italians' – for the old regional identities, from Sicily to the Veneto, were still as strong as the dialect differences between those areas. In 1861, only 2.5 per cent of the total Italian population spoke standard Italian.[145]

All the states in Europe made use of education to turn their citizens into nationals. Language tuition was a high priority everywhere, and often contested.[*] History, too, became a school subject in many European countries in the course of the century, often ousting religious education in the curriculum: the prime virtues to be taught in school were no longer religious in nature, but civic, and a shared historical consciousness was seen as instrumental in the process. A historical cult of national remembrance also made itself felt in the public spaces of Europe: everywhere memorials and monuments were built to remind citizens of their great shared past. In the process, a national canon of key historical facts and figures was elaborated from older dynastic and

---

[*] Among speakers of minority languages the use of the *signum* was much resented. Dating back to the pedagogical discipline of Jesuit education, the *signum* consisted in making the speaker of a banned dialect wear a sign (a piece of wood) around his neck, of which he could only rid himself by transferring it to someone else caught in the act of dialect-speaking; the last bearer at the end of the day was punished, and thus the task of policing language use was imposed on the pupils themselves. The system was used (and resented) in many countries. In many places, again, the enforcement of the 'national' language against regional languages led to activism and conflict; in Ireland, a 'Society for the preservation of the Irish language' was founded partly in reaction to attitudes like those of the Anglican bishop who had thoughtlessly expressed a hope that modern education would turn each Irish pupil into 'a happy English child' (Leerssen 1996c, 151).

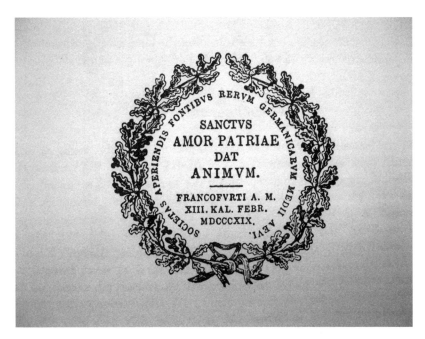

27. Seal of the Monumenta Germaniae Historica

regional sources, which featured prominently in public buildings, in paintings, pantheons and operas, and in school curricula.[146]

And everywhere the notion of love of the fatherland became the trump card among civic virtues. Nationality was not considered a political issue, but rather a transcendent moral imperative beyond politics. All different classes and political groups were to consider themselves united under the overriding ideal of shared nationhood. Here, too, an older, eighteenth-century virtue was updated into a new climate and given fresh intensification. The 'Love of Country' of Enlightenment Patriots was, following Fichte's moral-transcendent investment, given sacred qualities. The *'Marseillaise'* had already spoken, in its third couplet, of the *amour sacré de la patrie*. That same phrase was to form the catchline of an opera aria which sparked the Belgian rebellion of 1830 (see below, p. 192). And in Germany, a large, semi-state-sponsored effort to publish the ancient manuscript sources of German history, had for its seal an oak wreath with the motto *Sanctus amor patriae dat animum* – 'The sacred love of the fatherland inspires'.

There have been many comments on the extent to which nationalism in these decades takes the form of a 'secular religion'. To be sure, the new state takes on many of the symbols and rhetoric of religious worship – a worship of the national unity or the enduring principle of nationality; but more important is perhaps the fact that nationality thereby becomes a moral and even sacred notion, transcending all other concerns in politics or in the state. The revolutionary fervour of 1792 was echoed, ironically, by emperor Wilhelm II in 1914 when, in the course of his war-mongering chauvinism, he wanted to unite the entire country under his military leadership with the slogan *Ich*

28. Wartime postcard of Wilhelm II

kenne keine Parteien mehr, ich kenne nur noch Deutsche! ('I no longer recognize any parties, I only recognize Germans').

Nationalism as Unification

Germany

Deutschland? aber wo liegt es? asked Goethe in 1796 (ironic as usual). 'Germany? but where is it? I don't know where to find that land. Its learning begins where its politics end.' Metternich had a similar sense that neither Italy nor Germany constituted 'nations', and dryly stated that their names were at best cartographical, geographical notions:

> In my controversy with Lord Palmerston concerning the Italian question I made the statement, in the summer of 1847, that the national concept of 'Italy' was a geographical one, and my expression *l'Italie est un nom géographique*, which poisonously irritated Palmerston, has become a byword. More or less (as with all analogies) the same notion applies to Germany, as this is conceived subliminally with the people-at-large, and expressly among pure or calculating (i.e., honest or tricky) visionaries.[147]

Metternich's cynicism did not stop, of course, the unification and independence of a new state under the name of Italy; but as we have seen, even the author and minister Massimo D'Azeglio proclaimed shortly after the establishment of the new kingdom that 'now that Italy has been made, our task is to make the Italians'. A century later, at the establishment of the European Economic Community, De Gaulle still confided that there were only two well-established nation-states in the entire six-member EEC: France and the Netherlands; whereas the other four – which included, besides Belgium and Luxemburg, again Germany and Italy – were only nineteenth-century contrivances.

The German road to unification, from the dissolution of the First Empire to the proclamation of the Second, in 1871, is one of the great examples of the unificatory force of nationalism, as is the Italian *Risorgimento*. These processes can be, and have often been, described in terms of political interests, military force, dynastic ambition and political decision-making. But the driving power, behind all that, of cultural and ideological movements needs all the more to be emphasized here. The *Reichsgedanke* which actuated the Hohenzollern dynasty of Prussia was not just a hard-nosed, long-term dynastic agenda, but also and to a considerable extent the product of Romantic-historicist intellectuals. The last king of Prussia, Friedrich Wilhelm IV, who mounted the throne in 1840, was the product of an education imbued with national historicism; the last emperor, Wilhelm II (who reigned 1888-1918) no less so. What may have begun as the historical flattery of princes tutored by Romantic scholars was eventually internalized as political ideal by a good few of Europe's crowned heads.

The refusal to acquiesce in the dissolution of the *Reich* not only inspired the Romantic scholars like Von der Hagen, Aretin and Grimm, it also exerted a strong appeal in higher circles. Bavaria's *Walhalla*, previously mentioned, is a case in point: it marked, with classical columns and in marble dignity, the Eternal Germany from primitive antiquity to Goethe and after, and as Ludwig, its initiator, phrased it during his opening speech in 1842:

> May the Walhalla encourage the strength and growth of the
> German awareness! May all Germans, from whatever tribe
> they be, always feel that they have a common fatherland, and
> let each contribute as much as he can to its glorification![148]

The reference to many tribes with a common fatherland is portentous. We had already seen in discussing Fichte's *Reden an die deutsche Nation* that the realms and lands of Germany echoed the names and perpetuated the memory of the ancient Germanic tribes, from Saxons to Hessians and from Franks to Bavarians. A common German consciousness saw the unification as one between ancient divisions on the strength of a shared culture and the memory of a shared *Reich*. This mode of reasoning has later, famously, been couched in the phraseology of the Germans being a *Kulturnation* and developing ambitions to become a *Staatsnation*. The idea of a German language, literature and *Kultur* was self-evident; the idea that it could express itself as a German state was, to men like Goethe and Metternich, counter-intuitive.

If we see the nineteenth century as the translation period from *Kulturnation* to *Staatsnation* then obviously the process was more than just a dynastic-political rise of Prussia headed by the Hohenzollerns and led by Bismarck. Throughout the nineteenth century, Germany was held up as an ideal by its writers, intellectuals and artists. A particularly salient role was played by the Brothers Grimm, whose prestigious publications always carried the word *Deutsch* in their titles: from the German grammar to the German dictionary and including the German legal antiquities and the history of the German language. Jacob Grimm, who famously stated that he never in all his life loved anything as much as his fatherland, gave his inaugural lecture as professor at Göttingen University in 1830 on the topic *De desiderio patriae* – a remarkable text, probably unique in that it deploys the old, humanist medium of scholarly Latin for the formulation of a new, romantic ideology of national identity. One may translate *De desiderio patriae* either as 'On the love of the fatherland', or else as 'On the yearning for the fatherland' (i.e., homesickness[*]). The ambiguity is part of Grimm's point:

---

[*] Homesickness has been attested in texts from many different centuries and cultures (cf. Greverus 1972). It was diagnosed and given a name (initially the label 'nostalgia' was used) as a medical condition in the mid-to-late seventeenth century. It was seen as a type of melancholia or depression that resulted from one's removal away from home to foreign places, and to be cured by repatriation. Initially the condition was diagnosed among Swiss mercenary soldiers and British seamen. Thus, the

he argues that homesickness is a universal human affect, and that this fact proves that love of the fatherland is a universal, categorical human virtue. It is not a civic attitude cultivated or abandoned at will, but, like language, something which links the individual to a larger spiritual collective. And this, in turn, projects language as the first and fundamental part of our socialization as human beings: something which, imbued along with our mothers' milk, forms us at the very beginning of our lives. Language and nationality are, then, anthropological fundamentals. And this in turn justifies Grimm's definition of the fatherland in linguistic terms: the German's fatherland is wherever the German tongue is heard.[149] (Cf. also below, p. 179)

The philological-historicist dream of a united Germany started with the Wartburg festival of 1817 and culminated in 1848. It was, initially, at odds with the aristocratic absolutism of the Metternich-style reactionaries, and saw the new united Germany as incorporating some fundamental civil rights and a written constitution.

This dilemma points to an ambivalence at the very core of the national unification movement among German intellectuals – amongst whom we may count Arndt, the Grimms, Uhland and many others. On the one hand, they were deeply nostalgic, cultivating their romantic medievalism, glorifying the days of the old *Reich*. On the other hand, they were by no means reactionary: they believed in the emancipation of the citizen and rejected the reactionary programme of the German princes and Metternich. They cherished a firm belief in aboriginal tribal liberties – among these being a notion of local self-government, parliamentary institutions, and trial by jury – and they despised arbitrary power. To some extent, the defence of civil and 'national' (that is to say: collective-traditional) liberties makes these intellectuals democrats, radical liberals, and to some extent even precursors of social democracy.

On the other hand, the selfsame generation of intellectuals was imbued with a great deal of xenophobia and with a 'love of the fatherland' that was used to advocate territorial aggrandizement.[150] Belonging to the German *Kulturnation* was nothing short of a total commitment, involving particularly a hatred of everything French. Both Arndt and Jahn argued in so many words that hatred of things French was a moral imperative for any good German. The same vehement xenophobia and national chauvinism we find in another representative of this generation, Friedrich Christoph Dahlmann (1785-1860). He was later to be dismissed, together with the Grimms, from Göttingen University for refusing to accept arbitrary power; and during the Frankfurt Parliament he was one of the actual authors of the German draft constitution; but this selfsame champion of liberty had argued from his lectern at Kiel University, in the days of anti-Napoleonic resistance:

> Anyone who henceforth sees Germans and French merely as
> two opposing parties, both equally justified in pursuing their

---

conceptual rise of 'homesickness' in learned European discourse is linked to modernity in the guise of early-modern warfare or naval expansion, and early-modern medical science. It formed part of an emerging anthropology of human affect (a link between somatic and moral qualities) which reached its high point in the nineteenth century; cf. Leerssen 2002c.

cause; anyone who wants to speculate that, had he been born a Frenchman, he would act like them – anyone who compares this basely degenerated, oath-breaking, atheist, thieving nation with the noble, self-sacrificing German – such a one is a new-style Frenchman himself, wherever he was born, and deserves to be despised as such throughout Germany.[151]

Again, the generation of Grimm and Arndt, and their younger followers, linked their cultural idealism to a geopolitical expansionism that was of a highly belligerent, chauvinist nature. This is one of the contradictions that makes the ideology of the *Vormärz* so hard to assess for contemporary readers. A belief in national self-determination and individual liberties went hand-in-hand with a belief in the superior rights of Germany over its neighbours and in the historical rights of the German nation to coerce the unwilling. Being German conferred rights and imposed a destiny at the same time; in the ideology of the *Vormärz* we see the roots of democratic liberalism and social democracy alongside the roots of fascism and imperialism. In the Frankfurt Parliament of 1848, Grimm wanted to outlaw slavery in the proposed constitution and to include an article that anyone on German soil was *ipso facto* free; the same Grimm urged a war of conquest, on the same occasion, to take Schleswig and Jutland from Denmark, on the basis of obscure German-style dialect forms in the language spoken there (see below, p. 183-184).

The outstanding example of this ambivalence was the flamboyant character of Ernst August Hoffmann von Fallersleben (1798-1874). A poet of wit and facility, and an adept of Arndt and Grimm, he turned to the study of German (especially Low-German) medieval texts, and had considerable scholarly importance as a philologist in this line of learning. A typical representative of his Romantic generation, he undertook journeys across Europe, celebrating the rise of national-cultural consciousness everywhere.[*]

Like Arndt, the Grimms and Dahlmann, Hoffmann was one of those German-Romantic professors who between 1817 and 1848 were dismissed from their posts. After he had published a volume of scathing political-satirical verse, the Prussian government dismissed him from his chair at Breslau; Hoffmann became a wandering scholar. In his exile, he composed a song which expressed at the same time his homesickness, his belief in liberty, and his chauvinistic belief in the ideal and superiority of a Great United Germany. It was called the *Lied der Deutschen* or 'The Germans' Song', and later became Germany's national anthem:

> Germany, Germany above all, above everything in the world
> If for shelter and support it will fraternally stand together

---

[*] There is a significant poem dedicated to the Viennese-Slovene scholar Jernej Kopitar, at whose regular table in the inn 'Zum weissen Wolf' Hoffmann met representatives of the various emerging nationalities of the Balkans. Later in life, Hoffmann was to support, both through his textual scholarship and with his political verse, the Flemish Movement in Belgium (Deprez 1963; Hafner 1957).

From the Meuse to the Memel, from the Adige to the Belt
Germany, Germany above all, above everything in the
world![152]

The lyric has become a byword for a chauvinistic belief in superiority, and to some extent this reputation is not unjustified; the borders given to Hoffmann's ideal called 'Germany' are drawn widely, in expansionist-hegemonic fashion. Hoffmann claims much of the Low Countries east of the Meuse as German, and all of Schleswig-Holstein south of the Belt. All of the Southern Tyrol as far south as the Adige is claimed, and much of what now is Poland, as far as the Memel (a sea-arm near Königsberg/Kaliningrad). None of these rivers are named gratuitously: in each and every case they refer to actual territorial claims.

At the same time it would be wrong to see Hoffmann as a straightforward imperialist; this song was not written to be sung to the tune of stamping soldiers' boots. On the contrary: it expresses nostalgia and longing rather than greed, and the wide ambit given to the new Germany is, as it were, the spatial expression of an agenda of unity and democracy. For a *Vormärz* Romantic like Hoffmann, the cause of liberty was weakened in the German lands because these were broken up into so many monarchies and small realms. Within each of these petty realms, the power of the prince was great, the position of the populace weak and subordinate. Territorial integration would strengthen the hand of the people and weaken the grip of the princes. Hoffmann's Germany is a dream of fraternization across inner divisions, and within his ideal Germany, politics are to be dominated by the principles of Unity, Justice and Liberty. The third stanza (nowadays the official text of the German national anthem) accordingly reads:

Unity, Justice and Liberty for the German fatherland
Let us all work fraternally to that goal with hands and hearts
Unity, Justice and Liberty are the guarantors of bliss
Flourish in the glow of such bliss, flourish German fatherland![153]

Between the expansionist and chauvinist first stanza and the humane-democratic third stanza, Hoffmann's *Deutschlandlied* embodies the very ambiguity of the national-liberalism of his generation. It was to reach its apogee, and its ruin, in the Frankfurt Parliament or *Nationalversammlung* of 1848.

Taking place in a year that saw all European countries rocked by revolts, reforms and revolutions, the *Nationalversammlung* marks one of the pivotal points in nineteenth-century history. The fact that it was convened at all held a great promise among romantic, nationally minded German intellectuals. It opened the prospect of a unification of the various German lands into a federation or *Reich*, ideally to be glorified (and rooted in historical tradition) by a restored imperial crown, but also ensuring civil rights by means of a written constitution and a citizenry emancipated from the nobility's many prerogatives and privileges. From July 1848 onwards, the Parliament argued questions of civil rights, the constitution and the outline of a future united Germany.

From the beginning, however, deep tensions between conservative and progressive forces were only thinly glossed over by a shared rhetoric of National Freedom. Liberty for all Germans was demanded, and also the annexation of neighbouring territories such as Schleswig-Holstein. A particularly vexed question concerned the position of the Austrian Empire. This was resented for its closeness to the papacy, its Metternichian reputation, and the fact that it counted a majority of non-Germans (Hungarians, Slavs etc.) among its inhabitants. Ultimately, when a draft constitution for a new German Empire was drawn up, it was to leave Austria out of the equation, and the proposed German Empire was to be led by the Prussian Hohenzollerns. However, a *Reich* with a liberal Constitution was a contradiction in terms. Accordingly, when the imperial dignity was offered to the King of Prussia, it was rejected because it came from the hands of mere commoners. A proper emperor, it was felt, should be proclaimed by his kings and princes, not appointed by his subjects.

The 1848 rejection was a sore discomfiture for the Frankfurt delegation, which counted among its members the old, prestigious Romantic philologists (Arndt and Dahlmann), but which represented at that moment only a torn and thinned-out parliament. The Frankfurt Parliament, which was at best tolerated, at worst obstructed by the various German princes and Austria, was bypassed by the monarchists to its right and by the emerging socialists on its left, and ended in ignominy.

In subsequent years, Bismarck undertook to accomplish by 'blood and iron' (as he phrased it) the goal of imperial unification under Prussian leadership. Finally, in 1871, following the great Prussia-led victory over France, a new emperor was proclaimed by the assembled kings and princes of the Reich; this took place in, of all places, Louis XIV's Versailles.[*] (In his wartime diaries during the 1870 campaign, crown prince Friedrich was looking forward to this imperial *coup*, the end of what by that time he already called 'the fifty-six year interregnum'.[154]) In the same gesture, Germany re-annexed Strasbourg and the Alsace, mindful of the never-forgotten conquest by Louis XIV of 1681. A new German university was founded there, the leading scholars from all of Germany appointed on chairs there, in a policy to make Strasbourg and the Alsace once again a thoroughly German-minded area.[†]

Thus, even though the programme of German unification and of the re-establishment of the Reich was taken over by hard-nosed *Realpolitiker* after 1848, the cultural outline of the new Germany followed Hoffmann's semi-subversive song of 1841. Hoffmann's song had in turn been a variation of a true evergreen of nineteenth-century German political verse: Arndt's '*Was ist des Deutschen Vaterland*?' – 'Where lies the German's fatherland?'.

---

[*] The Versailles location was not only intended to humiliate the vanquished French enemy; it was also to have the emperor proclaimed on neutral territory and to spare the German princes a submissive journey to Berlin.

[†] Conversely, when the French retook Strasbourg and the Alsace, they closed down the German university there and put up a French flagship university in its place, clearly intending to undo the attempt at intellectual Germanization (Cf. Craig 1984).

GIUSEPPE MAZZINI
L'APOSTOLO DELL'UNITÀ ITALIANA

29. Giuseppe Mazzini

Jacob Grimm also practised linguistic geopolitics in the style of Hoffmann and Arndt. His inaugural lecture on 'Love of the fatherland' had concluded with a Latin phrase to the effect that everywhere where the German language was spoken, was *Germania* – including (as Arndt and Grimm both pointed out on various occasions) the funny-sounding semi-Germanic dialects on the frontiers such as Flemish, Dutch, Alsatian, and Jutland-Danish (cf. below, p. 178 ff.).

It all was, in effect, a reply to Goethe's question from 1796. 'Germany? but where is it?' The generation of philologists following Goethe answered that question in no uncertain terms on the basis of ethnic and linguistic geography. They territorialized culture, and their intellectual and poetic rhetoric provided, throughout the century, an ongoing, prestigious justification and rationalization of the emergence of a united German *Staatsnation*.

Italy

The process that saw the emergence of a unified Italy was, if anything, even more complex than that of Germany. It involved a collaboration of three political leaders of very different type: Giuseppe Garibaldi (1807-1882), a Romantic military leader; Count Cavour (1810-1861), an aristocratic diplomat, and Giuseppe Mazzini (1805-

1872), an ideologist and prophet of a Europe of Nations. Mazzini, a lifelong revolutionary democrat, is perhaps after Fichte the second most important architect of European nationalism.

Mazzini grew up in the period around Waterloo, and never accepted the restoration policies of 1815; he joined the *Carbonari*, a secret society of disaffected intellectuals, as a young man in 1828; he was arrested and briefly imprisoned in 1830 (the year that saw liberal revolutions in France, Belgium, Poland and elsewhere). In 1832 he founded a society, which he named *Giovine Italia* or 'Young Italy'. It proved enormously successful and influential, both within and outside Italy. Within Italy, the movement swelled to 60,000 members in a few years, and Mazzini tried a rash and abortive rebellion in 1833. Mazzini himself went into exile and spread his gospel of national self-determination. His programme of a 'Young Italy', with ardent, youthful idealists claiming their nation's liberties against the autocrats of the *ancien régime*, inspired similar movements elsewhere in Europe: from *Junges Deutschland* to Young Poland, Young Hungary and Young Ireland, eventually even giving its name to the reformist Young Turks. Mazzini himself wanted a federative solidarity between all these nationalist movements in a Young Europe; one of the first times that a pan-European vision was proposed, and directly inspiring Victor Hugo's vision of a 'United States of Europe'.[155] In Mazzini's view, no more wars or conflicts would be necessary if each state of Europe was the expression of its constituent nation's self-determination. It was a Romantic variation on the democratic unanimity envisaged by Rousseau, and the 'eternal peace' which Kant had predicted would arise from a Europe based on rational, free republics; it was a vision later proclaimed repeatedly in the period 1914-1918, when, in the run-up to the Versailles treaty, the 'war to end all wars' was thought to lead to a break-up of empires and a wholesome rearrangement of a Europe of nations great and small.

The vision was, as we can see from hindsight, based on a starry-eyed simplification and a denial of the geopolitical and demographic complexities of the real world. But it did, in the years 1830-1848, formulate a democratic, non-authoritarian and non-chauvinist programme for national self-determination much preferable to anything the Arndts and Grimms were devising north of the Alps. It also led, paradoxically, to an international network of nationalist movements, where activists in Hungary or Poland would support movements in Italy or vice versa. And ultimately, within Italy, the programme of Young Italy, despite frequent setbacks, defeats and internal quarrels, led to the emergence of a united, independent state.

This was achieved partly through the military genius of the wayward Garibaldi, partly through the canny negotiations of Cavour, who played off France against Austria at a particularly problematic juncture in European affairs. Austria, mistrusting Prussia's rise to dominance in the north, had refused to support Germany's claims on Schleswig-Holstein; this had even led to a Prussian-Austrian conflict at a time when Cavour, thanks to his stance in the Crimean War, had ensured French and British goodwill. Cavour made use of the occasion to lure a weakened Austria into conflict, having previously (secretly) ensured that France would remain neutral; as a result, he was able to achieve Northern Italian independence from Austria in 1861. Thus the national questions were 'wheels within wheels', involving Europe truly from the Belt to the Adige. One factor of particular complexity in all this was the status of Rome, ruled by the pope and supported (with varying degrees of real loyalty) by most Catholic monarchies. For the papacy, Rome was the Eternal City, capital of the Catholic church and indeed of Christianity at large; for Italian nationalists, it was the city of the old Roman Republic and Empire, and the only possible capital for a new, reconstituted Italy. Those two visions were clearly incompatible, and led to protracted complications and complexities.*

The price Cavour paid for French neutrality was the city of Nizza, which was ceded to France to become present-day Nice; another price was the fact that Italy was to become not a republic (which was a form of government detested and feared by the European powers) but a kingdom under the Sardinian king Vittorio Emmanuele. The Romantic Garibaldi could live with this: it was he who proclaimed Vittorio Emmanuele King in 1860 after he had landed in Sicily with his redshirts. Mazzini, however, a republican through and through, was deeply embittered by this turn of events and disassociated himself from the country he had helped create.

All this political wheeling and dealing should not, however, obscure the fact that the Italian *risorgimento* or 'resurgence' was carried, here as in Germany, by a wave of cultural consciousness-raising. The *risorgimento* was a deeply Romantic movement, carried by historians, poets, composers and historical novelists.[156] Massimo D'Azeglio who has been repeatedly quoted as stating the need to turn the people of Italy into Italians, had prepared the ground by writing historical novels in the style of Walter Scott, choosing significant periods from Italian history to proclaim his country's traditions and historical track record: *Ettore Fieramosca o la disfida di Barletta* (1833) is set in the 1503 conflict around the Spanish-Italian conquest of Naples against the French, and involves a question of honour which is consistently given nationalist symbolical value; *Niccolò de' Lapi, ovvero i Palleschi e i Piagnoni* (1841) is set in the Florence of Savonarola around that city's conquest by Charles V. Rossini glorified the Swiss national liberator William Tell in an opera; and Verdi's opera *Nabucco*, set in the Babylonian Exile of the tribes of Israel, contained a 'Slaves' Chorus' (*Va, pensiero*) that became a veritable hymn to national liberation everywhere in Europe. Verdi's name was written on the walls of Austrian-held Venice as an expression of Italian commitment: the name was understood as an acronym of Vittorio Emmanuele Re d'Italia.

It was Verdi, too, who composed his great 'Requiem' for the state funeral, in 1873, for the novelist who had perhaps done most to fire an Italian historical consciousness: Alessandro Manzoni (1785-1873) – incidentally, also D'Azeglio's father-in-law. Although his early career as a writer had been more oriented toward the drama (e.g. the history play *Il conte di Carmagnola*, 1828), he is famous as the greatest European adept of the Walter Scott-style historical novel, with his *I promessi sposi*. That work was

---

* Rome was forcibly taken in 1870; Pope Pius IX, who would not relinquish his claims and who in any case could not see his position as anything but a sovereign among sovereigns (never as a citizen of a secular country) locked himself up in his Vatican palaces, considering himself a prisoner there. The creation of an autonomous and extraterritorial Vatican in 1929, ensuring that the pope could remain an independent sovereign, finally put an end to this deadlock; it was a diplomatic success which massively strengthened the hand of Mussolini, under whose rule the deal was concluded. Generally Chadwick 1998.

one of the many Walter Scott adaptations across Europe playing a role of national consciousness-raising; but in Manzoni's case, there was an extra twist. He wrote the original version in 1825, in his native dialect of Northern Italy. Fifteen years later, he had moved to Florence, the city of Dante and the linguistic capital of Italian letters; and he decided to make his novel truly national (as opposed to regional) by re-writing it according to the Tuscan-Florentine standard. Manzoni made his novel Italian as his novel was part of the making of Italy.

Pan-movements

One of the more remarkable aspects of nineteenth-century unification nationalism is its tendency to spawn 'pan-movements' – projects to unite not just the fellow-members of one particular culture or language but indeed whole clusters or families of languages: the nationalism of language families.

The best-studied of these pan-movements is Pan-Slavism.[157] It aimed, not just at the emancipation and self-determination of various individual Slavic nations (Polish, Czech, Croat etc.) but of the Slavic race as a whole. We should realize that the mutual philological relations between the Slavic languages were as yet ill-understood. The number of Slavic languages was estimated, in the course of the eighteenth century, to run anywhere between one and seventeen; Albanian was thought of as a Slavic language, Bulgarian was not. Given the high degree of mutual intelligibility between neighbouring Slavic languages, there were (and still are) frequent debates as to whether two variants were closely related but different languages, or else two dialects of one and the same language.[*] Indeed, there was some cause to see Slavic as one large mega-language with a shifting number of dialect variations from Russian to Polish to Serbian. The ongoing use of Church Slavonic in the various Orthodox churches of Slavdom strengthened this notion.

The concept of a Slavic nation was first articulated by late-eighteenth-century critics and historians like Herder. Herder, in particular, dedicated some appreciative chapters to the European Slavs, whom he extolled as peaceful, long-suffering, morally exalted; an ethnotype that was to have great impact on nineteenth-century Slavic self-images. That the Slavs were united, not only by a common language and 'soul', but also by common aspirations, was evident in the works of early Slavic philologists like the Czech Josef Dobrovský and the Slovene Jernej Kopitar, both men of an outstanding Europe-wide reputation in the sphere of letters and learning; the two collaborated on the first scholarly grammar of ancient Slavic, which appeared under Dobrovský's name in 1822. Both worked in the Habsburg empire, both were Catholic (as opposed to Orthodox), and both saw the Habsburg capital of Vienna as the natural focus of Slavic

---

[*] In the course of the last two centuries, this debate has occurred regarding the relations between Bulgarian and Macedonian, Ukrainian and Ruthenian (Rusyn), Russian, Belorussian and Ukrainian, Serb and Croat, Slovene and Croat, Czech and Slovak. See below, pp. 166-167.

aspirations: from Polish Silesia to Croatia and Slovenia, the Habsburg crown had perhaps the greatest sample of Slavic nations under its aegis.

The resulting ideology is now usually known as 'Austro-Slavism'; it was soon to meet the competition of a different Pan-Slavic trend, one which looked to St. Petersburg rather than Vienna, to the Romanov tsar rather than the Habsburg emperor, and which accordingly is known as the 'russophile' or 'slavophile' trend. It was carried by Russian intellectuals, of course, but also by representatives of Orthodox Slavdom in Serbia and Bulgaria, and to a lesser extent by those Slovaks who felt uncomfortable with the idea that they were being subordinated to Czech dominance.[158]

Indeed, Slovakia may to some extent be seen as the very hub of early cultural Pan-Slavism. There is, to begin with, the Slovak poet Jan Kollár (1793-1852), who had studied in Jena and there imbued the legacy of Herder and the idealism of German Romanticism; he had participated in the Wartburg festivities of 1817. These ideas he used to formulate an explicit programme of Slavic cultural mutuality, and gave to the various Slavic nations a poem cycle which intensified the moral praise of Herder into a lyrical manifesto. A cycle of more than a hundred sonnets, his *Slavy dcera* ('Slava's daughter') at the same time celebrates his fraught love for a young woman whom he had met in Jena, and his transubstantiation of this yearning into a national worship of the personification of the Slavic race: the goddess Slava (whose name also means 'fame' or 'glory'). Built around the three rivers that define the Slavic world, the Saale, the Moldau and the Danube,[*] *Slavy dcera* is a lyrically intense bird's eye view of the world of Slavs, all of them yearning for a lost ideal and a distant desire. While the poetical and critical work of Kollár offered a collective-Slavic cultural inspiration to all readers from the Baltic to the Balkans, a common historical and archaeological foundation was offered by the Slovak scholar Pavol Šafárik (1795-1861). His studies on Slavic antiquity provided a common Slavic historical awareness to all Slavic nations.

The Pan-Slavic movement burst onto the political scene in 1848. In that fateful year, a Slavic Congress was held in Prague, with representatives from all Slavic nations (who between them often found they had to speak German because their various languages were not all that mutually intelligible after all).[159] This Congress must stand alongside the Frankfurt Parliament of the same year (above, p. 149) as one of the crucial assemblies of the mid-century. Indeed, the Prague meeting was set up partly to counterbalance Frankfurt: one of the prime movers, the widely respected Czech historian and activist František Palacký (1798-1876), had been invited to sit in the Frankfurt assembly as one of the representatives of the ancient kingdom of Bohemia, still one of the Habsburg crown lands and an important part of the ancient Holy Roman Empire. Palacký, in a significant move, decided that the ethnic difference between Slavs and Germans was such that the Bohemian Slavs (Czechs) could not and should not be adequately represented in a German assembly, and he decided to hold a separate Slavic

---

* The Saale, running close to Jena, also ran close to the most north-western of the Slavic languages: Sorbic. While the number of Sorbic speakers is insignificant, their status in early Pan-Slavism was very important, because they were highly educated, literate, and manifested their cultural presence with all the aplomb of German Romanticism.

congress in Prague.[160] (It should be remembered that Bohemia was culturally mixed, with a sizeable German-speaking population even in Prague – think Kafka – and that the Czech national movement was aimed primarily against the intra-Bohemian domination of Czech by German.)

The further vicissitudes of Pan-Slavism, dominated by a rift between the Austro-Slavic and the Russophile wing, and by the geopolitics of Habsburgs and Romanovs, need not concern us too closely here. Pan-Slavism neither fulfilled its Romantic-idealistic goal of a federation of free Slavic nations, nor did the ideal disappear. Many later developments were inspired by Pan-Slavic notions: emancipation movements in different Slavic regions, from Ukraine to Bulgaria and Macedonia. Some commentators have seen in Stalin's policies to create a belt of satellite states around his USSR a late, warped echo of Pan-Slavism. The papacy of Polish-born John Paul II (1978-2005) was certainly inspired by notions of Slavic identity and a Slavic moral mission.

More importantly, Pan-Slavism has bequeathed a tendency to hyphenate various Slavic nationalisms into federal initiatives. The union between Czechs and Slovaks is a case in point; the Yugoslav experiment another. Yugoslavia (the word means 'South-Slavia' as a union of the Slavic nations of the Western Balkans) finds its roots in a sub-branch of Austro-Slavism, the 'Illyrian Movement',[161] which burgeoned from the 1830s onwards, initiated by Slovene and Croat intellectuals who wished to see a union with neighbouring Bosnians, Serbs and Montenegrins. To that end, the unity of a 'Serbo-Croat' language was officially proclaimed in Vienna in 1850. The eventual establishment of a united kingdom of Slovenes, Croats and Serbs, eventually re-christened Yugoslavia, can be seen as a partial concretization of a subsidiary Pan-Slavic ideal. Yugoslavia was to some extent also seen as a Greater Serbia, as envisaged by the mid-nineteenth century politician Ilija Garašanin (1812-1874). The combination of 'Illyrian' cultural idealism and Garašanin's geopolitics proved impossible, here as in other cases: Yugoslavia included Macedonia, which has stronger cultural ties with Bulgaria than with Serbia, let alone Croatia; and it also included a sizeable Albanian (that is to say, non-Slavic) population, mainly because these inhabited a region (Kosovo) that had a huge symbolical importance in the Serb historical consciousness. These factors created strong centrifugal tendencies, besides the fact that even among the Slavic populations themselves, the different religious traditions (Catholic, Orthodox, Islamic) proved more difficult to unify than their linguistic kinship had suggested.

Another side effect of Pan-Slavism was that it inspired copycat movements elsewhere in Europe, such as Pan-Germanism and Pan-Celticism. Much as Slavic nationalism, including its Pan-Slavic outgrowth, had originally been inspired by Herder and by political Romanticism made in Germany, its influence was to echo back into German political thought. Of course, the German unification drive had always to some extent been implicitly Pan-Germanic or at least 'Great-German', or at least potentially so. In the linguistic expansionism of Arndt, Grimm and Hoffmann von Fallersleben it must be noted that their usage of *Deutsch* is always fuzzy: sometimes it means, specifically, the German language in the narrower sense of the term (also known as 'High German') – e.g. in the Grimms' great dictionary, the *Deutsches Wörterbuch*. At other times, however, the term *Deutsch* can mean nothing less than the entire Germanic language family, including Dutch and Frisian, and even Anglo-Saxon – thus in Jacob

Grimm's *Deutsche Grammatik*. On the basis of this elastic usage of 'German', outlying languages were repeatedly classified, first as Germanic, and then as part of a German complex as incorporated by Germany. This was the argument vis-à-vis Flemish, Dutch, Frisian and even Jutland-Danish.*

From the end of the nineteenth century onwards, there was actually a Pan-German movement, which was born among German-speaking Austrians eager to reunite with their northern neighbours (and break away from Austria's Central-European ties). In time this ethnic line of thought came to incorporate geopolitical ideals as well (e.g. control over the seaports at the mouths of the Rhine and Scheldt rivers, Rotterdam and Antwerp), and this brand of Pan-Germanic thought briefly became officially endorsed policy in 1940-1945.[162] Meanwhile, an alternative aggregation had been thought out in Flanders: that of a union of all Low-German dialect varieties spoken in the North-European plain from Dunkirk to Königsberg: Flemish, Dutch, *Plattdeutsch*.[163] This pan-movement was quickly marginalized. It does, however, testify to the ongoing presence of the associative force of nationalism as a project of uniting a dispersed *Kulturnation* into a single state. In the nineteenth- and twentieth-century case of Flanders and the Netherlands, there has been a long-standing movement of what is called 'Greater Netherlandism', stressing the fundamental cultural and linguistic unity between Flemish and Dutch. To some extent this Netherlandism has been officially and pragmatically enshrined in cross-border linguistic institutions (the *Taalunie*), in other cases it lives in associations dedicated to the closer cultural and/or political union between these two areas. There was, briefly, a flourish of this Greater Netherlandism under fascist auspices.[164]

Pan-Celticism, alongside Pan-Slavism and Pan-Germanism, emerged in the nineteenth century, largely as a network of Breton activists looking to Wales for moral and cultural support.[165] These contacts flourished from the late 1820s onwards, when Breton delegates were fêted at the Welsh cultural festival known as *Eisteddfod*. As the Breton movement gathered steam in the second half of the nineteenth century, it often looked to Welsh cultural festivals and institutions for inspiration, and continually stressed the fact that Brittany was not just an uncouth peripheral province within France, but part of a larger, Celtic whole. When, in the 1890s, Celtic-inspired revivals flourished in a *fin-de-siècle* atmosphere in Scotland and, above all, in Ireland, they meshed briefly with these Breton-Welsh connections under the common header of 'Celtic', and some Pan-Celtic conferences were held. There is still a Pan-Celtic movement in Europe, largely regionalist in tone, and nowadays enriched with the (philologically nonsensical) 'Ibero-Celtic' addition of Galicia. Pan-Celticism was never a serious political agenda in its own right, but did help to inspire cultural revival movements mutually and in regions like Cornwall and the Isle of Man, and to provide a wider solidarity support for violent nationalism in certain regions (e.g. IRA campaigns in Northern Ireland). There is still a street called Rue Bobby Sands in the

---

* Thus, among the c. 100 busts enshrined in the Bavarian Walhalla prior to 1914, celebrating men and women 'of German tongue', there are no less than twelve Dutch/Flemish figures, as well as the Swedish King Carl X Gustav.

Breton city of Nantes, named after the interned IRA terrorist who died on hunger strike in 1981.

Two pan-movements can be mentioned briefly, merely for the sake of completeness. Something calling itself Pan-Latinism was briefly inspired by the success of Pan-Slavism and German nationalism, in the mid-nineteenth century. Marginal, it still helped to legitimize thoughts about a *génie Latin* which set Western Europe off against the Slavic and Teutonic East and Centre.[166] The establishment, in 1883, of the *Alliance française*, dedicated to the spread and maintenance of French culture and the French language outside the borders of France proper, may be seen as an echo.[*] One should also note in passing a persistent, though non-dominant current in Walloon regionalism pleading for unification with France. Finally, a Turanian movement proclaimed the common roots and identities of all Turkish peoples, from the Balkans to Central Asia.[167]

The ongoing presence of nationalism as a unification ideology can still be registered in the German events of 1989. That year marked the end of one-party dictatorship in the German Democratic Republic, which for 45 years had been a Russian satellite state. Now, as democratic freedom was regained (as it was in Russia itself, in Poland, Hungary, Czechoslovakia and other countries in the region), hopes dawned for a removal of the Berlin Wall and the Iron Curtain, for free traffic from one Germany into the other, for long-separated friends and relatives to visit freely once more – a situation, in short, as between Dutch Limburg and Belgian Limburg, or between Bavaria and Tyrol. This, however, was not enough. The recuperation of liberty in East Germany was immediately translated into a unification drive territorially merging east and west. What is truly remarkable was the unquestioning automatism of this process; it was seen as self-evident, obvious, justified in itself and inherently, unarguably proper – almost a categorical necessity and certainly an overriding political priority. A century and a half after Hoffmann von Fallersleben, the notions of *Recht* and *Freiheit* were still led in tow by the overriding assumption of *Einigkeit*.

---

[*] The *Alliance française* was initially founded as an *Association nationale pour la propagation de la langue française dans les colonies et à l'étranger*. The administrative committee of 1884 includes Ernest Renan, Armand Colin, Ferdinand de Lesseps, Louis Pasteur and Jules Verne.

Nationalism as Separatism

The considerations that drove the French and Dutch states to tighten their communal centralism, and that drove Germans and Italians to seek unification in a common, culturally defined state, also drove cultural minorities away from the capitals from where they were governed. We may roughly distinguish two sub-types of this trend: those autonomist movements which harked back to ancient and still-remembered feudal independence (e.g. in Catalonia, Scotland, Hungary and Poland), and those which emerged with the discovery of a separate culture and identity among a local rustic populace (e.g. in Finland and the Baltic, or Bulgaria). The distinction between those two sub-types is gradual and tenuous: even the most illiterate and pre-modern peasantries were taught their national culture and 'roots' by intellectuals and activists from the gentry, or the professional and middle class, and even the most feudally inspired Romantic nationalists drew on the local colour of the native peasantry to underline the ancient realm's claim to continued separateness.

In itself there was nothing new in the fact that the imperial capitals of Europe had to cope with disaffected populations on their peripheries. The 'Congress' system that Metternich imposed after 1815 intended to subdue those restive provincials in the same gesture that should stifle all populist unrest: restoration of the monarch's central power also meant the imposition of obedience, not only of the rabble in the great metropolitan centres of Europe, but also in the provinces and margins. Whatever sedition or disaffection was going on in the outlying provinces had for centuries been a fact of life, part of the ongoing political push-and-pull of centrifugal resistance against central authority.

In the century following 1815, however, the rustic peasantry in the outlying provinces experienced a transformation: in many cases, its cultural, and specifically linguistic particularity gained for it a symbolic status which had been held in relatively low esteem before, but which now became nothing less than a badge of national identity. Peasant unrest, usually driven by oppression, exploitation, poverty and lack of legal status, was thereby transmuted into a national emancipation movement. Nationalism and the pursuit of national independence did not, of course, replace the old grievances of poverty and oppression; but it provided an indispensable focus for large-scale self-identification and for a sense of solidarity between peasantry and an emerging professional class or bourgeoisie.

A sample case: Ireland

A well-documented example is that of Ireland.[168] The subjugation of Ireland to the English Crown dates back, as we have seen, to the twelfth century. But the incorporation of Ireland into an English polity was never successful. Throughout the Middle Ages, the feudal tendency among great Irish nobles (including Anglo-Norman creations like the Fitzgerald Earls) to ignore royal suzerainty would take the shape of 'English' versus 'Irish' loyalties. Tudor campaigns for undivided supremacy would be resisted in a double religious-cum-national stance that neatly aligned the oppositions English-Irish and protestant-catholic. Even the civil wars of the 1640s, which in England itself divided Crown and Parliament, became, in Ireland, an anti-English war, uniting Gaelic septs and English recusants in a common cause, and drawing upon them the undifferentiating, ruinous fury of Cromwell's campaign. In the eighteenth century, a colonial-style landlord system had been installed which saw a small class of landowners exploiting the country and its underclass of cheap, native labour. The ruthless oppression and exploitation of the peasantry was to some extent part of a general *ancien régime* pattern, comparable to what one can find in France, Spain or certain German states; accordingly, the Enlightenment Patriots who vindicated a society based on virtue, and who moved towards a benevolent paternalism vis-à-vis the peasantry, form part of a European trend. Nonetheless, there was also a colonial element in this situation in that the underclass was defined, not just in terms of social standing, but also in terms of religion and ethnicity. The peasantry was always referred to as *native*, and even the benevolent interest of the professional, urban and landowning classes was often sparked by an antiquarian or exoticist interest in what made them different and quaint: the Gaelic language, their music, songs, myths, annals and historical antecedents.

A crucial transition towards Irish nationalism proper takes place between 1800 and 1830. By 1800, the Irish peasantry, pauperized into increasing illiteracy and maintaining its cultural and common awareness largely through oral, face-to-face local and regional networks, showed its opposition largely in inchoate agrarian revolts flaring up here and there and fed by a folklore of carnivalesque symbols – fictional soubriquets like 'Captain Swing', 'Captain Moonlight' or 'Captain Rock' were the collective pseudonyms for bands of rebellious peasants. The wider political import of this unrest was not ignored altogether: folksongs referred to current affairs, e.g. the American War of Independence, or the rise of Napoleon, and would often invoke the possibility of political liberation. But when folksongs and poems express a yearning for some messianic redeemer who would break their bondage, the character was as often mythical or formulaic as that it was informed by real, actual politics. The common insurrection of 1798, linking peasant activists with Jacobin democrats from Belfast and other cities, had been singularly unsuccessful.

In the decades following 1800, however, the peasantry was forged into an efficient mass movement, and into a powerful political leverage, by the charismatic leader Daniel O'Connell (1775-1847).[169] His campaigns resemble those of Mahatma Gandhi and Martin Luther King in that they mobilized a rural, dispersed population and used its unified presence as an amplification instrument for demands for legal reform. O'Connell's campaigns managed, in 1828, to wrest Catholic emancipation from an unwilling British government: all official disabilities were removed which had reduced Catholics (the overwhelming majority of the Irish population) to non-citizens. The underlying peasant grievances were not redressed.

O'Connell's campaign for economic and legal reform was overtaken by an actual nationalist movement. This later movement invoked, crucially, the right of the Irish nation to self-determination; the rallying cry was no longer one of social justice, or the redress of grievances, but the recognition of Ireland's different culture, ethnicity and historical consciousness, legitimizing a different national status. This national ideology drew together various source traditions:

– There was, to begin with, a tenuous and almost-extinct tradition of native 'bardic' learning, now restricted to some locally educated scribes, genealogists and versifiers; this tradition had been given some sponsorship from the 1730s onwards by colonial, Protestant antiquaries and was given semi-professional employment in the learned societies and institutions of the early 1800s.

– Alongside this native tradition, and linked to it, there was the legacy of a Gaelic-aristocratic historical consciousness as laid down in books produced in the Catholic monarchies of the continent by continentally educated gentry and clergy in the seventeenth and eighteenth century. These books were retrieved and reproduced for a wider readership within Ireland in the course of the nineteenth century.

– Thirdly, there was the antiquarian interest and scholarship that flourished throughout the British Isles from the 1760s onwards. This antiquarian interest provided a facilitating urban and middle-class ambience for the languishing tradition of native lore. In the course of the nineteenth century, it developed from the curious pursuit of eccentric gentlemen-of-leisure into an increasingly public and influential affair.

– To no small extent, this interest in the Gaelic antiquity and roots of Ireland caught hold of the imagination, and of public opinion, as a result of its literary dissemination. The verse of Tom Moore, the national tales of Lady Morgan and others, the many popularizing history books and journals (such as the *Dublin Penny Journal*) spread the self-image of an Irish nationality rooted in a Gaelic antiquity (and languishing under English rule) across an urban, readership which itself was on the increase.

By the 1840s, when new educational systems (now open to, and indeed dominated by, Catholic teaching orders) drew on Gaelic antiquity for their school materials, something like a Gaelic orientation had taken hold of the Irish public sphere. What is more, that public sphere had itself emerged as a result of urbanization, Catholic empowerment and the rise of new, cheap print. The successor generation to O'Connell, significantly, used newspapers, pamphlets and other print media to spread its message (whereas O'Connell himself had largely relied on physical gatherings, fundraising networks and mass meetings). The flagship of the new, nationalist media, founded in 1842, was called, fittingly, *The Nation*. Among its contributors were Romantic intellectuals of the type encountered throughout Europe at the time: poets, journalists, democrats, idealists. The best-remembered among them, Thomas Davis (1814-1845), wrote verse inspired by Romantic literary nationalism *à la* Körner and by the glories of Gaelic antiquity, and designed multimedia efforts to propagate this Romantic ideal of a lost Irish nationhood amongst the population-at-large: he outlined a projected gallery of historical paintings, a history of Ireland consisting of ballads, etcetera. His rousing song 'A Nation Once Again' became the informal battle hymn of the Irish nationalist movement.

In short, the years between Daniel O'Connell and Thomas Davis see the emergence of an autonomist national movement which, as opposed to older forms of anti-English resistance, is characterized by a number of features aligning it with national movements elsewhere in Europe. It is propagated by men of letters and often carried by urban activists; it invokes cultural rather than economic or legal arguments, especially the fact that Ireland is set apart from England by its Gaelic language and by the ethnic roots and historical memories of the Gaelic population; it spreads by means of urban sociability and print media, that is to say, by taking over the public sphere and mobilizing public opinion. Indeed, the success of a cultural and philological interest in mobilizing a national movement seems crucially to depend on its power to fire a public sphere; and in a country like Ireland, that public sphere was only just beginning to emerge from an older downtrodden peasantry.[170]

To the extent that a public sphere had existed in Ireland, it had conformed to the characteristics drawn up by Benedict Anderson (1983) and Jürgen Habermas (1990): focussed around public spaces with a potential of sociability and opinion-making, such as coffee houses, clubs and playhouses, and later also spawning a printed press carrying these opinions to a wide readership that took an interest in public affairs, without being physically present at the places of congregation. This Irish public sphere, however, had throughout the eighteenth century been an exclusively Protestant affair. Enlightenment Patriotism had been built around the urban, genteel associations, playhouses, and printing presses of eighteenth-century Dublin; democratic radicalism had crystallized around the Dissenting associations and publishers of Belfast; but in all this eighteenth-century development the mass of the Catholic population was almost wholly absent and unrepresented. Catholic public opinion, such as it was, took shape mostly in the complicity of local balladeering and the inchoate outbreaks of agitation and unrest. This continued into the nineteenth century, when local disaffection was given a nationwide organizational aggregation under O'Connell. But the capture of the Irish public sphere by a literate, empowered class of Irish Catholics was only made possible after the achievement of Catholic emancipation of 1828. Thus the rise of Irish nationalism may be said to follow, not so much that old chestnut, the 'rise of a middle class', as much as the capture of the public sphere by the mass of the newly enfranchised Catholic population with a Gaelic self-awareness (whose rise from the peasantry to the status of working- and middle-class was facilitated in the same process). No sooner was the public space opened up in this way for the bulk of the population, or it became the sounding board for a Gaelic, Catholic self-image of what it meant to be Irish.

Following the catastrophic potato famines of 1845-1849, the Gaelic-speaking population was almost eradicated as a result of starvation, emigration and demographic uprooting. Paradoxically, the Irish public sphere had at that point become so suffused with a Gaelic self-image, that in the second half of the century a Gaelic language revival took hold, which, though originally bourgeois and apolitical in nature, was soon infiltrated and taken over by militant republican-separatist nationalists, many of

30. Douglas Hyde (on Irish banknote)

them from the Irish diaspora in America.* The combination of republicanism and language revivalism led, finally, to a short-lived uprising in 1916, led mainly by educationalists, poets and white-collar workers, at which the Irish Republic was proclaimed 'In the name of God and the dead generations', and on the basis of an ongoing 'tradition of nationhood' asserted throughout the centuries by a succession of anti-English insurrections:

> Irishmen and Irishwomen: In the name of God and the dead generations from which she receives her tradition of nationhood, Ireland, through us, summons her children to her flag and strikes for her freedom.

The phraseology is interesting: whereas earlier, pre-nationalist declarations of independence such as the Dutch Act of Abjuration and the American Declaration of Independence had invoked timeless moral notions of right and justice, and had derived their authority from the fact that they were enacted on behalf of the common interests of all members of society, we see this nationalist declaration invoke the authority of historical trans-generational continuity and the principle of nationhood, and on that basis exercise authority over the population at large (addressed as the children of a personified Ireland).

The insurrection was quickly put down, but the harshness of the British response galvanized Irish public opinion and fed an insurrection which eventually led to the establishment of an autonomous Irish Free State. That Free State followed, immediately upon its independence, a strenuous Gaelicization policy that continued the cultural-nationalist activism of the year 1890-1920; it was aimed at re-establishing the Gaelic language and at replacing the iconography of the British administration by a

---

* In this respect (though not in others), Irish nationalism corresponds to what Gellner 1983 classifies as 'diaspora nationalism': a separatist movement supported by an emigrant population elsewhere. Support from the US for Croatian, Ukrainian, Armenian and Zionist causes falls under this heading as well.

wholly Gaelic-Irish one. When that Free State later proclaimed itself a Republic, its first president was, symbolically, the founder of the 1890s language revival movement, Douglas Hyde (1860-1949).

General features of national movements

The Irish developments outlined here are representative of many national movements throughout Europe. In many cases, national movements begin with cultural consciousness-raising, pursued and triggered by intellectuals, men of letters, philologists and scholars. Linguistic, philological, historical and folkloristic research salvages, inventorizes and displays cultural heritages which often have been denigrated or which have receded into the informal, unheeded recesses of private life, without status, without prestige, sometimes even without a name. The project that brings these cultural relics and traditions into view is often undertaken without immediate political agenda, purely for its own sake, often by romantically minded bookworm-scholars. Their role (the cultural carriers of national thought and nationalism) was more important than their relative obscurity indicates.

The Czech scholar Miroslav Hroch has defined this incipience of national movements as the 'phase A' of nationalism; phases B and C signal the widening agenda and appeal of such movements. In 'phase B', demands for social reform are formulated on the basis of that self-awareness which has now been culturally articulated. Once cultural traditions and elements such as languages have been instrumentalized to articulate a given aggregate of rustics into a nation, that nation so constituted can become the platform of social demands; these will, typically, combine economic, constitutional and cultural concerns, involving matters of education, social and economic improvement, and some degree of autonomy (locally devolved administration or self-government). 'Phase C', finally, denotes the spread and intensification into a mass movement resisting the power of the state and often formulating an agenda of full separatism.[171]

Hroch's 'phase model' is a generalized extrapolation from many different cases and does not claim to offer a universal, rigid, one-pattern-fits-all template. Still, its general outline holds, broadly speaking, for a great majority of European national movements as these arose in the nineteenth and early twentieth centuries. The Irish trajectory, too, exhibits the features of the three successive phases: from Lady Morgan's *National Tales* and Thomas Moore's *Irish Melodies* (in the 1810s and 1820s) to the rise of *The Nation* in the 1840s we can see the Irish question raised increasingly in terms of cultural and literary interest; from the Young Irelanders around *The Nation* to the radicalization of the language revival movement around 1900, the demands for economic and educational reform fit the pattern of a B-phase; leading to the C-phase of unrest and armed insurrection culminating in the achievement of independence in 1921.[*]

---

[*] The Irish case also illustrates the complexities beneath the ABC schematization: social unrest and violence were endemic in the Irish situation even before the 'phase A' verse of Thomas Moore; it fed and intensified the 'phase B' demands of Thomas Davis; and in 'Phase C', what has here been

Examples from elsewhere in Europe serve to illustrate the trend. The Flemish movement in Belgium started in the field of philological text editions and cultural journalism (phase A, roughly 1830-1844), then formulated increasingly stringent demands for linguistic emancipation in a Phase B (roughly 1845-1900), and eventually developed an anti-Belgian separatist wing in the first half of the twentieth century.[172] Further parallel cases abound.

In the context of this book, which after all wishes to trace a cultural history of nationalism, phase A nationalism is of primary relevance. It is not usually the phase with which nationalism studies are most closely concerned; nationalism scholars tend to see phase A as a prequel, an incubation period, a prologue before the Real Action starts. Such neglect is regrettable for various reasons, two of which will be highlighted here.

To begin with, the cultural concerns that dominate phase A do not cease when phases B and C swing into action. On the contrary: nationalism as an ideology is by definition predicated on a set of cultural assumptions and interests (linking language, history, tradition, ethnicity and identity), and these persistently continue to influence the agenda of nationalism, regardless of 'phase'.

Secondly, phase A (early cultural nationalism) is a pan-European affair – as European as the spread of Romanticism at the beginning of the nineteenth century. Cultural nationalists were in communication, exchanging scholarly insights, literary discoveries, working methods and ideas. Indeed, it is phase A that binds European nationalism into a specifically European network of nationalisms, spanning Iceland and Bulgaria, the Basque country and Finland. These cross-continental crosscurrents need more investigation; they have hitherto been neglected because each 'phase A' movement in cultural nationalism has been studied piecemeal, separately, within its own national context as the precursor of its own succeeding phase B.

Early cultural nationalism often coincides with the discovery of the nation's identity, something which might even be called its 'invention' or 'construction'. We see national movements arise in nineteenth-century Europe invoke a nationality that was not (or barely) known as such a hundred years previously. Bulgarians[173] were an almost-unnoticed group of eastern Balkan Slavs until the early 1800s; they had been left out of the great inventory of languages commissioned by Catherine the Great in 1786, and it

---

described as the 'radicalization of the language revival movement' might also be described as the 'culturalization of the resistance movement'. What is more, cultural concerns in the nineteenth century picked up on older Jacobite and counter-Reformation ideologies. In short: it is possible to trace across the three phases A, B and C both a long-term cultural agenda and a long-term insurrectionary tradition. None of this, however, invalidates a Hroch-style phase model if one wishes to situate Irish developments in the context and typology of nineteenth-century European nationalism. The militant leader Patrick Pearse (†1916) emerges from the language movement, not the other way around; the language movement was prepared by Thomas Davis's nationalist glorification of Gaelic culture, not the other way around; Davis's glorification of a Gaelic-rooted nation drew on the work of scholars such as John O'Donovan and George Petrie, and followed the example of Tom Moore, not the other way around. The progression from scholarship to activism is complex, but does have a specific vector and sequential logic.

31. 'Macedonia is Greece since ever': sticker used in Greek duty free shops in 1990s

took a number of non-Bulgarian philologists like the Serb Vuk Karadžić and the Ukrainian Yurii Venelin to point out their Slavic identity in the period 1810-1830. Until that time, the assumption was widespread that the dimly remembered Bulgarian realms of the Middle Ages descended from a non-Slavic tribe of invaders like Turks or Magyars. Bulgarians themselves were subjects of the Ottoman Empire and members of the (Greek-speaking) Orthodox *millet* (religious constituency). The Slavic language that they spoke was used for informal, private and semi-private conversation. Only very gradually did a manuscript history of the Bulgarian nation, originally written in 1762 by a Mount Athos monk, Paisi Hilendarski, begin to circulate in manuscript; only very gradually did local merchants, driven by a philanthropic desire to benefit their community, take educational initiatives. The first book printed in Bulgarian was a school primer, sponsored by a physician who had trained in Paris. A Bulgarian identity was recognized initially among merchant communities abroad, e.g. in Odessa, and often as the result of philological insights coming in from abroad. Characteristically, the first political manifestation of this budding Bulgarian awareness was not a drive for political autonomy against Ottoman rule, but a church reform movement within the Greek-dominated Orthodox *millet*. In short: the articulation of a Bulgarian identity was not the straightforward outgrowth of endemic and persistent ethnic roots and traditions, but something that was inspired from abroad, as part of a general macroregional ordering of cultural categories, and facilitated by the ambience of rising modernity, sociability and an incipient public sphere.

Just how the various populations in the Balkans have crystallized into the nationalities we know nowadays is a complex and interesting process. Eighteenth-century geography had no knowledge of 'Bulgarians' or 'Macedonians'; Petar Beron, the man who sponsored the first Bulgarian schoolbook in 1824, called himself, for want of a better term, a 'Thracian', using a term from classical antiquity that at least had the virtue of familiarity. Conversely, eighteenth-century geography habitually spoke of tribes such as 'Morlacks' and 'Dalmatians', terms which now no longer denote any national group. The categories of nationality in the Balkans were built on shifting sands. At some points we see Bulgarians and Macedonians regard themselves (and each other) as variants of one and the same language group, at other times they vehemently assert their separateness. Serbs and Croats proclaimed the unity of their 'Serbo-Croat' language in 1850; by 2000 separate dictionaries and grammars were being written for Serb, for Croat and even for Bosnian.[174] Readers will be familiar with the hotly contested appellation 'Macedonian' which is also claimed by Greeks as referring to an ethnically and territorially Hellenic, not Slavic, category. There are dispersed or non-territorial populations that are seen only as 'ethnic groups', without 'national' status: Vlachs and Roma.

All this illustrates that the emergence of national identities from an 'ethnic' substratum (as per Anthony Smith's model) is anything but straightforward, and amounts in many cases to a self-invention. Crucially, what is required is not just a sense of identity or self-image, but an act of articulation, a *naming*. This self-identification by a shared and recognized appellation denoting a fairly unambiguous aggregate is a well-established given in Europe's 'old states' (Portugal, France, Denmark); in the case of Germany and its adjoining Low Countries we have seen (p. 157 above) that there are various competing aggregation models (German unity with or without Austria, including the Low Countries or not, or with a neighbouring Greater Netherlandic or Pan-Low-German complex). The process of self-articulation is even more complex and turbulent elsewhere. A language and population must be *recognized*, identified by name and outline as something separate with a separate culture; and this in turn presupposes the availability of a public sphere, an 'imagined community', for the speakers of that language. In many national movements in Europe, all that was by no means a self-evident pre-given.

The Baltic nations present another case in point.[175] Ancient feudal and ecclesiastical divisions in that region knew territories and populations by names like Courland, Livland, Samogitia etcetera. The demotic languages spoken there were (alongside the prominent and widespread Yiddish) the almost invisible, disregarded vernaculars of poor peasants and serfs, overlaid with German, Polish and Russian.[176] The emergence of something like Latvian next to Lithuanian, or Estonian alongside those two, was not the straightforward instrumentalization of a well-demarcated, recognized individual ethnicity, but the result of deliberate (and often contested) acts of demarcation and identification. It only succeeded because the constituency was created at the same time as its ethnic label: a public sphere that was opened up, sensitized and mobilized by means of learned societies for the urban professionals,[*] choral societies for the emancipating rural peasantry, reading rooms and newspapers: new social platforms, new cultural media, creating a public sphere where only a rustic peasantry had existed before.

Particularly instructive in this respect is the case of Finland.[177] It had been an integral part of Sweden for centuries, and Swedish was the language of learned, trans-local communication everywhere in the land. Finnish had the status in 1800 that Saa-

---

[*] The intellectuals and professionals who were the harbingers of cultural interest in the Baltics and on the Balkans were often physicians or clergy (Orthodox in the Balkans, Protestant or Catholic in the Baltic). Their work brought them in touch with the vernacular-speaking people; their education gave them a literate interest in their language and culture.

mi (the language of the 'Lapps') has nowadays: known to exist, but not used in other than dialect-vernacular situations. The first Romantics evincing a Finnish national awareness were, in fact, Swedish speakers (much as in Ireland, most nationalists used English rather than Gaelic): Runeberg, Arwidsson and the Åbo school. The creation and propagation of something like a Finnish national awareness was, again, the result of cross-national, macroregional developments. Sweden had to cede Finland to Russia as part of the 1815 rearrangement of the European map. This caused some misgivings among Finnish intellectuals, who feared a more autocratic, Russian-oriented regime; on the other hand, it brought Finnish territories into closer contact with the adjoining lands in Karelia and Bothnia which were ethnically Finnish and which had been less deeply Swedified; a more 'authentic', unspoilt Finnish culture came into view.

One statement, made by the Romantic poet Adolf Ivar Arwidsson, is famous for hitting this nail on the head: 'We are no longer Swedes, we can never become Russians, therefore let us be Finns'. From the 1830s onwards, Finnish emerged from the shadow of Swedish as the language that embodied Finnishness. This process was given a huge boost, in the 1830s and 1840, by the publication of oral epic material collected by a country physician, Elias Lönnrot (1802-1884). His practice had taken him to far-flung Finnish-speaking villages, where long epic ballads were recited full of legendary and mythological material. Lönnrot, inspired by the Romantic philology of his times, collected and collated the oral fragments he noted down like a Finnish Grimm, and joined them into what he believed was their primordial epic cohesion. The result was *Kalevala*; published in expanding editions in 1835 and 1849, it was quickly hailed as 'the Finnish national epic', comparable to what Homer had been for the Greeks, or the Nibelungenlied for Germany. Alongside *Kalevala* (which grew and expanded in later editions as Lönnrot found more oral material that he fitted into his overall composite), Lönnrot collected a great corpus of other ballads and songs, published as the *Kanteletar*. These publications gave enormous prestige to Finnish as the backbone of the country's national, ethnic identity. Swedish-speaking Romantics were gradually sidelined (Arwidsson moved to Sweden, where he became keeper of the Royal Library at Stockholm), and the country's identity was subsumed under an ideal of Finnishness. The language, now recognized and de-stigmatized as a viable means of communication, spread across society; literacy in it increased as its status rose. Demands for Finnish education were made. People with Swedish names like Forstman changed these to Finnish forms like Yrjö Koskinen. Eventually, as the Russian empire itself became less and less tolerant of non-Russian minority cultures,[*] cultural demands hardened into social activism, and phase A nationalism led to its B and C continuations, culminating

---

[*] Since the 1830s, Russian leaders and intellectuals had invoked the principles of 'Orthodoxy, autocracy, and nationality' (*pravoslaviye, samoderzhaviye, i narodnost*). After Tsar Alexander III had mounted the throne in 1881, these became the guidelines of government policy, leading to an increased intolerance to non-Russian and/or non-Orthodox minorities, especially in the Polish/Baltic/Finnish dominions. The ensuing repressive policy of Russification in turn fanned national commitment among Ukrainians, Latvians, Lithuanians, Estonians and Finns.

in Finnish independence. In the Finnish republic, the publication day of Lönnrot's *Kalevala* is still annually celebrated as a national holiday.

A spin-off of Finnish developments was felt in Estonia: there, Lutheran German clergy, assembled in clubs and societies such as the Learned Society of Dorpat*, took an interest in Estonian folklore that was fanned by the achievements of Lönnrot in Finland. Lönnrot's *Kalevala* was held up as an enviable example for Estonian folklorists, and one of them, Friedrich Kreutzwald, fitted Estonian oral material together into a similarly conceived epic whole, the *Kalevipoeg* (1854).

Summing up

Centralization, unification and separatist nationalism all occurred more or less simultaneously in nineteenth-century Europe, and frequently affected each other. Russian centralization policy hardened cultural emancipation movements in Finland, Ukraine and the Baltic lands; French centralism provoked Breton regionalists into fostering ties with the 'Celtic brothers' in Wales; German nationalism, inspired by anti-Napoleonic resistance in Spain early on, itself inspired the Flemish language emancipation movement. Indeed one of the outstanding features of nationalism is that it is a supremely international affair, spilling from one country to another, spreading ideas, books, and symbols freely across the map, spawning copycat movements at great distance. Irish nationalism at one point was inspired by philhellenism (James Hardiman's 1831 *Irish Minstrelsy* cites the example of Fauriel's *Chants populaires de la Grèce moderne*), at another by Hungarian nationalism (Arthur Griffith's 1904 *The Resurrection of Hungary*). The point needs to be stressed: a national movement in a given country is not just the result of the circumstances obtaining within that country, but also inspired by the crisscrossing traffic of ideas all over Europe.

Why do I emphasize this point? Not only because it affects the way in which one should study nationalism (namely, on a comparative-European basis, with due attention to its cultural aspects), but also because it helps us to avoid unnecessary and even unhelpful distinctions in how we see nationalism. Nationalism might manifest itself differently in France than it does in Italy, differently in Germany than it does in Greece or Finland – but in each case, the underlying agenda is the same: to give the state a national foundation, and to adjust the state's territorial outline to its underlying cultural catchment area. Again, distinctions have been made between a 'Western' and an 'Eastern' type of nationalism, the former rational and liberal, the latter metaphysical

---

* Dorpat was the German name of present-day Tartu. The demarcation of public spaces often went as far as re-naming, not only streets, but even entire cities from their imperially imposed forms to native, vernacular ones. Laibach is now Ljubljana, Agram is now Zagreb, Neusatz is now Novi Sad, Pressburg Bratislava, Maryborough and Kingstown Portlaoise and Dún Laoghaire. In Finland, Åbo is now Turku, although Swedish is still a recognized second language in Finland, and the name Åbo is accordingly maintained. Language activism in Wales, Belgium and elsewhere still involves the contested forms of place names, and includes the graffiti-style blotting-out of place names on road signs in the resisted language.

and totalitarian – but in the Ukraine, the federalist ideals of Pan-Slavism are much more liberal and democratic than the totalitarian implications of French Jacobinism, at the opposite western end of Europe, with its ruthless, Spartan sense of what it means to be a citizen. The distinction between 'civic' and 'ethnic' nationalism – one derived from the democratic-republican heritage of Rousseau, the other from the cultural thought of Herder – is by no means useless, but would become unhelpful if we didn't realize that in most cases, national movements partake of both aspects: there are usually vestiges of civic libertarianism even in ethnic nationalism, and at the heart of civic nationalism there are often unstated ethnic assumptions as to who belongs, and who doesn't.[178]

The result of this Europe-wide activism was, eventually, a re-drawing of the European map. The chaotic opening decades of the twentieth century saw the downfall of imperial rule in Germany, Austria, Russia and Turkey, leading to the emergence of new states (sovereign or autonomous) from Finland and Norway to Ireland and Iceland across Europe's northern rim, and to Bulgaria and Albania in the south-east. Elsewhere, the emergence of regionalist or national movements was arrested but had nevertheless taken hold: in the Basque country, in Catalonia, in Flanders. The idea at the 1919 Paris Peace Conference was to ensure for each nation of Europe its self-determination; after all, it was partly for the sake of small, overrun countries like 'brave little Belgium' (as it had been called in British war propaganda) that the victorious powers had gone to war. The underlying, Mazzini-style reasoning was that once each nation-state was happy within its ethnic solidarity and in its political sovereignty, there would be fewer reasons to wage war, and the Great War might truly turn out to have been 'The war to end all wars'.

All this would seem, then, the run-up to a great rationalization of the European cultural-political landscape along the lines of a just and equitable 'self-determination of peoples'. But in fact, there was a major shadow side to all this. The translation of national emancipation programmes into territorial divisions, the move from culture into geopolitics, was deeply flawed; and deep at the heart of all national movements there were ancient ethnocentric and xenophobic attitudes that inexorably drove the ideology to the right and even the extreme right of the political spectrum.

The 'Versailles system' that emerged from the Paris Peace Conference (see below, 219 ff.) pretended, to some extent, to translate national cultural differences into national political frontiers. The next section will deal with the underlying flaws of this 'geopolitical mapping of cultural differences'.

Identity Rampant

The Nation's Sources, the State's Borders: Culture into Geopolitics

Irredentism

The term 'irredentism' is an offshoot of the Italian national movement, the *risorgimento*; it refers to the part of the Italian 'nation' still outside the free Italian state, not yet redeemed from foreign bondage. The yearning of the Slaves' Chorus in Verdi's *Nabucco* ('Va pensiero, sull'ali dorate') reverberated throughout Europe: lack of freedom was everywhere considered tantamount to *foreign* bondage, a domestic exile. Italy saw Italians outside its frontiers, under Habsburg rule, from Istria to Tyrol, and the agenda of independence was soon translated into an agenda of territorial expansion so as to embrace unredeemed Italy, *Italia Irredenta*, into the free homeland. One of the most arresting episodes of this irredentist urge is provided by the poet Gabriele D'Annunzio (1863-1938): originally a sensuous-sentimental poet, his elitism and adoration for the ideas of Nietzsche gradually made him list to the ideology of authoritarianism and fascism.[*] He took a strongly belligerent stance in the First World War. He lost an eye, and staged the remarkable stunt of dropping propaganda leaflets on Vienna in 1918. Himself a heroic and charismatic fighter pilot, his fighter squadron was called '*La Serenissima*', a reference to Venice (until recently part of the Habsburg empire).[†] After the war, D'Annunzio went as far as seizing, like a newfangled Garibaldi, the Istrian town of Rijeka/Fiume with a 700-strong band of followers, proclaiming himself *Duce* of the new territory.[179] And successfully so: although the arrangements made at the Paris Peace Conference had stipulated otherwise, Fiume was subsequently attached to Italy.

Irredentism is by no means unique to the Italian case. In almost every instance where a national independence movement achieves territorial incorporation as a new state, there will be disputes as to the territorial outlines of that state. In each case, the logic of nationalism will urge a territorial expansion so as to include all fellow-nationals within the new state's territory. Additionally, once established frontiers have been raised as an issue owing to national movements, the demands of geopolitics will often also lead to expansionist claims. Thus, as has been mentioned, the Prime Minis-

---

[*] A similar trend can be noticed in the development of the Irish poet William Butler Yeats (1865-1939); also, the case of Stefan George (1868-1933) shows some similarities. The fascist sympathies of these closely contemporary, elitist *fin-de-siècle* poets were inspired by their distaste of modern-style democracy, but at the same time they were also kept in check to some extent by their elitism. While they endorsed the fascist creed of the Strong Leader, they despised the populism inherent in fascist movements. For Yeats: Foster 1997-2003, McCormack 2005; for George: Strodthof 1976.

[†] Pilots were seen as the most gallant of 'supermen', acquiring considerable charisma – the early rise and status of Hermann Goering was largely due to his reputation as a fighter 'ace' in the First World War; and Yeats celebrated the heroism of the fighter pilots repeatedly in his poems.

ter of a newly independent Serbia, Ilija Garašanin, formulated a Draft Plan (*nacarta-nije*) in the late 1840s calling for a Greater Serbia, based, not only on the national (anti-Ottoman) ideal of a united Slavic-Orthodox state in the Balkans, but also on the geopolitical needs for Serbia to have seaports at the Adriatic and elsewhere.

The most pronounced example of irredentism in Europe is probably the case of Greece. The independent state established in the 1820s and consolidated in 1832 as the Kingdom of the Hellenes originally covered little more than the Peloponnese, with Navplion for its capital. Attica and the rest of Southern Greece, as well as a number of islands, merged into the independent Greece in subsequent decades, and the capital was accordingly moved to Athens. Throughout the nineteenth century, more norther-ly regions (Arcadia, Macedonian lands around Salonika including the Chalcedonica peninsulas, parts of Epirus and Thrace) followed suit, and on the islands (like Crete) there was a strong urge among ethnic Hellenes towards *enosis* or 'unification'. In the later parts of the century, this expansion seemed to follow a historicist logic: known as the *Megali idea* or 'Great Concept', it envisaged bringing all ethnic Greeks together into a mighty state that would revive the traditions of Alexander the Great and the Byzantine Empire.[180] Since Greeks were, at that time, a far-flung diaspora with settle-ments (like the Armenians) throughout the Ottoman-ruled Levant, the ultimate bor-ders of the new Greater Greece allowed for considerable latitude: there were Hellenic colonies on the shores of the Black Sea, throughout Anatolia (in particular in the coastal cities), even in Alexandria and Cairo. The more idealistic irredentists dreamed of a re-conquest of Istanbul/Constantinople, and a re-dedication of its main mosque, the Hagia Sophia, to Christian worship under the Ecumenical Patriarch. All crises of the crumbling Ottoman empire were exploited towards this end, and in 1920, briefly, Greek armies held not only the territory of what is now Greece but also a considerable portion of Western Anatolia around the city of Smyrna/Izmir.[181] (In the event, the Anatolian conquest was recaptured by the Turkish army, and the demarcation between Greece and Turkey was settled in a traumatic population-exchange, the first and by no means the least of the ethnic cleansings in the region.)

Thus the establishment of a successful separatist movement may with gradual logic shift into an irredentist expansion: a partial realization of national-separatist goals is achieved by establishing a territorial 'foothold', from where the continuing secessionist agenda is pursued further. In quite the opposite corner of Europe, Ireland, we see how the establishment of a Free State was grudgingly accepted by a part of the nationalist movement as a 'second best' solution, in that a northern part of Ireland (in Ulster) was left within the United Kingdom. A more fundamentalist wing of the national move-ment refused to accept this compromise, resulting in a civil war within the new Free State; both wings, however, considered the Ulster partition as an unsatisfactory stop-gap measure and continued to lay claim to the entire territory of the island of Ireland.

The unresolved problems of national frontiers have been, in each and every case, the fly in the ointment of national self-determination. They continue to addle public affairs in Europe, albeit in different degrees of intensity. The South Tyrolean problem, fairly harsh throughout the 1950s and 1960s, has found some accommodation in a multicultural regional policy;[182] tensions still ride high in the Istrian and Triestine borderlands between Italy and Slovenia. Sharper conflicts persist between Greece and

Turkey (and on the island of Cyprus), and in Northern Ireland. The splitting-up of Yugoslavia into various ethnic regions has been notoriously, and tragically, intractable. In every case, it appears that the territorial demarcation and 'mapping' of cultural identities is highly problematic, and tends to call forth more problems than it sets out to solve.

The incommensurability of 'frontiers'

Political frontiers are of a wholly different nature than cultural borders.[183] A frontier between states will mark off different sovereign, mutually exclusive jurisdictions in an absolute, black-and-white fashion. Five metres on one side of a border post, I am subject to the laws of one state, five metres beyond, I am bound by the wholly different laws of a wholly different state. There is no gradual transition, no grey in-between-zone: political frontiers are razor sharp and absolute.

Cultural borders, on the other hand, are almost never of this nature. They are usually many miles 'thick', consisting of a mixed population where one language area or cultural catchment area gradually shades into another, and where the people are either familiar with both cultures, or else exhibit a mixed in-between-form. Languages shade into each other by way of dialect variants or hybrid creolizations, and borderlands usually exhibit a measure both of bilingualism and of diglossia (i.e. there are two, or more, languages current in the area, and many speakers are themselves fluent in both of them). Religions will usually coexist in territorial proximity and with intermingled populations, sometimes (as in the case of Albania) even sharing the same sacred locations in different liturgical contexts.[184] Orthodox, Catholic and Islamic are intermingled in Bosnia, Protestant and Catholic in Belfast; speakers of Danish and German are a *mixum gatherum* in Schleswig, as are speakers of German, Italian and Ladin in Alto Adige (Southern Tyrol), or speakers of Netherlandic and French in Brussels.

A territorial division of such mixed regions is almost never clear-cut; it will, at best, separate a 51 per cent majority 'over here' from a 49 per cent minority 'over there' by tortuously meandering and deeply resented, contested frontiers. These, in turn, are open to manipulation; the accusation of gerrymandering (outlining electoral districts in such a way as to let certain groups carry more voting weight than others) is never far off and frequently justified.

As a political model, nationalism has two main flaws. One is the uncertain idea of what a 'nation' actually *is*. (I shall address this problem, and some of its consequences, in the next chapter.) The other is the blithe and naive assumption that it is possible to translate cultural identity, however defined, into sovereign territories. If, in the definition of the great scholar Ernest Gellner, nationalism can be defined as the attempt to achieve congruence between the cultural and the political unit, i.e. to map political frontiers onto cultural borders, then on scrutiny we must conclude that this is as impossible as to measure the outline of a flock of starlings with a pair of calipers. Yet that is what the ideology of nationalism sets out to do: to fix in politics the profile of culture. And who will expect nationalists to confine their nation in restricted, narrow frontiers that embrace only one part of the nation and exclude other parts? Irredentism is not an anomalous derailment of nationalism, but its logical and almost unavoidable extension.

The logical transmutation of nationalism into irredentism can be traced in the pronouncements of national activists: it is they who, after first having identified and vindicated a cultural identity, then propose to give that identity a political expression and a right to self-determination. In the process, they make a crucial step from the moral and intellectual sphere to a demarcation of territory.

Culture is like the weather. It affects all of us but belongs to no one and to no place. It manifests itself a set of behavioural choices and preferences transmitted across generations, involving religion, language, values and historical memories. Culture is not in itself territorial; its geographical outlines need be no more fixed than those of vegetarianism, Quakerism or Jewishness. A language is not a geographical fixture like a mountain range or a coastline: it moves wherever its speakers move. Heinrich Heine, German poet living in Paris, called the German language his 'portable fatherland'. Many cultures live in diasporas; many cities, even in early modern and nineteenth-century Europe, are receptacles for the influx of many different cultures. To vindicate the rights of a culture is, then, not itself a territorial demand. Indeed, in Central and Eastern Europe the various 'phase A' beginnings of national movements were located extraterritorially, in the multi-ethnic cities of those multi-ethnic empires. Bulgarian, Greek and Serbian cultural activists started their work in places like Odessa, Vienna, Budapest, Istanbul.

The nationalist translation of cultural emancipation demands into a political agenda involves, crucially, a step towards territorialization; and in most cases, this is where a fatefully agonistic note sets in. Douglas Hyde vindicated Gaelic traditions and the Gaelic language in a programme which he himself considered 'purely cultural', and, as such, above party politics; at the same time, his proclamation that Ireland was, 'and has always been, Celtic to the core', had to dismiss the troublesome fact that this view was not shared by the British-oriented, Protestant population of Ulster. They were mentioned and dismissed in a breezy semi-sentence ('in spite of some Saxon admixture in the North-East').[185] Irish nationalism always claimed two things which, in their incompatibility, reflect the incompatibility of culture and territorialism: one the one hand, it asserts the difference of Ireland from England on the basis of Ireland's rootedness in an aboriginally Celtic culture; on the other hand, it claims to speak for all of Ireland. The Protestants of Ulster fall between the cracks of those two claims: they are part of the Irish territory, but are not rooted in aboriginally Celtic culture. The result is a dilemma: to include Ulster in an independent Ireland would be to ride roughshod over its Protestants' self-identification and express wishes; to leave Ulster out of such an Ireland, and within a United Kingdom, is to do the same thing to that region's nationalist Catholics. Are Ulster Catholics a minority within Ulster, or part of a majority within Ireland-as-a-whole? Are Ulster Protestants a minority within Ireland, or part of a majority within the United Kingdom? The question is unanswerable and must in any case come to terms with the fact that Irish-oriented Catholics and British-oriented Protestants live in close (though not friendly) proximity, and that to separate them territorially would be like drawing a dividing line between the black and white pebbles on a beach.

The role of the philologists: Tongue, tribe and territory

The ideal of mapping culture into territories is, then, a chimera. But where does it come from? Leaving aside the older European patterns of reconciling the 'law of the land' (*ius soli*) with the 'law of the bloodline' (*ius sanguinis*),[*] or of settling religious divisions, the origin seems to lie, once again, in the historicist backlash against Napoleonic upheavals. Once again we may take as a case in point the German cultural critic Ernst Moritz Arndt.

Arndt, whom we have repeatedly encountered as the spokesman of anti-French attitudes in early-nineteenth-century Germany, had written a 'rebel song' during the anti-Napoleonic insurrection which became almost the unofficial national anthem of pre-Bismarck Germany. It was called *Was ist des Deutschen Vaterland*, 'What is the German's fatherland?', repeating that pregnant question in every stanza, taking a bird's eye view of all the German lands and regions, from the sea coast to the Alps, one after the other, and concluding, each and every time: 'Nay! his fatherland is greater than that!' The German's fatherland, so Arndt argued, was greater than any separate region; it was the sum total of all of them, *das ganze Deutschland*, circumscribed by the furthest reach of the German language:

> As far and wide as the German language is heard
> Singing the praises of God on high:
> That is where it should be!
> That, bold German, you may call yours!

This blunt equation of language and territory, squarely countering Goethe's ironic *Deutschland, aber wo liegt es?*, was to echo throughout German nineteenth-century history. The song was a favourite on the repertoire of any male choir, sung at frequent sociable and political gatherings, and its impact was such that thirty-five years later, when the elderly Arndt was a member of the Frankfurt Parliament, the assembly spon-

---

* Fundamentally, that distinction concerns the question whether a person is governed by the laws of his tribe, or by the laws of his dwelling place. Usually, the latter (*ius soli*, law of the land) applies: a Dutchman in Austria is subject to Austrian, not Dutch law. *Ius sanguinis* has historically been most important in cases of royal succession: the genealogical/tribal descent of the royal house might decide whether succession through the female line is, or is not permitted. Again, *ius sanguinis* lies behind the constitutional right of any ethnic German, or any Jew, to claim German or Israeli citizenship. In Belgium, the arrangement of linguistic rights has vacillated between the two modes: at times, the use of either Flemish or French was legally permissible anywhere throughout Belgium, depending on the preference of the citizen concerned; this 'personality principle' has by and large been replaced by a 'territoriality principle', where Flemish is the legally established language of the north, French of the south.

taneously gave him an ovation and a vote of thanks, citing, in particular, this one song.[186]

Arndt's *Was ist des Deutschen Vaterland* reverberated in many other patriotic songs of the nineteenth century, each of them becoming national, nationalist 'classics': Hoffmann von Fallersleben's *Lied der Deutschen* also, as we have seen, subsumes the inner divisions of a fragmented complex of German statelets into an amply drawn *Deutschland*; and in particular the river Rhine was claimed as the main artery and bulwark of a greater 'Germany' in songs like Nicolaus Becker's *Rheinlied* ('The French shall not lay their hands upon that free, German Rhine'). Max Schneckenburger's *Die Wacht am Rhein* also served as a German national anthem in the nineteenth century: 'Dear fatherland, you may rest easy, firm stands the Guard on the Rhine'.

All of these songs stake geopolitical claims as to the territory and outline of a beloved 'Germany'. Arndt himself showed how these claims were in fact defined and drawn up; and here we notice, once again, that the influence of culture on politics involves, not only a straightforward adoption of poetic ideals by political leaders, but also a transmission through the field of learning and scholarship. In Arndt's writings, influential as they were on public opinion, his song and his activist prose formed only the tip of a pyramid which had, for its base, the genre of learned-antiquarian disquisition. Arndt himself had straddled the gap between cultural criticism and political activism repeatedly in his various pamphlet disquisitions, most famous among them the brochure proclaiming the Rhine 'Germany's river, not Germany's border' (*Der Rhein, Teutschlands Strom, nicht Teutschlands Gränze*, 1812). It cast its influence over German negotiators at the Congress of Vienna, where the geopolitical feature of the German states would be decided briefly afterwards. Prussia then obtained its Rhineland Provinces; but how far were these to reach? Arndt felt strongly that the Alsace, with Strasbourg, ought to become German again, and also the entire Rhine basin, from Basel to Rotterdam and Antwerp. This went against the French claims on the Alsace, and the establishment of an independent kingdom of the Netherlands as a strong buffer state between France and Germany.*

Arndt wanted to see Germany's western border run from Dunkirk through the Ardennes to Luxembourg and Saarbrücken, in effect annexing the entire modern-day Benelux and Alsace-Lorraine. Characteristically, his arguments were a combination of raw geopolitical power-calculations (Germany needed shipping control over the Rhine and would profit from access to the sea by way of Antwerp and Rotterdam) and historicist and philological learning: The Low Countries had formerly been part of the Holy Roman Empire; it had been a mistake to release the United Provinces into independent sovereignty in 1648; the language spoken in all these territories was Dutch, or Flemish, or some other such dialect with might properly be classified as 'German';

---

* That new Kingdom of the Netherlands, in the ambition of its monarch-designate (a scion of the Orange-Nassau dynasty), should for its south-eastern frontier have the Rhine as far south as Koblenz (where the Moselle was to form its southern border from Koblenz to Luxembourg). In the event, the new kingdom came to occupy the territory of what nowadays are the Benelux countries.

and the tribes which had inhabited these parts in ancient times, Franks and others, had been Germanic tribes.

With this mode of reasoning, Arndt set in motion three important intellectual trends: the translation of cultural and ethnographic patterns (like language and ancient tribal habitations) into contemporary political and territorial claims; a remarkably fuzzy usage of the concept of language to include, at will, neighbouring languages as mere dialect variations; and a tendency to look to the past as justification, and even to see the most ancient past (that of primitive tribal periods) as the most fundamentally and transhistorically valid. This last point foreshadows a tendency to argue, not only from history, but even from ethnographical patterns – a trend which will be more amply discussed below.

Arndt returned to his linguistic-historical-ethnographic claims time and again throughout the course of his long career. He ceaselessly vindicated the right of Germany to annex Alsace-Lorraine, the Low Countries, and Schleswig-Holstein, and each time argued for the historical necessity and the political justification of these regions reverting to the German motherland from which they had branched off. The fact that, upon his acclamation at the Frankfurt Parliament, he was appointed to that body's Committee for Foreign Relations indicates the potential leverage of his ideas.

In the realm of learning, Arndt's views were taken over by an entire generation of philologically minded intellectuals. Among them, Jacob Grimm soon became a leading personality. Grimm follows Arndt in linking the language and the nation, the linguistic and the ethnic category. German is as German speaks. In a famous definition from the mid-1840s, Grimm explicitly linked the two:

> Let me begin with the simple question, What is a people? –
> and reply with the equally simple answer: A people is the
> sum total of persons speaking the same language.[187]

Like Arndt (and most philological scholars of his generation), Grimm was deliberately vague, however, as to what formed, or did not form, part of the 'German' language. In his *Deutsches Wörterbuch*, the concept covered only standard German: that 'High German' that was consolidated by Luther's Bible translation. (For this reason, Grimm and fellow-Protestants always celebrated Luther as the true champion, both of German identity and or German morality, these two being interconnected concepts: not only had Luther resisted Roman corruption, he had also cut short the enervation of the German language by an insidious Latinity.) However, in the *Deutsche Grammatik*, we see that the term *Deutsch* covers all the Germanic languages of Europe: from ancient Gothic to Anglo-Saxon, from Icelandic to Frisian and Flemish – all of this centring, of course, around the German language in the narrower sense of the word, which is thereby canonized into the linchpin and gravitational core of this linguistic cluster. Much as German unification nationalism was an attempt to gather all the German lands into a great whole, the logic of that project tended to great-German expansionism: to gather all those areas which could be called 'German', in however elastic a meaning, into the motherland. Both in German unification and in German expansionism, philologists set the agenda.

32. Jacob Grimm

Whenever a terminological obfuscation concerning the outlines of the term and the language area of 'German' occurs, it will be in order to extend rather than to diminish the hegemonic claims of High German amidst its adjoining Germanic sister languages. What people speak in Holland, in Flanders, in Friesland or in Jutland can be easily grouped, foggily, as 'Low Germanic' or 'Low German', kindred languages, or possibly variants of German-in-the-larger-sense, or possibly dialects in a subaltern satellite relationship to German-proper... Thus, linguistic problems of taxonomy (where does dialect variation stop, and a separate different language begin?) shade into problems of the catchment area of the German nation, its identity and its fatherland. Throughout the nineteenth century, this was to place an intellectual mortgage on two German borderlands in particular: the Low Countries in the West, and Schleswig-Holstein in the North.

The first overt sign of Grimm's expansionist 'linguistic geopolitics' came in his confrontation with the great Danish scholar Rasmus Rask (1787-1832), as early as 1812. It is now generally recognized that Rask was a major influence on the linguistic development of the young Grimm. Grimm read Rask's grammatical work, which contained first descriptions of what is now known as the 'Germanic consonantal shifts', as well as ideas on *Umlaut* and *Ablaut*, after having himself published the first volume of his German grammar; such was the importance of Rask's insights for what Grimm set out to do, that he revised this first volume and introduced the systematic analysis of consonantal shifts, now known as 'Grimm's Laws' (cf. below, p. 260).

Rask and Grimm were to prove rivals rather than collaborators, however, and much of this was a national Danish-German rivalry. It was announced as early as 1812, when a young Grimm reviewed Rask's Icelandic/Old-Norse grammar of 1811. The following remarkable passage is worth quoting in full:

> Each individuality is sacred, also in language; it is to be
> hoped that even the smallest, least-regarded dialect (which
> certainly will harbour unobtrusive advantages over the great-
> est and most prestigious languages) be left to itself, its own
> nature, without coercion. The value of Danish is beyond
> question: that important language which, by virtue of its
> outstanding output, commands the respect of ourselves as
> much as of its own speakers. It is praiseworthy in the Danish
> people that they resist the open intrusion of German words
> and phrases; yet it would be foolish to believe that a million
> and a half people (all of Scandinavia numbers no more than 5
> million) can close themselves off against the irresistible influ-
> ence of a language, spoken by 32 million and closely related,
> which great minds have now set alight for ages to come; or to
> believe that an awareness of this overpowering superiority
> should count, in Denmark, as something dishonourable.
> German culture and literature holds sway in no ignoble fash-
> ion: in Lower Saxony and in Austria it is appreciated by peo-
> ple who nonetheless cherish their local dialect (with which,
> by the way, we do not wish to compare Danish). The best
> minds of Denmark have seen rightly and acted wisely: they
> know that they belong to German literature as much as it
> belongs to them.

Grimm then proceeds to vindicate German authors as being superior to the Danish ones, and concludes:

> This effusion concerning our language and literature may
> seem to some overly long and ill-mannered, I nevertheless
> considered it just and necessary. It must have pained every
> German to see, even in recent days, from a recent public de-
> cree of the Danish government that in the German-speaking
> lands under its rule the German language is to be gradually
> discouraged, repressed even. Is it not reasonable, O thou
> German, that the language, which in the cradle thou hast

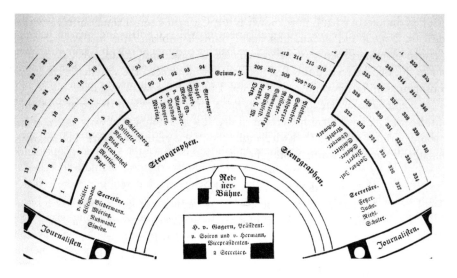

33. Seating arrangement at the Frankfurt Nationalversammlung.

drunk in from the sweet murmurings of thy mother, together
with her milk, should be dear and precious to thee?!* [188]

As an old man, Grimm (like Arndt) was to stick to his attitudes of the 1810s. The relationship with Rask had from an early moment gone sour over the irreconcilable national loyalties of both scholars; and in German-Danish relations generally, the question of Schleswig-Holstein, already alluded to in the fragment quoted above, was to remain a vexed and contentious issue. The Danish government deployed policies of cultural centralization as did other European states at the time, and wished to curb the ancient heteronomy of Holstein (which was only linked to Denmark in a personal union, and also formed part of the German Confederation). Danish centralization measures were much resented among German speakers in Holstein and elsewhere in Germany, Arndt and Grimm taking the lead. Things came to a head when in 1844 the Estates of Holstein declared the duchies of Schleswig and Holstein independent of the Danish Crown; Denmark retorted by placing the wayward province under direct, central rule (1846-1848), which in turn provoked the first Danish-Prussian War (1848-1850).[189]

The events of the 1840s were spurred on to no small extent by a nationalist groundswell in German public opinion. It was here that Arndt and Grimm played

---

* The concluding rhetorical question is paraphrased from Justus Georg Schottelius (1612-1676), an early legal scholar, grammarian and lexicographer, who sought to purify the German language; a figure who obviously appealed to Grimm during the period of Napoleonic domination. Grimm later included the quotation in his Deutsches Wörterbuch (s.v. *Gesäusel*).

prominent roles. This can be gauged from their stance in the portentous *Nationalversammlung* of 1848; the Frankfurt Parliament in which scholars and men of learning, like Dahlmann, Arndt and Grimm played such a prominent role. It was in this *Nationalversammlung* that Arndt was acclaimed in a spontaneous vote of thanks for his patriotic verse; it was in this *Nationalversammlung* that Grimm was given a seat all of his own, directly opposite the Speaker, in the central aisle between the Right and the Left, symbolizing his transcendent importance for the nation-at-large.

In the *Nationalversammlung's* deliberations, both Arndt and Grimm spoke repeatedly on the German right to support and indeed embrace the German people under foreign rule. Grimm went as far as to propose a motion that war should be declared on the kingdom of Denmark until all rights to Schleswig and Holstein were ceded to Germany. What makes this intervention truly remarkable is Grimm's historical justification. He declares, in the course of his speech, that he believes in a long-term historical grounding for national policies, and refers to painstaking research undertaken by him as to the antiquity of the lands in question. In the course of these somewhat breathless and rambling remarks, Grimm proffers the usual mixture of linguistic and antiquarian-ethnographic arguments, the usual confusion as to his chosen ethnic names and categories, and the direct transmutation from tribal antiquity and historical memory into territorial claims:

> I have immersed myself for a long time in research concern-
> ing the history of those northern regions, and I have come to
> conclusions which are in part very different from what was
> accepted until now. [...] according to my research, the Jutes,
> which until now have been considered the indigenous inha-
> bitants of the northern half of the peninsula, these Jutes were
> also an originally Germanic tribe – to the extent that we are
> in a position to oppose Germanic tribes and Scandinavian
> ones. But what memories does the history of that northern
> region evoke! From there, even before the Christian year-
> count, did those two peoples swarm out who filled the
> mighty Romans with insurmountable fears, the Kimbrians
> and Teutons, who carry the same name as we do. Should that
> not be a cause for just pride? Truly, other nations would not
> tolerate even a sod to be taken off the dwelling-place of their
> renowned ancestors.[190]

Not even a sod from the land of our renowned ancestors... that is the irredentism, based, not on present-day population data, but on historical memories, which drives Serbian claims to Kosovo and Zionist claims to all of *Eretz Israel*. Land has been invested with deeply ingrained collective-historical memories and therefore, no matter what demographic changes have occurred in the meantime, continues to 'belong', both in a moral and in a geopolitical sense, to the present-day descendants of the erstwhile inhabitants: as an inheritance.

Readers will also have noted the equivocation between 'Germanic' and 'Scandinavian', which are, yet are not, seen as distinct categories. As a result the Danish inhabitants of Jutland are lifted out of the Scandinavian, Nordic category, and included in the 'German(ic)' one, even though Grimm admits at the same time that 'Scandinavian' and 'Germanic' are as distinct as the left-hand and right-hand-side of a glass of water. And the 'research' that underpins this remarkable, and (according to Grimm) new scientific insight? The claim is portentous; Grimm, after all, spoke as the greatest philological scholar of his generation, respected far and wide throughout Europe, the man who had discovered 'Grimm's laws' and who had opened the treasure-house of the Fairy Tales, with literally dozens of honorary doctorates, academy memberships and book dedications to his name. Surely a claim to scientific proof as to the radically German nature, not only of Schleswig-Holstein, but of the entire peninsula of Jutland, from such a source, counted for much. Grimm does not deliver any substantiation for this claim in his parliamentary harangue; but we find the background worked out more fully in a book that appeared in the selfsame year 1848: the *Geschichte der deutschen Sprache*. The surprisingly small rabbit that Grimm pulls out of his irredentist hat consists of a dialect feature in Jutland Danish (the article being placed before, not after the noun) which he considers a sign of Saxon/German (as opposed to Danish/Scandinavian) roots.

This book shows the Grimm of 1848 to be essentially the same fatherland-loving Grimm of his 1830 inaugural lecture at Göttingen, and of the 1812 review of Rask. It surveys the various dialects and variants of the German complex, aligning each dialect with an ancient tribe and linking, consistently, ethnic and linguistic categories. Grimm not only surveys the dialects of German in the narrow (High-German) sense (Franks, Hessians, Saxons etc.) but also of 'neighbouring and deep-down related nations' (*die sprachen der uns benachbarten und urverwandten völker*). It is here that he political intentions become obvious. As he himself phrases it in his dedication to Gervinus: 'This is, for one who can read from its contents the tasks and dangers facing our fatherland, a thoroughly political book.' Grimm sees warnings in history: 'Lorraine, Alsace, Switzerland, Belgium and Holland have been alienated from our realm, though [*and here he makes a tell-tale reservation:*] one does not wish to say: irrevocably so.' Here as elsewhere, Grimm testifies to a desire to see these abandoned regions return to the German fold – much in the spirit of Arndt. And the same goes for Denmark:

> Much as recent quarrels between Danes and Swedes have
> awakened the slumbering sense of their close relationship, so
> too our current tiff with the Scandinavians will give way to a
> fraternal bond, as required insistently by the community of
> languages. If a grand association [between Germany and
> Scandinavia] be given internal divisions, should the proble-
> matic peninsula [Jutland, JL] not be given wholly to the con-
> tinent, as demanded by history, nature and position? How
> could the Jutes not return to their ancient attachment to the
> Angles and Saxons, the Danes [of the islands, JL] to that of

the Goths [of southern Sweden, JL]? Once Germany has been given its new form, Denmark cannot possibly continue to exist it is present form.[191]

Elsewhere in the book, Grimm returns to this historical necessity:

> Not only among the nations themselves, also in the languages they speak there is an unavoidable gravitation towards central points. The desire for a unification of all tribes, now so vividly awakened, will not cease. I consider it probable, and also wholesome for all 'German' peoples, that in the next centuries the Dutch people will move over to the High German language, and the Danes will move over to Swedish. I believe that this process has been set in motion by the separation of Belgium from Holland and that of Norway from Denmark.* It stands to reason that a Dutchman will rather become German than French, and a Dane rather Swedish than German. Moreover, the language of the mountains and uplands deserves to conquer that of the low-lying plane.[192]

The relation between cultural and political nationalism is complex but fundamental. In some measure, poetry and learning provided a reservoir of propaganda and rhetoric for politicians. In some measure, also, poets and artists (like Körner or Arndt) were actively motivated by nationalist fervour in their choice of topics, and actively attempted either to influence public opinion or the spheres of political decision-making. But crucially, also, the field of learning and of cultural reflection, led by a professionalizing class of academic scholars whose prestige was growing year by year, made assumptions about the territoriality of culture thinkable, explicit; turned them from abstract speculations into a deliberate and explicit set of theses and models, and thus made them available for political instrumentalization; in many cases, deliberately so. Nineteenth-century philologists stood with one leg in the field of literature and learning, with another in the arena of politics and its emerging institutions. They were in large measure the go-betweens, the transmitting agents, from one sphere to the other.

---

* In 1830, Belgium had seceded from the Netherlands (as established in 1815). Denmark had lost its ancient province of Norway to Sweden in 1815 as a part of post-Napoleonic border adjustments. (In the same process, Sweden had lost its ancient Finnish province to Russia.)

The Nationalization of Culture

Ritual, symbols, public space, material culture

The world of learning shared what by the mid-century had become an all-pervasive dominance, in all sectors of public life, of nationalist commitment. Love of the fatherland, the celebration of one's nation, was proclaimed and practised everywhere as a fundamental precept in public morality.

In its rituals and ceremonies, the state itself cultivated a nostalgic pomp and circumstance, which in some cases dated back to the feudal-cum-religious protocol of the pious Middle Ages, and which in other cases was patently contrived – with many in-between shades. The papacy in the Vatican was particularly tenacious in its maintenance of ancient forms and rites (which need not surprise us, since that is what churches are for), and in the course of the nineteenth century became more and more stringently opposed to all forms of 'modern error'; in this opposition against modernity, and in particular against the formation of nation-states based on the idea of self-determination, the Popes fostered devotional movements across Europe, including the Marian cult which involved the noteworthy apparitions at Lourdes.[*]

As we have noted, the Restoration King Charles X, in France, actually reinstated the medieval ritual of being anointed at Rheims Cathedral, and he performed the old, quasi-magical rite of touching scrofula patients in the belief that the King's touch could heal this disease. Authentic though these rituals were, they looked odd and anachronistic in the nineteenth-century context.

In many other cases, public ceremony was retrieved from a limbo of semi-oblivion, or even created out of nothing like a fictional 'might-have-been'. The visit of King George IV to his Scottish capital of Edinburgh in 1822 (already briefly referred to, p. 134) is a good case in point.[193] Under the stage management of Walter Scott, the occasion was used for a celebration of Highland Scottishness and its reconciliation with the modern British monarchy. Tartans, kilt and bagpipes, which had dropped out of fashion and in any case only belonged to the remote moors and glens of the Highlands, now inundated Edinburgh society; leading families were told that, if they wanted to join the social razzmatazz, they ought to retrieve their clannish roots and colours as soon as possible (these were provided by tartan manufacturers in case none were known). All this marked the definitive adoption of Highland local colour as representing the true Scottish identity, and also marked the beginning of a new love

---

[*] The papacy opposed nationalism, which (in its Italian manifestation) formed a direct threat to the pope's power over Rome and the Papal States. This led to some tensions in those states where Catholicism formed a popular basis for nationalist agitation, e.g. in Poland, Croatia and Ireland. Notwithstanding, the traditionalist, devotional campaigns of the papacy resemble a nationalist movement in their appeal to grass root loyalty and their cultivation of a group identity with the help of idealist and historicist rhetoric. Cf. generally Chadwick 1998.

186

affair between the British monarchy and the Scottish highlands; and it was, on the whole, spurious and artificial, owing more to Scott's Romantic-historical poetic vision that to real precedent. Political life came to imitate Romantic-nationalist art.

By the end of the century, this self-dramatization of political ritual in terms of nostalgic traditional kitsch was prevalent all over Europe. What had been feudal custom was recycled as populist pageantry. When Holland's Queen Wilhelmina came of age in 1898, she was given a gold-painted carriage by the city of Amsterdam. It was wholly in a retro-historicist eighteenth-century design (at a time when automobiles were already becoming available), and accordingly was driven by coachmen and servants in fake eighteenth-century dress, complete with three-cornered hats. It is still used in this travestied counterchronological manner when the monarch opens the annual session of Parliament.[194]

At the same time, the dynastic trappings of the ancient ruling houses of Europe were themselves becoming 'national', less and less linked to the person or the household of the monarch and more generally symbolizing the nation-state of which the monarch formed the crown. Statues and public monuments had originally been put up to celebrate royal glories; in the course of the nineteenth century they became increasingly 'national' rather than dynastic.[195] Thus, the triumphal arch* on the Place St. Denis had been erected to the *gloire* of Louis XIV; the one on the Étoile, of Napoleonic vintage, celebrated the armed feats of the nation-at-large, something which was made all the more obvious in the twentieth century when ashes from an unknown soldier were enshrined under it. Flags (having originally been above all military and naval signals, or heraldic displays of a commander[†]) became the badge of national sovereignty, and from the French Revolution onwards a tricolour design usually signalled a democratic or republican ideal. Likewise, national anthems became, in the course of the nineteenth century, precisely that. In the late eighteenth century, songs in praise of a monarchical figurehead had been used to express and heighten patriotic fervour – thus in the cases of the Dutch *Wilhelmus*, the English 'God Save the King' and the Austrian *Gott beschütze Franz den Kaiser*. From the *Marseillaise* onwards, topical anthems celebrating liberty, independence or nationality became, first informally and later increasingly formally, the official statement of a nation's presence at a public gathering. German national anthems included, in the course of the nineteenth century, Arndt's *Was ist des Deutschen Vaterland*, Schneckenburger's *Die Wacht am Rhein*,

---

* The prototype is, of course, from Roman antiquity: the two outstanding examples are the triumphal arches of Titus and Constantine on the Roman Forum. Pre-1789 monuments fell back on Roman prototypes (the equestrian statue of Marcus Aurelius, commemorative columns) or else on religious monumentalization (e.g. saints' statues). A certain amount of Egyptian 'sampling' (obelisks, pyramids) crept into the European monumental style in the course of the seventeenth and eighteenth centuries.

† Traditionally, captured flags were (like field guns) highly prized military trophies, often displayed in important churches (e.g. the *Invalides* in Paris, or many English cathedrals) or in government buildings (the meeting hall of the Dutch Estates General). A vestige of their old function is kept alive in the British tradition of *Trooping the Colour*.

the Prussian-dynastic *Heil Dir im Siegeskranz*, finally settling on Hoffmann von Fallersleben's *Lied der Deutschen*.

Almost all national anthems in Europe are of nineteenth-century vintage; many of them originated as pieces of patriotic verse that, set to music, acquired wide popularity. The oldest national anthem in Europe is the Dutch one, dating back to a song in defence of the leader of the insurrection against Spain, William the Silent; but it only gradually acquired the status of national anthem in the course of the nineteenth and early twentieth century, ousting as such a specially composed hymn from the 1810s, Hendrik Tollens's 'In Whose Veins Netherlandic Blood Flows'. Interestingly, the Dutch monarch Beatrix (a distant and collateral descendant of William the Silent) in 2004 briefly attempted to restore the dynastic nature of the *Wilhelmus* by ordering that it should only be used as the national anthem in the presence of herself or some other representative of the royal household. The general outcry was such that this brief attempt was swiftly retracted: the anthem was obviously felt to be a national, rather than a dynastic heirloom.

Along with flag and national anthem, other symbols of national identity emerged with the modernization of the nation-state. The system of national banks as it crystallized in Europe, and the increasingly successful use of banknotes rather than coins, brought a national iconography into everyone's pocket or handbag – quite literally so. Whereas coins (now minted by national banks, and legal tender only in their country of origin) continued an older design involving relief-portraits of monarchs in profile, or else a heraldic device, banknotes swiftly became the carriers, not just of royal portraits, but of 'national' scenes, landscapes and buildings, or of portraits of Great Figures from the nation's cultural history. The same national-iconographic use can be encountered on postage stamps; all of this forming an insidious, hardly noticed but omnipresent form of 'banal nationalism'.[196]

In the field of painting and sculpture, themes from national history had become dominant, celebrating the glories and glorifying the tragedies from the nation's annals. The public spaces of the mid-century were suffused by this visual rendition of the national past: on the walls of public buildings in commissioned historical paintings and murals; on the streets in the form of statues and national monuments; and in the very city-scapes by the great vogue for a national-historicist architecture that gave quasi-Gothic or quasi-Renaissance form to new buildings, and carefully restored old, decrepit buildings to their ancient glory – or even to an overblown exaggeration of what that ancient glory was fondly imagined to have been.[197] Following individual initiatives towards 'restoration' in the early century (The Marienburg in Prussia, the St. Denis chapel near Paris), the mid-century moved into overdrive when it came to cultivating the traditional heritage of the national public space. The Romantic poet Prosper Mérimée had been placed in a position to survey all ancient buildings in France and drew up a 'hit list' for what became a monument protection and restoration campaign. Foremost in this was the celebrated architect Viollet-le-Duc, whose name is linked to the restoration of the church at Vézelay, of Notre Dame and of the Sainte-Chapelle in Paris, of the entire city works of Carcassonne, and who may be considered almost single-handedly responsible for much of the 'medieval' architecture that has reached us by way of the nineteenth century.[198] His neo-Gothic taste would

34. Budapest Parliament (on Hungarian banknote)

embellish rather than diminish the quaint style of the crumbling originals; that neo-gothicism is even more pronounced in his Dutch adept Cuypers, or in the leading Victorian architect Pugin. And where the medieval original was lacking as such, the modern architect could easily supply a simulacrum. The National Museum (*Rijksmuseum*) in Amsterdam, the Houses of Parliament in Westminster and in Budapest, olde-worlde though they appear, are in fact nineteenth-century designs, as 'authentic' as the Castle of Sleeping Beauty in Disneyland. Indeed, that Disney-castle has been cloned from another nineteenth-century quasi-medieval counterfeit, Bavaria's Neuschwanstein. Another such counterfeit is Balmoral Castle, Scottish home of the British monarchs. It is striking that this historicist retro-architecture was used most lavishly for those buildings which were considered to have a public function (national museums, universities and academies, main railway stations, government buildings, royal residences), and which were therefore most obviously anchored in a post-Napoleonic modernity and most in need of a (spurious) historicist legitimation.

The most outstanding example of gothicism *redivivus* is doubtless Cologne Cathedral.[199] Abandoned and left unfinished in the fifteenth century, it had for centuries stood as an incomplete hulk on the city skyline, dominated by an inert and abandoned builders' crane. In the fervently nationalist climate of the nineteenth century, it was decided that this sign of German medieval greatness on the Rhine (again the geopolitical note creeps in), a counterpart to the cathedral of French-dominated Strasbourg, should be restored, and indeed finished. Under Prussian sponsorship, but with much jealously obtruded support from Bavaria, a completion of Cologne Cathedral was undertaken from the mid-1840s onwards. The work was finally completed in 1880. Symbolically, the great bells that were hung in its towers were cast from the French field guns captured in the 1870-1871 war, and to its rear the old/new cathedral was linked to the eastern bank of the Rhine by a new steel-girder railway bridge, dominated by a monument to the Emperor and the victory over France.

The public spaces in Europe from the mid-nineteenth century onwards were dominated by an incessant barrage of national self-historicization: old buildings restored and maintained, new buildings in old style, and monuments recalling the past on squares and eye-catching locations. Even the names of the public spaces became a lexicon for national history: new streets and boulevards (and railway or metro stations) were named, old street and squares were re-named, to honour national heroes or key events. The cities thematized into everyday living space that national history which everywhere was placed on the school curriculum.[200]

The nineteenth century also witnesses the rise of museums dedicated to enshrining the nation's heirlooms.[201] Their roots lie in the private collections of rich connoisseurs from the early modern period onwards. Originally dedicated, without much systematization, to whatever was rare or unusual (the so-called *Wunderkammer*), such collections came to include, not only exotic collectibles, but also fine manuscripts, books and paintings. Foremost among these collectors were, of course, the reigning princes of Europe; their private collections form the backbone of almost every National Library and National Museum in existence today. Not that these collections were so very 'private' as the modern use of that term may suggest: even in the eighteenth century, it was accepted and normal for visitors – even strangers, travellers passing through on their journey – to ask permission to view paintings in a private collection, and in eighteenth-century Saxony a special day in the week was set aside for the general public to come and view the Elector's gallery.

In the course of the nineteenth century, these collections of manuscripts, paintings and rare items began to drift from private to public ownership. This may be traced back, as so many other things, to the events surrounding the French Revolution and the Napoleonic Empire. French troops had pillaged the private collections of the princes whom they had driven away, and much of this was taken to Paris, where the Louvre was the great receptacle of it all. After the fall of Napoleon, many princes made a point of requesting the return of their artworks, which, in the process, became matters of international diplomacy. The Pope, for instance, sent the sculptor Canova to Paris to obtain the return of the classical statuary looted from the Vatican; Jacob Grimm was sent to obtain the return of the manuscripts of the Hessian court library. The collection in what is now the *Mauritshuis* in The Hague, a former collection of the stadholder, was likewise retrieved from a Parisian sojourn. In the following decades, control and maintenance were entrusted to public bodies, and access became as regulated and public as we know it nowadays, by means of standard opening hours and the sale of tickets. In the same process, museums obtained the added function of demonstrating nationality. The original collections had been nationally a-specific (much as one can still find a Vermeer or an El Greco in any important museum anywhere in the world); but in the long, slow process of collection reorganization that started after 1800, a national-gravitational pull made itself felt. National museums and libraries felt a special interest in acquiring, keeping, or re-acquiring, specimens of national importance. (Most countries, today, have legal provision against the exportation of antiquities considered to be of national importance.)

The return of the Palatinate book collection and of the *Codex Manesse* to Heidelberg is a case in point. Originally, this had been the private library of the Count Palatine on the Rhine; it had been purloined as war booty in the seventeenth century, most of it ending up in the Vatican Library, and its chief jewel, the great collection of medieval courtly poetry known as the *Codex Manesse*, ending up in the Royal Library in Paris. Wilhelm von Humboldt negotiated for the return of the Vatican holdings in the 1810s; and after a century of agitation, the German government managed to acquire, through an intermediary, the *Codex Manesse* in 1880, ensuring its return to Heidelberg. Meanwhile, however, the Heidelberg repository was no longer a Count's private collection, but the city's university library – a tell-tale transition from private to public ownership. A similar 'nationalization' pattern in the transition from private to public can be seen in the case of the Stowe Manuscripts; originally the property of the Duke of Buckingham, the collection eventually ended up in the British Museum, but its rich fund of Gaelic manuscripts was given to the Royal Irish Academy. The more important historical manuscripts came to be edited, either by learned associations (the Royal Irish Academy spawned a few of such edition-oriented associations), or, in the case of material of 'national' historical importance, in state-sponsored source editions. Flagship among these is, of course, the huge *Monumenta Germaniae Historica*; in France, a special state institute for the technique of document editing was founded in 1821, the august *Ecole des Chartes*. All this signalled the official ('national', state-endorsed) importance of historical material, and provided a professional career for many philologists, historians and men of learning who would previously have pursued their interests only as a hobby. Practically all great historians and philologists of the nineteenth century have somewhere on their CV an appointment as librarian or archivist.

The museumization of artefacts and artworks shows the same trend as that of the libraries and archives. The curios and collectibles of erstwhile *Wunderkammer* become museums of antiquities and ethnography, containing, not only antique heirlooms and materials looted from the colonies, but also archeological remains gaining increasing importance for the light they shed on the nation's early, unwritten history. Such museums (the National Museum of Ireland is a good case in point) acquire their materials from private collections, are placed under public administration (in this case, the core collection was formed by the Royal Irish Academy) and become 'national' in a double sense: in that, in addition to their scholarly function, they are open to (and indeed maintained for the educational benefit of) the public-at-large, and in that they showcase specifically those materials which throw light on the nation's antiquity. In the realm of painting, 'national galleries' and museums obtain that status for a similar combination of reasons; the best example here being probably the Dutch *Rijksmuseum*, which has its proudest collection in the 'national' school, the Flemish and Dutch masters, and which is housed in a building that, in historicist neo-Renaissance style, displays itself as a shrine to the artistic and learned accomplishments of the Dutch nation, with commemorative names and displays on its outside walls. Fittingly, the *Rijksmuseum* is located in one of those late-nineteenth-century city developments where all the streets are themselves named after the poets, painters and admirals of the Dutch Golden Age.[202]

Thus far I have only surveyed the cultivation of highly-valorized practices and artefacts among the elite section of the nation-state. However, 'high' culture by itself tends to be cosmopolitan. Monteverdi and Handel belong to concert halls all the world over; Caravaggio and Rembrandt are not tethered to their country of origin, nor can classical ballet be understood only in a proper national setting. The nationalization of culture inevitably involves, therefore, a return to roots – not only historical roots, but also social ones. The case of the 'national schools' of musical composition illustrates this point.[203] To be sure, all composers from the European metropolitan centres follow the classical mode of European music, in their choice of instrumentation, and basic available features of diatonic melody, harmonization and time signature. Any listener who enjoys De Falla can enjoy Borodin: for all their Spanish or Russian local colour these composers share a classical-western paradigm that sets them apart from Arabic or Japanese music or from Indian *raga*.

But within the Europe-wide framework of the metropolitan tradition, composers did begin to turn to 'national' models, beginning with Weber in Germany, Glinka in Russia and Smetana in Bohemia. It was later (towards the end of the nineteenth and in the beginning of the twentieth century) to lead to the emergence of 'national' schools of composition everywhere in Europe, from Vaughan Williams in Britain to Sibelius in Finland and from De Falla in Spain to Kalomiris in Greece, or even Komitas Vartabed in Armenia. Music, like all fields of culture, 'went national'.[*]

It was the multimedia spectacle of grand opera that became the most powerful nation-building instrument from the field of music. Often on national themes, they glorified nationality, supported the growth of national consciousness in places like Hungary and Italy, and indeed it was one such opera that in fact kicked off a national revolt: Auber's *La muette de Portici*. This now-forgotten work contained an aria beginning with the line *'Amour sacré de la patrie'* (itself, as pointed out above, an echo from one of the stanzas of the *Marseillaise*), and in itself was nothing more than a piece of the hackneyed, all-pervasive piety that protestations of national love of the fatherland had become. However, in the politically charged atmosphere of the city of Brussels where the opera was performed in 1830, the aria sparked off anti-Dutch riots, eventually broadening out into the Belgian secession from the Netherlands. Not only in its

---

* Precisely what this involved, remains a fascinating topic for future research; it would require a study of various factors. There are the titles deliberately evoking nationality (Chopin's *polonaises* and *mazurkas*, Liszt's 'Hungarian Rhapsodies', Smetana's 'Moldau'); there are the pieces written for national purposes (Grieg's 'Peer Gynt Suite', Tchaikovsky's '1812 Overture' or, less prominently, Verdi's 'Requiem', composed for the state funeral of the novelist Alessandro Manzoni); there are composers' critical writings and comments (e.g. the critical prose of Cui, Wagner and Vaughan Williams); there is the institutional role played in the *conservatoires* and academies by musician-composers such as D'Indy and Charles Villiers Stanford; the folk music interests of Bartók and Percy Grainger; and last but not least literary materials and libretti used for operas, e.g. Verdi's 'Sicilian Vespers', Musorgksy's 'Boris Godunov' (after Pushkin), Wagner's 'Ring des Nibelungen'.

stylistic register, then, did music 'go national', but also is its close links with nationalist discourse and verbal rhetoric.

The foremost assertion of nationality in music was by drawing on local, non-classical traditions; this fashion started around the mid-nineteenth century and flourished well beyond the Romantic period into the twentieth, the latest and perhaps greatest example being Béla Bartók (1881-1945). Ralph Vaughan Williams (1872-1958) uses the harmonies and stately measures of English plainchant alongside the modal or pentatonic register of English folksong; Manuel de Falla (1876-1946) invokes flamencos, fandangos and other forms of popular Spanish music. This alerts us to the fact that the notion of 'nationality' involves two dovetailing principles: [1] it deliberately sets out to distinguish itself from the general classic-cosmopolitan norm and [2] it uses, for that purpose, elements from the nation's non-classical popular (folk) music.

The nationalist 'cultivation of culture' always involved a deliberate turning towards the demotic, popular roots of the nation. While 'high' culture was transnational, the true identity of the nation was found, so it was felt, among the common folk – not, to be sure, the uprooted and pauperized masses in the inner cities (although Michelet, Hugo and Dickens did describe, with a fond sense of identification, the urban poor in their history-books and novels) but particularly the rustic peasantry: people who, in the countryside, has largely been bypassed by the modernization trends of the past decades, and who were nostalgically imagined to maintain, informally and without being aware of it, the old traditions and ancient customs and practices of the nations.

To be sure, this view is to a large extent a romantic idyll, a matter of stereotyping. As such, it is linked to that great sense of loss and nostalgia which followed in the wake of historical change and modernization. The countryside with its peasantry was seen, not as a part of modern society, but as a surviving timeless community. Famously schematized as a fundamental opposition by the late-nineteenth-century sociologist Ferdinand Tönnies in his classic *Gemeinschaft und Gesellschaft* (1881), society (*Gesellschaft*) was seen as large-scale, anonymous, with social contacts mediatized and with social control entrusted to an apparatus of officials. It afforded great social mobility and dynamism, and great liberty of movement and action to the individual, but at the cost of solitude and harsh indifference. The community (*Gemeinschaft*), by contrast, was seen as small-scale, tightly integrated, with direct face-to-face social contacts and direct, communal social control. It afforded little or no social mobility, perpetuated ancient, ingrained social divisions, hemming the individual into a preordained position; this being mitigated, however, by a high degree of mutual solidarity and support.

In this view, the *Gemeinschaft* was a leftover from the premodern, pre-urban past, now being overtaken by the modernity of urban, industrialized society. The entire nineteenth century (and the twentieth as well) constantly felt that the traditions of the ancient countryside were on the verge of disappearing, swept aside by the tide of history and modernity;[204] as a result, the countryside and its *Gemeinschaft* and its closeness to nature were nostalgically and idyllically invoked throughout the century everywhere in Europe. An entire register and genre of writing, that of the rustic novel, is dedicated to it. It began in the aftermath of Romanticism and has continued unabated in popularity to this very day. In France, George Sand's *La Mare au diable* has led, by way of Gabriel Chevallier's *Clochemerle*, to the novels by Marcel Pagnol (*L'eau des collines,* which in turn has become iconic in the filmed version). In England, the opposition society-community is played out in the seminal novella by George Eliot, *Silas Marner.* Thomas Hardy's evocation of an English countryside, sombre as it was, led to its glorification by the so-called 'Georgian' poets, the films of Powell and Pressburger, and even recent novels like Graham Swift's *Waterland.* In Germany, the genre of the *Dorfgeschichte* or *Dorfsidylle* starts with the novella *Die Judenbuche* by Annette von Droste-Hülshoff, leads to a huge lower-middle-brow activity in *Heimat*-fiction and cinema in the mid-twentieth-century, recently transformed in Edgar Reitz's film cycles entitled *Heimat*.

The best case in point is a passage in Tolstoy's great *War and Peace* (1865-69).[*] It is centred around aristocratic circles in the capital and their purgatorial experience of the Napoleonic invasion of 1812, and consistently sees the redemption in these trials as coming from the plain Russian peasantry. The quiet, pious suffering of the old soldier Karatayev ('the very personification of all that was Russian'), which finally redeems the soul-torn Pierre Bezukhov, is one example. There is also a formative experience in the countryside for the young noblewoman Natasha Rostov. She has had a thoroughly cosmopolitan-French, aristocratic upbringing in the city, and has avidly learned the dances of the court balls and the drawing room. At one point, however, she finds herself, after a sleigh-ride on a country holiday, in the company of rustics who sing traditional songs and dance traditional dances. And this, in Tolstoy's sentimental idealism, speaks directly to Natasha's Russian blood, to some atavistic, genetically inherited familiarity with the national culture that no foreign-style education has been able to stifle:

> The hearts of Nikolai and Natasha thrilled in rhythm with
> the steady beat, thrilled with the sober gaiety of the song [...]
> 'Lovely, lovely! Go on, Uncle, go on!' cried Natasha as soon
> as he came to a stop. Jumping up from her place she hugged
> and kissed him. 'Oh Nikolai, Nikolai!' she said, turning to
> her brother as though words failed to describe the wonder of
> it all. [...]
> 'Uncle' rose, and it was as though there were two men in
> him, one of whom smiled a grave smile at the merry fellow,
> while the merry fellow struck a naïve, formal pose preparatory to a folk-dance.

---

[*] The Russian title is more evocative: *Vaina i mir*, where *mir* (the name also of a space station from the last days of the USSR) has, not only the primary meaning 'peace', but also the subliminal meanings 'the world' and 'a traditional village community' – this entire range of meanings collapsing into a composite semantic effect of a peacefully ordered 'small world', and how it was broken by Napoleon's war. The *Heimat*-style notion of the 'small world' – the village as a microcosm of larger moral and political relations – is a nostalgic favourite, used explicitly by the Italian humorist Giovannino Guareschi for his *Don Camillo* stories.

'Now then, niece!' he exclaimed, waving to Natasha the hand
that had just struck a chord.

Natasha flung off the shawl that had been wrapped around
her, ran forward facing 'Uncle', and setting her arms akimbo
made a motion with her shoulders and waited.

Where, how and when could this young countess, who had
had a French émigrée for governess, have imbibed from the
Russian air she breathed the spirit of that dance? Where had
she picked up that manner which the *pas de châle*, one might
have supposed, would have effaced long ago? But the spirit
and the movements were the very ones – inimitable, un-
teachable, Russian – which 'Uncle' had expected of her. [...]
Her performance was so perfect, so absolutely perfect, that
Anisya Fiodorovna, who had at once handed her the kerchief
she needed for the dance, had tears in her eyes, though she
laughed as she watched the slender, graceful countess, reared
in silks and velvets, in another world than hers, who was yet
able to understand all that was in Anisya and in Anisya's
father and mother and aunt, and in every Russian man and
woman.[205]

Rustic popular culture is canonized into the very essence and bedrock of the national
identity. This is a trope that governs all of Europe in the course of the century. That
century had, after all, been heralded by Herder's celebration of the spontaneous grace
of popular verse and folksong, had begun in music with the new genre of the *Lied*, had
seen the cultivation of simple ballad-forms by Romantics from Goethe to Wordsworth, and was dominated in its early years by the massively influential folksong collections of Arnim and Brentano (*Des Knaben Wunderhorn*, 1806) followed by the even
more influential folktale collections of the Brothers Grimm. The new scholarly discipline of folklore studies flourished in the wake of these romantic interests: tales, proverbs, ballads were collected everywhere, from Russia (Afanasev) to Sicily (Pitrè) and
Norway (Asbjørnsen and Moe). Festivals, rituals, superstitions and customs were in-
ventorized in a sort of ethnography-turned-inward; traditional dress, farmhouse architecture, dialects and folk dances; all this became a search for the cultural mainspring of
the nation, old, primeval, untainted by foreign or modern admixture, by exchange or
by cosmopolitization. In the simple, rustic manners of the humble folk, the purest
echoes of the nation's primitive culture might yet be discerned. 'Representative' rustics
henceforth became the symbolic representatives of the nation's true identity – witness
the case of Volendam in Holland.[206] The first folk museums opened towards the end
of the century, to salvage and display the remains of a countryside *Gemeinschaft*
doomed to oblivion but indispensable for the nation's self-image. In nationalist revival
movements, a return to folkways and an idealized solidarity between the primeval
peasantry and the latter-day nationalist activist dominated; for example, in Ireland,
where urban language revivalists would make regular excursions to the countryside in
order to hear Gaelic still spoken by native speakers and to regenerate themselves in a

35. Volendam fisherman as Dutch prototype
(from P.J. Meertens & Anne de Vries, De Nederlandse volkskarakters, *1938)*

well of pure nationality undefiled by that English influence from which they wished to cleanse themselves. Such countryside excursions are discussed, with some authorial irony, in James Joyce's story 'The Dead', and their attitudes (a curious combination of primitivist exoticism and nationalist self-identification) are reflected in a contemporary press report:

> No greater treat can be in store for the Gaedhilgeoir [Gaelic
> language revivalist, JL], than to travel from Galway west
> through Bearna, Spiddal, and Cashla to Connemara, to hear
> the Gaelic growing in volume and richness as he proceeds, till
> at last the English language is as unknown as it was in the
> days of Maev [a mythical queen, JL]. [...] it would be difficult
> to find a finer race of Irish-speaking men and women than
> these peasants of Iar-Connaught [...] We have seen old men
> with fine characteristic features who could recite Ossianic
> tales and the poems of Raftery and Wallace by the hour, full

at the same time, of ready wit and good, practical sense, living amid those stony wastes and confronting their daily difficulties with firm and determined eyes, and treading the ground that bore them with the self-confidence born of successful struggle. [...] Brown-faced, weather-beaten women who would carry a hundred-weight of oats home on their shoulders, and give you a kindly smile in passing. Young women of queenly build and fine oval features, the most beautiful, they say, in Ireland, and indeed in the wide world. Young men and boys with laughing eyes, full of youthful vigour and enterprise [...] Families of twelve or fifteen, all with beautiful teeth and exuberant health, joined in the closest bonds of affection – such is this Western Race, with its Gaelic speech and its boundless possibilities.[207]

The national self-image and its articulation in literature and learning

What we see in operation here is the political instrumentalization of an idealized national self-image. That self-image had been retrieved from ancient sources, updated and perpetuated in new cultural practices, and used propagandistically in public space to proclaim the nation's identity and presence. The most important fields where this process occurred were, of course, those of literature and learning. The evocation of a national-popular culture whose traditions link the present with the past is to a large extent also a projection on the part of literati and folklorists; we have encountered the names, famous in literature, of the Grimms, Walter Scott and Tolstoy.

Nationally minded literature in the nineteenth century brought together a variety of source traditions and genres. One of these was the popular, orally transmitted verse and narrative of premodern communities – the sort of folktale and folk ballad inventoried by the likes of Herder, Grimm, Afanasev and Asbjørnsen/Moe. It was realized that the oral traditions of even illiterate societies could be of great moral and poetical richness. Thus the Romantic taste for oral literature led to the collection of material, precisely, from marginal peripheries in Europe – and these were precisely the peripheries which in the course of the nineteenth century made a bid for national autonomies. Norway, where Asbjørnsen and Moe worked, is a case in point; we have also come across the role of literature-collecting in the case of emerging Finnish nationalism; but nowhere was the salvage of folk literature as politically important as on the Balkans. Songs from Greek *klephts* (mountain-dwelling outlaws at odds with the Ottoman regime) were popular among West-European philhellenes, foremost among them Werner von Haxthausen (an associate of Arnim/Brentano and of the Grimm brothers) and the Frenchman Claude Fauriel, who brought out a hugely influential collection of *Chants populaires de la Grèce moderne* in 1824 – the year that Byron died in the Greek war of independence.

No less important was a collection brought out by a Serbian who had fled to Vienna in 1810 following a failed insurrection, Vuk Stefanović Karadžić (1787-1864). He was befriended and tutored by the scholar and librarian Jernej Kopitar, himself Slovene by birth. Under Kopitar's guidance and influence, Vuk became the Jacob Grimm of Serbia.[208] He published a Serb grammar, reformed the Serbian language and alphabet, and presented his nation's culture to the European literary world by publishing its oral epic poetry. This collection, speedily brought to the attention of Grimm, circulated through Europe, not only in Slavic and Pan-Slavic circles, but also in German and French translation, providing Romantic literati everywhere with a veritable modern example of epic greatness couched in stark, straightforward, popular language. Soon, Serb oral epic began to be seen as having a type of proto-Homeric quality, something which demonstrated a collective heroic imagination on the cusp of developing an epic literary presence. The view of such oral balladry as being 'epic in an embryonic stage' raised its literary prestige, and matched the aspiration of the people in question as being a 'nation in an embryonic stage', a people on the cusp of taking its place among the European nations. Thus, for cultures without an established literary tradition, the possession of a proto-epic oral tradition was a powerful trump card in their bid for national status. It is for this reason that in some cases, balladry collected in folklore-style fieldwork was subsequently arranged or manipulated to give it an epic cohesion; thus in the case of the Finnish *Kalevala* and the Estonian *Kalevipoeg*.

Following Grimm's celebration of Vuk and of the *Kalevala*, the notion became widespread that in order to be a nation, one had to show both a separate, independent language and a foundational epic. Much as the classical literatures had Homer and Virgil, Italian had Dante, England had Shakespeare and Portugal Camões, so every nation needed its foundational epic. Where none was found, collections of ancient balladry could have the same function: in the Serbian, Finnish and Estonian cases, but also in the so-called *Dainos* of Lithuania and Latvia, or in the Breton balladry edited as *Barzaz Breiz* in the 1830s.[209]

In other cases, modern foundational epics were manufactured either in verse or in prose. Latvia saw the publication of a long epic poem called *Lāčplēsis* or 'The Bear-Slayer' in 1888; written by Andrejs Pumpurs, it may originally have been intended as a manipulated sample of 'authentic' balladry, but it was eventually published, with greater honesty, as an original composition. Its national-foundational importance for the emergence of a Latvian self-consciousness was none the less for all that.[210] The same may be said of the importance of Taras Shevchenko's poetry and balladry for the emergence of Ukrainian nationalism.[211] It invoked the native, national-Ukrainian traditions of Cossacks, *hetman*-leaders and wandering beggar-poets, but in the form of original poetic compositions rather than as the folk specimens collected by Vuk or the Macedonian Miladinov brothers. In Slovenia, again, a deliberate attempt to create a national epic poem was Prešeren's *Baptism on the Savica*, written in the 1830s in folk metre on a collective theme from medieval Slovene history (the victory of Christianity over native Slavic paganism).[212]

In such cases, we see the tradition of oral folk poetry meet, and merge with, the classical genre of the epic. In the course of the nineteenth century the genre of the 'national epic' came to be seen as the reflection of the moment when a nation, through a collective-heroic experience remembered in literary form, took its place on the stage of world history. The term *Nationalepos* was used by the Grimms as early as 1810 for

36. Vuk Karadžić (on Yugoslav banknote)

the German *Nibelungenlied*, which (as we have seen) was first published for a modern audience in 1807 and on which Wagner was eventually to base his opera cycle *Der Ring des Nibelungen*.[213]

The roots of the nation were, after all, not only celebrated in the epic dramas, poems and novels of romantically minded authors – a veritable deluge of manuscripts was coming to light, many of them genuine and some of them forged, containing texts with early-medieval material. Most of the early medieval 'foundational texts' of Europe were, in fact, rediscovered after centuries of oblivion by scholars of the Grimm generation, and presented to an awed national readership as the mainspring of the nation's literature. The *Nibelungenlied* in Germany; *Beowulf* for England (first published in 1815); the *Chanson de Roland* for France (first published in 1836); *Karel ende Elegast*, the *Reinaert* story, and the Servatius legend for Dutch (first published in 1824, 1836 and 1858 respectively): all those texts which we now unquestioningly place in the very first opening chapters of the respective literary histories, as dating from the early dawn of the nation's literary presence, were in fact, after centuries of oblivion, let loose upon the reading public in the days of Walter Scott and Jacob Grimm.[214]

A historicist 'return to the national sources' involved, accordingly, a great linguistic and textual inventory project. Philologists edited early literary texts, often with the added historical bonus that these illustrated the manners and customs of the nation's ancestors. Legal scholars everywhere in Europe undertook a publication of ancient jurisprudential sources, and in the process exerted much influence on medieval studies; and historians, too, were given the important task of retrieving the nation's historical sources from their manuscripts holdings and publishing them in systematic printed form. We have noted the foundation of the great project of the *Monumenta Germaniae Historica*, the edition of manuscript sources concerning Charlemagne's Empire; Britain followed suit with a historical source edition known as the *Rolls Series*, and similar endeavours were undertaken in many European countries. These were seen as affairs of state, under state supervision, and indeed this was necessary because such projects were huge and monumental indeed, too large to be undertaken by individuals, covering hundreds of large printed volumes published over a time-span covering many, many decades.

A side effect of all these textual retrievals was the rise of the great national dictionary. The great dictionaries of the European languages were by and large undertaken in the national climate of the nineteenth century. Earlier models reach back, by way of the English and French dictionaries of Dr Johnson and the *Académie française*, to the true European point of origin: the 1583 Italian *vocabolario* edited by the *Accademia della Crusca* of the city of Florence. This Renaissance prototype of dictionaries was impelled towards a new (fifth), comprehensive edition during the Napoleonic occupation, in 1811; and when the first volume finally appeared, in 1863, it was dedicated to the new Italian king, Vittorio Emmanuele, and carried a preface full of the resounding rhetoric of *risorgimento* nationalism.[215] Large, comprehensive dictionaries on a historical-philological basis were undertaken all over nineteenth-century Europe: the Netherlands, England (what was to become known as the Oxford English Dictionary) and Russia (the work of the lexicographer Dal'); but the flagship of them all was, of course, the *Deutsches Wörterbuch* of the Grimm Brothers. Its logo carried the image of an angel holding, on a scroll, the opening line of the Gospel of St. John: '*Im Anfang war das Wort*' ('In the beginning was the word'). This encapsulated the deeply held belief that language was at the very root of human identity, individual and collective, and gave this philological-anthropological axiom a Biblical aura. The angelic figure was, for all that, wreathed in oak leaves – symbolic of Germany.[216]

The Grimms' Dictionary became the repository of the entire linguistic stock-in-trade of German identity. Its volume on the letter 'K' made clear that the German language was to be cleaned of the Latin 'C' (even Jacob Grimm's name was changed to Jakob; much as the names of the cities of Cöln (Cologne), Coblenz and Cassel became Köln, Koblenz and Kassel). The effeminate Latinity of the C was replaced by the rough-hewn Teutonic masculinity of the K.* As a dictionary, the enterprise was to run for more than a century; its final, 32nd volume appeared in 1960. Similar in scope and girth were the Dutch and English spin-offs. Such lexicographical enterprises (and they were pursued all around Europe, on a correspondingly smaller scale, for the smaller languages) helped to unify spelling, were used to purify the language of foreign (and, as such, resented) intrusions and to spread a unified standard form among all its speakers.[217]

What form this standard should take was not in all cases clear. The relation between standard and dialect variants was sometimes contested, principles of spelling led in almost all countries to heated debate, and even the choice of letter-type (cf. below, pp. 258-259) was a politically charged issue. Denmark was driven by anti-German feelings to abandon its old reliance on the gothic-style 'Fraktur'-letter and change over to the Roman type; Romanian similarly switched from Cyrillic to Roman when it

---

* Similar Teutonic language politics affected England. The Latinate term 'preface' spawned, among Germanically minded writers, the alternative word 'foreword' (first used in 1842). The study of popular culture wanted to avoid the Latinate words 'popular' and 'culture', and as a result devised the neologism 'folklore' (first used in 1846).

37. Vignette on title page of Grimms' German dictionary

wanted to demonstrate its close linguistic relation with the Romance languages of Western Europe; and in Turkey, the modernizing programme of Atatürk involved the abolition of the Arabic script that had been standard in Ottoman days. In the cases of non-standardized subaltern languages, a curious dilemma played itself out time and again. In choosing a standard to revive and propagate, was one to use the literary language of olden days, pure and prestigious, but now old-fashioned and obsolete; or was one to use the contemporary spoken language of the people, widespread and often-encountered, but often irregular, restricted to the lower classes and shot through with foreign loanwords? The first and most fundamental of such debates took place in Greece, where a battle raged between those who advocated a purified, classical Greek (*katharevousa*) and those who endorsed the popular speech of the common people (*demotic*).[218] So, too, in Ireland, where the revival of Gaelic had to choose between the old, complex, literary language and 'the speech of the people' (*caint na ndaoine*); and in Catalan, the choice has taken the almost Coca-Cola-style form of an opposition between 'Catalan Classic' and 'Catalan Lite'. The problem (or something like it) was never resolved in Norway, where to this day two standards of Norwegian compete with each other.

Such debates straddled the spheres of linguistics and the common interests of the public-at-large, and were among the issues that turned linguists and philologists into men of public importance. But not only did their academic activities shade over into the realm of public affairs – they also inspired, and often participated, in the literary field. Many of the philologists and historians of the Romantic generation also tried their hand at literary genres like drama and the novel. National drama harked back to the classical and classicist tragedy, usually commemorating the acts of an individual protagonist rather than a collective-heroic moment. In the seventeenth and eighteenth century, historical characters celebrated in literature included the Cid (Corneille), Mohammed (Voltaire) and Cato (Addison). In the course of the Patriotic eighteenth century, the choice of heroes became gradually more oriented towards the register of the 'champion of the nation's liberty': from Henry Brooke's play *Gustavus Vasa* (1739; on the hero who made Sweden independent from Danish rule and founded the Swedish royal dynasty) to Schiller's play *Wilhelm Tell* (1804). In a parallel trend, dramas began to look for their themes, not to an international canon of Great Men from classical antiquity or world history, but specifically to material from the nation's own past. A lodestar was Shakespeare, who had treated English history, particularly the medieval dynastic wars as described in Holinshed's Chronicles. From Goethe (*Götz von Berlichingen*, 1773) onwards, we see attempts to found a 'national drama' on the theatrical re-working of national mythical or historical material. Such initiatives reach from Copenhagen, where sagas and heroic ballads were turned into theatre by Oehlenschläger, to Serbia, where a hero from the medieval battle of Kosovo, Miloš Obilić, was made the protagonist of a play. That 1828 play, by Jovan Serija Popović, had taken the topic from an 1823 history-book, and it marks the beginning of the intense historicist preoccupation of Serbia with Kosovo. Kosovo obtained mythical status in Serb national consciousness as the site of that great medieval battle when Serbia, tragically and heroically alone among nations, was defeated in attempting to defend the Christian territories against the rising power of the Ottoman Empire. Much as the First World War poet Rupert Brooke wrote:

> If I should die, think only this of me:
> There is some corner in a foreign field
> That is forever England

– so too Kosovo was claimed as being forever Serbia, notwithstanding a large proportion of Albanians in the territory's subsequent population.

But the epic celebration of ancient battles and defining moments in the nation's history was not limited to the classical genre of the tragedy. A new genre proved far more suited to express this epic romanticism, and that was the novel; and here, once again, we encounter the towering figure of Sir Walter Scott.

As a genre, the novel was caught between the sensationalist fiction of the 'romance' (example: Mary Shelley's *Frankenstein*) and the demure realism of the novel-proper (example: Jane Austen's *Emma*). Scott brought the two poles together by creating a psychologically realistic, plausible story with the colour and incident of a violent historical setting – which, in turn, he scrupulously documented from available archival sources.[219] Before he created the historical novel, Scott had already drawn on the adventurous local colour of historical settings in his romantic verse ballads; and he was, as I have pointed out, an antiquary/historian of considerable reputation. It was, however, as the father of the historical novel that Scott reached his greatest and most lasting fame, with Europe-wide bestsellers and classics such as *Waverley, The Heart of Midlothian, Ivanhoe, Quentin Durward* and many others.

Scott's historical novels describe, each of them, moments of crisis and discord in the nation's history, as witnessed through the eyes of a Romantic protagonist, and usually leading to a harmonious reconciliation. In setting out this plotline at repeated points through Scottish and British history, Scott narrates the past as an ongoing process of conflict-resolution and gradual, step-by-step national integration. The narratives probably appealed most because they addressed moments of the collective past in which at least his primary audience felt personally interested, and also because he brought this past to life by providing countless small details on ordinary, daily life in those distant days.

Scott's novels were widely copied as a genre throughout Europe, becoming the most outstanding and appealing way of approaching the past in literature. Usually based on fairly solid historical documentation, to which the novelist would explicitly refer in the course of his book, it gave the reader a sense of reality and plausibility as well as entertainment. The format was used even in America, where Fenimore Cooper outlined his Leatherstocking novels (most famously among them *The Last of the Mohicans*, 1826) as a Walter Scott-style reflection on late colonial history. In Russia, Pushkin used the materials he had used for his historical study of the Pugachev Rebellion for his *Captain's Daughter* (1836). Scott's influence is still felt in Tolstoy's *War and Peace*, likewise a narrative of national regeneration after a crisis, focussed through the private fate of likeable, ingénu protagonists.

In many countries, the genre of the historical novel offers one of the first attempts to chart the national past in a romantic narrative. An outstanding case in point is *The Lion of Flanders* (*De Leeuw van Vlaenderen*) by Hendrik Conscience (1838), which thematizes the resistance of the Flemish cities against French feudal oppression. The book culminates in the celebration of a 1302 battle (largely forgotten until then), whose commemoration has, since it was immortalized in this novel, developed into the national feast day of Flanders.[220] In all these repercussions of Scott, a national intent and impact is obvious.[*]

National-historical narratives swirled through the public sphere, all over Europe, and in great and relentless density. Historians like Michelet wrote 'national' histories, competing with Scott for the attention of readers and using Romantic effects like melodramatic narrative and shrill oppositions between the Good (national heroes) the Bad (foreign oppressors) and the Ugly (traitors).[221] Such Romantic historians became nation-builders in most European countries, not least in Central and Eastern Europe.[222] Their histories were often accompanied by novels on the same theme: the Portuguese Alexandre Herculano not only wrote extensive Michelet-style histories of Portugal, but also Walter Scott-style historical novels set in the Middle Ages. Novels themselves were turned into theatre plays, or provided the basis for opera libretti. Historical scenes were celebrated in paintings and monuments. All of society, the entire public sphere was immersed neck-deep in a nonstop multimedia cult of national self-articulation and self-celebration.

---

[*] Nineteenth-century historical novels generally address the writer's 'own' national history, but there is a sub-genre thematizing the history of early Christianity: Chateaubriand's *Les martyrs* (1809) to Bulwer-Lytton's *The Last Days of Pompeii* (1834) and Sienkiewicz's *Quo Vadis* (1896).

Ethnic Nationalism and Racism

Language and race

Is there something like a 'racial memory' in Natasha Rostov, who can perform a Russian folk dance without ever having been taught the steps? Tolstoy almost seems to imply as much. In the literature of the nineteenth century, the plain people are the guardians of the authentic cultural heritage of the nation, passing it on informally from generation to generation, in settings that are as intimate, as physical as the suckling of infants by their mothers and the acquisition of the native language in that most intimate of circumstances. We repeatedly encounter, in the nineteenth century, narrative themes where national continuity is presented as some demotic-popular inheritance, persisting unnoticed below the level of the governing elite.

This is a Romantic continuation of the 'democratic primitivism' we have traced in a previous chapter. While aristocrats were celebrating their unmixed 'blue blood', democrats countered by taking pride in their descent from the nation's tribal ancestors. This is already noticeable in a 'dig' that Sieyès took, in *Qu'est-ce le Tiers État?* against those aristocrats who claimed that they owned France by virtue of their descent from the Frankish conquerors. Sieyès countered: 'Sons of the Gauls and the Romans! Why don't we send these self-proclaimed heirs of the Franks back to the forests of Franconia? Our blood is worth as much as theirs.' From that moment onwards, there was a tendency to see the 'Franks' as the importers of aristocratic privilege, whereas the true, democratic traditions of France were the secret possession of the Gaulish-descended bedrock of the population, oppressed by church and nobility, but organized in communes and finally vindicated in the French Revolution.[223] That biological vision was already present in a early generation of post-Revolution Romantic historians, such as the Thierry brothers and Jules Michelet;[224] in 1829 the ethnographer W.F. Edwards even tried to put these historical theses to the test by trying to assess, through cranial measurement, which parts of the French population had Gaulish ancestry.

The 'Gaulish myth' (affectionately mocked nowadays in the comic strips of *Astérix le Gaulois*) became dominant in the mid-nineteenth century, specifically with the monomaniac historian Henri Martin, who saw in every admirable aspect of French history the persistence of the true democratic spirit of the ancient Gauls. His ethnic-populist view of French history was popularized in the hugely popular thrillers by the mid-century novelist Eugène Sue, e.g. *Le juif errant* and *Les mystères du peuple*. Like *The Da Vinci Code* of their day (which they anticipate in many respects), these conspiracy-theory novels traced century-long plots and understandings running underneath the surface of history-as-we-know-it, usually involving a transgenerational struggle between the forces of oppression (the church, the nobility) and a filiation of proletarian heroes of liberty. In *Les mystères du peuple*, the heroes (representing the true French nation-at-large) are a proletarian family with Breton-Gaulish roots, which

38. Les mystères du peuple: *leering Frankish lord importuning Gaulish maiden*

has kept, over the centuries, the records of their oppression at the hands of the ruthless powers of church and state, and the messianic promise of future liberation. These records of oppression usually involve the (pictorially illustrated) sexual exploitation and torture of young, beautiful, victimized women. Sue pornographically indulges in the scenes of oppression he sets out to denounce.

To see history as a battlefield, even in modern times, of inimical national bloodlines was a vision made popular, above all, by (again!) Walter Scott. Scott's *Ivanhoe* re-activated the old English political myth of the 'Norman yoke' when he described the cultural and linguistic *apartheid* of medieval England. Under a feudal, French-speaking oppression at the hands of the Norman-French aristocracy, Scott evoked the persistence of a dogged, native Englishness in the persons of the oppressed Saxons. Scott uses the narrative scheme to offer, once again, interesting facts from cultural history. As one of the characters observes, the native Saxon-Germanic names for animals and cattle have, under Norman rule, been restricted to the vocabulary of the farm: ox, swine, sheep and calf. As soon as these animals are turned into the meat that graces the nobles' tables, their names turn French: ox becomes beef (*boeuf*), swine becomes pork (*porc*), sheep becomes mutton (*mouton*), calf becomes veal (*veau*).

GERMANIC			ROMANCE
German	English		French
	Saxon (*farm animal*)	Norman (*meat dish*)	
Schwein	swine	pork	porc
Ochse	ox	beef	boeuf
Kalb	calf	veal	veau
Schaf	sheep	mutton	mouton

It was with such facts and insights that Scott delighted his readers. Meanwhile, his view of an English medieval history dominated by tribal conflict became something of a formula for historians. Thierry used it for his *Histoire de la conquête de l'Angleterre par les Normands*, and Kervyn de Lettenhove, a Belgian adept of Thierry's, saw Flemish history as a transgenerational battle between freedom-loving, oppressed Flemings and haughty, French conquerors – a formula which in the politics of nineteenth-century Belgium, riddled with Flemish grievances about the supremacy of French throughout the state, was nothing short of explosive.[*]

What is striking in Scott's vignette is also the link between language and racial descent. The two are so closely intertwined that it goes almost without saying; apparently the strong link between linguistic and racial entity was not a monopoly of German philologists like Arndt and Grimm, but had already affected Scott by 1820.

Just how strongly felt the ethnic status of language was, may be judged from a passage from 1806 by the renowned scholar Wilhelm von Humboldt:

> Most of the circumstances that accompany the life of a nation (residence, climate, religion, political constitution, manners and customs) can be, as it were, separated from it, and one can, even in the case of intense exchange, separate out what influence they have exerted and undergone. But one aspect is of a wholly different order, and that is language. It is the breath, the very soul of the nation, appearing everywhere

---

[*] It was radicalized when the novelist Hendrik Conscience, himself an old Walter Scott follower, expounded a theory (in his novel 'The Carles of Flanders', *De Kerels van Vlaanderen*, 1871) that rebellious 'Churls' or 'Carles' (*kerels*) mentioned in mediaeval sources were in fact an ethnic tribe, related to the Saxons, and that class conflict in medieval Flanders was in fact a racial, tribal war. This in turn inspired a young student, Albrecht Rodenbach (who died at the age of 24, before he could reach a more sober or mature stance) to pen some vehement and radical verse promising a re-emergence of the old Carle ideals. That verse entered into the rhetoric of the more extreme wings of Flemish nationalism. Leerssen 2006a; Van Houtte 1898; Van Houtte 1934.

in tandem with it, and (whether it be considered as something that has exerted, or else undergone, historical influences) setting the limits of what can be known about it.[225]

Language is more than a communication tool, it is the very substance of a nation's identity. It determines how a nation articulates its presence in the world, it is the carrier that determines the outline of the nation's moral existence; it may be called the nation's moral DNA, its 'operating system'.[226]

This may help to explain Grimm's equation between language and ethnicity. In his view, the Germanic races had at one pointed swarmed out to occupy all of Europe; some of these, like the Anglo-Saxons, had maintained their language even in the newly settled territories, but others had not. The Ostrogoths and Longobards who settled in Italy; the Visigoths who settled in Spain; the Franks and Burgundians who settled in Gaul: all these had abandoned their original Germanic tongue and had adopted the Roman (vulgar Latin) of their new homeland, eventually becoming speakers of Italian, Spanish, French. For Grimm (who had deep mistrust of the French, and of Europe's Catholic southern countries in general), this was to the highest degree sinful, a fall from grace; he went as far as calling it a 'self-forgetfulness' (*Selbvergessenheit*), and even a form of degeneration (*Entartung*).

That last choice of word is fateful. The present-day reader may recognize in it the Nazi denunciation of modern art as 'degenerate' (*entartete Kunst*); in its root sense it means, not just 'dropped to an increasingly low and despicable level', but 'dropped away from its proper *genus*', its proper category. To adopt a language other than the native one means to abandon one's roots and real identity, and thereby to sink to a lower life form.

Do I read too much into Grimm's use of an incidental word? I do not think so. Grimm, as a philologist, was always strongly aware of the root meaning of the words he used, and although he is altogether innocent of the phraseology of the Third Reich, he did testify to a sense that it is despicable and corrupt to compromise racial and linguistic purity. He felt, for instance, that Jews had no role to play in the philological cultivation of the German language.[227]

In any case, the link between race and language was not just Grimm's, it prevailed everywhere in Europe by the mid-century. Cranial measurement was the scientific flavour of the day: it involved measuring the relative height, width and depth of skulls, the resulting ratio giving an index that was used to classify people anthropologically. Scholars were deeply interested in the racial, tribal past of Europe and of humanity at large; some of them would look at physical features (cranial index, skin colour, etc.), others would look at language. The two were considered complementary; language and race were two sides of the same coin. In trying to trace the roots and descent of the human race, a 'family tree' model was used to schematize degrees of similarity and difference; this genealogical classification of diversity made use of racial and linguistic data indiscriminately. The Welsh antiquary Samuel Prichard,[228] author of a *Physical History of Man* (1813) attempted to trace *The Eastern Origin of the Celtic Nations* (1831) by moving with equal ease in the fields of anthropology and linguistics. Another adept of the new learning, Nicholas Wiseman, tellingly spoke of 'philological and physiognomical ethnography' as 'sister sciences'[229] – that is to say that the ethnographical study of the descent of human races could be studied complementarily on the basis of linguistic (philological) evidence or on the basis of physical features (physiognomy). In the decades between Grimm and Darwin, family trees and genealogical models would be drawn up both for the relationship between different languages and between different animal species.[230]

Indeed, one German scholar, the prominent August Schleicher,* did precisely that: he set up, on the basis of Grimm-style comparative linguistics, a family tree of languages which was very close indeed to the model of Darwin. Much as in the animal kingdom, the vertebrate animals would see successive branchings of fishes, amphibians, reptiles, mammals and birds (these then subdividing into genera and species, such as rodents and canines: rats and rabbits, foxes and wolves), so the Indo-European languages were viewed as a tree with Indo-Iranian, Slavic, Germanic and other branches forming out of a common trunk at various stages, and subdividing into finer boughs (languages) and twigs (dialects). Family trees (or, in the technical parlance, a 'phylogenetic model') became the one-size-fits-all mode for viewing the world and its complexities.

Later that century, prominent philologists became embarrassed by the popular link between racial ethnography and comparative linguistics. One of them pointed out:

> To me an ethnologist who speaks of the Aryan race, Aryan blood, Aryan eyes and hair, is as great a sinner as a linguist who speaks of a dolichocephalic dictionary or a brachycephalic grammar.† It is worse than a Babylonian confusion of tongues – it is downright theft. We have made our own terminology for the classification of languages; let ethnologists make their own for the classification of skulls, and hair, and blood.[231]

But in reality, that confusion was something that the linguists and philologists had wilfully caused, and indulged in, themselves; it was the straightforward consequence of a mode of thought that was at the heart of the 'phylogenetic' way of looking at humanity and at the world. For one thing, linguistics used the names of countries and regions to refer to specific languages (English, Spanish, Danish, Polish...) but blithely used the names of races to refer to language families (Germanic, Slavic, Celtic, Semitic; and even, as a parallel to the word 'Indo-European', the portentous name of

---

* Schleicher himself (1821-1868) is known for his dictum 'language is the audible form of thought; thinking is the silent form of language' (*Sprache ist lautes denken, Denken ist lautloses Sprechen*). He was a specialist in Lithuanian (indeed, he was among the first to draw attention to that language's scientific importance) and in the Slavic languages, but lost his chair at Prague University in 1857, after Czech students there had militated at his German arrogance (Bynon 2001; Lefmann 1870).

† 'Dolichocephalic' and 'brachycephalic' are terms from cranial measurement, i.e. from physical anthropology, referring to the relative width, height and depth of a skull-shape.

'Aryan'[*]). It was not that people had begun to confuse the scientific terminology of language and of race; scientists had systematically brought linguistic and racial vocabulary together into a single anthropological category. A case in point is the scholar Robert Gordon Latham, who worked both in the ethnological and in the philological field. Alongside his publications of the history of the English language and literature he wrote works such as *The Natural History of the Varieties of Man* (1850), *The Ethnology of Europe* (1852) and *The Nationalities of Europe* (1863).

The impact of physical anthropology

That anthropological study of linguistic-cum-racial diversity moved, accordingly, from a cultural definition of nationality (language and shared traditions, customs and historical memories) towards a genetic-biological, racial one: the nation was defined, in this view, by shared descent, a common inheritance passed along a physical bloodline. To be sure, we have seen that the term and the idea of 'nation' had always been ambiguous between the registers of culture and race, from Biblical sources and the Middle Ages onwards; but the 'life sciences' of the nineteenth century were beginning to develop a type of biological determinism of a new order. We can trace that development by taking, as a sample case, the line from Lavater to Lombroso.[232] The Swiss clergyman Johann Caspar Lavater (1741-1801) had, in typical late-eighteenth-century fashion, attempted to give a characterological systematization of facial traits. We still speak of 'sensuous lips', or a 'strong/weak chin': certain features of the face have a traditional prejudice attached to them as to the character of the person in question. This old superstition of the 'face as the mirror of the soul' was classified and systematized by Lavater; in particular, he drew attention to the fact that the line from nose-bridge to chin, in the classical ideal of beauty, ought to be as perpendicular as possible; the more it receded, the more it made the bearer's profile resemble, not a Greek god, but an ape or a 'fishface'.

Lavaterian physiognomy was, of course, Eurocentric and led, as we shall see, to a pictorial register of denigration: vilification (often racist) would henceforth draw on the pictorial stereotypes of a heavy eyebrow, small close-set eyes, a gorilla-style ('prognathous') lower jaw, long upper lip and small snub nose. Even so, it should be borne in mind that Lavater did not intend this. He wrote as a sentimental, pietist protestant and as a philanthropically minded Patriot; and he asserted that in all its variations, all human faces were still, as the Bible had phrased it, in the image of their Maker.

---

* Aryan is a word from the Indo-Iranian languages referring to the tribes that settled in the Indian subcontinent, bringing their Indo-European languages with them (Benveniste 1969). The word became popular from c. 1840 onwards as a linguistic-cum-racial appellation, particularly in Britain with its imperial-Indian connections, and spread from there to Germany (where is became a fundamental concept in Hitlerite racist thought.) We continue to see such odd confusions between geographical and racial names e.g. in the appellation 'Caucasian' (common in the US) for 'someone of white-European descent' – echoing the typology (based on a combination of linguistics and cranial measurement) by Johann Friedrich Blumenbach (1752-1840).

Such pious reservations were wholly forgotten when, a century later, the criminal psychiatrist Cesare Lombroso attempted to give a typology of 'the criminal type'. He studied photographs of detainees and the skulls of executed convicts, and came up with a facial index indicating, from physical features, the criminal proclivities within. Behaviour was increasingly explained from physical type, much as the 'character' of certain dogs is considered to be a typical feature of their 'race': friendly labradors and aggressive pitbulls. Science was reducing human culture to the brute facts of nature. And the same line of 'scientific' thinking was applied to European nations and to races. Lombroso himself published a disquisition on *L'uomo bianco e l'uomo di colore* in 1871. Everywhere in Europe, long-standing racist stereotypes were now solemnly rehearsed as if they were 'scientifically proven facts'.

Philology, Grimm-style, from its early days had always shown an ambition to become a type of national anthropology. Grimm himself could look to any type of data (language, folktales, legal sources, medieval epics, proverbs) to conduct something called *Germanistik*, which, for him, meant the scientific study of what gave the German race its culture and identity.[233] His interests moved at times very close to something that Carl Gustav Jung would later refer to as a 'collective racial subconscious'. Much as language programmed a nation's worldview, so its spiritual life was expressed in its literature and its manners and customs; conversely, the study of language, literature, manners and customs was mainly intended to gain an insight into the nation's soul.

Later successors were to spell out this national-psychological 'hidden agenda' at the root of Grimm-style philology. The ultimate generator of cultural difference was the 'national character' or 'race soul', so it was believed, and people set out to elucidate these slippery concepts from their cultural traces. National psychology was launched by Moritz Lazarus and Heymann Steinthal, who founded, in 1860, a Review for National Psychology and Linguistics (*Zeitschrift für Völkersychologie und Sprachwissenschaft* – a tell-tale title). Wilhelm Wundt, for his part, likewise extended linguistics into the realm of national characterology in his massive and influential ten-volume *Völkerpsychologie* (1900-1920), which, according to its subtitle, pretended to be 'an investigation of the developmental laws of language, myth and morals' (*eine Untersuchung der Entwicklungsgesetze von Sprache, Mythus und Sitte*).

Modern readers, when turning to such publications, will immediately realize that they contain nothing but farragos of prejudice, stereotype and ethnocentrism, presented in pseudo-scientific vocabulary: men like Lombroso are the forerunners of the 'mad scientists' often caricatured in Hollywood movies and spoofs, but lugubriously real in the cases of certain Nazi doctors. It can only be through lack of familiarity with the actual substance of these nineteenth-century would-be-scientists that they are still credited nowadays as founding fathers of social or experimental psychology and anthropology; they are, rather, the initial myth-mongers that had to be exorcised before anthropology and social psychology could move to a properly scientific modus operandi.[*]

---

[*] On nineteenth-century anthropology: Stocking 1987. The process of decontaminating the idea of culture from racial essentialism has been arduous and has not everywhere been successful. *Pace* Kalmar 1987, the influence of Lazarus and Steinthal on Franz Boas, and (through Boas) on American

The nineteenth-century 'anthropology of cultural diversity' was dominated by one fundamental question: was there, in humanity, such a thing as a common origin at all? Traditionally, the Bible had taught the story of a single point of origin: the nuclear family of Adam and Eve, and again the nuclear family of Noah and his three sons, from which all of humanity had fanned out. Accordingly, those scholars who had had a theological connection or training would tend to emphasize that all diversity was ultimately a historically grown diversification of a common stock, and that all races, no matter how different, still reflected their common creation in God's image. Representatives of this 'monogenist' line of thought included erudite clergymen like Herder or Lavater, and many British scholars such as Prichard (in England, the position of the Anglican church in the world of learning and in the universities was strong.) However, this common-human view of a single origin was difficult to reconcile with the deeply felt sense that some races were superior to others, as much as humans are superior to animals. Europeans went so far in their sense of racial superiority that they refused to acknowledge family ties with 'inferior' fellow-humans. As early as 1789, the antiquary John Pinkerton stated:

> It is a self-evident proposition that the Author of nature, as
> he formed great varieties in the same species of plants, and of
> animals, so he also gave various races of men as inhabitants of
> several countries: a Tartar, a Negro, an American, &c. &c.,
> differ as much from a German, as a bull-dog, or lap-dog, or a
> shepherd's cur, from a pointer. The differences are radical,
> and such as no climate or chance would produce; and it may
> be expected that as science advances, able writers will give us
> a complete system of the many different races of man.[234]

As the Biblical account of the origin of nations and languages was eroded and supplanted by the Grimm-Darwinian model, the old monogenism was likewise replaced by a 'polygenist' view, which would stress the radical differences between the human races rather than their common origin or features. In particular, polygenism was a scientific rationalization for European, white ethnocentrism and racism.

What became especially pronounced in a polygenist ideology of ethnic authenticity and purity, was the abhorrence of interracial exchange: mixture and hybridity. We have seen a cult of German authenticity and unmixedness in the thought of Fichte and Grimm; with them, it is still largely a celebration of the fact that Germans maintained their ancient institutions and language – in short, their culture. But in the ethnographically minded climate of the 1830s and 1840 the abhorrence of decadence,

---

anthropology in general, has been less than felicitous. Boas's notion of culture does, in fact, appear as a watered-down euphemism for what in the nineteenth century had been more bluntly called *Volksgeist*. A tendency towards ethnic essentialism and determinism has continued to bedevil experimental psychology and mid-twentieth-century anthropology alike.

Entartung and loss-of-identity became also a physical one, involving, not culture or language, but bloodlines and physical (racial) descent.

The great architect of this European cult of racial purity was a French nobleman, Count Arthur de Gobineau (1816-1882).[235] As a nobleman, he had perhaps been habituated early on to an aristocratic glorification of 'pure descent', of unmixed 'blue blood' – which involved also a horror of the *mésalliance* or 'improper marriage' whereby the descendant of a noble bloodline would betray that inheritance by marrying a social inferior. Gobineau's thought may be seen as an application of such aristocratic exclusiveness to racial/ethnic categories. His *Essai sur l'inégalité des races humaines* (1853-1855) takes it as a given that among and between the various human societies (the word 'race' is already an unquestioned, quasi-anthropological category) there are various levels of achievement and nobility, and that some are 'higher' than others. Gobineau's main argument is, that in this situation, the very worst thing to happen for a society is 'miscegenation' or racial mixture. This will lead to a physical degeneracy where the higher achievements of the one race are tainted and corrupted by the lower features of the other.[*]

Human intolerance often tends to fixate on instances where clear-cut categories are blurred or crossed: social upstarts (between classes); homosexuals (between the sexes); and indeed people of mixed racial origin, 'half-bloods'. In nineteenth-century racial thought, this last aspect becomes all-dominant. Miscegenation, so it is believed, will lead to degeneracy. Not only is this seen as a moral betrayal (as with Grimm's linguistic *Entartung*), it is also magnified into a biological threat. If humanity is the end result of a Darwinian evolution, then degeneracy is the potential threat that such evolution can be reversed, that later generations will revert to the brutish and inferior standards of bygone ages of lower races. A particular phobia was that of atavism, 'relapsing to the primitive stage of development of one's distant ancestors'. The inner ape, or Neanderthal-style caveman, is still latently present within the modern gentleman, as the case of Dr Jekyll and Mr Hyde (in Stevenson's classic parable) shows. In many novels of the later nineteenth century, the figure of the *dégénéré* is a stock character: the last product of a refined family, who is genetically burdened and prone to weakness, to sexual perversion and other forms of immorality.[236]

Even Down syndrome was originally seen as a form of atavism. People afflicted with this chromosomal disorder have limited intelligence and physically they are often characterized by a fold in the eyelid. It is for this reason that the physician who first diagnosed the condition as such, Dr John Langdon Down (after whom it is now named) named it 'Mongolism'. The fold in the eyelid reminded him of a similar feature in the Mongol races. Down accordingly interpreted this as a sign that the person in question

---

[*] As Pinkerton's reference to dogs indicates, another source tradition for Gobineau's thought may have been the tradition of breeding animals, and especially the thoroughbreeding of horses. Systematic breeding of horses, cattle and dogs had been pursued since the seventeenth century, and had led to a discourse linking physical appearance, 'character' and purity of descent. Cf. Schmölders 1995 and 1998.

had reverted back to the low, primitive developmental stage of an older race such as it still existed in its original form in Asia.[237]

One of the side effects of the new ideology of racial purity was a freshly increased intolerance towards Jews. As 'Semites' they were considered representatives of an alien race residing within European society, and as such posing a constant threat to the racial purity of the nations of Europe and their collective strength. Antisemitism was nothing new, of course, but in Western Europe it now became rationalized by a quasi-scientific thought of racism, and it took on the new form of conspiracy theories fed by a phobic concern for ethnic purity. The *Protocols of the Elders of Zion* are a good illustration of this.[238] Originally formulated as a lurid quasi-fictional speculative plot element in a pulp thriller (again, the genre that runs from Eugène Sue to *The Da Vinci Code*), it purported to represent a secret Jewish plot to take control of economic and political affairs worldwide. Its fictional origins were soon forgotten, the text was spread as if it were a genuine document, and it has remained a key ingredient in paranoid antisemitic propaganda ever since. But despite its worldwide currency and continuing use (most recently in Idi Amin's Uganda and in some Arab-Islamic states, as well as certain white-supremacy websites), its origins reflects firmly and clearly the decadence-obsessed climate of late-nineteenth-century Europe. Antisemitism likewise made itself felt in the enormous, long-drawn-out scandal that polarized French society from 1894 until 1906 and after, known as the Dreyfus affair. A Jewish officer, Alfred Dreyfus, was accused (falsely) of espionage and treason, and condemned after a high-publicity trial – something which in the fervently patriotic climate of the post-1870 years touched a particularly raw nerve in French public opinion. Those who believed in Dreyfus's innocence and denounced a miscarriage of justice had to argue that the truth had been twisted by the Army authorities – thus placing a Jewish individual in polar opposition to the representatives of France's hope for national regeneration. Successive court cases dragged on for more than a decade, traumatizing and dividing public opinion, and fanning the flame of French antisemitism, which, notwithstanding the experience of Nazi occupation in the years 1940-1944, has remained strong in the French extreme right ever since.

Although the cult of racial purity, linked to an increasingly rabid antisemitism, culminated in the genocidal policies of the Third Reich, it is important to realize that its roots involve all of Europe, France and Britain no less than Germany itself. Indeed, German racism may with some justice be said to have been introduced from French and English sources: 'Gobinism' had become popular all over Europe; calls for 'eugenics' (the biological improvement of the national gene pool by means of selective procreation) were widespread in many countries; and Britain in particular was in the grip of a racial debate involving the 'Celtic' or 'Germanic' roots of English culture.[*] Following national-ethnographic studies like Robert Knox's *The Races of Men* (1850,

---

* Eugenics originates with the work of Francis Galton (a nephew of Darwin, knighted in 1909): *Hereditary genius* (1869) and *Natural inheritance* (1889). The mathematician Karl Pearson did much to propagate Galton's thought by attempting to prove the Darwinian principle of natural selection by a mathematical-statistical population analysis (Gould 1981).

39. Eugène Delacroix: 'Liberty leading the people' (1830)

with many reprints after 1862) and John Beddoe's *The Races of Britain* (1885),[239] it was an Englishman, Houston Stewart Chamberlain, who introduced Gobineau's theories of racial purity and the evils of miscegenation into Germany, when he married into the family of the celebrated composer Richard Wagner. It is through the Wagner circle that Gobinism was grafted onto the Fichte-style myth of Germanic purity. Chamberlain himself wrote a Gobineau-style book on racial purity, *Der Mythus des neunzehnten Jahrhunderts* (1899); Wagner wrote essays denouncing Jews as alien and detrimental parasites in German culture; and all this was strengthened by Austrian thinkers who felt that the multi-ethnicity of the Habsburg empire was a fatal weakening of its German strength.[240] It is in these circles that the roots of Hitlerite racism must be sought: the Nazi policies of the 1930s and early 1940s, including the Nuremberg laws against interracial marriage and the removal of Jews as foreign vermin from the German body politic, were the militaristically organized implementation of notions dreamed up by tweed-clad, upper-middle-class backroom philosophers of the previous generation.

Even the actual physical extermination of the Jews was in its origins an application of Gobineau-style eugenics. The main phobia being that of atavism and decadence, it was felt that nations and societies ought to be selective in their breeding. Offspring for 'superior' individuals was to be encouraged, offspring for 'inferior' specimens was to be counteracted. Such eugenics were not peculiar to Nazi totalitarianism: they became popular in the United States early on. In Sweden, well into this century, young girls from a socially undesirable background (or what the authorities chose to consider as such) were sterilized, without their knowledge or consent. The first victims of categorical sterilization and extermination in Nazi Germany, and the first victims of indus-

40. Physiognomy of hate propaganda:
the enemy (Irish, German, bolshevik) as ape-man

trialized gassing in purpose-built gas chambers, were, accordingly, ethnic Germans: inmates of asylums for lunatics and mentally retarded people. It was only subsequently that these homicidal procedures, first implemented to weed out undesirable elements in the German gene-pool, were applied, at an unimaginably larger scale, to the 'Final Solution of the Jewish Question'.[241]

Nazi Germany is no stand-alone singularity: it is, rather, the most extreme outgrowth of patterns that were widespread across Europe. It does, however, represent the most extreme case of defining a nation as a physical group, a race: that is, after all, what *völkisch* means in Nazi parlance (cf. below, p. 234). What all fascists shared was a profound preoccupation with national purity and homogeneity, a phobic fear of degeneration and decadence, and a belief that decadence could be counteracted by strong leadership and a total, military-style obedience to that leadership.

Racial discipline

The nationalist ideology shows, over the course of the nineteenth century, a slow, inexorable shift from the left of the political spectrum towards the right. Pictorially speaking, nationalism in the 1820s is Delacroix: the artist who showed philhellenic sympathies in his Chios painting, and democratic-republican ideals in his 'Liberty Leading the People'. By the twentieth century, the pictorial expression of nationalism is in ethnic hate caricatures showing the despised enemy nation as gorilla-style King Kong monsters: Irish, Germans, Bolsheviks or African-Americans; they all have a bestial barbarism oozing from their ape-like features.[242]

Many factors contribute to this shift of nationalism to the right. Most fundamentally, nationalism changed in status from an anti-government opposition force to a propaganda tool wielded by governments to justify state hegemonism; also, national thought was infected by the discourse of biological determinism, race, the spectre of 'decadence' and degeneration, and the new cult of the authoritarian, heroic leader.

The slow emergence of the phobia of degeneration we have traced as a side effect of the cult of authenticity and purity, from Fichte to Gobineau and onwards. In post-1871 France, army doctors reported in worried terms that the physical stalwartness of recruits seemed to be on the decline, signalling a fatal physical weakening of the French population. In Italy, organized crime in Sicily was blamed on the racial inferiority of the Sicilians. Similar worries cropped up in Britain: the various colonial wars in southern Africa showed that natives and Boers were surprisingly difficult opponents of Empire's armed might; Zulu and Tutsi warriors were celebrated, even in the colonial-imperialist stories of Henry Rider Haggard (*King Solomon's Mines*, 1895) as enviable examples of 'noble savages'. An officer in the South African service, Baden Powell, decided to hold up colonial natives as a primitivist role model for the inner-city boys of England; the Boy Scout movement was the result. Hardiness, a paramilitary organization, stalwart masculine comradeship, a love of uniforms and learning how to tie knots: this Victorian survival-gaming was quite obviously intended to regenerate a youth lacking fresh air and exercise, and exposed to the dangers of sex and alcohol.[243]

The need for regeneration was expressed urgently by two seminal books: Max Nordau's *Degeneration* (*Entartung*, 1892-1893) and Oswald Spengler's *The Decline of the West* (*Der Untergang des Abendlandes*, 1918-1923). Both authors signalled a weakening of an old, worldly-wise and decrepit Europe, burdened by its long and increasingly a-moral history. *Fin de siècle* Europe seemed to consist of self-styled 'decadent' poets such as Baudelaire, Huysmans, Villiers de l'Isle-Adam ('Life? I've got my servant to do that for me') and Aubrey Beardsley; Oscar Wilde's tale *The Picture of Dorian Gray* (1891) contrasted the elegant refinement of dandyism and aestheticism with a hidden moral corruption; novelists like Eça de Queirós, Thomas Mann and Louis Couperus traced elite families in decay: *Os Maias* (1881), *Buddenbrooks: Zerfall einer Familie* (1901), *De boeken der kleine zielen* (1901-1903); the fashion was for occult societies, the use of drugs and absinthe, and a taste for perverse sexuality (Leopold von Sacher-Masoch, *Venus im Pelz*, 1869). As Nordau wrote:

> The degenerates are not always criminals, prostitutes, anar-
> chists and certified lunatics. Often they are writers and ar-
> tists. But these show the same spiritual – and often also phy-
> sical – traits as their anthropological relatives, who satisfy
> their unhealthy urges with the serial-killer's knife and the ter-
> rorist's dynamite-stick rather than with the pen or paint-
> brush.[244]

Europe was facing a corrupt old age, was becoming a Dirty Old Man. Stevenson's parable of Dr Jekyll and Mr Hyde seemed to have a real-life fulfilment in the bloody career of Jack the Ripper. Europe would soon, so the worried prediction ran, be overtaken and overrun by the savages of the colonies, who were less educated but in better physical shape. Emperor Wilhelm II of Germany had an apocalyptic vision of Europe facing the onslaught of the 'Yellow Peril', which echoed in the later anti-Asian hate images of Sax Rohmer's *Fu Manchu* thrillers and in the 'Dr. No' figure of James Bond fame. What was needed was not an arms race but a campaign of regeneration. Youth movements like the Boy Scouts were one aspect. Another harked back to the old *Turnverein* tradition of Jahn. Many nationalist movements had sports clubs: the Gaelic Athletic Organization in Ireland,[245] the Czech and Polish *Sokol* clubs, the mountaineering *excursionistas* in Catalonia. These partly functioned as cover organizations for nationalist mobilization and paramilitary training, partly they were inspired by the thought that national moves to independence also involved the physical regeneration of a strong, healthy people. The rhetoric of the Irish nationalist William Smith O'Brien is typical:

> The world is a-weary with pessimism. It has lost its inno-
> cence. It is losing its faith in most things here or hereafter.
> [...] For this poison of moral and intellectual despair which is
> creeping through a sad world's veins, what cheerier antidote
> is within reach than the living tide of health, and hope, and
> simplicity and hilarity, the breezy objectiveness and stoutness
> of muscle, and ardour or emotion which flows full and warm
> through the heroic myths of the men of Erin?[246]

The old Roman motto *mens sana in corpore sano* ('a healthy mind in a healthy body') seemed to be transmuted into *natio sana in republica forte*. Robustness was needed, cold showers and military drill. It was the last permutation of the old Tacitus-style ideal of manly *virtus*, with some Spartan overtones. It led to the cult of physical discipline that was a central part of fascist and Nazi movements.[247]

There is nothing inherently pernicious in giving young kids holidays outdoors and teaching them how to tie knots and other life skills; on the contrary. What could tip such regeneration movements from innocent and even wholesome physical exercise into something altogether more sinister was the way its cult of the physical could mesh, in the years 1920-1940, with militaristic authoritarianism, with a reliance on the myth of the heroic leader-figure (what in Nazi parlance was called the *Führerprinzip*). True regeneration was to be found in totally dedicating oneself to the superior wisdom, insight and power of the leader – *duce, Führer, caudillo*, whatever. This cult of the heroic leader, who like a Nietzschean Superman sensed his nation's needs and the necessities of History, had been prepared by the transcendent philosophy of Hegel, had been formulated into a programme of moral duty by Thomas Carlyle, and gave nationalism, from the 1870s onwards, its strong anti-democratic, authoritarian direction.[248] It was felt most strongly in destabilized countries; but a certain anti-democratic joy of corporatism, duty, uniforms and militaristic organization was also noticeable in stable states and also in Catholic organizations. Communist organizations also used the same formula everywhere (and it is remarkable how vulnerable that ideology proved to personality cults, the veneration of heroic leaders).

All these diverse factors played into the rightward shift of national thought and nationalism. The Romantic celebration of cultural difference, and the Revolution's assertion of popular sovereignty, moved into the authoritarian and corporatist extreme right of the political spectrum, became the driving force of the massed fanatics led by Mussolini, Hitler, and their imitators.

Versailles* and After

The Great War, the War to End All Wars, was the ruinous culmination of the European 'Balance of Power' doctrine. From the days of Louis XIV onwards, and indeed foreshadowed by the terms of the 1648 Treaty of Westphalia, there had been a tendency for states to form strategic alliances in order to counterbalance the overwhelming superiority of a mighty neighbour. In the century between 1813 and 1914, a dual system of two balancing alliances had emerged, that of a Central-European 'Axis' bracketed by a French-British-Russian *entente*. The resulting domino effect, which inexorably led from the Sarajevo incident to the battles of Tannenberg and Verdun, is notorious. Also notorious is the huge, industrialized scale of the warfare: this was no longer a 'continuation of diplomacy by other means' (as war had been for Clausewitz), no longer the backing up of international confrontation by an armed campaign, but a life-and-death struggle between entire nations. The social, economic and ideological investment in the Great War was total. Propaganda and jingoism were capable of penetrating society to a far greater extent than in the previous century, and a frenzy of national hatred was whipped up from all quarters to make this, morally no less than in other respects, an almost 'total war'. German professors and intellectuals issued proclamations in support of German right, might and superiority; British noble and royal families like Battenberg and Saxe-Coburg-Gotha were compelled to change their names to the more patriotically sounding Mountbatten and Windsor. Slogans like *Gott strafe England* and *Hang the Kaiser* suffused the public sphere. The national fanaticism of the First and Second World Wars can only compare to the religious fanaticism of the Crusades and the Wars of Religion, illustrating once more that nationalism had taken the place, ideologically and socially, of religion as a mobilizing force.

Even as the military events unfolded, it was obvious that the Great War would mark a fundamental shift in the European state system. The British entry into the war was motivated and proclaimed as a defence of Belgium and of small states whose violated neutrality had been guaranteed internationally. The various nationalities of the Romanov and Habsburg Empires had by now developed active and ambitious national emancipation movements, all of which were to use the military deadlock of the great imperial war to proclaim self-government. As the Tsar's empire crumbled after 1917, its peripheral dominions in the Polish/Baltic area all seized the opportunity. In Central and South-Eastern Europe, minority nations in the borderlands of the Austro-

---

* I use 'Versailles' as shorthand for the entire set of arrangements that brought the First World War to a close. A cessation of hostilities had been agreed in Compiègne in 1918. The Paris Peace Conference formally brought the war to an end, leading to the Treaties of Versailles (for Germany), of Saint-Germain (Austria), of Trianon (Hungary), of Neuilly (Bulgaria) and Sèvres (Ottoman Empire); these are often grouped collectively under the name of the Versailles Treaty. A separate arrangement with Russia had been made in the Treaty of Brest-Litovsk. For the various texts cited here, cf. (unless otherwise indicated) Treaty 1947 and Martin 1924.

Hungarian and Ottoman empires did likewise, hyphenating themselves into Czecho-Slovak and Serbo-Croat alliances. Again, at the other end of Europe, a symbolic gesture towards a nationalist uprising was staged in Dublin in 1916, suppressed for the nonce but re-erupting in an insurrectionary campaign in 1919. Even in British war propaganda, the argument was made that after the war a 'Europe of Nations' should re-establish state divisions on the principle of nationality, thereby removing the ethnic tensions that had triggered the confrontation on the Balkans.

This late echo of Mazzini-style thought was carried into the highest circles of political policy-making as a result of Leon Dominian's book *The Frontiers of Language and Nationality in Europe*. It was rooted in the European tradition of mixing geography, anthropology and linguistics, and arguing that states should ideally reflect the racial/linguistic profile of their populations. Published for the American Geographical Association of New York in 1917, it introduced this tradition of 'ethnic geopolitics' into a society that had been dominated by race feeling during the previous decades, and that was now on the brink of entering the First World War. The introduction by Madison Grant (author of the notorious *The Passing of the Great Race*, 1916, a racist classic[249]) regretted the 'prevailing lack of race consciousness in Europe' and urged the idea that language was the essential factor in 'the creation of national union and nationality'. How ingrained and blatant the habit had become of extrapolating from culture to geopolitics, may appear from the following excerpt, which also illustrates how Vuk Karadžić's romantic-philological folksong-collecting of the 1810s was to have unforeseen, enormous political repercussions a century later:

> The *pjesme* [epic ballad, JL] voices Serbia's national aspirations once more in the storm and stress of new afflictions. Its accents ring so true, that the geographer, in search of Serbian boundaries, tries in vain to discover a surer guide to delimitation. From the Adriatic to the Western walls of the Balkan ranges, from Croatia to Macedonia, the guzlar's ballad is the symbol of national solidarity. His tunes live within the heart and upon the lips of every Serbian. The *pjesme* may therefore be fittingly considered the measure and index of a nationality whose fibre it has stirred. To make Serbian territory coincide with the regional extension of the *pjesme* implies the defining of the Serbian national area. And Serbia is only one among many countries to which this method of delimitation is applicable.[250]

The American success of this book was to reverberate back into European affairs. When the conclusion of the Great War was negotiated in 1918-1919, the doctrine of the 'self-determination of peoples' became a guiding principle. It formed part of the American brief for the Paris Peace Conference, Woodrow Wilson's famous 'fourteen points', many of which involved the principle of nationality and of national self-determination. Multi-ethnic empires were to be broken up in order to make the establish-

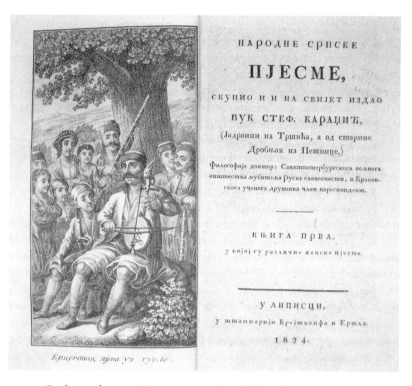

НАРОДНЕ СРПСКЕ

ПЈЕСМЕ,

СКУПИО И И НА СВИЈЕТ ИЗДАО

ВУК СТЕФ. КАРАЏИЋ,

(Јадранин из Тршића, а од старине
Дробњак из Петнице,)

Философије доктор; Санктпетербургскога волнога
општества лубителя Руске словесности, и Краков-
скога ученога друштва члeн кореспондент.

КЊИГА ПРВА,

у којој су различне женске пјесме.

У ЛИПИСЦИ,

у штампарији Брејткопфа и Ертла.

1824.

Ерцеговац, пјена уз гусле.

41. Guzlar performing: Frontispiece to Karadžić's collection, 1824 edition.

ment of nation-states possible. Thus point 8 restores Alsace-Lorraine from German to French control, and 9 through 13 of Wilson's 'fourteen points' read:

> 9. A readjustment of the frontiers of Italy should be effected along clearly recognizable lines of nationality.
> 10. The peoples of Austria-Hungary, whose place among the nations we wish to see safeguarded and assured, should be accorded the freest opportunity to autonomous development.
> 11. Rumania, Serbia, and Montenegro should be evacuated; occupied territories restored; Serbia accorded free and secure access to the sea; and the relations of the several Balkan states to one another determined by friendly counsel along historically established lines of allegiance and nationality; and international guarantees of the political and economic independence and territorial integrity of the several Balkan states should be entered into.
> 12. The Turkish portion of the present Ottoman Empire should be assured a secure sovereignty, but the other nationalities which are now under Turkish rule should be assured

an undoubted security of life and an absolutely unmolested opportunity of autonomous development, and the Dardanelles should be permanently opened as a free passage to the ships and commerce of all nations under international guarantees.

13. An independent Polish state should be erected which should include the territories inhabited by indisputably Polish populations, which should be assured a free and secure access to the sea, and whose political and economic independence and territorial integrity should be guaranteed by international covenant.

The principle of national self-determination was to be enshrined thirty years later in the Charter of the United Nations: Chapter 1, Article 2 stipulates the aim to 'develop friendly relations among nations based on respect for the principle of equal rights and self-determination of peoples, and to take other appropriate measures to strengthen universal peace'.

But what were the nationalities whose right to self-determination was now enshrined in international law? Arguably, for Wilson and the American negotiators, the nationalities were precisely that amalgam of race and language that had been described by Dominian. We can see Dominian's book, and its vitriolic denunciation of the Turkish racial character,* quoted by the King-Crane Commission (appointed by Wilson during the Paris Peace Conference to prepare the settlement of erstwhile Ottoman dominions). The romantic pipe dream to make political frontiers coincide with cultural-linguistic discontinuities was made official policy. Thus a memoir addressed to German negotiators in 1919 pointed out:

> Every territorial settlement of the Treaty of Peace has been determined upon after the most careful and laboured consideration of all the religious, racial and linguistic factors in each particular country. The legitimate hopes of peoples long under alien rule have been heard; and the decisions in each case have been founded upon the principle, explicitly enunciated in the same address: that 'All well-defined national aspirations shall be accorded the utmost satisfaction that can be accorded them without introducing new or perpetuating old elements of discord and antagonism that would be likely in time to break the peace of Europe and consequently of the world.'[251]

The most striking aspect of the principle of national self-determination is the partiality with which it was applied. It was used as a crowbar in order to break up the van-

---

* It should be kept in mind that the author was Armenian, and wrote his book under the shadow of the Armenian genocide, knowledge of which was then only just beginning to emerge.

quished empires in Central and Eastern Europe, but its application in the West was not envisaged. Belgium severely prosecuted those who, during the years 1914-1918, had advocated Flemish emancipation (some of whom had collaborated with the German occupiers for the purpose); the independence of Ireland was only grudgingly conceded in subsequent years; regional minority movements in Spain and France got little or no room for their autonomist ambitions. Even within Eastern and Central Europe the principle of nationality was only used insofar as it served other purposes. Strategic or geopolitical considerations (e.g. access to the Danube or to the sea) often overrode the ethnicity of disputed areas. And in any case, the idea that state borders could reflect ethnic population patterns was, in Central and Eastern Europe of all places, an impossible chimera. In transferring Transylvania from Hungary to Romania, the only effect was that the area no longer represented a Romanian minority under Hungarian rule, but rather a Hungarian minority under Romanian rule – not to mention the other nationalities, neither Romanian nor Magyar, inhabiting the area. Even in a relatively straightforward case such as Schleswig-Holstein, with its mixed Danish- or German-speaking population (and a sprinkling of Frisian), prosperous and socially stable, the plebiscites that eventually settled the area's preponderant ethnicity (and hence, the question as to which state it should belong to) were a vexed affair. Deeper into the heart of the European continent, many areas, indeed, comported four, five or more nationalities intermingled socially and geographically: Vojvodina, Bucovina, the Banat, Ruthenia... to pretend that these could be assigned to one nation-state or another on the principle of national self-determination was either naive or hypocritical.

The 'Versailles system' has often been blamed for the rise of German revanchism in its Nazi guise. It should also be realized that it created as many ethno-geographic problem areas as it aimed to resolve. Hitler's early successes in international affairs were to a large extent based on the ethno-geopolitical policies that had dominated 'Versailles' and that could now be turned into a weapon of nationalist German aggrandizement: the Rhineland, union with Austria, the issues of the Sudetenland and Danzig/Gdańsk.

Nonetheless, 'Versailles' laid down the blueprint of the Europe of nation-states of the twentieth century. To some extent it formed the political enactment of the nationalist ideals of many nineteenth-century movements. Countries like Ireland, Iceland, Finland, the Baltic states, the various South-Slavic states, Albania, Czechia/Slovakia, and so on: all these either obtained their first independence or achieved their territorial outline in 1919. Remarkably, after decades of totalitarian submergence from the 1930s until 1989, many of them (like the Baltic states) reverted after 1989 to the outline that they had first received in the period 1919-1925. (The great exception being, of course, Poland, whose territory has shifted westward.) The Versailles system has consistently provided a mental frame for the European nation-state throughout the twentieth century; even the emergence of an independent Ukraine afer 1993 re-enacts a brief interval of independence, achieved in 1919, and never quite forgotten or abandoned since.

A good many European states date their independence back to nineteenth-century national movements finally recognized in the years following the First World War. These states tend to reflect the linguistic/ethnic principle of nationality emphatically in their political structures and symbolism. The constitutions of such states tend to stipulate, in their preambles or opening articles, that they are based on a cultural identity as expressed in a national language. A massive repartitioning of Europe's demographic space, begun by the Romantics and philologists of Napoleonic times, was given constitutional embodiment in the Versailles system.

Aftermath and Conclusions:
Twentieth-Century Issues

Tethering National Sovereignty:
Transnationalism and Internationalism

Ernest Renan and the critique of national determinism

The fourteenth of Woodrow Wilson's 'fourteen points' envisaged a system of international association in order to guarantee the peaceful coexistence of the self-determining nationalities now achieving statehood. It stipulated that:

> A general association of nations must be formed under specific covenants for the purpose of affording mutual guarantees of political independence and territorial integrity to great and small states alike.

The idea that no nation-state is an island, but that they form part of a system that can ideally control itself was to lead to the ill-fated League of Nations. It has roots as long as the history of nationalism itself: it was foreshadowed by Mazzini's (and Victor Hugo's) ideal that the nationalities of Europe, once sovereign, should cluster into a 'United States of Europe'; and we may even see a forerunner of this notion in Immanuel Kant's project for an 'Everlasting Peace'. *

The League of Nations was notoriously unsuccessful in achieving peace and stability after Versailles; the system derailed with the rise of the totalitarian states in Europe. At the same time, its underlying goal was kept alive in other forms of international association and mutual control such as the United Nations and the European Union. The need to counteract a chauvinistic, hegemonistic nationalism by limiting the unilateralist sovereignty of the nation-state is an ongoing concern in twentieth-century Europe, and its immediate origins may be found in one of the most influential and oft-quoted essays of the last two centuries, Ernest Renan's *Qu'est-ce qu'une nation?* of 1882.[252]

Renan himself (1823-1892) was one of the leading French intellectuals of his day. Originally trained to become a priest, he had, upon losing his faith, gained fame with a remarkable life of Christ (*Vie de Jésus*, 1863), and established himself as an agnostic intellectual as well as a specialist in the culture and spirituality of the Middle East; his

---

* Kant had argued that war is only waged if at least one of the belligerents is a despotic state. Rationally run republics or states (so Kant's Enlightenment view had it) will settle disputes through negotiation or other peaceful means. Remarkably, a bird's-eye view of European wars in the last centuries seems, by and large, to bear out this tenet: one is hard put to find examples of actual wars flaring up between two democracies.

42. Ernest Renan

standing as an Orientalist was high, although he lost his chair at the Collège de France for a while for political reasons.

Intellectually, Renan was a child of his time. With other intellectuals like Hippolyte Taine he believed that scientific progress and a scientific mode of thinking would come to dominate human affairs; and a quasi-ethnographical belief in the racial under-pinning of culture formed part of that 'scientific' outlook. Hippolyte Taine, famously, believed that literary history could be written on the basis of the underlying para-meters of race, geographical location and historical context. Renan himself applied this type of ethnological determinism to the Celtic literature of Brittany, his own home region, in influential essays such as *La littérature des races celtiques* (1854).[253]

Racially deterministic scientism also linked Renan to German scholarship, which he admired and from which he took inspiration. A crisis in this outlook occurred after the Franco-Prussian war of 1870-1871, which culminated in the German annexation of Alsace-Lorraine. That annexation continued, as we have seen, a centuries-old geopolitical tug of war over the region. In the strident German triumphalism of the time, however, it was also rationalized as the necessary adjustment of political frontiers to their underlying ethnic patterns. Alsace and Strasbourg were Germanic (so it was argued) in their architecture, their viticulture, their local speech and other ethnographical factors, and must therefore necessarily form part of the state which incorporated that Germanic identity.

That ethnic-determinist rationalization cut no ice, however, in France. Strasbourg, including its white wine, its half-timbered houses and its German *patois*, had been French since the days of Louis XIV; it had been the birthplace of the *Marseillaise* and of the revolutionary general Kléber, as Lorraine had been the birthplace of Jeanne d'Arc; it had, over the past centuries, become enmeshed in the tapestry of France's historical weal and woe, and the annexation was felt by the French (and by most Alsatians) as a brutal amputation.

Renan's essay *Qu'est-ce qu'une nation?* never once mentions Strasbourg, or Alsace-Lorraine. Its phraseology is that of a courteous, if slightly sarcastic, theoretical disquisition on the determinants of that complex thing, 'national identity'; yet Renan takes issue with a determinism that he qualifies, time and again, as a product of 'German' thought (conveniently ignoring how much that thought had also been carried by Frenchmen like Taine and himself), and taking, at least in his theoretical position, an anti-German stance. That the practical implications of that stance were anti-German, too, and that they amounted to a rebuttal of the German claims on Alsace-Lorraine, is obvious but never explicitly stated. This attempt to generalize beyond the contentious issue of the day is not just a rhetorical ploy; it does makes Renan's line of reasoning all the stronger, lifts the essay out of the context of French-German antagonism and has ensured its status, well into the twentieth century and beyond. It is one of the key arguments against the beliefs, so rampantly predominant by the late nineteenth century, that culture and identity are determined by descent, and that the state should incorporate an underlying ethnicity.

What is a nation? Renan reviews the various answers to that question which were dominant at the time. To begin with, he rejects the semantic slippage between nation and race. Against the ideology of racal purity he points out that all of Europe, for the entire duration of its recorded history, has been a melting pot of tribes crisscrossing the map and cohabiting in the various corners of the continent. The idea that any modern individual or nation could be the pure and unmixed offspring of the tribes of antiquity, across all the intervening centuries of migration and intermixture, he dismisses as an implausible fiction. France has emerged from Gauls, Romans and Franks, England from Saxons, Normans and Danes; the national bloodlines of Europe are a cocktail of different ancestries.

Other historical determinants of nationality are likewise surveyed and dismissed. Geography (riverbeds and mountain ranges) may influence international traffic, they do not impose national cohesion. Language spills across various nationalities whilst a single nation like the Swiss may straddle diverse languages. The same goes for religion. And the fiscal-administrative rule of a state is not in itself enough to establish a common identity. Nationality lies, if anywhere, with the people's own sense of identity, their self-identification, and no single circumstance can directly determine that collective attitude (Renan speaks of '*un principe spirituel, un état d'âme*'): nationality is a state of mind.

It is at this point that Renan formulates his alternative to the determinism which he attacks. It is, precisely, the will of the people concerned: their choice to identify in one way rather than another. In an interesting echo of Rousseau's *volonté générale*, Renan's idea of nationality, of 'what makes a nation', is the principle of collective choice; in so doing, Renan opposes to determinism what we now call 'voluntarism'. One belongs to a nation because implicitly or explicitly that is what one chooses to do; the collectivity of a nation is a mutual sense of belonging and togetherness, which is tacitly affirmed from day to day in one's implicit allegiance; the famous phrase Renan uses is that of '*un plébiscite de tous les jours*', a 'plebiscite renewed from day to day'. This moral allegiance or solidarity is in turn inspired, not by any determining external factor such as race or geography, but by common interests and shared experiences. Nationality is a social choice rather than an anthropological category.

Renan's argument in favour of social choice was to a large extent a tactical, ad hoc one. The idea of a 'plebiscite' is not merely a metaphor for the general will of the people, it also echoes specific calls to let the status of Alsace-Lorraine be decided, not by the warring capitals Berlin and Paris, but by the people concerned (and Renan knew full well that the people concerned would overwhelmingly support a French rather than a German appurtenance). The decision of national status by plebiscite had been tried before, incidentally: the inhabitants of Avignon and the Franche-Comté had decided in such a way to join France in 1791.[254] Similarly, in those decades, the absorption (*enosis*) of the Ionian islands and Crete into an expanding Greece proceeded on the basis of a locally established free choice rather than as a result of geopolitics enforced from the metropolis. In the subsequent century, the plebiscite would remain a reliable instrument to settle conflicts in disputed border regions; from the 1920 Schleswig-Holstein settlement to the 2006 declaration of Montenegrin independence fom Serbia.

But, aside from this deliberate political aim, Renan's notion of plebiscite crucially formulated the idea that nationality is not a question of identity, but of identification. As Renan himself clearly saw, this identification is a history-driven process which over the course of time is subject to historical change. Solidarity can grow on the basis of shared glories and, more importantly, shared suffering; national unity can only be established if the memories of ancient strife and old divisions are allowed to be laid to rest.

Indeed, in an almost prophetical gesture, Renan predicted that the progress of the historical sciences might unearth old, almost-forgotten intra-national grievances which, if re-actualized and re-remembered might threaten the moral cohesion of the nation-state. At the time when Renan wrote this, he was thinking of the blood-stained records of French history itself: the anti-Cathar and anti-Albigensian crusades of the Middle Ages; the ruthless suppression of Protestantism from the St. Bartholomew's Day massacre to the extirpation of the *Camisards* in the Cevennes; the memory of the 1790s Vendée wars. (In fact, some of these events were already feeding into regionalist anti-French resentment in the Languedoc and in Brittany at the time.) But more generally, Renan's observation predicts with remarkable insight the end of the triumphalist mode of monumental-nationalist history-writing, and the rise of the 'traumatic paradigm' in the twentieth-century collective-historical consciousness. State commemorations have adopted the mode of mourning into their celebrations: under the *Arc de Triomphe* now lie the ashes of the Unknown Soldier, and national monuments now tend to pay respect to history's victims rather than to celebrate history's conquering heroes. The framework of 'the nation' in history-writing and in historical consciousness has receded. Other groups and aggregates (class, regions, community, gender, race) have come to take exception to the grand national narratives and claim the right to tell the story of the past from their subordinate point of view and from their experience – an experience, often, of marginalization, oppression or persecution.[255] Thus the rise of 'identity politics', predicted with so much foresight by Renan as a refusal to let bygones be bygones, a refusal to sink own's partial grievances into the general consensus, occured initially as part of a weakening of the totalizing vision of nationalism.

Most fundamentally, however, the influence of Renan lies in his rebuttal of the determinist vision of ethnic nationalism. If, by and large in contemporary Europe, the tenets of ethnic nationalism are viewed with scepticism and suspicion, then credit is due to the lone voice that was first raised against them during their heyday of the 1880s.

Renan's widening influence

Twentieth-century manifestations of anti-nationalism, following Renan, were often motivated directly by pacifism. The national fanaticism of warfare since Napoleon (already described in terms of moral denunciation in Tolstoy's *War and Peace*) had made one thing clear: if the nation was everything in public affairs, it was also the Leviathan that waged wars and destroyed entire generations. Bertha von Suttner's *Die Waffen nieder!* of 1889 set a trend. The fact that Alfred Nobel dedicated part of his estate to the establishment of a Peace Prize (awarded to Suttner in 1905) consolidated that trend, as did the series of the The Hague Peace Conferences, undertaken in 1899 on the initiative of Tsar Nicholas II and funded by the American industrialist and philanthropist Andrew Carnegie.[*]

Although all this well-meaning elite pacifism failed to stop the carnage of the Balkan Wars and the First World War, those conflicts did demonstrate how urgent the need had become to limit the nation-states' power of chauvinist belligerence. In 1914, many thinkers had welcomed the war as a glorious occasion to rejuvenate and re-heroicize Europe; the Irish nationalist Patrick Pearse echoed the sentiments of his generation all over Europe when he wrote:

> The last sixteen months have been the most glorious in the
> history of Europe. Heroism has come back to the earth. [...]
> the people themselves have gone to battle because to each the

---

[*] In 1907, the Peace Palace in The Hague was built, and today houses the International Court of Human Rights, set up under the auspices of the United Nations and known nowadays largely for its Yugoslavia tribunal (Eyffinger 2006). Currently, the attempt to expand the court with an International Criminal Court for the prosecution of war crimes worldwide has notoriously met with resistance from the United States.

old voice that speaks out of the soil of a nation has spoken
anew. Each fights for the fatherland. [...] It is good for the
world that such things should be done. The old heart of the
earth needed to be warmed with the red wine of the battlefield. Such august homage was never before offered to God as
this, the homage of millions of lives given gladly for love of
country.[256]

At the outbreak of the war, and maybe even still in December 1915, when Pearse wrote
this, such a sentiment was still an acceptable rhetorical continuation of nineteenth-
century romantic attitudes, sharpened by the prevailing fear of decadence and degeneration; a few years later it had become an obscenity. The horrors of the mud-clogged
trenches, with their barbed wire, their poison gas, their artillery barrages, splintered
forests and endless casualty lists, spread far and wide into society-at-large by new media such as press and photography.[257] Press coverage was followed by artistic representations of what war could inflict, in the poems of Wilfred Owen, the novels of
Remarque and Hašek, the drawings of Otto Dix. All this cast a pall over the old
Romantic glorification of the military and of warfare. Even at the Paris Peace Conference, there were those who realized that the settlement of the war should be more
than an exercise in punishing the losers,[*] and that the root of the problem lay in the
exaggerated national chauvinism that had come to dominate international relations.
The diplomat and scholar Carlile Aylmer Macartney (1895-1979) who had participated
as a young man in the Paris Peace Conference, published his important study *Nation
States and National Minorities* in 1934, when the delayed flaws of the Versailles system
were becoming painfully obvious in Germany and Central Europe. By that time, too,
internationalism and pacifism had been placed on a new footing by initiatives such as
the aforementioned League of Nations, and the Pan-European Movement of Count
Richard Coudenhove-Kalergi (1894-1972). Although Coudenhove-Kalergi's movement
was elitist and inefficient, it did catch the imagination of certain politicians, such as
Aristide Briand and Winston Churchill, and may have sown some of the seeds that
were, one World War later, to inspire the initiative towards a deliberately transnational
European Community.[258]

The attempts of politicians to tie down that destructive giant of the unilateralist
nation-state (much like Lilliputians trussing Gulliver with hundreds of small threads)

---

* Who were 'the losers' anyway? The Versailles Treaty uses a curious formula in the opening
section of the part dealing with reparations (section VIII, kindly brought to my attention by Wim
Roobol): 'The Allied and Associated Governments affirm and Germany accepts the responsibility of
Germany and her allies for causing all the loss and damage to which the Allied and Associated
Governments and their nationals have been subjected as a consequence of the war imposed upon
them by the aggression of Germany and her allies.' Asymmetrically, a set of governments (represent-
ing states and their nationals) is juxtaposed with an abstract and undifferentiated principle called
'Germany', which embodies the continuity (and continuing responsibility) between the vanished
Wilhelminian *Reich* that had started the war in 1914, and the government that signed the treaty in
1919. The standard work on this 'continuity principle', Marek 1968, does not address this case.

eventually culminated in Jean Monnet's insightful programme to pool the West-European resources of coal and steel internationally. If Europe's heavy industry were to be placed under the control of an international community regulating its raw materials, coal and steel, then unilateral re-armament would be a thing of the past forever. The European Community of Coal and Steel, thus established in 1952, was to give a firm basis to the French-German tandem, and later led to the European Economic Community and the European Union by way of the Treaties of Rome (1958), of Maastricht (1993), of Amsterdam (1999), and of Nice (2003).

This diplomatic-political initiative was flanked by, and inspired by, a more moral-intellectual drive, which we can trace back, by various filiations, to Ernest Renan's critique of nationalism. One of the disseminators of Renan's thought was the French sociologist Marcel Mauss, author of *Nation, nationalité, internationalisme* (1920); another was the aforementioned Macartney, who participated in a highly influential British think-tank, the Royal Institute for International Affairs at Oxford, led by the historian E.H. Carr. Faced with the rise of Hitlerism in the 1930, this institute produced a seminal analysis of the nationalist ideology, entitled *Nationalism*, in 1939. (Carr himself published, in 1945, a brief tract with the hopeful title *Nationalism and After.*) Among the collaborators was also a rising young scholar from Prague, the polyglot Hans Kohn (1891-1971), who, after he had emigrated to the United States, was to become an early associate of the Foreign Policy Research Institute and one of the twentieth century's greatest historians and analysts of nationalism.[*] Such anti-totalitarian internationalism eventually found its political expression in another European-wide organization, the Council of Europe, established in 1949, and dedicated primarily to the defence and European integration of human rights, parliamentary democracy and the rule of law. In addition, the Council of Europe proclaimed its internationalist roots in its aim to 'promote awareness of a European identity based on shared values and cutting across different cultures.'

The recoil from totalitarianism

Obviously, the rejection of determinist ethnic nationalism and national chauvinism became a matter of urgency after the rise of fascist dictatorships in the mid-century. Many European countries were affected, from Portugal to Romania. Even in the more stable states of Northern and Western Europe, fascist movements played a strident and sometimes prominent role in politics in the 1920s and 1930s. They flourished to a degree under Nazi aegis when the continental democracies were occupied after Hitler's campaigns of 1939-1940.

---

[*] Born in Prague, Kohn had been active in Zionist student organizations. He received a Doctor of Law degree from the German University in Prague. In the First World War, he became a prisoner of war and was interned in Samarkand and Khaborovsk, Krasnoyarsk and Irkutsk in Siberia until 1920. In the following years he lived and worked in Paris, London and Palestine; in 1929 he moved to the US.

Although there are differences of degree between the authoritarian corporatism of falangist and fascist dictatorships on the one hand, and the racial-collective *völkisch* ideologies of National Socialism, these extreme right-wing ideologies all shared an exaggerated belief in the primacy of nationality, overriding all concerns of individual liberty and cultivating a deliberate intolerance of others. The deterministic views of ethnic nationalism were exaggerated into the various forms of pseudo-science that flourished under these regimes. The National-Socialist idea of nationality is more or less *sui generis* and one had best call it by its own self-styled appellation: that of *völkisch*. Although racism is present in almost all fascist movements,[259] the *völkisch* way of seeing the nation as a biological community is in a league of its own. In its view, the history of the *Volk* is thoroughly determined, in its larger patterns, by its innate and cultivated temperament and by its purity and collective solidarity, and in its crises, by the willpower of its leaders and their capacity to understand the patterns and necessities of the historical juncture. Thus, the *völkisch* historical vision often concentrates on single, powerful historical figures and their entourage, while there is also a tendency to go into large geo-anthropological abstractions. Karl Haushofer's notorious *Geopolitik* explained national destinies with the geological and geographical morphological features of their areas of settlement and their *Lebensraum*. Similarly, the most typical exponent of *völkisch* history-writing, the pursuit of *Volksgeschichte*, tended towards a historical geography of national settlements and migrations. The names by which these studies were called usually involve a purported link between the timeless principle of ethnicity and the equally a-historical framework of space. *Volkstum-* and *Deutschtumforschung* (the study of 'nationality' and 'Germanness') hinged on the concepts of *Volk* and *Raum* (landscape-space): *Raumforschung, Volks- und Raumgeschichte*.[260] The overriding interest was always to celebrate the perennial sameness of the Germanic tribes, from archaic roots to Hitlerite rebirth: the enduring link between the Germans' racial lineage and their land (*Blut und Boden*). This cult of *völkisch* identity was an important contributing factor in the Third Reich's policy of genocide as an instrument of national purity and total control.[261]

Following these bloodbaths, Europeans in the second half of the twentieth century had to confront Renan's evocation of a blood-stained, traumatic history with a disconcerted sense of massive, unremitting barbarism lurking under the appearance of civilization. The Christian Middle Ages had spawned the Crusades and the witch craze; the rise of modernity had seen the wars of religion and the devastating imperial delusions of Louis XIV, Napoleon and Wilhelm; Europe's colonial and imperial expansion involved the huge, centuries-long genocide and ethnocide of slavery and the slave trade; and at least numerically the death toll of Nazi rule was mirrored in the vast homicidal track record of Stalinism. In the second half of the twentieth century then, Western Europe, staggering out of the ruins of the Second World War, faced the dual task of anti-totalitarianism and the defence of individuals and minorities against the authority of the state. (In the East, communist rule was to extend the period of totalitarian tyranny for another half-century.) It is not for nothing that the trans- and international organizations set up in the late 1940s all linked the notion of international cooperation with the principle of respect for human rights.[*]

---

* The implicit stipulation of democratic rule can be seen at work in the track record of the EEC and European Union. Dictatorships like Franco's Spain and Salazar's Portugal were excluded from membership, and only acceded after their transition to parliamentary democracy. Greek applications for membership were unacceptable while that country was under the regime of a military junta in the early 1970s. In 2000, the rise of Jörg Haider's extreme right-wing FPÖ to government in Austria (already a member state of the EU) led to the country's informal isolation in European affairs; and even the candidacy of Jean-Marie Le Pen in France's presidential elections of 2002 immediately led the French media to reflect on France's total isolation in European affairs should he be elected. Negotiations with prospective members from post-Communist countries (as well as Turkey) have again brought the issue of human rights to the front as an implicit but fundamentally important principle in the EU.

Postnationalism

The internationalist and anti-totalitarian recoil from national chauvinism dominated Western Europe throughout the Cold War. Increasingly, European cooperation dominated the agenda; the future lay in a healing of old wounds and international European harmony. What is more, the period 1945-1989 was almost unique in European history for the stability of its international frontiers. No other half-century can be found in which the outline of the states and the trajectory of their dividing borders was so rigidly and unchangingly fixed. For someone who grew up in these immediate post-war decades, the impression might well be that states had now found their lasting, definitive geographical expression and that Europe henceforth was to be a neat jigsaw puzzle of seamlessly interlocking states, each comprising an unambiguous nationality and territory. Despite some anomalies (a divided Germany and an isolated Berlin foremost among them), all potential territorial conflicts were resolutely kept in deep freeze, since any destabilization could trigger a devastating nuclear war between the two superpowers, the US and the USSR. The time of international rivalry and territorial conquest, which had ruled the fluctuations of the European map for so long, seemed over; nationalism, self-denounced as a result of its perverse ideological excesses of the mid-century, seemed as dead an ideology as the belief in witchcraft. Even so, some specifically national issues continued to make their presence felt.

Decolonization

Famously, the twentieth century was the time of de-colonization; the first European state to be confronted with this process had been Spain, which, following the early-nineteenth-century campaigns of Simon Bolívar[*] in Latin America, experienced the loss of its last overseas colonies in 1898 as a time of national trauma and a point of recalibration for a sense of Spanish identity. In the course of the following century, Britain was to lose its empire in India/Pakistan and its colonies and dominions in Africa, the Caribbean and the Pacific; the Netherlands their East Indies (Indonesia) and Surinam; France its possessions in Indochina and North Africa; Belgium its Congo colony; Portugal, Angola and Mozambique. This process of de-colonization has been extensively studied and may very roughly be explained from two or three key factors: the drastic weakening of the European states as a result of their internecine wars, linked to the fact that the superpowers which came to dominate world affairs

---

[*] Simon de Bolívar (1783-1830), celebrated throughout Latin America as *El libertador*, stands at the beginning of the independence of Colombia, Venezuela, Ecuador and Peru; Bolivia has been named after him. His profile as a national liberation campaigner (astutely exploiting the Napoleon-inflicted weakness of Spain around 1810) fits that of others who were inspired by an Enlightenment sense of civic patriotism and liberty: Pasquale Paoli in Corsica, Washington in North America, Kosciuszko in Poland, O'Connell in Ireland, and, as a belated example perhaps, Garibaldi in Italy.

after 1945 were themselves averse to colonialism; and the emergence of a modern-trained elite of local intellectuals who could rally popular discontent behind a realistic political agenda of self-determination.

For the anticolonial activists, the pursuit of independence constituted a national agenda, and as a result the decolonization process has been studied as a form of nationalism. It is, however, a moot point whether Sukarno, Gandhi, Nkrumah, Nyerere, Ho Chi Minh, Senghor, Bourguiba and Ben Bella (to name just a few of the many independence leaders in Europe's colonies) can be compared to the likes of Pearse, Kossuth, Rakovski, Velestinlis or Alecsandri.* European nationalism as it has been studied here was always the political application of a cultural programme. It involved the political instrumentalization of a sense of nationality rooted in cultural patterns and triggered by a programme of cultural consciousness-raising. The twentieth-century pursuit of independence in the European colonies started from an agenda of political justice and economic empowerment, and while we can often see a cultural policy of sorts (e.g. literacy programmes), these tend to be largely educational and rarely aimed at the political instrumentalization of cultural identity. Most leaders were content to draw the boundaries of their emerging stages according to the frontiers imposed by colonial administrators, surrounding territories including many cultures and languages, and establishing states often using the colonial language as its official one (Spanish, Portuguese, English or French). The concept of language-based nationality counted for little; if anything the concept of race was thematized, in the overriding binary 'black versus white' terms that had defined colonial denigration and expropriation. Many leaders, moreover, were motivated by ideologies that stood apart from the European patterns; influential thinkers were Marx, Gramsci and the Caribbean-born Frantz Fanon (1925-1961). If European nationalism had been driven by Romantic idealism, anticolonialism tended to rest its case on the tenets and rhetoric of a radical liberalism, Marxism, or religions such as Hinduism or Islam.

In all these respects, then, decolonization in the twentieth century represented something structurally different from European nationalism. Nonetheless, the process had an impact within Europe as well. To begin with, the colonial empires of the nineteenth century had to re-imagine themselves as nation-states: the process that started with the Spanish 'generation of 1898' (Unamuno, Ortega y Gasset), and that can also be registered in the period 1945-1965 in Britain. Between the independence of India and Pakistan and the humiliation of the Suez crisis, Britain underwent a powerful process of national identity-seeking, expressed in the pageantry of Elizabeth II's coronation in 1953 (and the proclamation of a self-styled generation of 'new Elizabethans', harking back to the Shakespeares, Raleighs and Drakes of Elizabeth I's reign), in the ironic domesticity of John Betjeman's poetry, in the introspective preoccupations of the cinema of Powell and Pressburger and the Ealing Studios. What for the colonies

---

* A possible in-between figure is Archbishop Makarios of Cyprus, who in some respects conforms to patterns of Hellenic, Church-driven, anti-Turkish nationalism, and in other respects conforms to the pattern of global decolonization (e.g. his participation in the non-aligned movement of Sukarno and Tito).

themselves was an emancipation, was felt by the European states as a loss, an amputation, which played into a general sense of disorientation caused by wartime destruction.

The mid-twentieth century has been described generally as a period of relentless modernity, the time of Sartre and Beckett; there is yet a history to be written of the no less important wave of popular nostalgia that formed its counterpart in these decades: the *Heimatfilme* (cinematic 'homeland idylls') of Adenauer's Germany; the *piccolo mondo* in which Giovannino Guareschi reduced Italy's political clashes to the level of village brawls between Don Camillo and Peppone; the Agatha Christie novels and Ealing comedies affectionately mocking the lovingly invoked sterotypical Englishness of their subject-matter; the wry evocation of a *douce France* in Chevallier's novel *Clochemerle* (1934; film version, 1948) and in the semi-bohemian *chansons* of Georges Brassens. All these cozy manifestations of middlebrow nostalgia reflect an almost deliberate attempt *not* to mention the war or the colonial dismemberment of the former empires. Remarkably, these nationally nostalgic productions were internationally popular across Europe: the French film productions of the Italian Don Camillo stories were eagerly viewed in Germany and Holland, and everyone, from Lisbon to Lübeck, knew Miss Marple. The German *Heimatfilm* was less popular internationally, owing to a general impopularity of things German, but the formula reached a world audience in the *Sissi* films and in *The Sound of Music* (itself a closely faithful American remake of *Die Trapp-Familie*, 1956).[262]

Radical anti-hegemonist critiques from emancipating ex-colonies washed back into Europe in the course of the 1960s, and did affect European national movements. Militant separatists in Northern Ireland (the IRA) and the Basque Country (ETA) took inspiration from Civil Rights movements in America and from Liberation Front nationalism in Vietnam, Cuba and Palestine; as a result they changed, in a generation shift starting around 1968, their ideology away from romantic-idealist celebrations of their homeland, its culture, its traditions and its yearning for a return to the Golden Age of prelapsarian independence. The new generation of ETA and IRA militants were inspired by the likes of Che Guevara and Ho Chi Minh, read Mao and Marx, and saw their insurgence as an 'armed struggle' in which they spearheaded the people at large. Their military tactics, training and armament were likewise taken from a common worldwide market of liberation front warriors and insurrectionists.

As the names of ETA and IRA indicate, separatist activism had not died out in Europe after 1945. In the streets of Bilbao and Belfast, enmity between a repressive state (Franco's Spain and unionist Ulster) and a disaffected national minority continued unabated throughout the postwar decades. The centuries-long conflict between Greece and Turkey played itself out once more, in Cyprus, where it was overlaid by the added factor of anti-British decolonization. Nationalism was still around, but in the provinces and peripheries, and drawing on new discourses and ideologies.

In the selfsame provinces and peripheries, the nostalgia of the postwar decades took the form, after 1968, of a new regionalism. Cultural minorities found a new audience and a new platform with the renewed popularity of folk music and 'folk rock' (the Breton harp player Alan Stivell is a good example of this generational shift from old-style Breton regionalism into the 1970s), and became linked with a youth culture that also embraced ecological, anti-militaristic and generally countercultural issues. Against a free-market, middle-class Europe of enterprises and governments, stood a 'Europe of regions' where people ate wholefood, wore homespuns, advocated solar energy and celebrated rustic traditions. Paradoxically, rustic nostalgia became a form of social criticism;[263] and in many cases, this social criticism on a regional basis was grafted onto long-standing cultural differences and cultural movements with nineteenth-century culture-nationalistic roots, e.g. in Wales, Brittany, Catalonia, Corsica, Friesland and elsewhere. Again, in some cases this regionalist activism could confront state centralism in acts of occasional, minor violence: holiday homes were burned in anti-tourist campaigns in Wales; clashes over Welsh- or Breton-language media or education occurred. By the end of the 1980s, there were regionalist 'green' networks operative across Europe, and regional politics and particularisms were beginning to be discussed in the 'postcolonial' terms of marginalization and centre-periphery imbalance.

This trend towards regionalization profited from a general weakening of the power of the sovereign state in Europe. As we have seen, European states had united in a European Community which in its various embodiments (EEC, EC, EU) became increasingly powerful and siphoned off ever-larger portions of national sovereignty towards its institutions. The 'seepage of sovereignty' proceeded not only in an upwards direction (towards 'Brussels'), but also downward, towards the regions and border zones. One of the side effects of European integration was the increase of regional diversity within the member states, weakened as the autonomy of their own centres became. Cross-border local and regional cooperation (e.g. between Strasbourg and Baden-Baden, or between Lyon and Lombardy) became progressively easier as the borders between France, Germany and Italy lost their incisive and divisive force, and traffic between these places could afford to bypass the national capitals of Paris, Bonn and Rome.[264] Local Scottish authorities were in a position to mount European lobbies for control over 'their' North Sea oil reserves, bypassing and at some point wrong-footing the British Prime Minister Thatcher. Regions grew in strength as a side effect of European integration and of the weakening of nation-state centralism. Indeed even during the Cold War years Belgium witnessed the beginnings of an irreversible drift from a centralized state to a federative structure of different language communities, Flemish and French-speaking. An administrative frontier was drawn up in 1962, and the Belgian state has since then consistently ceded more and more powers to its Flemish and Francophone constituent parts.

When the end of the Cold War led to a general thaw in constitutional relations, this trend towards regionalization gathered speed. Spain has moved from Franco-style strict centralism to a high degree of cultural federalism, recognizing the linguistic and administrative autonomy of regions such as the Basque Country, Catalonia and Galicia. In Britain, devolution granted linguistic and then political rights to Wales and to Scotland, involving the installation of regional parliaments. In Italy, a populist 'Northern League' or *Lega Nord* began to attack the unitary Italian state in which they saw an economically and socially mature north hampered down by the poverty and sloth of the south of the country. (The party's own politics and rhetoric failed, however, to demonstrate that alleged northern maturity and superiority which they invoked for themselves.)

At the same time, the Council of Europe has become increasingly proactive in the matter of intra-state regional and ethnic minorities, going as far as to issue a charter for the protection of regional and minority languages, which is now ratified by the requisite majority of member-states. In short: cultural identity politics have in some form or other remained on the agenda in Western Europe throughout the second half of the twentieth century. Reports about the demise of nationalism, heard occasionally in the 1970s and 1980s, were definitely premature – as the events following the end of the Cold War would demonstrate. Before we turn to that most recent period in the history of national thought in Europe, we must, however, address one thorny issue. Is the persistence of regionalism and cultural particularism in the minorities and peripheries of Europe a countermovement against, or else a vestige of, nationalism?

Heteronomy: Against cultural atomism

The question of regionalism and sub-nationalism is troublesome. In some demonstrated instances, regionalism (e.g. in Brittany) is historically descended from, or has historically anticipated, nationalist movements, and in some cases, again, regionalism can take a worrying form of separatist xenophobia and intolerance – e.g. in the Italian Lega Nord and in extreme Flemish nationalism. One must also question the wisdom of wishing to define and split up cultures in ever-finer, ever-purer and ever-more-unmixed subgroups, and to demand separate autonomy for each of these separate subgroups. A crumbling of states to the unworkable level of mini-statelets merely to satisfy a sense of cultural separateness amongst their inhabitants seems unwise. From Latvia (with its Russian population) and Moldova (with its intransigent Transdniestrian region) to Catalonia (where there are Castilian-speaking Spaniards as well as Catalans), we shall always find that minorities, once liberated from the clasp of their masters, will prove to include yet smaller mini-minorities that had been hidden from sight before. Nor is it reasonable to assume that at some fundamental level we will refine our cultural and social divisions down to an atomic (no-longer-divisible) level of homogeneity, as if the smallest communities would exhibit an ideal uniformity of culture and consensus. The community consists, not of people agreeing in all things and in all choices, but of people arguing out their differences. Social and cultural conflicts are not the monopoly of large states; they occur also in regions, provinces, cities and villages. And the intensity of conflict does not diminish at the smaller scale. The worst atrocities in the Bosnian war of the 1990s took place at village level. Village politics are, if anything, more antagonistic than state politics, and the bitterest enmities occur within the tightest communities, even within families. Not even at the level of the individual do we see consensus and unity of purpose: a single human will feel differently at age 50 than at age 17, may feel differently about things on a Monday morning than on a Saturday afternoon, and will have mixed feelings and mood vacillations about a good many things in life. The term 'individual' in its Latin root sense ('not divisible, a fundamental unit') is a misnomer; and the idea that at some small, communitarian level cultural difference resolves itself into undifferentiated homogeneity is a chimera. A dangerous chimera at that, because it may inspire us with the desire to measure our human, quarrelsome states against an ant-hill ideal of homogeneity and undifferentiatedness; as if the best states were those without minorities...

The inner diversity of the state will not resolve itself into unitary, homogenous, undifferentiated building-blocks if we subdivide it: at each level of subdivision we will encounter fresh diversity and the chimerical lure to resolve *that* by subdividing still further, ad infinitum. Regionalism in Europe must, in other words, resist the siren call of separatism. The response I would like to put forward as the most workable one is that of *heteronomy* – by which I mean the very opposite of autonomy. Regional, intra-state diversity is a given. To try and rationalize it away by granting autonomy to the component regions is shortsighted and counterproductive; like a car driver low on fuel who drives faster so as to reach the petrol station sooner. If by autonomy we mean the existence of separate laws for separate polities, it may be better to consider the alternative, heteronomy: the subsidiary co-existence of different laws within one and the same state. States should be tolerant enough of their minorities to allow them the liberty of their specificity; in making legal provisions for the cultural diversity within their borders, the state will also reduce the disaffection of its regions and minorities, will forestall differences being exacerbated into conflicts, will ensure the civic allegiance of even those citizens and taxpayers whose culture differs from that of the capital. The implementation of the European Charter for Regional and Minority Languages envisages precisely this: that linguistic difference within a state will be accommodated and acknowledged in national legislation, and will be prevented from becoming either an object of state repression or a focus of separatist disaffection. The most coherent states may in the future well be those that are most flexible about their inner diversity, and most efficient in giving citizens a civic, rather than a cultural, focus for their shared loyalty and solidarity.

Neonationalism: After the Cold War

The communist regimes lost their grip on Eastern Europe from 1989 onwards. As the example of Germany shows (where the retrieval of political liberty was immediately translated into the reflex towards territorial unification), national thought, in various gradations of intensity, filled the ideological vacuum. The USSR crumbled into the nationalities that had already asserted their autonomy between 1900 and 1920: the Baltic states, Ukraine and even Belarus immediately made use of the weakening of central rule to set up autonomous governments. The federation of Yugoslavia proved too weak to survive the death of Tito and of one-party rule, and crumbled into its constituent nationalities. The process was relatively painless for Slovenia but led to violent conflict on the frontiers of Serbia, involving gruesome civil war along ethnic lines in Bosnia-Hercegovina. Serbia, the strongest member of the Yugoslav complex, used the greatest force in that conflict, but overplayed its hand. It emerged from the war as a weakened and isolated pariah state, unable to stem the secessionist tendencies in Kosovo and Montenegro; even the northern, ethnically mixed province of Vojvodina has shown strong tendencies to dissociate itself from Belgrade. Meanwhile, a similar centrifugal tendency, though much more peacefully resolved, led to the break-up between the Czech Republic and Slovakia. The 'hyphenated' nationalities that had emerged from nineteenth-century Pan-Slavism (Serbo-Croat, Czecho-Slovak[265]) fissioned into their component parts.

The re-emergence of ethnic nationalism was also noticeable in the emergence of right-wing ethnonationalist parties in these post-communist countries; remarkably, they often sheltered, or colluded with, erstwhile communist cadres. While these developments are ominous, and a measure of the lack of stability and civic harmony in Central and Eastern Europe, they are not peculiar to that region. The resurgence of nationalism, and of ethnic nationalism, is occurring all over Europe, also in the west.

Although Western Europe never underwent the traumatic decades of communist rule and had a longer tradition of civic stability, nationalism would here, too, make its mark in the course of the 1990s. The first sign of this was a growing Euroscepticism, from the late 1980s onwards. The 1993 Treaty of Maastricht seemed to mark the high tide of European integrationism, and even in the run-up to it there were signs that the agenda of federal or confederal integration was losing its momentum. The long rule of Thatcherite Toryism in Britain made Euroscepticism a recognizable political stance, located largely on the right wing of the Conservative Party. Euroscepticism tended to stress the Atlantic ties with the USA, was supported in particular by the mutual sympathies between Republican Presidents and the European centre-right;* it also sup-

---

* Conversely, Europeanism always carried a certain amount of anti-Americanism with it, ever since the days when Charles De Gaulle had thought of Europe as a French-dominated power base alongside the US. Significantly, this anti-American Europeanism was strongest when Republicans with an aggressive foreign policy occupied the White House (Nixon, Reagan, Bush), and relaxed

ported, largely for geopolitical reasons, and not necessarily in order to fortify a separate European position, EU membership for NATO partners such as Turkey.

Euroscepticism argued, in particular, that European integration might be detrimental to national sovereignty and national identity. It represented relations with 'Brussels' increasingly in 'us versus them' terms, and represented the European administration as an alien, Kafkaesque, overblown bureaucracy threatening traditional and harmonious, national communities. Instead of a European Union (feared as a 'superstate'), Eurosceptics would prefer to see a loose economic working association of a 'Europe of nations'. In other words: resistance against the development of the European integration process was couched in the rhetoric of nationality and national identity. Integration gestures such as the establishment of a common currency were in many cases resisted as an attack on the 'national' currency, as a loss of a cherished symbol of national sovereignty and identity.

To a significant extent, Eurosceptic rhetoric reflected a general, and growing, populist mistrust between citizen and government – a political malaise which has come to affect intra-national affairs in many Western European countries since ca. 2000, and of which Eurosceptic feelings in the 1980s and early 1990s were only the first, early warnings.[266] It must also be added that this populism was irresponsibly exploited by political parties trying (like the Thatcherite Tories) to obtain street credibility with the electorate. Thus, the 2004 European elections in the Netherlands saw all political parties wage Eurosceptic campaigns (with the exception only of the small social-liberal D66), asking for votes 'so as to make a defiantly Dutch voice heard in Brussels'. In an eyebrow-raising turnaround, those selfsame political parties asked the selfsame electorate the next year, 2005, to endorse the European draft constitution. The fact that this constitution was so resoundingly rejected marked, then, not only a Euro-weariness among Dutch voters, but also a credibility problem for the mainstream parties, which was further illustrated by the rise (and murder) of the populist leader Pim Fortuyn – much as the long-indulged Euroscepticism of the Conservative Party in Britain triggered, eventually, the establishment of the populist UK Independence Party.

Ironically, by the time the Maastricht Treaty was concluded, the European Union had already taken steps to exclude, explicitly, national cultures from the integration process. The 'cultural paragraph' in the Maastricht Treaty stipulated this, but even earlier, a ruling of the European Court had ensured that matters of national cultural identity were exempt from the integrationist rules and measures of the European Union.† Even so, 'Europe' and 'national identity' came, over the 1990s, to be seen

---

whenever America was led by a mellower or Democratic presidency, especially during the Clinton years.

† In a ruling dated 28 November 1989, the Court ruled in a conflict between the Republic of Ireland and the Dutch-born artist and art teacher Anita Groener. Groener found it difficult to obtain tenure in her teaching post as a result of not having a working knowledge of the Irish-Gaelic language, and argued that this (largely formalistic) linguistic requirement contravened her right as a European citizen to settle and work in a European member state. The Court ruled that a constitutional arrangement aimed at maintaining an aspect of national culture and identity overruled such European rights of employment.

increasingly as contradictory terms, and the ill-fated attempt to have the various European Treaties rearranged into a constitution, to be endorsed by the European electorate, foundered as a result.

National thought, the unwillingness to embed one's national citizenship into a larger, European one, here presents itself largely as a form of political agoraphobia: a preference for the comfortable enclosure of the community and for the domesticity of one's own nation-state. However, even within that nation-state, the wide world has made inroads, and led to the same reflex of populist agoraphobia. The presence of a large contingent of immigrants, from the 1960s onwards, triggered xenophobic reflexes throughout Western Europe. An early indication was the strident speech delivered by the maverick Tory politician Enoch Powell as early as 1968, calling for an end to immigration from Britain's former colonies and Commonwealth partners (Pakistan, the West Indies) because otherwise ethnic tension would lead to 'rivers of blood'. Powell was promptly disciplined and sidelined by his party, but his rhetoric proves, from hindsight, to have been an early straw in the wind for the direction that xenophobia was to take thirty years later.* Most European countries saw an influx of non-Europeans from their African and Asian ex-colonies. In addition, migrant workers from Turkey, Morocco and elsewhere settled in Northern European countries like Germany, France, Belgium and the Netherlands; and alongside these two migrant streams, there were asylum seekers from the many dictatorial and tyrannical regimes of the world.

This demographic influx was not easily accommodated. It ran concurrently with, but should not be confused with, a trend towards 'globalization' (which in many cases meant Americanization). People were on the whole willing to try out the more benevolent sides of cultural exchange. Exotic foods, colourful fashions, unusual types of music and dance: all this was embraced gladly. The actual presence of people led to increased social tensions and provided also a new flashpoint in the general sense of civic malaise affecting Western Europe in the 1990s: a rallying point around which populism and xenophobia crystallized.

The case of Flanders is illustrative in this respect. Flemish politics well into the 1980s was dominated almost exclusively by Belgium's communitarian conflict: the uneasy relations between Belgium's two halves, Flemish and French-speaking. Although the major grievances had been settled, remaining issues (the linguistic status of the Brussels suburbs and of rural villages along the linguistic frontier) continued to irk; even the matter of the allocation of tax money, road works and traffic fines across the language border could become a 'communitarian' issue. The most strident vindication of Flemish rights, and denunciations of Walloon greed and iniquity, traditionally came from the far right. Significantly, however, that far right fixed on a different hate-focus in the course of the 1990s: immigrant workers, especially from Islamic countries. The right-wing propaganda of xenophobic denunciation has shifted its attention from French-speaking Belgian authorities to first- and second-generation Islamic immigrants.

---

* The text of Powell's 'rivers of blood' speech can still be found on extremist right-wing websites like those of Britain's National Front, where it enjoys an obviously inspirational status.

Likewise in France, the *Front national* of Jean-Marie Le Pen, rooted in a tradition of extreme Catholic conservatism with corporatist or fascist sympathies, has morphed into a movement against African and Islamic immigrants. Here (as in Holland) the Islamic headscarf has become a symbolic flashpoint and has accordingly been heavily burdened with contradictory significations: for some, it is the sign of female submission to a hidebound patriarchal-Islamic traditionalism, also involving other practices such as arranged marriages and female genital mutilation; for others, it is the proud proclamation of a cultural tradition freely embraced and displayed in the teeth of intolerant assimilationism. Both interpretations can be encountered both within and outside the Muslim communities now established in Western Europe.[267]

'Multiculturalism', particularly in the social encounter between traditional Islam and Europe's established Enlightenment values (the separation of church and state, freedom of conscience for the individual, the epistemic superiority of critical and scientific thought over religious belief) is proving a very difficult challenge. In many instances, it brings out the worst in both camps: those advocating 'Enlightenment values' often do so with remarkable ethnocentric arrogance, while Islamic immigrants often entrench themselves in an inward-looking, self-righteous intransigence. A middle ground is difficult to establish; all the more so, since global conflicts focussing around the Middle East place the European debate under a heavy mortgage. Europe is often perceived, by disaffected Muslims, as a Western accomplice to American hegemonism in the Middle East; conversely, denunciations of the West's military ruthlessness in Iraq and in the Palestinian occupied territories sometimes slide into the rhetoric of crass *jihad*ism and antisemitism. At the same time, the ongoing flux of immigrants, either economic work-seekers from Eastern Europe and North Africa, or else asylum seekers from further afield, is continuing to put pressure on European resources and flexibility; social unrest and xenophobic populism (often invoking nationalist nostrums like 'our own nation first') are increasing. The widespread unwillingness to consider Turkish membership in the European Union is a result of this tension. One should avoid terms like the 'clash of civilizations' because, like Enoch Powell's 'rivers of blood' speech, these incendiary slogans are self-fulfilling prophecies, exacerbating the very conflict they claim to warn against, and blaming the victims of racism for the intolerance they are said to provoke. Even so, European states, which for centuries have been habituated to consider themselves the political incorporation of an underlying nationality (and which as a result had basked in the self-delusion of internal, undifferentiated cultural homogeneity), are facing a difficult challenge indeed: to sort out which moral, social and political values are constitutionally nonnegotiable, and which ones are culturally relative and open to future change.

The most egregious result of these developments has been the rejuvenation of the extreme ethnonationalist right. In the 1970s, the extreme right-wing parties of Europe were not only marginal in the political spectrum, they were also demographically marginal, in that they were composed almost wholly of ex-Nazis and old fascists, who stubbornly clung to their totalitarian nostalgia rationalized by large doses of Holocaust denial. The NPD in Germany may count as an example, with a leader like Adolf von Thadden, or figures such as the Belgian fascist leader Léon Degrelle in his exile in Franco Spain, or the old widow Rost van Tonningen in Holland: *Ewiggestrige*, nostal-

43. Recent Dutch racist cartoon: a sticker removed from a public Dutch location by the author in 2005. Underneath the cartoon-style ethnic caricatures features a Germanic rune with crossed swords, with neo-Nazi connotations.

gic for the days of mid-century fascism. Twenty years later, the demographic constituency of the extreme right has drawn in a new, young generation of skinheads, bootboys and disaffected young males. Under the new agenda of anti-Islamic xenophobia these have swelled the ranks of the aging antisemites, still using the runic symbols, the rhetoric and the violent racist ethnocentrism of their seniors. The extreme right in Europe, which for decades looked like a dying-out, spent force, has managed to infect a new generation – both in Western Europe and in the former communist countries. A pull to the nationalist right has also affected the mainstream parties in various countries, and has led to a new propagation of national themes in the public sphere, such as the televised popular elections of 'the Greatest German/Englishman/Dutchman',[*] and widespread calls to re-nationalize the history curriculum taught in schools.

---

* The event as it took shape in the Dutch media was particularly embarrassing. It involved questions in the media whether or not Anne Frank qualified as 'Dutch' (since her father had been a refugee from Nazi Germany). Although the question was quickly, and rightly, dismissed as misguided and offensive – it is not the possession of a valid passport that ensures one's place in a nation's history – the disquieting point remains that similar questions were never raised concerning other non-carriers of a Dutch passport such as William of Orange. In the event, and to the extreme discomfiture of the programme-makers, a populist campaign ensured that the most votes for Greatest Dutchman of All Times went to the rabble-rousing politician Pim Fortuyn (murdered in 2001 and godfather of the new ethnocentrist right in The Netherlands). The episode shows that those who sow the national wind may reap the nationalist storm.

One can only point out these recent trends; there are no simple solutions. The experience of national thought and nationalism over the past two centuries does make it possible, however, to point out with some confidence that a retrenchment into monoculturalism, although psychologically understandable, is no long-term social solution; on the contrary. It is also possible, on the basis of a historical understanding of the present predicament, to identify some issues which Europeans cannot afford to neglect. The accommodation of new cultural and ethnic traditions in European society must be disentangled from the global conflicts in and around the Middle East. The European state must redefine what it stands for, socially and culturally: how much adaptation and integrative effort can be reasonably expected from new arrivals, and how much flexibility is due to the cultural and religious traditions newly established on European soil. Most of all, European states must define to which extent they have a role to play in cultural affairs and cultural conflicts. It may be necessary for European states to stop being nation-states; maybe the state's self-imposed mission of incorporating a 'national identity' was not such a bright idea to begin with. National thought affects, not just the position of the state amidst its neighbours, but also the position of the state vis-à-vis its own citizens.

From Nation-State to Civic State?

The impact of national thought in European history can be registered most fore-groundedly and fundamentally in the idea of the 'nation-state', the hyphenation of the concepts of 'nation' and 'state'.[268] It is an ideal that emerges from the cultural thought of Herder and the social thought of Rousseau and that rises to dominance in the course of the nineteenth century. Earlier conceptions of the state did not invoke the concept of nationality as an intrinsic principle: the oldest, and by no means the least successful state in Europe, Switzerland, antedates the rise of the nationality concept. Conversely, when as late as 1813, a newly-created Kingdom of the Netherlands was being set up in the run-up to the Congress of Vienna, its future monarch, William of Orange-Nassau, envisaged it as stretching from Koblenz to Dunkirk, involving three different languages across a swathe of territories without common historical experience – a mode of thinking that was obviously dynastic-territorial and, even in 1813, still pre-national.[269]

Fundamentally (these home truths bear repeating at this point), the state is a fiscal-administrative organization claiming sovereignty and the right to coerce its citizens. The principle of sovereignty and the right to coerce (what Max Weber called the 'monopoly on legitimate violence') may be conflated, but such conflation is dangerous and will lead to a 'hawkish', even despotic state exercising arbitrary power on the basis of might rather than right. Sovereignty ought to be understood, not just as the state's right to act freely as it pleases, but as the principle that restrictions on how to act can come from no external source and can only be freely self-imposed by the state itself on itself (e.g. through constitutional or legal stipulations or by the ratification of international treaties). The self-imposition of limits on the state's authority and on its freedom of behaviour is an exercise of sovereignty, not a reduction of it; it is a measure of the state's commitment to the rule of law. Any refusal to commit to self-restriction is not an assertion of the state's sovereignty but a slippage towards despotism.

Within those parameters, some primary functions of the modern state are: to collect taxes and spend these on policies approved by the taxpayers; and to provide a legal system to protect its citizens so as to manage their mutual conflicts. Traditionally, the state has also maintained or placed under its supervision important infrastructures of general use, such as an army/navy; roads, water management and vital services; health care and education; a central bank and monetary currency.

None of these functions need involve any sense of cultural identity. The state is a working community of taxpayers controlling how and on what issues their taxes are spent, and by what laws their social relations are governed. The German philosopher Jürgen Habermas has argued, to my mind convincingly, that this alone can provide a sense of solidarity between taxpaying citizens, deriving from a joint stake in the *res publica* and a shared sense of purpose in the state's public sphere (or *Öffentlichkeit*). Habermas defines this as *Verfassungspatriotismus* or 'constitutional patriotism'.[270] Given the present climate in which citizens' moral and cultural allegiances are becoming so diverse (for that is in part what 'multiculturalism' will necessarily entail), it seems that the idea of *Verfassungspatriotismus* gains fresh importance and even urgency. When Renan spoke of the elements that inspire a sense of national solidarity, he highlighted the communality of historical experience (having gone through a shared and jointly remembered set of triumphs and traumas). That historical communality is no longer an automatic given; what binds citizens and fellow-nationals nowadays must be a communality of political responsibilities, a shared membership and participation in the same public sphere.

Interestingly this was largely the basis on which the European Union was set up. The European Union could never claim to embody a single nation; its *raison d'être* lay (and continues to lie) rather in its conflict management and its provision of enabling infrastructures. For decades, the European Union's lack of a *national* identity, its incapacity of claiming citizen's national allegiance, was seen as a lacuna, a failure even. However, that apparent failure has perhaps hidden from view the Union's slow, unglamorous but solid success in creating, not only shared infrastuctures, but also a common public sphere, a shared *Öffentlichkeit,* over the past decades.[271]

Now that the failure to command a united 'national' loyalty has also proved itself to be a problem, not just at the European level, but also within the individual European member states, the need for a fresh *Verfassungspatriotismus* may be pondered at the national level as well. The vexed question of church-state relations bears this out.

One experience which has been common to many European states over the past two centuries was the problematical relationship between church and state – the two institutions which have always commanded the strongest loyalty amongst their constituents, and whose claims to loyalty have in many cases been entangled in bitter competition. Even the apparent church-state harmonization model of Britain with its 'established' national churches has only been achieved at the cost of the sectarian divisions dominating the seventeenth and eighteenth century, and still persisting in Ulster; and the nationally mobilizing role of Orthodoxy in Greece, Cyprus and Serbia does not imply an absence of conflict or of divided loyalties in those areas. The strict separation of church and state in France, conversely, and the notion of the state's *laicité*, has for centuries sparked major social conflicts in the field of education. The present clashes over manifestations of Islam in the French public sphere are, in a way, a continuation over the republic's clashes with Catholicism in the previous two centuries; something similar might be said of the Dutch experience, where the nineteenth-century religious diffraction of society (*verzuiling*) was no less vehement or divisive than are the contemporary conflicts surrounding the presence of Islam. In all Western countries, a renewed rise of Christian fundamentalism (including renewed discussions on the teaching of Darwinism at school) shows that the debate concerns, fundamentally, the status of revealed religion in the state's public sphere and instruments.

In all these debates it should be realized that the phrase of a separation between church and state, or a state's *laicité*, is in fact a misnomer. The state is not simply the counterpart of the church, or of religion; it has, in fact set up a different church, a different religion to compete with Christianity and which is now competing with Islam. That religion is the cult of nationality. From the medieval conflict between pope and emperor; from the moment that Henry VIII claimed the headship of the Church of England; from the moment Robespierre set up a state religion of the *Être suprême*; from the moment Pius IX faced the emerging nation-states in his campaign of ultramontanism and Bismarck faced Rome in an aptly named *Kulturkampf*; throughout these centuries of crisis, political leaders have sought to divert their populaces' religious reverence into national loyalty. Early monarchs claimed mantic, thaumaturgic powers; later states have claimed a similar moral, ethical command over their subject's sense of piety. The extent to which nationalism mimics the liturgies and rituals of religion is well known. The symbols of the state in the course of the nineteenth century were set up to command an almost numinous reverence and fervour; the lessons of the nation's history were taught in schools in lieu of the Ten Commandments and the Bible; the shrines of national history were made sites of pilgrimage and worship; the notion of 'my country, right or wrong' turned national loyalty into a moral tenet. In many national movements, the call went out explicitly to forget or transcend religious ('sectarian') differences and to unite in the name of a common nationality: the histories of Illyrianism and of Irish nationalism offer examples, having urged the common cause of nationality as transcending the differences between Catholic and Orthodox, or Catholic and Protestant. A Cretan exhortation from the mid-nineteenth century proclaimed that 'Orthodox or Muslim, we are all Hellenes'.[272] In short, national thought arose in competition to that older focus of collective loyalty, religion.

The nation-state that resulted from these developments has had a mixed track record in cultural history. With its centralist organizing powers, it has undoubtedly given institutional fixity to the main languages, literatures and history-narratives of Europe; by the same token it has tended to marginalize all those languages, literatures and history-narratives that failed to fit the state-endorsed patterns. The rich cultural diversity in dress, architecture and language, that characterized so many European countries, has declined over the past centuries. To be sure, one does not want to indulge in nostalgic-regionalist hand-wringing: the de-diversification of European culture is to a large extent the result of an autonomous modernizing process, eagerly embraced by members of all cultures and communities, which went hand-in-hand with the increase in health, longevity and prosperity; and it has been to a large extent a transnational trend (nowadays presenting itself as a process of 'Americanization' rather than 'nationalization or 'Europeanization'). Even so, the point remains that the European nation-state, given its ideological origins and historical track record, is by no means ideally equipped to accommodate cultural diversity within its borders; a cultural diversity which has increased and deepened brusquely over the past two decades.

The statement that nationalism is a secular religion may sound threadbare, but its truth deserves pondering. If European states have, for the past 200 years, adopted the principle of a freedom of conscience and a separation between church and state (meaning that the coercive powers of the state should not be applied in matters of religion, and that religions should not arrogate any coercive powers which are now the state's monopoly), then the logical extension of that principle would be to contemplate now a separation between state and nationality: to reduce the state to its core business, to disable its coercive powers in matters of language and culture (with all its patterns, traditions and identifications).

Given the increasing multiculturalism and multi-ethnicity of our societies, the state should, I suggest, abandon its old reliance on nationality as its enabling principle, and revert from the outworn ideal of the nation-state to that of the *civic state*. Once the state moves into such a civic, post-national phase, it may on that basis, and with fresh credibility, expect and even claim a 'constitutional patriotism' from its citizens. The state has no call to incorporate or represent any given specific cultural tradition. It has only the duty to maintain its laws and protect all citizens and cultures under its aegis from persecution, repression or discrimination. This may not in itself ensure absolute and ideal harmony; but then again, the pursuit of absolute and ideal harmony, even if it were not a chimera (which in any case could never be achieved by the ostrich-policy of national monoculturalism), is not the duty of the state. The mere suppression of injustice and intolerance is already a sufficiently heavy task.

Appendices

Languages, Alphabets, Dialects and Language Politics

Our default image of Europe is a modular one, consisting of countries neatly fitting together like pieces in a jigsaw puzzle, each with its own colour and shape, each fitted snugly against neighbouring pieces with different colours. The names of states, of peoples and of languages in most cases are homonyms, which reinforces this neat modular template: in Germany live the Germans who speak German, in Portugal live the Portuguese who speak Portuguese, in Denmark live the Danes who speak Danish, etcetera. Even though everyone realizes that this is a simplification (as becomes immediately obvious from the cases of Britain, Belgium and Switzerland), our knowledge of the *non-congruence* between states and language areas is on the whole far less specific than it should be. Of the European states, only a very few can be considered monolingual: e.g. Iceland and Portugal. Practically all states have different languages and language areas within their borders.

It is useful, therefore, to outline a linguistic profile of Europe to counterbalance the overriding and insidiously distortive trend to organize cultural patterns by nation-state. In the following outline, I do not take into account the languages which have recently become established in various parts of Europe as a result of post-1945 immigration (Berber, Arabic, Hindi, Sranan Tongo, etc.).

Non-Indo-European languages

Most of the languages of Europe belong to the great 'Indo-European' language family.[*]
Some languages, however, stand apart from that Indo-European group. These include:
– Saami (the language of the Saami of Lapland, in Northern Finland, Sweden and Norway);
– Finnish and its related neighbour, Estonian;
– Hungarian;
– Turkish (also spoken on Cyprus and by communities in Greece, Bulgaria and Macedonia);
– Maltese (related to the Arabic dialects of North Africa);
– Basque;
– and Hebrew (the liturgical language of the Jews).

These languages are mutually unrelated, except in the case of Finnish/Estonian and Hungarian – their mutual relatedness is, however, remote.

---

[*] There are also non-European languages belonging to the Indo-European group: e.g. Persian (Farsi, Iranian) and Hindi.

Non-Indo-European languages: Hebrew*, Basque, Estonian, Finnish, Hungarian, Maltese, Saami, Turkish		
Indo-European languages	Separate Indo-European languages: Albanian, Greek, Latvian, Lithuanian, Roma/Sinti	
	Celtic	Gaulish* Irish Gaelic, Scots Galic Welsh, Breton
	Germanic	Danish, Icelandic, Faroese, Norwegian (2 var.), Swedish English, Frisian, German, Netherlandic (Dutch/Flemish) smaller/regional variants incl. Luxemburgish, Yiddish
	Slavic	Church Slavonic* Belorussian, Russian, Rusyn/Ukrainian Czech, Polish, Slovak Bosnian/Croat/Serbian, Bulgarian, Macedonian, Slovene
	Romance	Latin* French, Italian (incl. impt. dialect variants), Portuguese, Romanian, Spanish Catalan, Corsican, Galego, Occitan/Provençal, Rhaeto-Romance, Sardinian numerous smaller regional variants
* extinct or liturgical		

Individually separate Indo-European languages

The Indo-European languages of Europe fall, on the whole, into four main branches: the Celtic, Germanic, Slavic and Romance clusters. However, some Indo-European languages stand apart from these four main clusters, and take up an individually separate position. These are:

- Albanian (also spoken in Northern Greece, Serbia, Montenegro and Macedonia; there is also a variant spoken in Southern Italy);
- Greek (also spoken in Cyprus and in various diaspora communities);
- Lithuanian and its related neighbour, Latvian;
- Roma and Sinti (the languages of the Roma or Sinti 'gypsies', in diverse variants).

Celtic

The Celtic languages are the remnant of what once was a large group of languages (including the extinct Gaulish), now spoken on the Atlantic coastlands of North-Western Europe. They include:

- Irish Gaelic and its related neighbour Scots Gaelic;

- Welsh and its related neighbour Breton.

Germanic

The Germanic languages cover an area from the Swiss and Austrian Alps to the North Cape and Iceland. They include:
- The Scandinavian or 'Nordic' group: Swedish, Danish, Norwegian (in two main variants[*]), Icelandic and Faroese (the language of the Faroe Islands);
- The others: English, Frisian, Netherlandic (with a Flemish and a Dutch variant), German;
- Smaller variants (some of which are uncertainly classed as 'dialects' or regional languages); they include Yiddish (the language of the Ashkenazi Jews of North-Central Europe), Plattdeutsch (and the adjoining 'Low Saxon' dialects of the north-eastern Netherlands), Luxemburgish (a Franconian dialect now the official language of Luxembourg).

Slavic

The Slavic languages fall into three main groups; distinctions within these groups are often open to debate and fluctuation:
- The East-Slavic Group: Russian, Belorussian, Ukrainian (with a Ruthenian or 'Rusyn' offshoot);
- The West-Slavic group: Polish, Czech and its related neighbour Slovak;
- The South Slavic group: Slovene, Bosnian/Croat/Serbian, Bulgarian and its related neighbour Macedonian.

The Orthodox speakers of the Slavic languages share an older form of 'Church Slavonic' as a liturgical language. The East-Slavic and West-Slavic groups adjoin each other: Slavic languages are spoken in a continuous territory from Gdańsk to Vladivostok. The South Slavic languages are located on the Balkan peninsula. They are separated from the other Slavic-speaking territories by a belt of different, non-Slavic languages along the Danube from Vienna to the Black Sea: German (in Austria), Hungarian, Romanian. (Non-Slavic languages on the Balkans also include Turkish, Greek, Albanian, Vlach and Roma.)

Romance

The Romance languages include some major national languages and a large number of small and not easily distinguished dialects or regional languages, in a great curve reach-

---

* The variants, previously known as *Riksmål* and *Landsmål* and now known as *Bokmål* and *Nynorsk*, derive ultimately from two separate attempts, undertaken in the mid-nineteenth century, to give the dialects of Norway a more specifically non-Danish standardization.

ing from the English Channel to Gibraltar and the Northern Mediterranean. They include:

- French;
- Occitan (also known as Provençal);
- Catalan with a Valencian variant;
- Spanish;
- Galego;
- Portuguese;
- Corsican;
- Sardinian;
- Italian (with many important regional differentiations);
- Rhaeto-Romance (the Romance language of some Swiss cantons, with an offshoot in the Italian alps called Ladin);
- Romanian (an isolated Romance language on the eastern Balkans);
- Vlach (also known as Arumanian, spoken by isolated populations in the Southern Balkans: Macedonia and Northern Greece);
- and Ladino (the Spanish-derived language of the Mediterranean's Sephardic Jews).

Latin, the language of ancient Rome from which all the Romance languages derive, is still in use as a liturgical language in the Roman Catholic church.

The lists above are not exhaustive. Smaller dialects and regional variants exist in their dozens: Karaim, Sorbic, Walloon, Schwyzerdütsch, Asturian, revived Cornish, Limburgs, etc. etc. A complete survey is given on the *Ethnologue* website: www.ethnologue.org.

The languages enumerated here number ca. 55. Some 5-10 of these are in use only for liturgical purposes, or only among very restricted and dwindling groups of speakers. Of the remainder, ca. 30-35 (depending on the way of counting) are the official or co-official languages of an independent state. That means that between a third and a quarter of the European languages are only regionally recognized, or not at all.

Scripts and alphabets

Five main alphabets have been in use in Europe over the last two centuries. Their use is not distributed according to language but rather a result of church history.

- Arabic, the language and alphabet of the Koran, is used throughout the Islamic world, also for non-Arabic languages like Iranian, and it was used as the official Turkish alphabet of the Ottoman Empire (that is to say, also in South-Eastern Europe) until 1928. In South-Western Europe, the mural inscriptions in the Alhambra of Granada still testify to the use of the Arabic script in Moorish Spain.
- The Hebrew alphabet is still used for liturgical purposes, for modern-day revived Hebrew (the language of Israel), and, during the nineteenth and early twentieth centuries, for Yiddish.

- The Greek alphabet, once the alphabet of ancient Greece and of the Eastern Roman Empire, is still used for the Greek language (official in Greece and Cyprus) and in the Greek-Orthodox church.
- Slavic Orthodox churches, and the Slavic languages belonging to the Orthodox world, use the Cyrillic alphabet derived from the Greek by Cyrillus and Methodius.[*]
- Western Christianity uses the Latin alphabet.

This means that some closely related neighbouring Slavic languages use different alphabets, depending on the religion involved. Croat uses the Latin alphabet, the very closely related Serbian uses Cyrillic. Polish uses Latin, the (not so dissimilar) Belorussian uses Cyrillic. Ukrainian uses Cyrillic, its twin Rusyn uses Latin. Romanian switched from Cyrillic to Latin when, in the course of the nineteenth century, it chose to emphasize its western roots rather than its Orthodox religion.

In the Renaissance, around the time of the invention of print, a classically based form of the Latin alphabet was reconstituted by Italian humanists, now the standard western letter (which is why the names of some fonts still employ names like 'Roman' or 'Italic'; illustration 8 furnishes an example). Meanwhile, manuscript variants had taken hold elsewhere in Western Europe. These remained in use even after the invention of print, especially in Protestant countries which were unwilling to adopt to the Italian-humanist style. Thus, in Germany the 'gothic' *Fraktur* remained the standard letter until the mid-twentieth century;[273] that same letter was also used in Denmark until the mid-nineteenth century. 'Black letters' were likewise used for English and Dutch throughout the sixteenth and seventeenth centuries. Irish-Gaelic maintained its own manuscript-derived letter type until the mid-twentieth century. Examples of these Northern European variants can be found in illustrations 4, 5, 28 and 30.

The historicity of linguistic taxonomy

The Indo-European model of relationships outlined here was unknown until the early nineteenth century, and only elaborated in a slow process. In the Middle Ages, the Old Testament story of Noah's survival of the Deluge, and the list of tribes descended from his sons Sem, Cham and Japhet (Genesis X-XII) led to the assumption that the total number of 'nations' and languages was 72, and that Hebrew was the central and oldest of them all.[274] Over the course of the sixteenth and seventeenth centuries, the comparison of languages (often for purposes of Bible exegesis and Bible translation) led to the realization that certain languages were more closely related than others; family resemblances between the Romance languages, or the Germanic ones, were recognized. Even so, especially during the eighteenth century, the axiomatic centrality

---

[*] Glagolitic, a forerunner of Cyrillic, was and still is sporadically in use in the north-western Balkans. Cyrillic is also used for a number of different languages spoken in parts of the former Russian Empire (Ossetian, Kyrgyz, Uzbek).

of Hebrew and the increasing acquaintance with exotic, non-European languages led to linguistic confusion and speculation.[275] A breakthrough came when Sir William Jones realized that Sanskrit was more closely related to European languages like Greek, Latin and English than either Hebrew or Turkish. This led to the 'Indo-European' model of language relationships, first propounded by Jones and his circle, and subsequently by Friedrich Schlegel.[276] The development of a comparative method, involving Rasmus Rask, Jacob Grimm and Franz Bopp, placed comparative linguistics on a scientific footing; the formulation of 'Grimm's Laws' around 1820 (systematizing consonant shifts marking the branchings between and within language families) was a triumph of the comparative-historical method, raised linguistics to the status of a prestigious science and made Grimm's name as one of Europe's foremost scholars.[*]

In subsequent decades, between 1820 and 1860, problematic languages like Albanian, Lithuanian and the Celtic languages found their place in this Indo-European family tree. It is important to realize that this process, which covered the first half of the nineteenth century, coincided not only with the rise of other comparative modes of science, but also with the rise of nationalism. On the one hand, it overlaps with the rise of comparative ethnography; on the other, the great scientific prestige of comparative linguistics added to the prestige of language as the alleged essence of national identity.[277]

Languages and dialects: Difference or distinction?

Asturian, Walloon or Limburgish: are these dialect variants of Spanish, French and Netherlandic, or are they separate languages? This is a vexed question. Among linguists, the consensus is that there are no hard, measurable criteria according to which a linguistic variant be given the status of 'dialect' or of 'language'. The joke one often hears is that 'a language is a dialect with a government and an army'– indicating that external (political) circumstances rather than intrinsic features determine the linguistic status of a given variant. As a result, linguists have declared this taxonomical problem

---

[*] The Germanic language family split off from, and can be distinguished from, the other Indo-European languages by a typical shift from initial *p* and *c* to *f* and *ch* or *h*. Thus, against Latin *pes*, *plenus* and *pater* we see German *Fuss*, *voll* and *Vater* (or English *foot*, *full* and *father*), while against Latin *cor*, *centum* and *cornu* we see German *Herz*, *hundert* and *Horn* (English *heart*, *hundred* and *horn*). Similarly, German has at a later point branched off from other Germanic languages by shifting from *p* to *pf*, and from *t* to *ts*: German *Apfel*, *Sumpf*, *Katze* and *Hitze* stand against *apple*, *swamp*, *cat* and *heat*. What is more, this systematization of changes allows us to date them: the word *Fuss* must have been part of the German lexicon from very ancient times, the word *Pforte* must have entered more recently (otherwise it would have morphed into *Forte*, along with *Fuss*) while words like *Professor* and *Pension*, unaffected by any of these changes, obviously only became part of the German language after all such sound-shifts had played themselves out. For the impact in linguistic science of this method, cf. Davies 1998, 83-97 ('Historicism, organicism and the scientific model').

'out of bounds', and will make no distinction in principle between dialect difference and language difference.[*]

The extent of linguistic difference is hard to measure. We can sense, informally but with great obviousness, that Danish and Norwegian are closely related, while Breton and French are very different, but to quantify and measure this distance in objective, non-impressionistic terms, is extremely difficult. Recently, interesting attempts have been made to quantify linguistic distance on the basis of statistical methods, but the methodology used here is still imperfect (it tends to privilege phonetics and pronunciation, over syntax, grammar, and lexical variation). Even so, the results tend to confirm and in some measure objectively quantify people's informal impressions concerning dialect variation and linguistic distance.[278]

The problem remains that, while some dialect variations are considerable (e.g. between the German spoken in Lübeck, Berlin, Munich or Bern, or the English spoken in the working class areas of Glasgow and London) some languages are extremely closely related (so that they can, with less or more effort, be mutually comprehensible): Danish and Norwegian, Belorussian and Ukrainian. As a result, there have at various points in history been shifts of opinion as to whether certain closely related neighbouring idioms should be seen as different languages or as two dialects of a single language: Serb and Croat, Bulgarian and Macedonian, Dutch and Flemish.

Outside the technical realm of linguistics, in general everyday usage, a clear distinction is made between 'a language' and 'a dialect'. Language relates to dialect as country relates to province or region, or as species relates to race. Differences between languages are generally considered to be discrete, absolute and codified, whereas dialects are considered to be shifting variations within a given language. Thus, while linguists have pointed out that there are no fundamental *differences* between the classifications 'dialect' and 'language', people at large tend to make a *distinction*. The distinction involves factors that are, indeed, close to the idea of 'having an army and a government'. Among the informal, often non-explicit elements that play into the language/dialect distinction involve matters such as the following:

A *language* is the official means of communication of a state. As such, it has wide currency and an officially regulated standard taught in schools, and an extensive written practice. It has a long-standing record in its written form and a body of literature; it is used for non-trivial topics. A *dialect*, by contrast, is the non-official means of communication for a community or region; it has limited currency and is passed on without educational institutions, in the informal privacy of the home situation. It is often oral and rarely written, its usage is often limited to homely matters of family and

---

[*] All the same, even among linguists one often encounters ingrained attitudes which indicate that they, too, informally distinguish between dialect variation on the one hand, and language difference on the other. 'Creolization' patterns or the effects of infants' dual language acquisition, for instance, are rarely, if ever, studied between dialect variations, and usually between separate languages. Also, although 'register shifts' (when a speaker moves between dialects or sociolects) are not the same as 'code switching' (when a speaker changes from using one language to another), it is not really argued at at what point one shifts into the other.

community life. Its history is unrecorded and there is no important literary corpus written in it.

This distinction obviously raises borderline cases. There are 'non-official' languages which nonetheless have an important historical and literary presence: Provençal or Frisian; the dialects of certain large cities (Cologne, Vienna, Rome) have become the carrier of a lively and prestigious city culture. As a result, we see that the distinction is not absolute, but that it can shift over time. Luxemburgish and Afrikaans were seen as 'mere' dialects a century ago and have now the status of 'a language'. The court language of sixteenth-century Scotland (a Scots variant next to the English of England) was demoted to the status of a mere dialect between 1600 and 1750: the rustic speech of lower-class characers in Walter Scott novels.

The distinction between dialect and language seems to revolve around to the criterion that languages (as opposed to dialects) are the vehicles of communication of a *public sphere* (in Jürgen Habermas's sense of that term): any form of communication that is used for non-trivial purposes in situations that are beyond the type of face-to-face contact which characterizes private or small-scale communitarian settings, can lay claim to the social status of a language. Thus, while there is no real criterion to pinpoint an *objective difference* between dialect status and language status, we can certainly identify a generally accepted criterion governing the *social distinction* between the two. For that reason, the attempt to have one's local idiom raised from the status of private/communitarian dialect to the public status of language is often a prime concern of language revival movements and regionalist or national movements.

Language politics across the centuries: Outre-Meuse, medieval and contemporary

I wish to make a final clarification regarding the status of language arguments in political thought, and the question to which extent these are part of the nationalist ideology or not. It has emerged from the foregoing pages that language concerns were central to nationalist thought. European nationalism is fundamentally a nineteenth-century ideology addressing the relations between culture and politics, and wishing to map the outlines of the modern state onto the territorial pattern of culture – in particular, language. Yet at the same time, the preoccupation with language and with linguistic rights and purity is also older than its nationalistic investment. There are various examples of language improvers and language purists from the seventeenth and eighteenth centuries, and early declarations of love for one's native tongue – examples gratefully quoted by their successors, nineteenth-century linguistic nationalists such as the German Grimm and the Fleming Jan Frans Willems. Much as 'love of the fatherland' is an affect that can be traced back to periods long before the emergence of nationalism-proper, so too language concerns have a history long antedating the rise of nationalism. It is all the more important to clarify what remains constant, and what is variable, in the political use of language arguments before and after the rise of nationalism.

Modern nationalism crucially considers language the very core of ethnicity. That this should be so is understandable: the German Romantics who were instrumental in shaping and disseminating the ideology also formulated a language philosophy which saw a nation's language as the very breath of its moral essence. The Flemish dictum that 'the language is the nation entire' (*de tael is gantsch het volk*), coined by the poet Prudens Van Duyse (1804-1859), and used both as a motto and as a name for an influential association for Flemish cultural emancipation established in 1836, sums up this all-pervasive attitude. For nineteenth-century nationalists, the badge, hallmark and indeed the substance of national specificity consisted in the presence of a national language.

Accordingly, linguistic discrimination is always deeply resented and tends to inflame nationalist anger like nothing else. The Flemish Movement for example is and has been, centrally, a linguistic emancipation movement, fanned at every step by the marginalization and subordination of Netherlandic in the Belgian state. Among the most galvanizing moments in that movement's history are acts of linguistic injustice, in particular a notorious murder trial (1863) held entirely in French, although the Flemish defendants, Coucke and Goethals, were ignorant of that language.[279] The resulting miscarriage of justice (the defendants were condemned to death and executed, and, as later appeared, innocently so) did much to fan the vehemence of the Flemish movement. Similar cases are known from the same period from other European minority languages, such as Welsh or Irish Gaelic. Monoglot Welsh- and Irish-speaking subjects were interrogated and judged by uncomprehending British authorities displaying arrogant linguistic heedlessness, which in turn provoked widespread and deeply felt indignation and fanned nationalist activism.

We can trace such legal-linguistic concerns back much further than the beginning of Romantic linguistic philosophy or modern nationalism. The case I want to highlight comes from the Belgian area; in fact from an area notorious for its linguistic clashes in the 1970s and 1980s: the area in the city triangle between Maastricht, Liège and Aachen.

For centuries, this has been a borderland where the Netherlandic, German and French languages meet. The three cities are and have since Carolingian times been fixed in their linguistic appurtenance: Netherlandic for Maastricht, Francophone for Liège, German for Aachen. These cities' linguistic spheres of influence have waxed and waned over time, but not by much. In present-day Belgium, the heart of this city triangle has been contested terrain between Flanders and Wallonia. The Voer area (Fr. *Fourons*) was transferred from the French-speaking province of Liège to the Netherlandic-speaking province of Limburg in 1962 as part of a nationwide politico-linguistic arrangement. The local population by and large shares a Limburgish dialect close to Low-German (also spoken in the adjoining Dutch and German countryside), but is sharply divided on what they consider their 'official' language of choice, philologically related Netherlandic or sociologically accustomed French. This division, which was aligned with long-standing political factionalism in the local communities, accordingly split the population along 'pro-Flemish' versus 'pro-Walloon' lines of allegiance. This discord in turn obtained a symbolic value in national politics. As a result, the picaresque faction-fights and brawls of these rural villages escalated under nationwide participation to bring down the Belgian national government in 1987.[280]

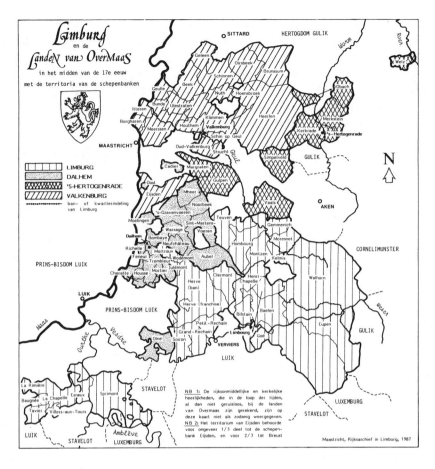

44. Map of pre-modern Outre-Meuse

Remarkably, we notice that an equally touchy sense of linguistic identity and linguistic difference was at work in precisely the same area as long ago as the fourteenth to sixteenth century. The area in question was at that time a feudal lordship, the county of Dalhem, which was ruled from Brussels by the dukes of Brabant, and called by them the 'Lands across the Meuse' (*Outre-Meuse*). Brabant as a duchy was bilingual in administration, and Outre-Meuse Dalhem as a county was bilingual in population: the languages were *Romance* (forerunner of the present-day French, possibly with Walloon dialect colouration) and *Diets* (forerunner of present-day Netherlandic); the border between them has shifted little over the centuries. The nearest urban and administrative centre, the town of Limbourg, kept law books in both languages for the administration of court hearings in higher appeal.[281]

In the course of the late Middle Ages and early modern period, we see repeated attempts from the Brabant authorities in Brussels to rationalize the administrative structure of this outlying county. The first attempt occurred shortly after the Duchy of Brabant had been taken over by the House of Burgundy between 1396 and 1406. The new ducal chancery requested (in Latin) that each local village court write down its customs and legal traditions and forward them to Brussels. (The move was evidently intended to suppress the tendency among the local village courts to lodge higher appeal cases with nearby non-Brabant courts such as Aachen.[282])

An interesting pattern emerges from the replies forwarded to Brussels by the local village courts: they all dutifully record their local customs and by-laws, but in each case stipulate jealously that they administer law in their own language (as the case may be, in Romance or Diets). What is more, many replies emphatically tell the Brussels authorities that they expect to conduct their correspondence with the ducal capital in their own language and will accept no letters or communication in any other language.[283]

Over the next centuries, renewed instances of centralization and regularization call forth similar reactions. By the seventeenth century, the Brabant authorities have gone so far as to recognize two separate county courts: one for the Romance-speaking population at the town of Dalhem, one for the Diets-speaking population at the county's old fiscal centre, 's-Gravenvoeren (Fouron-le-Comte). And the story does not end there: when, as a result of the independence of the United Provinces, the county of Dalhem was to be partitioned between Spanish and Dutch states in the wake of the Treaty of Westphalia (1648-1662), the ensuing, long-negotiated division turned out to follow the line of the jurisdiction of these two county courts and, accordingly, of the linguistic frontier.[284]

Nor does the case stop even there. We encounter the selfsame sensitivities when, in the 1790s, the territories, now conquered by the French Republic, were being divided into the administrative units called *départements*. The demarcation between the *département de l'Ourthe* (with Liège for its centre) and the *département de la Meuse Inférieure* (with Maastricht for its centre) cut across ancient feudal divisions. In the process, French-speaking towns like Visé (mid-way between Maastricht and Liège) evinced a strong preference for Liège. Conversely, the territory of the ancient county of Loon (Looz), including cities like Hasselt and Tongeren, argued strenuously to be released from its centuries-old tie with the city of Liège, and to be attached to the Maastricht *département*, because (so it was argued) the Netherlandic language united the inhabitants of Hasselt and Tongeren with Maastricht, and rendered them aliens in Liège. In the event, the wishes of the inhabitants, based on linguistic kinship, were granted.[285] The departmental border between the Ourthe and the Lower Meuse was mapped, to no small extent, onto a linguistic identification. And east of the Meuse, this departmental border became the state frontier between the Netherlands and Belgium in 1830.

That would appear a textbook illustration of nationalism as defined by Ernest Gellner: political borders are being mapped on to cultural (linguistic) ones. Much as an administrative linguistic frontier was drawn in 1962 to divide the quarrelling Flemish and Walloon factions in modern day-Belgium, so too a political border drawn up in 1648-1662 and again in 1794 followed a linguistic trajectory – in all these cases involving the town of Dalhem and the village of 's-Gravenvoeren. And in each case, and again in the linguistic clashes of the 1980s, the locals repeatedly, strenuously and suspiciously informed the distant Brussels authorities that they will only conduct business in their own language.

However, despite the obvious parallel between this case and Gellner's definition of nationalism (the congruence between political and cultural frontiers), the ancient county of Dalhem squarely fails to fit Gellner's modernist chronology, and instead comes to us from the most rustic backwardness of the Outre-Meuse periphery of the medieval duchy of Brabant.

Still, much as this case forces us to reconsider Gellnerian modernism, I would not like to see it as a straightforward confirmation of primordialism (the theory that nationalism and national feeling predates the nineteenth century). We would make a grave error if we see the pre-modern linguistic assertiveness of the local village courts in the same light as nineteenth- and twentieth-century national-linguistic activism, as something that was actuated, across the centuries, by the selfsame stance.

As we have seen, nineteenth-century nationalism invokes language as a cardinally important factor in a self-other distinction, between nations and neighbours, in a 'horizontal' dynamic of 'othering' and identification across the European cultural landscape. This, I believe, is a specifically modern, latter-day usage. It overlays the far older, and persistent, 'vertical' dynamics of asserting local or particular rights vis-à-vis a central authority. There, tensions and distinctions take shape, not across a culturally diverse landscape, but across a social spectrum of power, privilege, and customary rights. The fifteenth-century *échevins* of Cheratte who state that they conduct business in Romance, and the sixteenth-century village court of Mheer which lets it be known that its language is Diets, do not oppose *each other*, but jointly assert their right to local particularism against the suzerain ducal authorities in Brussels.

This distinction between 'horizontal' (geocultural) and 'vertical' (socio-political) language assertion is crucial, and superficial similarities between fifteenth- and twentieth-century data should not blind us to this important difference. The 'vertical' assertion of language rights against a distant feudal authority is a matter of local particularism, the defence of customary rights against the threat of arbitrary government and power arrogation, part and parcel of feudal politics. Its thrust is not towards any notion of autonomy, but rather towards what I term 'heteronomy': the recognition and acceptance of diverse cultures and administrative régimes within the state. Such heteronomic assertions of local customary rights fed into revolts against centralizing arrogations of arbitrary feudal power, such as we see in the Low Countries and Switzerland; as such they are a source tradition of the rise of the modern civic state; but one source tradition among many, and not to be conflated with modern nationalism. Heteronomism is, if anything, a forerunner of modern democratic and federalist thought.

To that extent, the case of Outre-Meuse illustrates the danger of anachronistically spotting similarities across centuries and of magnifying similarity into sameness. However, there is also another conclusion to be drawn. The 'horizontal', modern-nationalistic invocation of language has not abrogated or displaced the older, 'vertical' one. The right to speak one's own language to one's government is obviously felt as a natural right in the fifteenth century,[*] and it continues undiminished in the nine-teenth century (and indeed the twentieth and twenty-first). Court cases incomprehen-sible to the defendant would today still cause outrage; the spectre of a European cen-tral government at Brussels, heedless of the cultures and languages of the European Union's various member states, continues to cause apprehension. Under a modern overlay of 'horizontal' (inter-ethnic) language conflict, the older 'vertical' assertion (be-tween speakers and government) is as forceful as ever. There are powerful cultural-political, identitarian forces at work which can antedate, by centuries, the rise of na-tionalism in the stricter, modern sense of the term, and which can furnish modern movements with very ancient ammunition.

By the same token, language activism ought to be carefully distinguished in its horizontal and vertical dimensions (and their complex interactions). Not all language arguments and linguistic apprehensions expressed in modern-day Europe are actuated by nationalism or nationalist xenophobia. In many countries, Euro-scepticism is dri-ven by a fear that an alien 'Brussels' may, in an alien tongue, dominate one's domestic affairs. That is not just an example of national-chauvinist, hidebound tunnel vision: it reflects a centuries-long vindication of the right to speak one's own language with one's own government. It is democratic, not necessarily xenophobic. A sense of linguistic identity is older than the nationalist ideology; it has become entangled in the discourse of nationalism but does not form an intrinsic part of it. Crucially important, then, for a sober and sane analysis of such conflicts, is the distinction whether these are 'hori-zontal', between inimical nations, countries, or antagonistic groups, or 'vertical', be-tween citizens and their authorities.

---

* It need not surprise us that the county of Flanders and the duchy of Brabant used this insistence of linguistic rights as a political instrument vis-à-vis Burgundian overlords between 1400 and 1500 (Willemyns 1994); or that Charles V, upon being sworn in as king in the *Cortes* of his various Spanish realms, had to pledge himself repeatedly to using the Spanish language.

Source References

NB: These references are also meant to indicate 'suggested further reading'. I have extensively relied on, without separately noting, general surveys and studies (cf. below, notes 1-6) and on a number of reference works. Whenever I trace the changing semantics of our cultural and political vocabulary, I have made use of the *Oxford English Dictionary*. For biographical background information, I have made use of the *Dictionary of National Biography* and of the old *Allgemeine Deutsche Biographie*. For the details of historical developments, a very useful reference book was Raymond Pearson's *The Longman Companion to European Nationalism, 1789-1920* (London: Longman, 1994), now unfortunately out of print. In my summaries or paraphrases from widely known and readily-available primary sources (such as Montesquieu's *De l'Esprit des Lois*, Fichte's *Reden an die deutsche Nation* and Wordsworth's Preface to the *Lyrical Ballads*), I have dispensed with specific source-references; these have been given only in the case of literal quotations.

1. The classic authorities in nationalism studies, mentioned here and in the next pages, are Anderson 1983, Breuilly 1993, Gellner 1983, Kedourie 1960, Kohn 1946 and 1967, Hobsbawm 1990, Smith 1971, 1986, 1991, 1998. An excellent survey of the history of nationalism studies is Lawrence 2005. For the debates around Gellner's work and his 'modernist' thesis, see also Hall 1998.

2. In this respect, the approach applied here is an application of the comparatist specialism of 'imagology', the study of cross-cultural perceptions and stereotypes as formulated in literature. For imagology, cf. Dyserinck 1991 and 2002, Leerssen 2000, and the website www.hum.uva.nl/images; also the recent Beller & Leerssen 2007.

3. For instance, Agnew 1993 and Bugge 1994 (on Czechia), Alvárez Junco 2001 (Spain), Balcells 1991 (Catalonia), Boyce 1991 (Ireland), Citron 1987 (France), Faensen 1980 and Skendi 1967 (Albania), Fewster 2006 (Finland), Herzfeld 1986 (Greece), Juaristi 1998 (Basque), Krapauskas 2000 (Lithuania), Lindheim & Luckyj 1996 (Ukraine), Samuel 1989 and 1994-1998 (Britain), Eile 2003 and Walicki 1994 (Poland). In addition there have, in the wake of Nora 1997, been various projects on the formula of *lieux de mémoire* (Feldbæk 1991-92 for Denmark, François & Schulze 2001 for Germany, Isnenghi 1996-97 for Italy). Such studies, though not separately referred to in the following book, have been very useful and informative and are here gratefully acknowledged.

4. Examples of such macroregional or comparative studies are Alén Garabato 2005, Baycroft & Hewitson 2006, Berding 1994, Cubitt 1998, Eade 1983, Giesen 1991, Loit 1985, Michel 1995, Mitchison 1980, Reiter 1983, Řezník & Sleváková 1997, Teich & Porter 1993. Again, I am deeply indebted to these collections, although there is little occasion to source-reference them specifically in the following pages.

5. I have taken the definition of a comparative analysis as 'studying a multinational object from a supranational perspective' from Hugo Dyserinck's programmatic outline of Comparative Literature: Dyserinck 1991. This approach has so far been most successfully applied in thematically focused studies, e.g. involving art history (Flacke 1998), literary history (Rubulis 1970, or the ongoing comparatist project Cornis-Pope & Neubauer 2004 ff.); music history (White & Murphy 2001), university history (Rüegg 2004), history writing (Deletant & Hanak 1988, and the ongoing project *Writing National Histories in Europe*, coordinated by Stefan Berger and Chris Lorenz), the history of language reforms, language philosophy and linguistics (Auroux *et*

al 2000-01, Caussat *et al* 1996, Fodor & Hagège 1983-1994 Schieffelin *et al* 1998, van der Sijs 1999), the history of racial thought and tribal origin-myths (Geary 2002, Juaristi 2000, Poliakov 1987), or the role of intellectuals (Suny & Kennedy 1999).

6. Sperber 1990 and 1996. The epidemiological model of Sperber, describing the geographical and social spread of ideas and representations is if these are self-replicating units of 'contagious behaviour', was foreshadowed by André Siegfried's analysis of ideology diffusion, *Itinéraires de contagion: Épidemies et idéologies* (posthumously published in 1960). Cf. also Hägerstrand 1967 (kindly brought to my attention by Willibrord Rutten).

7. For the declaration of Arbroath, cf. also Barrow 2003.

8. Generally Hoppenbrouwers 2006 and the sources gathered there. For other reflections on the idea of nationality in the Middle Ages, see Beumann 1986; Post 1953; Zientara 1986. For the notion of the realm as a community, cf. S. Reynolds 1983 and 1984.

9. Le Goff 1988, 58. Cf. generally also Thomas 1984 and Yamamoto 2000.

10. Most recently on Moritoen's *Kerelslied*: Brinkman 2002 and 2004.

11. Williams 1981, 66 (the original Gaelic on p. 2).

12. The distinction between an ordered, regulated Within and an unruly, wild Outside is already implied in Heraclitus's dictum that 'the people must fight for their law as for their city wall'; cf. Kahn 1979, 59; also Eijsbouts 1993; Leerssen 1999.

13. Benveniste 1969, 1: 313. Le Goff 1988, however, holds that the word 'no doubt comes from the expression *silva forestis*, a forest under the jurisdiction of a royal tribunal (*forum*)', indicating its separate legal status (52, 110).

14. On the imagining of the forest and of Forest Law, cf. Marienstras 1969. Also, Young 1979.

15. Saunders 1993.

16. Savage 1933.

17. Hoffmann 1983.

18. Generally, Leerssen 1995 and 1996b.

19. Quoted in Giraldus Cambrensis 1978, 144, 146.

20. Hassig 1995; Mason 1990. Also Friedman 1981.

21. Giraldus Cambrensis 1982, 166.

22. Ibid., 162-163.

23. The case for courtliness and classical learning to have been revived in courtly-clerical circles has been made for continental Europe by Jaeger 1985.

24. For the impact of Giraldus on subsequent representations, see Rambo 1994.

25. Bernheimer 1952, 20. Cf. also White 1978, 150-182 ('The Forms of Wildness: Archeology of an Idea').

26. Generally Ellis 1998a and 1988b, Crawford 1993; Leerssen 1994. Also, Connors 2001. For slightly later developments, Canny 2001.

27. Richard Stanyhurst, in Holinshed's *Chronicles* (1577), quoted and commented Leerssen 1996b, 43. Cf. also Jackson 1973; Lennon 1994.

28. Davies 1612, 114-115.

29. 11-13 James I, c.5. Statutes 1786, 1: 441.

30. The standard work, itself a 'classic', is Lovejoy & Boas 1935.

31. Caesar 1917, 3 (the original Latin on p. 2).

32. Decharneux 1995; Van der Linden 1930.

33. This is why the old *Catholic Encyclopaedia* (1909 ed.) sees this council as the beginning of 'nationalism'; see the entry 'Constance, Council of'. This 1909 edition of the *Catholic Encyclopaedia* is online at http://www.newadvent.org/cathen/index.html (last updated 6 October 2005; visited 26 June 2006). For the Councils of Constance and Basel this encyclopaedia is as informative as it is (of course) biased.

34. Leupen 1998.

35. Borst 1995, vol. III/1: 985; Poliakov 1987; Mörke 1996, 118n.

36. Generally, Clark 1921; L.D. Reynolds 1983, and Reynolds & Wilson 1991. Also the introduction to Tacitus 1970, 119-125.

37. Tacitus 1970, 157-161.

38. This interdependence of auto-image and hetero-image is one of the fundamental features of ethnotypes and of national image-formation, well established in the field of imagology; cf. Dyserinck 1991 and 2002, Leerssen 2000, and the website www.hum.uva.nl/images.

39. Iuvenalis 2004, 234-235.

40. Borst 1995, III:/1: 969-970; Haitsma Mulier 1974.

41. Lehmann 1983. Also Borchardt 1971, Kuehnemund 1953; von See 1994; Unverfehrt 1981; Wes 1980.

42. The Loeb edition emends 'barditum' (the variant found only in the Vatican MS 4468, in itself an authoritative one) to 'barritum' or 'baritum': 'sunt illis haec quoque carmina, quorum relatu, quem baritum vocant, accendunt animos futuraeque pugnae fortunam ipso cantu augurantur' (cap. 3).

43. von der Dunk 2000, 69.

44. Schöffer 1975; Tilmans 1993; van der Woud 1990.

45. Generally, Kliger 1952. On Alfred the Great, Parker 2007.

46. 'En 1480, un Français a, à coup sûr, des ancêtres gaulois qu'il ne possédait pas en 1400': Pomian 1997, 2265, quoting Beaune 1985.

47. Kelley 1973; Reynolds 1931.

48. Viallaneix & Ehrard 1982; Leerssen 1989; Pomian 1997. For Hotman, see also the contribution by Dubois in Viallanneix & Ehrard 1982, 19-28.

49. The phrase and concept come, of course, from Fink 1962.

50. On the early history of European borders and their linearization and rationalization: Genicot 1970; Guenée 1997; Nordman 1997.

51. Wolf 1968, 403-404. Generally on Vauban, the excellent biography by Virol 2003.

52. Black 1997, 1-17. Cf also Bagrow 1985; Harley & Woodward 1987; Woodward 1987.

53. Chaytor 1966.

54. Thurville-Petre 1996.

55. 'El idioma analítico de John Wilkins', orig. in *Otras inquisiciones* (1952). Borges 1985, 3: 109-113. In the original: 'los animales se dividen en (a) pertenecientes al Emperador, (b) embalsamados, (c) amaestrados, (d) lechones, (e) sirenas, (f) fabulosos, (g) perros sueltos, (h) incluidos en esta clasificación, (i) que se agitan come locos, (j) innumerables, (k) dibujados con un pinsél finísimo de pelo de camello, (l) etcétera, (m) que acaban de romper el jarrón, (n) que de lejos parecen moscas' (111).

56. Scaliger 1964, lib. III, cap. 17; and cf. Zach 1987. In the original: 'Asianorum luxus, Africanorum perfidia, Europaeorum (hoc enim volo mihi dari) acritas. [...] Montani asperi: Campestres molliores, desides. [...] Germani fortes, simplices, animarum prodigi, veri amici, verique hostes. Suetii, Noruegii, Gruntlandii, Gotti, belluae. Scoti non minus. Angli, perfidi, inflati, feri, contemptores, irrisores, factiosi, alieni sibiipsis, bellicosi coacti, servi ut ne serviant, Dei contemptores. Galli ad rem attenti, mobiles, leves, humani, hospitales, prodigi, lauti, bellicosi, hostium contemptores, atque adcirco sui negligentes, imparati, audaces, cedentes labori, equites omni longe optimi. Hispanis victus asper somi, alienis mensis largi, alacres bibaces, loquaces, iactrabundi, fastus tartareus, supercilium cerbereum, avaritia immanis, paupertate fortes, fidei firmitas ex precio, omnibius nationaibus & invidentes & invisi. Una natio illos superat animi pravitate, magnitudine vincitur, Ligures.'

57. Leerssen 1991.

58. Amossy & Delon 1999; Amossy & Rosen 1982; Zach 1987. Also, Morgan 1986.

59. Genette 1969.

60. La Mesnardière 1972, 122-123; also quoted in Zach 1987, 104.

61. Stanzel 1974a; Stanzel 1974b; Stanzel 1987.

62. Jauß 1999; also Seidel & Pongratz 1971.
63. The following section is deeply indebted to Van Delft 1993.
64. Generally Smeed 1985.
65. López de Abiada 2004, 15.
66. Amidst the sizeable body of commentary on this object, I highlight Stanzel 1997; Stanzel, Weiler, & Zacharasiewicz 1999.
67. The fundamental work on the topic is Zacharasiewicz 1977.
68. Reynolds 1931.
69. Lord 1975, 626.
70. Mossner 1980.
71. Cf. Leerssen 1987.
72. Shackleton 1962; on Montesquieu's influence, Romani 1998. By the end of the century, this 'temperamental' view of constitutional systems had already become a generally accepted commonplace. The Swiss essayist Johann Georg Zimmermann, author of a widely read treatise of 'National Pride' (*Von dem Nationalstolze*) argues that 'a wild, impetuous and restless person finds happiness in democracy; a quiet, sage and virtuous person in an aristocracy; and a flexible, ambitious but adaptable spirit is best suited to a monarchy' (quoted from the 1760 ed. in Leerssen 1996b, 386). In the original: 'Ein wilder, ungestümer und unruhiger Kopf findet sich in der Demokratie glücklich; ein stiller, vernünftiger und tugendhafter Mensch in der Aristocratie; ein biegsamer, ehrgeitziger, aber nach den Umständen sich selbst überwindender Geist, in der Monarchie'.
73. Hayman 1971. The pivotal texts are Part III, esp. Book XIV ('Des lois dans le rapport qu'elles ont avec la nature du climat') of *De l'esprit des lois*, in Montesquieu 1964, 613 ff., and Hume's essay 'Of National Characters', which first appeared in the revised edition of the *Moral and Political Essays* of 1748; in Hume 1964, 3: 244 ff.
74. Diderot & D'Alembert 1777, s.v. *Caractère* and *Nation*, respectively. In the original: 'Le caractère d'une nation consiste dans une certaine disposition habituelle de l'âme, qui est plus commune chez une nation que chez une autre, quoique cette disposition ne se rencontre pas dans tous les membres qui composent la nation: ainsi le caractère des François est la légereté, la gaieté, la sociabilité, l'amour de leurs rois & de la monarchie même, &c.'; 'Chaque nation a son caractère particulier: c'est une espèce de proverbe que de dire, léger comme un françois, jaloux comme un italien, grave comme un espagnol, méchant comme un anglois, fier comme un écossois, ivrogne comme un allemand, paresseux comme un irlandois, fourbe comme un grec, &c.'
75. Locke 1960; for the context, generally Harris 1994.
76. Robbins 1959.
77. Generally Troost 2005.
78. The following section presents a case already addressed in Leerssen 1988, and is deeply indebted to Venturi 1971; Viroli 1995, Goodwin 1979 and Robbins 1959. The notion of democratic revolutions takes up the argument of Palmer 1959. References to the semantic shifts of operative terms all are taken from the OED.
79. *A Voyage to Brobdingnag*, ch. 7.
80. Venturi 1971, 72.
81. Quoted from Leeb 1973, 78.
82. Generally Goodwin 1979, 106-112. Also Fitzpatrick 1987.
83. The amount of literature on Rousseau is vast. For the themes of virtue and democracy developed here, see Damrosch 2005; Reisert 2003; Trousson 2003.
84. Ozouf 1997.
85. On Sieyès, see generally Bredin 1988. Also Kohn 1967, 27-34.
86. A recent biography is Scurr 2006.

87. Saint-Just, report 'Sur la police générale de le République', 15 April 1794; quoted Bredin 1988, 300-301. In the original: 'Un homme révolutionnaire est inflexible, mais il est sensé, il est frugal, il est simple, sans afficher le luxe de la fausse modestie; il est l'irréconciliable ennemi de toute mensonge, de toute indulgence, de toute affectation; comme son but est de voir triompher la Révolution, il ne la censure jamais, mais il condamne ses ennemis sans l'envelopper avec eux; il ne l'outrage point, mais il l'éclaire, et, jaloux de sa pureté, il s'observe quand il en parle par respect pour elle; il prétend moins être l'égal de l'autorité, qui est la loi, que l'égal des hommes, et surtout des malheureux.Un homme révolutionnaire est plein d'honneur; il est policé sans fadeur, mais par franchise, et parce qu'il est en paix avec son propre coeur; il croit que la groissièreté est une marque de tromperie et de remords, et qu'elle déguise la fausseté sous l'emportement. Les aristocrates parlent et agissent avec tyrannie: l'homme révolution-naire est intraitable aux méchants, mais il est sensible; il est si jaloux de la gloire de sa patrie et de la liberté, qu'il ne fait rien inconsidérément; il court dans les combats, il poursuit les coupables, et défend l'innocene devant les tribunaux; il dit la vérité afin qu'elle instruise, et non pas afin qu'elle outrage; il sait que pour que la Révolution s'affermisse il faut être aussi bon qu'on était méchant autrefois; sa probité n'est pas une finesse de l'esprit, mais une qualité du coeur et une chose bien entendue. Marat était doux dans son ménage; il n'épouvantait que les traîtres: J.-J. Rousseau était révolutionnaire, et n'était pas insolent sans doute. J'en conclus que l'homme révolutionnaire est un héros de bon sens et de probité.'

88. Cartledge 2001. Also: Rawson 1969.

89. Cartledge 2002.

90. The idea of an emerging public sphere in these decades follows, of course, Habermas 1990.

91. Genette 1969, 73. In the original: 'Cette «opinion», réelle ou supposée, c'est assez précisément ce que l'on nommerait aujourd'hui une idéologie, c'est-à-dire un corps de maximes et de préjugés qui constitue tout à la fois une vision du monde et un système de valeurs.'

92. I have surveyed the patriotism evinced in a fair number of such sentimental comedies in Leerssen 1996b, 102-136.

93. Babcock 1931; Halliday 1957. Also Meehan 1975.

94. This is the famous phrase in the final section of the *Hamburgische Dramaturgie*, mentioning 'den gutherzigen Einfall, den Deutschen ein Nationaltheater zu verschaffen, weil wir Deutsche noch keine Nation sind!' (Lessing 1988, 4: 484).

95. Friedrich Schiller, *Die Schaubühne als eine moralische Anstalt betrachtet* (lecture read in Mannheim, 1784. Schiller 1970, 11-12. In the original: 'Unmöglich kann ich hier den grossen Einfluss übergehen, den eine gute stehende Bühne auf den Geist der Nation haben würde. National-geist eines Volks nenne ich die Ähnlichkeit und Übereinstimmung seiner Meinungen und Neigungen bei Gegenständen, worüber eine andere Nation anders meint und empfindet. Nur der Schaubühne ist es möglich, diese Übereinstimmung in einem hohen Grad zu bewirken, weil sie das ganze Gebiet des menschlichen Lebens durchwandert, alle Situationen des Lebens erschöpft und in alle Winkel des Herzens hinunter leuchtet; weil sie alle Stände und Klassen in sich vereinigt und den gebahntesten Weg zum Verstand und zum Herzen hat. [...] wenn wir es erlebten, eine Nationalbühne zu haben, so würden wir auch eine Nation. Was kettete Griechenland so fest aneinander? Was zog das Volk so unwiderstehlich nach seiner Bühne? – Nichts anders als der vaterländische Inhalt der Stücke, der griechische Geist, das grosse überwältigende Interesse, des Staats, der besseren Menschheit, das in denselbigen ath-mete.' – I have used the word 'public-mindedness' to render Schiller's term *vaterländisch*, which roughly corresponds to the term 'patriotic' as discussed earlier in this chapter. Schiller's argument, too, needs to be safeguarded from retrospective anachronism: it is not yet part of the genre of 'calls for a national literature' such as we see it flourish after the Schlegel brothers, in the nineteenth century. *Vaterländisch* in this context has no ethnic-chauvinist overtones whatsoever, and refers only to a civic-minded interest in the well-being of society at large. Similarly, the term 'Nationalgeist' as used by Schiller should by no means be confused with

later coinages such as *Volksgeist*; it means 'public climate, public spirit'. In his Jena lecture on the legislators of ancient Greece, Schiller praises ancient Sparta for inculcating such a public spirit and uses terms like *vaterländisch* and *Nationalgeist* to describe it, almost celebrating the ascendancy of the public over the private. 'All acts [in ancient Sparta] became public acts. Under the gaze of the nation, youth grew to adulthood and old age declined into senility. Incessantly, the Spartan looked upon Sparta as Sparta looked upon him. He was witness to everything, and everything was witness to his life. The desire for fame was given incessant stimulation, the public spirit [*Nationalgeist*] continuous nourishment. The idea of the fatherland and of a fatherlandish interest was intertwined with the most intimate life of all its citizens.'

96. See also Isaiah Berlin's assessment: Berlin 2000.

97. This seminal work of English poetical Romanticism (a collaboration between Wordsworth and Coleridge) is programmatic in both words of its title. To begin with, it sees the true function of poetry to be *lyrical* (rather than dramatic, narrative or otherwise), i.e. to express emotions and motivated by what Wordsworth in his preface (added to the 1802 edition) famously called 'a spontaneous overflow of powerful feeling'. Moreover, the work gravitates towards the register of *balladry*, i.e. a simple, homely form, unadorned and of a demure rhetorical register, couched in a natural, non-artificial and spontaneous 'language really used by men'. In all these respects, Wordsworth stands indebted, unknowingly, to Herder.

98. Herder, *Auch eine Philosophie der Geschichte zur Bildung der Menschheit*, in Herder 1982, 3: 105. In the original: 'Wie elend, als es noch Nationen und Nationalcharakter gab! Was für wechselseitiger Hass, Abneigung gegen die Fremden, Festsetzung auf seinen Mittelpunkt, väterliche Vorurteile, Hangen an der Erdscholle, an der wir geboren sind und auf der wir verwesen sollen! Einheimische Denkart, enger Kreis von Ideen, ewige Barbarei! Bei uns sind gottlob alle Nationalcharaktere ausgelöscht, wir lieben uns alle, oder vielmehr keiner bedarf's den andern zu lieben; wir gehen miteinander um, sind einander völlig gleich – gesittet, höflich, glückselig, haben zwar keinen Vaterland, keine Unsern, für die wir leben, aber sind Menschenfreunde und Weltbürger. Schon jetzt alle Regenten Europas, bald werden wir alle die französische Sprache reden! Und denn – Glückseligkeit! – es fängt wieder die Güldne Zeit an, "da hatte alle Welt einerlei Zunge und Sprache, wird eine Herde und ein Hirte werden!" Nationalcharaktere, wo seid ihr?'

99. Walder 1948; also, more generally, Hartmann 2001. The secularization of the monasteries led to an enormous re-inventory of their libraries, which were relocated to the German capitals – especially Munich, which as a result came to have one of the richest libraries of Europe; Hacker 2000. Many medieval manuscripts were found in the process, cf. here p. 199.

100. Jolles 1936. On German Romanticism, also Kluckhohn 1961; Ziolkowski 1990 and Verschoor 1928. The links between anti-Revolutionary politics, Romanticism and national thought are complex. See, generally, Eade 1983.

101. There is, as yet, no good, modern scholarly biography of this contradictory and intriguing figure; nor is there even a proper edition of his works or correspondence. I have traced some of his activities in Leerssen 2006a. Also, Pundt 1935 and Schäfer & Schawe 1971.

102. Schmidt 1994.

103. Cepl-Kaufmann & Johanning 2003; Pabst 2003.

104. Thus in the first installment of *Geist der Zeit* (1805). In the original: 'Ihr also seid das würdige Volk, ihr, die ihr Europa um seine schönsten Hoffnungen betrogen habt, ihr wollt die Beglücker und die Herren anderer sein, die ihr wieder die kriechendsten und elendsten Sklaven geworden seid?'

105. A good impression is given in Pinkard 2000, which amply demonstrates the formative influence of Hölderlin on Hegel's early development. The status of Schiller, not just as a poet and playwright, but as a thinker and intellectual amidst his contemporaries, comes to the fore in Herbert Scurla's 1984 biography of Wilhelm v. Humboldt.

106. Cf also Krügel 1914.
107. Bauer 1908.
108. Kleist 1975, 1: 232-235 and 283-310. In the original: 'Nur der Franzmann zeigt sich noch / in dem deutschen Reiche / Bruder, nehmt die Keule doch / Dass er gleichfalls weiche' and 'Alles, was ihr Fuss betreten, / Färbt mit ihren Knochen weiss, / Welchen Rab und Fuchs verschmähten, / Gebet ihn den Fischen Preis, / Dämmt den Rhein mit ihren Leichen, / Lasst, gestäuft von ihrem Bein, / Ihn um Pfalz und Trier weichen / Und ihn dann die Grenze sein! / Eine Jagdlust, wie wenn Schützen / Auf dem Spur dem Wolfe sitzen! / Schlagt sie tot! Das Weltgericht / Fragt Euch nach den Gründen nicht!'
109. In addition to the Arminius literature mentioned in note 41 above, cf. also Stephens 1983.
110. Schlegel 1988, 7-8. In the original: 'Wichtig vor allen Dingen für die ganze fernere Entwickelung, ja für das ganze geistige Dasein einer Nation erscheint es auf diesem historischen, die Völker nach ihrem Wert vergleichenden Standpunkte, daß ein Volk große National-Erinnerungen hat, welche sich sch meistens noch in den dunkeln Zeiten seines ersten Ursprungs verlieren, und welche zu erhalten und zu verherrlichen das vorzüglichste Geschäft der Dichtkunst ist. Solche National-Erinnerungen, das herrlichste Erbteil, das ein Volk haben kann, sind ein Vorzug, der durch nichts anders ersetzt werden kann; und wenn ein Volk dadurch, daß es eine große Vergangenheit, daß es solche Erinnerungen aus uralter Vorzeit, daß es mit einem Wort eine Poesie hat, sich selbst in seinem Gefühle erhoben und gleichsam geadelt findet, so wird es eben dadurch auch in unserm Auge und Urteil auf eine höhere Stufe gestellt.'
111. Schilling 2000.
112. Lange 1954, 260. In the original: 'Religion, Gebet, Liebe zum Regenten, zum Vaterland, zur Tugend, sind nichts anderes als Poesie, keine Herzenserhebung ohne poetische Stimmung. Wer nur nach kalter Berechung handelt, wird ein starrer Egoist. Auf Poesie ist die Sicherheit der Throne gegründet.'
113. Generally, Bann 1995; Fritzsche 2004.
114. Ozouf 1997.
115. Hanske & Traeger 1992.
116. Aretin 1803. In the original: 'Nun sind es gerade tausend Jahre, dass Karl der Grosse das deutsche Kaiserthum gegründet hat. Ich rufe dieses Faktum nicht darum in das Gedächtnis meiner Leser zurück, um sie auf den erstaunungswürdigen Wechsel der Dinge während dieses Zeitraumes aufmerksam zu machen, oder um ihre Betrachtungen auf neuere Ereignisse zu lenken, die eben diesem Kaiserthum nach tausendjähriger Existenz den Umsturz zu drohen geschienen hatten; – diese und ähnliche Reflexionen überlasse ich den Politikern. – Meine Absicht ist nur, eine literarische Jubelfeier jener grossen Begebenheit zu halten, und hierzu giebt mir ein merkwürdiges altdeutsches Manuskript, welches ich in der uralten Abtey Weihenstephan bey Freisingen einsehen und benutzen konnte (und das nunmehr mit allen übrigen literarischen Schätzen der baier. Abteien in die hiesige Bibliothek gewandert ist), eine erwünschte Gelegenheit.'
117. von der Hagen 1824. In the original: 'Wie man zu des Tacitus Zeiten die Altrömische Sprache der Republik wieder hervor zu rufen strebte: so ist auch jetzt, mitten unter den zerreißendsten Stürmen, in Deutschland die Liebe zu der Sprache und den Werken unserer ehrenfesten Altvordern rege und thätig, und es scheint, als suche man in der Vergangenheit und Dichtung, was in der Gegenwart schmerzlich untergeht.' Cf. generally Leerssen 2004a.
118. Ehrismann 1975.
119. Von der Hagen 1824. In the original: 'in der schmachvollsten Zeit des Vaterlandes eine wahre Herzstärkung und eine hohe Verheißung der Wiedekehr deutscher Weltherrlichkeit.'
120. Friemel 1990.
121. This section is based on material more amply treated in Leerssen 2004a; Leerssen 2006a.

122. On that term, cf. Leerssen 2006b. Also: Wyss 1979, Jordan 1999 and Küttler, Rüsen, & Schulin 1997.

123. From Scherer's article on Jacob Grimm in the AdB; in the original: 'das Sein aus dem Werden zu begreifen.' For Grimm's debt to Savigny, see also Schoof 1953. On Savigny's career: Denneler 1985 and the sources cited there.

124. Grimm 1864-90, 2: 75-133 ('Über das finnische Epos') 75. In the original: 'Unter den drei dichtungsarten fällt zu beurtheilen keine schwerer als das epos, denn die lyrische poesie aus dem menschlichen herzen selbst aufsteigend wendet sich unmittelbar an unser gemüt und wird aus allen zeiten zu allen verstanden; die dramatische strebt das vergangne in die empfindungsweise, gleichsam sprache der gegenwart umzusetzen und ist, wo ihr das gelingt, in ihrer wirkung unfehlbar [...] um die epische poesie aber steht es weit anders, in der vergangenheit geboren reicht sie aus dieser bis zu uns herüber, ohne ihre eigne natur fahren zu lassen, wir haben, wenn wir sie genieszen wollen, uns in gans geschwundene umstände zu versetzen.' [capitalization *sic*].

125. Eliot 1960.

126. Generally, Brown 1979, Chandler 1970 and Rigney 2001.

127. For a good visualization, cf. Moretti 1998.

128. This magically healing power of the 'Royal Touch' dates back to primitive-magical notions on the superhuman charisma of royalty. The practice had fallen out of use in the course of the eighteenth century. Dr Johnson, as a boy, had been touched by Queen Anne for scrofula, known as 'the King's Evil'. The formula used in France was 'The King touches you, may God heal you'. The standard work on supernatural charisma attributed to royals is Bloch 1924; more work remains to be done on the Romantic-historicist background of its final revival in the 1820s in France. On Saint-Denis: Beaune 1997.

129. Boockmann 1982; Frühwald 1983; Knapp 1990.

130. Drentje 2006, Van der Wal 1983.

131. Hansen 1976; Hettling & Nolte 1993; Malettke 1992. For a restrained view of the affair of the 'Göttingen Seven', see von See 1999.

132. Touchard 1968.

133. Konstantinou 1992; Noe 1994; Spencer 1986.

134. For Ireland: Boyce 1991; Hutchinson 1987; Kee 1972; Leerssen 1996c; MacDonagh 1983. For the Balkans: Daskalov 2004; Faensen 1980; Jelavich 1983; Lord 1963; Reiter 1983; Todorova 1997.

135. Cf. also Nipperdey 1968.

136. Prebble 2000.

137. Nichols 1996, 41. Generally: Ridoux 2001.

138. On the *Marseillaise*, composed in Strasbourg in 1792, see Vovelle 1997. The quoted lines in the original: 'Allons enfants de la Patrie / Le jour de gloire est arrivé! / Contre nous de la tyrannie / L'étendard sanglant est levé / Entendez-vous dans les campagnes / Mugir ces féroces soldats? / Ils viennent jusque dans vos bras / Égorger vos fils, vos compagnes! / Aux armes, citoyens, formez vos bataillons, / Marchons, marchons! Qu'un sang impur abreuve nos sillons! / Que veut cette horde d'esclaves, / De traîtres, de rois conjurés ? / Pour qui ces ignobles entraves, / Ces fers dès longtemps préparés? / Français, pour nous, ah ! quel outrage / Quels transports il doit exciter! / C'est nous qu'on ose méditer / De rendre à l'antique esclavage. / Aux armes, citoyens, formez vos bataillons, / Marchons, marchons! Qu'un sang impur abreuve nos sillons!' There are five more stanzas.

139. The standard work on the linguistic policies of the République is de Certeau, Julia, & Revel 1975. The various quoted texts can also be found in the internet: www.languefrancaise.net/dossiers/. In the original: 'Nous n'avons plus de provinces, et nous avons encore environ trente patois qui en rappellent les noms.' 'Le fédéralisme et la superstition parlent bas-breton; l'émigration et la haine de la République parlent allemand; la contre-révolution parle l'italien, et le

fanatisme parle le basque. Cassons ces instruments de dommage et d'erreur.' 'Mais au moins on peut uniformer le langage d'une grande nation, de manière que tous les citoyens qui la composent puissent sans obstacle se communiquer leurs pensées. Cette entreprise, qui ne fut pleinement exécutée chez aucun peuple, est digne du peuple français, qui centralise toutes les branches de l'organisation sociale et qui doit être jaloux de consacrer au plutôt, dans une République une et indivisible, l'usage unique et invariable de la langue de la liberté.'

140. Quoted in Revel 1997, 2924-2925. In the original: 'Il faut espérer que tôt ou tard la Révolution amènera le bienfait d'un costume national et que le voyageur, en passant d'un département à un autre, ne croira plus se trouver chez des peuples différents. A voir les habitants du département du Nord, ceux du Finistère auprès de ceux du Bas-Rhin, ceux de la Seine-Inférieure auprès de ceux du Var, croirait-on que ce fût la même nation?'

141. It was still in full force by the late nineteenth century, witness Eugene Weber's classic study *Peasants into Frenchmen*: Weber 1976.

142. Such influences in political culture are studied nowadays under the heading of 'cultural transfer': Espagne 1990; for an example, see Jourdan 2004.

143. The classic study is Knippenberg & de Pater 1988; also, Van der Burg 2007.

144. Roberts 1998; Williams 1980; Williams 1985. Also Jones 1998.

145. Eley & Suny 1996, 7. Generally also Kramer 1983-1994.

146. Gillis 1994.

147. Metternich to Prokesch, 1849; printed in *Aus dem nachlasse des Grafen Prokesch-Osten. Briefwechsel mit Herrn von Gentz und Fürsten Metternich* (Wien, 1881), 2:343. Quoted in Georg Buchmann, *Geflügelte Worte: Der Citatenschatz des deutschen Volkes* (19th ed. Berlin 1898), 537-538, online at http://aronsson.se/buchmann/0572.html. In the original: 'Ich habe in meiner Controverse mit Lord Palmerston in den italienischen Fragen im Sommer 1847 den Ausspruch gefällt, dass der nationale Begriff «Italien» ein geographischer sei, und mein Ausspruch, *l'Italie est un nom géographique*, welcher Palmerston giftig ärgerte, hat sich das Bürgerrecht erworben. Mehr oder weniger – wie dies auf alle Vergleiche passt – gilt derselbe Begriff für das Deutschland, welches bei der Menge in der zweiten Linie der Gefühle und der Strebungen steht, während es von reinen oder berechnenden Phantasten (also von ehrlichen und kniffigen) auf die oberste Stelle erhoben wird.'

148. The statement is engraved on a stone in the grounds. In the original: 'Möchte Walhalla förderlich sein der Erstarkung und der Vermehrung Deutschen Sinnes! Möchten alle Deutschen, welchen Stammes sie auch seien, immer fühlen, dass sie gemeinsames Vaterland haben. Und jeder trage bei, soviel er vermag, zu dessen Verherrlichung!'

149. Grimm 1864-1890, 5:480, 6:411.

150. Cf. Leerssen 2006a, 97-98.

151. Quoted in Bleuel 1968, 17. In the original: 'Wer unter uns in Zukunft noch Franzosen und Deutsche bloß als zwei feindliche Parteien betrachtet, die mit gleichem Rechte hadern, wer noch vernünftelt, daß, wenn er als Franzose geboren wäre, er es ebenso machen würde – wer noch dieses von einer besseren Vorzeit so (schmählich) entartete, dieses meineidige, gottesleugnerische, raubgierige Volk dem edlen aufopfernden Sinn der Deutschen vergleicht, der ist ein Franzose neuester Art, wo er auch geboren worden, und verdient in Deutschland als solcher geachtet zu werden.'

152. In the original: 'Deutschland, Deutschland über alles, über alles in der Welt, / Wenn es stets zu Schutz und Trutze brüderlich zusammenhält / Von der Maas bis an die Memel, von der Etsch bis an den Belt. / Deutschland, Deutschland über alles, über alles in der Welt!' Generally on Hoffmann: Andrée 1972; Behr 1999; von Wintzingerode-Knorr 1999. On the *Lied der Deutschen*: Grewe 1982.

153. In the original: 'Einigkeit und Recht und Freiheit für das deutsche Vaterland! / Danach lasst uns alle streben brüderlich mit Herz und Hand! / Einigkeit und Recht und Freiheit sind des Glückes Unterpfand; / Blüh im Glanze dieses Glückes, blühe, deutsches Vaterland!'

154. Hampe 1936, 79, quoting the crown prince's diary for 3 December 1870, looking forward to 'die Beendigung des fünfundsechzigjährigen Interregnums'.

155. Bruyning 1990. Also, McMenamin 1997.

156. The early, cultural phase of the *risorgimento* has been comparatively less thoroughly researched than the period after 1848. For a profile of the various historians of the romantic-nationalist generation, see Bruyning 1995.

157. Kohn 1960; Milojković-Djurić 1994.

158. For Slovak nationalism, see Brock 1976.

159. Haselsteiner 2000; Moritsch 2000; Orton 1978.

160. Mout 1996; Štaif 1997; Zacek 1970. On Czech nationalism, generally, Agnew 1993; Hanak 1988; Vlnas & Hojda 1998.

161. Despatalovic 1975.

162. Chickering 1984; Loock 1969. On the earlier, cultural roots of Greater German thought, see Leerssen 2006a; Loock 1969.

163. Simons 1980.

164. Wils 1994.

165. Ellis 1993; Constantine 2007.

166. The founding text of this trend was a paranoid tract written anonymously by Cyprien Robert, who had succeeded Adam Mickiewicz to the chair of Slavic philology at the Collège de France: Robert 1860.

167. Landau 1981.

168. Generally, Leerssen 1996b; Leerssen 1996c.

169. For O'Connell, MacDonagh 1991.

170. Leerssen 2002a.

171. Hroch 1968; Hroch 1985.

172. Fredericq 1906; NEVB 1998.

173. Sampimon 2006.

174. Lučić 2002.

175. Generally, Kirby 1995; Loit 1985.

176. The complexities are visualized in Magocsi 1995, maps 27a, 30, 32a, 33. Cf. also Teunissen & Steegh 2003.

177. Kemiläinen 1997; Kemiläinen 1998; Klinge 1980; Klinge 1993; also Fewster 2006.

178. The various oppositions between different types of nationalism derive from Hans Kohn's work. An excellent survey of these different analytical schools in nationalism studies is given by Lawrence 2005. A no less excellent attempt to transcend such binaries (undertaken, significantly, on a comparative-European basis) is the recent collection Baycroft & Hewitson 2006, with the programmatic editors' introduction on pp. 1-16.

179. Ledeen 1977.

180. The *megali idea* was proposed most strenuously by the influential figure of Ioannis Kolettis (1773-1847); cf. Clogg 2002, 46-51 and 244-245.

181. M.L. Smith 1998.

182. Markusse 1996.

183. Cf. Simanowski 1998, Leerssen 1993b.

184. Duyzings 2000.

185. Hyde 1994. On Hyde, see Ó Glaisne 1991 and (more in the mode of a-critical adulation) Dunleavy & Dunleavy 1991.

186. In the original: 'So weit die deutsche Zunge klingt / Und Gott im Himmel Lieder singt / Das soll es seyn! / Das, wackrer Deutscher, nenne dein.' More on Arndt and this song in Leerssen 2006a; on his acclamation in the Frankfurt *Nationalversammlung*: *ibid.*, 131-132, 212 following Wigard 1848-1850, 1: 27.

187. Grimm 1864-1890, 7: 557. In the original: 'Lassen Sie mich mit der einfachen frage anheben: was ist ein volk? und ebenso einfach antworten: ein volk ist der inbegriff von menschen, welche dieselbe sprache reden.' [capitalization *sic*] This was part of Grimm's opening speech as president of the first Congress of Germanisten, held in Frankfurt in 1846 and often seen as a scholarly warming-up exercise for the 1848 *Nationalversammlung*. Cf. Fürbeth *et al* 1999; Netzer 2006; Verhandlungen 1847; Verhandlungen 1848.

188. Grimm 1864-1890, 4: 73. In the original: 'Jede individualität soll heilig gehalten werden, auch in der sprache; es ist zu wünschen, dasz auch der kleinste, verachteste dialect, weil es gewisz vor dem grösten und geehrtesten heimliche vorzüge voraushaben wird, nur sich selbst und seiner natur überlassen bleibe und keine gewaltsamkeit erdulde. von dem werth einer so bedeutenden, durch treffliche werke uns, wie den eingeborenen achtbar erscheinenden sprache, wie die dänische ist, braucht gar keine rede zu sein. daran sind die Dänen untadelhaft, dasz sie dem offenen eindringen deutscher wörter und phrasen einhalt thun; allein thöricht wäre es, zu glauben, 1½ millionen menschen (der ganze norden zählt deren nicht fünf) könnten sich dem unaufhaltsamen zuströmen einer von 32 millionen gesprochenen nah verwandten sprache, welche die grösten geister gleichsam für alle zeiten angezündet haben, eigentlich verschlieszen, so dasz das gefühl dieser übermacht in Dänemark für eine unehre gelten sollte. die deutsche literatur herscht [*sic*] auf keine unedle weise, der Niedersachse wie der Österreicher freut sich ihrer und behält dennoch seine mundart lieb und werth, mit denen wir die dänische übrigens nicht vergleichen. die geistreichsten Dänen haben das rechte empfunden und gethan, sie wissen, dasz sie der deutschen literatur eben so gehören, als diese ihnen. [...] diese ergieszung über unsere sprache und literatur, wenn sie einigen zu lang und ungehörig erscheinen sollte, hat uns gerecht und nothwendig geschienen, es hat jedem Deutschen schmerzhaft sein müssen, zumal jetzt, aus einer neulich erschienenen, öffentlichen verordnung der dänischen regierung zu ersehen, dasz in den ihr untergebenen deutschredenden ländern die deutsche sprache nach und nach gedrückt und wohl unterdrückt werden soll. «ist es nicht billig, du Deutscher, dasz die sprache, welche du in der wiege aus dem süszen vorgeschwätze deiner mutter sammt der milch eingesogen, bei dir lieb und werth gehalten werde!»' [capitalization *sic*]

189. Cf. Demandt 1990.

190. Wigard 1848-1850, 1:289-290. In the original: 'Ich habe mich seit langer Zeit in genaue Untersuchungen eingelassen über die Geschichte jener nördlichen Gegenden, und bin dadurch auf Ergebnisse gelangt, die von den bisherigen zum Theil vollkommen abweichen. [...] dass nach meinen Untersuchungen die Jüten, welche jetzt für die Bewohner des nördlichen Theils der Halbinsel gelten, dass diese Jüten ebensowohl ein ursprünglich germanischer Volksstamm waren, insofern wir befugt sind, germanische Volksstämme den scandinavischen entgegenzustellen. Aber welche Erinnerungen weckt nicht die Geschichte dieser nördlichen Gegend! Von dort sind schon vor dem Beginn unserer Zeitrechnung die beiden Völker ausgegangen, welche den mächtigen Römern unüberwindlichen Schrecken einflössten, die Cimbern und Teutonen, die mit uns gleichen Namen führen. Sollte das nicht gerechten Stolz anfachen, und wahrhaftig! andere Völker würden das nicht dulden, dass von dem Wohnsitze ihrer ruhmvollen Vorfahren auch nur eine Scholle breit jemals abgetreten werden dürfe.'

191. Grimm 1880, dedication to Gervinus, dated 11 June 1848. In the original: 'Und wie aus der letzten feindschaft zwischen Schweden und Dänen der schlummernde trieb ihres engen verbandes erwacht ist, wird auch unser gegenwärtiger hader mit den Scandinaviern sich umwandeln zu brüderlichem bunde zwischen uns und ihnen, welchen der sprache gemeinschaft laut begehrt. wie sollte dann, wenn der grosze verein sich binnenmarken setzt, die streitige halbinsel nicht ganz zum festen lande geschlagen werden, was geschichte, natur und lage fordert, wie sollten nicht die Jüten zum alten anschlusz an Angeln und Sachsen, die Dänen zu dem an den Gothen wiederkehren? sobald Deutschland sich umgestaltet kann Dänemark unmöglich wie vorher bestehn.' [capitalization *sic*] Generally Storost 1988.

192. *Ibid.*, 580-81. In the original: 'wie in den völkern selbst thut sich auch in den sprachen, die sie reden, eine unausweichliche anziehungskraft der schwerpuncte kund, und lebhaft erwachte sehnsucht nach fester einigung aller sich zugewandten stämme wird nicht nachlassen. einen übertritt der Niederländer zur hochdeutschen sprache, der Dänen zur schwedischen halte ich in den nächsten jahrhunderten sowohl für wahrscheinlich, als allen deutschen völkern für heilsam, und glaube daß ihm durch die Lostrennung Belgiens von Holland, Norwegens von Dänemark vorgearbeitet wird: es leuchtet ein, daß dem Niederländer lieber sein muß deutsch als französisch, dem Dänen lieber schwedisch als deutsch zu werden. auch verdient die sprache der berge und höhen zu siegen über die der flachen ebene.' [capitalization *sic*]

193. Prebble 2000. Also Hugh Trevor-Roper's contribution to Hobsbawm & Ranger 1983, 15-42 ('The Invention of Tradition: The Highland Tradition of Scotland').

194. Rössing 1898.

195. Nipperdey 1968; on the earlier history of monuments, see von der Dunk 1997; von der Dunk 1999; Jourdan 1997.

196. That term is, of course, from Billig 1995. For the national iconography on banknotes, see Helleiner 2003; Pointon 1998, Unwin & Hewitt 2001 and Brion & Moreau 2001.

197. The case of Belgium has been well studied: Ogonovsky-Steffens 1999; Tollebeek & Verschaffel 1999; Tollebeek & Verschaffel 2000; Tollebeek & Verschaffel 2004; Verschaffel 1999. A comparative survey: Flacke 1998.

198. Fermigier 1997; Foucart 1997; Mérimée 1971.

199. Borger 1980; Klein 1980; Nipperdey 1986; Zink 1982.

200. On the professionalization and educational instrumentalization of history, see den Boer 1987.

201. Boswell & Evans 1999.

202. Bank 1990; van der Ham 2006.

203. There is as yet no large-scale comparative analysis. An influential early pointer was Dahlhaus 1974; since then, important contributions to the topic in have been made in Samson 2002 and Taruskin 2005. Taruskin is also the author of the article 'Nationalism' in the *New Grove Dictionary of Music and Musicians* (Grove Music Online, www.grovemusic.com, accessed 1 July 2006). See also Lajosi 2005.

204. Cf. Williams 1973.

205. Tolstoy 1957, 1, 603-604. The characterization of Karatayev: 2, 1150.

206. De Jong 1994; De Jong 2001.

207. 'The West's Awake', *Celtia*, 2 #9 (September 1902), 129-130.

208. There is a great body of research on Karadžić, most of it in Serbian and some in German; a good English-language biography is Wilson 1970. On Kopitar: Pogačnik 1978, Lukan 1995 and 2000, and most recently, Merchiers 2005.

209. Guiomar 1997; Kokare 1985.

210. Pumpurs 1988; Viķe-Freiberga 1985.

211. Lawrynenko 1962; Lindheim & Luckyj 1996; Mijakovs'kyj 1962; Zaitsev 1988.

212. Leerssen 2002b; Paternu 1993.

213. Ehrismann 1975.

214. Leerssen 2004b.

215. Vocabolario 1863-1923; Engler 2000; von Polenz 2000.

216. Kochs 1967.

217. On language purism generally: the many essays collected in van der Sijs 1999. The process of standardization has been described in the massive collection Fodor & Hagège 1983-1994.

218. Hering 1987. The dilemma is phrased by Fishman 1973 as a choice between 'language as the link with the glorious past' and 'language as the link with authenticity'.

219. Rigney 2001; Rigney 2004.

220. Gobbers 1990; Tollebeek 1995.

221. Rigney 1990.

222. Deletant & Hanak 1988.
223. Leerssen 1989; Poliakov 1987.
224. Rearick 1974.
225. *Latium und Hellas*, in Humboldt 1973, 6. In the original: 'Die meisten das Leben einer Nation begleitenden Umstände, der Wohnort, das Klima, die Religion, die Staatsverfassung, die Sitten und Gebräuche, lassen sich gewissermassen von ihr trennen, es kann, selbst bei reger Wechselwirkung noch, was sie an Bildung gaben und empfingen, gewissermassen abgesondert werden. Allein einer ist von durchaus verschiedener Natur, ist der Odem, die Seele der Nation selbst, erscheint überall in gleichem Schritte mit ihr, und führt, man mag ihn als wirkend oder gewirkt ansehen, die Untersuchung nur in einem beständigen Kreise herum – die Sprache.' Other linguistic writings of Humboldt are collected in Humboldt 1994.
226. Auroux *et al* 2000-2001; Caussat, Adamski, & Crépon 1996.
227. We can piece this attitude together from Grimm 1864-1890, and the dedications in Grimm 1834 and Grimm 1880 (to Lachmann and Gervinus, respectively). The antisemitic bent is expressed in a vicious private letter long kept out of the edited correspondence but quoted in Van Driel & Noordegraaf 1998: 99-100, following Hass-Zumkehr 1995.
228. Cf. Augstein 1997.
229. Wiseman 1866, 34-39.
230. Dayrat 2003.
231. Max Müller as quoted in MacDougall 1982, 121.; cf. also Poliakov 1987, 289-295. There are many disclaimers in this style, even from the great champion of Darwinism, Julian Huxley; see 'Professor Huxley on Political Ethnology', *Anthropological Review*, 28 (January 1870), 197-204.
232. Cf. the classic Gould 1981; also, Agazzi & Beller 1998 and Caroli 1995.
233. Behland 1967; Janota 1980; Schmidt 2000; Sørensen 1999.
234. John Pinkerton, *An Enquiry into the History of Scotland Preceding the Reign of Malcolm III.* (1789) vol 2 p. 33. Pinkerton was notorious for his ethnic chauvinism. His specific hypothesis concerned 'the inveterate inferiority of the Celtic race. He affirms that the 'Irish, the Scottish highlanders, the Welsh, the Bretons, and the Spanish Biscayans' are the only surviving aborigines of Europe, and that their features, history, actions, and manners indicate a fatal moral and intellectual weakness, rendering them incapable of susceptibility to the higher influences of civilisation. Throughout the work facts are subordinated to preconceived theories.' (Comments taken fom the article on Pinkerton in the *Dictionary of National Biography*). On the distinction monogenist-polygenist, cf. Gould 1981.
235. Biddiss 1970.
236. Pick 1989.
237. Down put this case in a paper entitled 'Observations on an Ethnic Classification of Idiots' (1866). Banton 1987, 26 and Gould 1981, 134-135.
238. Ben-Itto 1998.
239. Generally, Stepan 1982.
240. Poliakov 1987, 245-288; for French developments: Winock 1982, Thiesse 1999, 174-179. For Chamberlain: Field 1981.
241. Browning 2005.
242. Curtis 1997; Keen 1986.
243. France: Weber 1976; Sicily: Dickie 2004; Britain (Rider Haggard to the Boy Scouts movement): Rosenthal 1986.
244. In the original: 'Die Entarteten sind nicht immer Verbrecher, Prostituierte, Anarchisten und erklärte Wahnsinige. Sie sind manchmal Schriftsteller und Künstler. Aber diese weisen dieselben geistigen – und meist auch leiblichen – Züge auf wie diejenigen der nämlichen anthropologischen Familie, die ihre ungesunden Triebe mit dem Messer des Meuchelmörders oder der Patrone des Dynamit-Gesellen statt mit der Feder oder mit dem Pinsel befriedigen.'

245. Mandle 1987.
246. Quoted Leerssen 1996c, 193-195.
247. Mosse 1975; Theleweit 1980.
248. Bentley 1957.
249. On the adoption of Anglo-Saxonist racism in America, see Horsman 1981.
250. Quoted Kedourie 1960, 122-123.
251. Quoted Woolf 1996. The clarification was needed because the German negotiators saw Allied conditions as an unwarranted sharpening of Wilson's Fourteen Points.
252. There are many editions. The one used here, Renan 1994, is based on Renan 1948.
253. On Renan's influence, cf. Leerssen 1996a; McCormack 1985. Taine's theory of *race, milieu, moment* as determinants of a national literature was made in the introduction to his *Histoire de la littérature anglaise* of 1864: Espagne & Werner 1994, 461-477 (Michel Espagne, 'Taine et la notion de littérature nationale').
254. Kemiläinen 1971.
255. For the notion of a 'traumatic paradigm', see Valensi 2000; generally: Berkhofer 1995.
256. Pearse n.d., 216. On Pearse, see Edwards 1977.
257. Winter 1995.
258. Fleury 1998; Oudin 1987; Ziegerhofer-Prettenthaler 2004.
259. Pisanty 2006 presents a case: the Italian fascist review *La difesa della razza* ('The Defence of the Race').
260. Hettling 2003; Hirsch 2005; von Klimó 2004; Oberkrone 1993. On Haushofer and *Geopolitik*: Ebeling 1994, Murphy 1997.
261. From amidst the enormous amount of literature, I mention only Browning 2005.
262. On the *Heimatfilm* generally Höfig 1973.
263. Greverus & Haindl 1983.
264. Generally, Knippenberg & Markusse 1999.
265. Hamm 1987; Short 1996.
266. I argued this in Leerssen 1993a.
267. A refreshingly different perspective is offered by the ethnographer Germaine Tillion: Tillion 1966, brought to my attention by Ieme van der Poel.
268. Roobol 1998.
269. Emmer 1937.
270. Habermas 1992, 1998.
271. Habermas 1990, 2001.
272. The Greek government sent the following declaration to Crete (perceived as Islamic) on the occasion of the 1821 rising: 'For your houses are besides ours, and you wear the same clothes as us, and you have the same boldness, and the same gait, and the same language. For all these reasons you must join us, so that we can all live together like good fellow citizens [...] for deep down you are not Orientals, or Arabs, you are rather true Cretans and you have Greek blood': Detorakis 1994, 262.
273. Hartmann 1999.
274. Borst 1995.
275. Droixhe 1978.
276. Aarsleff 1967.
277. Auroux *et al* 2000-2001; Bynon 2001; Collinge 2001; Ringmacher 2001; Rousseau 2001; Schieffelin, Woolard, & Kroskrity 1998; Sherwood 1996; Short 1996, Swiggers & Desmet 1996; Swiggers & Desmet 2000. Also, Caussat, Adamski, & Crépon 1996.
278. Cf. Heeringa 2004.
279. Fredericq 1906, 100. A parallel Irish case were the Maamtrasna murders of 1882.
280. Van Laar 1986.
281. Ceyssens 1929; de Ryckel 1980; Verkooren 1916-1961.

282. On attempts by the Brabant dukes to curb higher appeal to non-Brabant courts, see Nève 1972.
283. The materials are cited in Janssen de Limpens 1977.
284. Haas 1978. The influence of linguistic differences and resulting different local jurisdictions is cited 262 n. 35.
285. Hardenberg & Nuyens 1946, xiii-xiv.

Bibliography

Aarsleff, Hans (1967). *The Study of Language in England, 1780-1860* (Princeton, NJ: Princeton University Press).

Agazzi, Elena; Manfred Beller (eds.) (1998). *Evidenze e ambiguità della fisionomia umana. Studi sul XVIIIe e XIX secolo* (Viareggio: Baroni).

Agnew, Hugh LeCaine (1993). *Origins of the Czech National Renascence* (Pittsburgh: University of Pittsburgh Press).

Alén Garabato, Carmen (ed.) (2005). *L'éveil des nationalités et les revendications linguistiques en Europe* (Paris: L'Harmattan).

Alvárez Junco, José (2001). *Mater dolorosa. La idea de España en el siglo XIX* (Madrid: Taurus).

Amossy, Ruth; Michel Delon (eds.) (1999). *Critique et légitimité du préjugé (XVIIIe-XXe siècle)* (Bruxelles: Editions de l'Université de Bruxelles).

Amossy, Ruth; Elisheva Rosen (1982). *Les discours du cliché* (Paris: SEDES).

Anderson, Benedict (1983). *Imagined Communities: Reflections on the Origin and Spread of Nationalism* (London: Verso).

Andrée, Fritz (1972). *Hoffmann von Fallersleben. Des Dichters Leben, Wirken und Gedenkstätten in Word und Bild* (2nd ed.; Fallersleben: Hoffmann von Fallersleben-Gesellschaft).

Arens, William (1979). *The Man-Eating Myth: Anthropology and Anthropophagy* (Oxford: Oxford University Press).

Arens, William (1986). *The Original Sin: Incest and its Meaning* (Oxford: Oxford University Press).

Aretin, J. Chr. von (1803). *Älteste Sage über die Geburt und Jugend Karls des Grossen* (München).

Augstein, Hannah Franziska (1997). 'Linguistics and Politics in the Early 19th Century: James Cowles Prichard's Moral Philology', *History of European Ideas*, 23 #1: 1-18.

Auroux, Sylvain; E.F.K. Koerner; Hans-Josef Niederehe; Kees Versteegh (eds.) (2000-2001). *History of the Language Sciences. An International Handbook on the Evolution of the Study of Language from the Beginnings to the Present* (2 vols; Berlin: De Gruyter).

Ayçoberry, Pierre; Marc Ferro (eds.) (1981). *Une histoire du Rhin* (Paris: Ramsay).

Babcock, Robert Witbeck (1931). *The Genesis of Shakespeare Idolatry, 1766-1799: A Study of English Criticism of the Late Eighteenth Century* (Chapel Hill, NC: University of North Carolina Press).

Bagrow, Leo (1985 [1944]). *History of Cartography* (rev./enl. R.A. Skelton; Chicago: Precedent).

Balcells, Albert (1991). *El nacionalisme catalán* (Madrid: Histori 16).

Bank, J.Th.M. (1990). *Het roemrijk vaderland: Cultureel nationalisme in Nederland in de negentiende eeuw* ('s-Gravenhage: Sdu).

Bank, J.Th.M.; Mathijsen, Marita (eds.) (2006). *Plaatsen van herinnering: Nederland in de negentiende eeuw* (Amsterdam: Bert Bakker).

Bann, Stephen (1995). *Romanticism and the Rise of History* (Boston, MA: Twayne).

Banton, Michael (1987). *Racial Theories* (Cambridge: Cambridge University Press).

Barrow, Geoffrey (ed.) (2003). *The Declaration of Arbroath: History, Significance, Setting* (Edinburgh: Society of Antiquaries of Scotland).

Bauer, Johannes (1908). *Schleiermacher als patriotischer Prediger. Ein Beitrag zur Geschichte der nationalen Erhebung vor hundert Jahren* (Giessen).

Baycroft, Timothy; Mark Hewitson (eds.) (2006). *What is a Nation? Europe 1789-1914* (Oxford: Oxford University Press).

Beaune, Colette (1985). *Naissance de la nation France* (Paris: Gallimard).

Beaune, Colette (1997). 'Les sanctuaires royaux: De Saint-Denis à Saint-Michel et Saint-Léonard', in Nora, 1: 625-648.

Béguin, Albert (1946). *L'âme romantique et le rêve: Essai sur le Romantisme allemand et la poésie française* (Paris: Corti).

Behland, Max (1967). 'Nationale und nationalistische Tendenzen in Vorreden zu wissenschaftlichen Werken', in *Nationalismus in Germanistik und Dichtung. Dokumentation des Germanistentages in München vom 17. bis 22. Oktober 1966*, ed. B. von Wiese & R. Henß (Berlin: Schmidt): 334-346.

Behr, Hans-Joachim (1999). 'Eilige Philologie. Hoffmann von Fallersleben als Editor mittelalterlicher Texte', in *August Heinrich Hoffmann von Fallersleben 1798-1998. Festschrift zum 200. Geburtstag*, ed. H.-J. Behr, H. Blume & E. Rohse (Bielefeld: Verlag für Regionalgeschichte): 169-181.

Beller, Manfred; Joep Leerssen (eds.) (2007). *Imagology: The cultural construction and literary representation of national characters. A critical survey* (Amsterdam: Rodopi).

Ben-Itto, Hadassa (1998). *«Die Protokolle der Weisen von Zion»: Anatomie einer Fälschung* (trl. H. Ettinger & J. Lochner; Berlin: Aufbau).

Bentley, Eric (1957). *A Century of Hero-Worship: A Study of the Idea of Heroism in Carlyle and Nietzsche, with Notes on Wagner, Spengler, Stefan George, and D.H. Lawrence* (Boston, MA: Beacon).

Benveniste, Emile (1969). *Le vocabulaire des institutions indo-européennes* (2 vols; Paris: Minuit).

Berding, Helmut (ed.) (1994). *Nationales Bewußtsein und kollektive Identität. Studien zur Entwicklung des kollektiven Bewußtseins in der Neuzeit, 2* (Frankfurt: Suhrkamp).

Berkhofer, Robert F., Jr (1995). *Beyond the Great Story: History as Text and Discourse* (Cambridge, MA: Harvard University Press).

Berlin, Isaiah (1990). *The Crooked Timber of Humanity: Chapters in the History of Ideas* (ed. Henry Hardy; London: Murray).

Berlin, Isaiah (2000). *Three Critics of the Enlightenment: Vico, Hamann, Herder* (ed. Henry Hardy; London: Pimlico).

Bernheimer, Richard (1952). *Wild Men in the Middle Ages: A Study in Art, Sentiment and Demonology* (Cambridge, MA: Harvard University Press).

Beumann, Helmut (1986). 'Zur Nationenbildung im Mittelalter', in *Studien zur Geschichte des neunzehnten Jahrhunderts*, ed. O. Dann (München: Oldenbourg), 14: 21-34.

Biddiss, Michael D. (1970). *Father of Racist Ideology. The Social and Political Thought of Count Gobineau* (London: Weidenfeld & Nicholson).

Billig, Michael (1995). *Banal Nationalism* (London: Sage).

Black, Jeremy (1997). *Maps and History. Constructing Images of the Past* (New Haven, CT: Yale University Press).

Bleuel, Hans Peter (1968). *Deutschlands Bekenner. Professoren zwischen Kaiserreich und Diktatur* (Bern: Scherz).

Bloch, Marc (1924). *Les rois thaumaturges: Etude sur le caractère surnaturel attribué à la puissance royale, particulièrement en France et en Angleterre* (Strasbourg: Istra).

Bluhm, Lothar (1997). *Die Brüder Grimm und der Beginn der Deutschen Philologie: Eine Studie zu Kommunikation und Wissenschaftsbildung im frühen 19. Jahrhundert* (Hildesheim: Weidmann).

den Boer, Pim (1987). *Geschiedenis als beroep. De professionalisering van de geschiedbeoefening in Frankrijk (1818-1914)* (Nijmegen: SUN).

Boockmann, Hartmut (1982). *Die Marienburg im 19. Jahrhundert* (Wien: Propyläen).

Borchardt, Frank L. (1971). *German Antiquity in Renaissance Myth* (Baltimore: Johns Hopkins Press).

Borger, Hugo (1980). *Der Kölner Dom im Jahrhundert seiner Vollendung* (3 vols; Köln: Museen der Stadt Köln).

Borges, Jorge Luis (1985). *Prosa completa* (5 vols; Barcelona: Bruguera).

Borst, Arno (1995). *Der Turmbau von Babel. Geschichte der Meinungen über Ursprung und Vielfalt der Sprachen und Völker* (4 in 6 vols; München: dtv).

Boswell, David; Jessica Evans (eds.) (1999). *Representing the Nation: A Reader. Histories, Heritage and Museums* (London: Routledge).

Boureau, Alain (1995). *Le droit de cuissage: La fabrication d'un mythe (XIIIe-XXe siècle)* (Paris: Albin Michel).

Boyce, D. George (1991). *Nationalism in Ireland* (2nd ed.; London: Routledge).

Bredin, Jean-Denis (1988). *Sieyès: La clé de la Révolution française* (Paris: Fallois).

Breuilly, John (1993 [1982]). *Nationalism and the State* (Manchester: Manchester University Press).

Brinkman, Herman (2002). 'Het kerelslied: Van historielied tot lyriek van het beschavingsoffensief', *Queeste,* 9 #2: 98-116.

Brinkman, Herman (2004). 'Een lied van hoon en eerwraak: «Ruters» contra «kerels» in het Gruuthuse-handschrift', *Queeste,* 11 #1: 1-43.

Brion, René; Jean-Louis Moreau (2001). *Het bankbiljet in alle staten. Van het eerste bankpapier tot de Euro* (Antwerpen: Mercatorfonds).

Brock, Peter (1976). *The Slovak National Awakening: An Essay in the Intellectual History of East Central Europe* (Toronto: University of Toronto Press).

Brown, David (1979). *Walter Scott and the Historical Imagination* (London: Routledge & Kegan Paul).

Browning, Christopher R. (2005). *The Origins of the Final Solution: The Evolution of Nazi Jewish Policy, September 1939 – March 1942* (London: Arrow).

Brunner, Horst (2000). 'Jacob Grimm (1785-1863)', in *Wissenschaftsgeschichte der Germanistik in Porträts,* ed. C. König, H.-H. Müller & W. Röcke (Berlin: Walter de Gruyter): 11-19.

Bruyning, Lucas (1990). 'The United States of Europe: An Italian Invention?', *Yearbook of European Studies,* 3: 55-66.

Bruyning, Lucas (1995). 'Europa in de Italiaanse geschiedschrijving van de eerste helft van de negentiende eeuw' (doctoral thesis, Amsterdam: Universiteit van Amsterdam).

Bugge, Peter (1994). 'Czech nation-buiding, national self-perception and politics 1780-1914' (doctoral thesis, University of Aarhus).

Burg, Martijn van der (2007). 'Nederland onder Franse invloed: Cultuurtransfer en staatsvorming in de napoleontische tijd, 1799-1813' (doctoral thesis, University of Amsterdam).

Bynon, Theodora (2001). 'The Synthesis of Comparative and Historical Indo-European Studies: August Schleicher', in Auroux *et al,* 2: 1223-1239.

Caesar, C. Iulius (1917). *The Gallic War* (ed./trl. H.J. Edwards; Cambridge, MA: Harvard University Press).

Canny, Nicholas (2001). *Making Ireland British, 1580-1650* (Oxford: Oxford University Press).

Caroli, Flavio (1995). *Storia della fisiognomica. Arte e psicologia da Leonardo a Freud* (Milano: Mondadori).

Cartledge, Paul (2001). *Spartan Reflections* (London: Duckworth).

Cartledge, Paul (2002). 'To Die For?', *History Today,* 52 #8: 19-25.

Caussat, Pierre; Dariusz Adamski; Marc Crépon (eds.) (1996). *La langue source de la nation: Messianismes séculiers en Europe centrale et orientale (du XVIIIe au XXe siècle)* (Sprimont: Mardaga).

Cepl-Kaufmann, Gertrude; Antje Johanning (2003). *Mythos Rhein. Kulturgeschichte eines Stroms* (Darmstadt: Primus).

de Certeau, Michel; Dominique Julia; Jacques Revel (1975). *Une politique de la langue. La Révolution française et les patois* (Paris: Gallimard).

Ceyssens, J. (1929). *Les bans, seigneuries laïques et immunités ecclésiastiques du Pays de Dalhem, spécialement au XVe siècle* (Liège: Printing Co.).

Chadwick, Owen (1998). *A History of the Popes, 1830-1914* (Oxford: Clarendon).

Chandler, Alice (1970). 'Origins of Medievalism: Scott', in *A Dream of Order: The Medieval Ideal in Nineteenth-Century English Literature* (Lincoln: University of Nebraska Press): 12-51.

Chaytor, H.J. (1966). *From Script to Print: An Introduction to Medieval Vernacular Literature* (London: Sidgwick & Jackson).

Chickering, Roger (1984). *We Men Who Feel Most German: A Cultural Study of the Pan-German League, 1886-1914* (Boston: Allen & Unwin).

Citron, Suzanne (1987). *Le mythe national. L'histoire de France en question* (Paris: Les éditions ouvrières).

Clark, Albert C. (1921). 'The Reappearance of the Texts of the Classics', *The Library*, 4th ser. vol. 2 #1: 13-42.

Clogg, R. (2002 [1992]). *A Concise History of Greece* (2nd ed.; Cambridge: Cambridge University Press).

Collinge, N.E. (2001). 'The Introduction of the Historical Principle into the Study of Languages: Grimm', in Auroux *et al*, 2: 1210-1223.

Connors, Seán (2001). *Mapping Ireland: From Kingdoms to Counties* (Dublin: Mercier).

Constantine, Mary-Ann (2007). *The truth against the world: Iolo Morganwg and romantic forgery* (Cardiff: University of Wales Press).

Cornis-Pope, Marcel; John Neubauer (eds.) (2004-). *History of the Literary Cultures of East-Central Europe: Junctures and Disjunctures in the 19th and 20th Centuries* (5 vols; Amsterdam: Benjamins).

Craig, John E. (1984). *Scholarship and Nation Building: The Universities of Strasbourg and Alsatian Society, 1870-1939* (Chicago: University of Chicago Press).

Crawford, Jon G. (1993). *Anglicizing the Government of Ireland: The Irish Privy Council and the Expansion of Tudor Rule, 1556-1578* (Dublin: Irish Academic Press).

Cubitt, Geoffrey (ed.) (1998). *Imagining Nations* (Manchester: Manchester University Press).

Curtis, L.P. (1997). *Apes and Angels. The Irishman in Victorian Caricature* (revised ed.; Washington, D.C.: Smithsonian Institution).

Dahlhaus, Carl (1974). 'Die Idee des Nationalismus in der Musik', in *Zwischen Romantik und Moderne. Vier Studien zur Musikgeschichte des späteren 19. Jahrhunderts* (München: Katzbichler): 74-92.

Damrosch, Leo (2005). *Jean-Jacques Rousseau* (Boston, MA: Houghton Mifflin).

Daskalov, Rumen (2004). *The Making of a Nation in the Balkans. Historiography of the Bulgarian Revival* (Budapest: Central European University Press).

Davies, Anna Morpurgo (1998). *Nineteenth-Century Linguistics* (London: Longman).

Davies, Sir John (1612). *A Discoverie of the True Causes why Ireland was Never Entirely Subdued Untill the Beginning of His Majesties Happy Raigne* (London).

Dayrat, Benoît (2003). 'The Roots of Phylogeny: How Did Haeckel Build his Tree?', *Systematic Biology*, 52 #4: 515-527.

Decharneux, Baudoin (1995). 'Les Anciens Belges', in *Les grands mythes de l'histoire de Belgique, de Flandre et de Wallonie*, ed. A. Morelli (Bruxelles: Vie ouvrière): 21-34.

Deletant, Dennis; Harry Hanak (eds.) (1988). *Historians as Nation-Builders. Central and South-East Europe* (London: Macmillan / School of Slavonic and East European Studies).

Demandt, Alexander et al. (1990). *Deutschlands Grenzen in der Geschichte* (München: Beck).

Denecke, Ludwig (1971). *Jacob Grimm und sein Bruder Wilhelm* (Stuttgart: Metzler).

Denneler, Iris (1985). *Friedrich Karl von Savigny* (Berlin: Stapp).

Deprez, Ada (ed.) (1963). *Briefwisseling van Jan Frans Willems en Hoffmann von Fallersleben (1836-1843)* (Gent: Seminarie voor Nederlandse Literatuurstudie der Rijksuniversiteit te Gent).

Despatalović, Elinor Murray (1975). *Ljudevit Gaj and the Illyrian Movement* (Boulder: East European Quarterly).

Detorakis, Theocharis E. (1994). *History of Crete* (trl. J.C. Davis; Iraklion: no publ.).

de Deugd, Cornelis (1966). *Het metafysisch grondpatroon van het romantische literaire denken: De fenomenologie van een geestesgesteldheid* (Groningen: Wolters).

Dickie, John (2004). *Cosa Nostra. A History of the Sicilian Mafia* (London: Hodder & Stoughton).

Diderot, Denis; Jean Baptiste D'Alembert (eds.) (1777). *Encyclopédie, ou dictionnaire raisonné des sciences, des arts et des métiers* (3rd ed.; Genève).

Drentje, Jan (2006). 'Den Haag: Het Plein', in Bank & Mathijsen, 148-161.

van Driel, Lodewijk; Jan Noordegraaf (1998). *De Vries en Te Winkel: een duografie* (Den Haag: Sdu).

Droixhe, Daniel (1978). *La linguistique et l'appel de l'histoire (1600-1800): Rationalisme et révolutions positivistes* (Genève: Droz).

von der Dunk, Thomas H. (1997). 'Vom Fürstenkultbild zum Untertanendenkmal: Öffentliche Monumente in Brandenburg-Preußen im 17. und 18. Jahrhundert', *Forschungen zur brandenburgischen und preußischen Geschichte,* 7 #2: 177-210.

von der Dunk, Thomas H. (1999). *Das deutsche Denkmal. Eine Geschichte in Bronze und Stein vom Hochmittelalter bis zum Barock* (Köln: Böhlau).

von der Dunk, Thomas H. (2000). *De schaduw van het Teutoburgerwoud. Een Duitse politieke zedenschets van tien eeuwen* (Amsterdam: Amsterdam University Press).

Dunleavy, Janet Egleson; Gareth W. Dunleavy (1991). *Douglas Hyde: A Maker of Modern Ireland* (Berkeley, CA: University of California Press).

Duyzings, Ger (2000). *Religion and the Politics of Identity in Kosovo* (London: Hurst).

Dyserinck, Hugo (1991 [1979]). *Komparatistik. Eine Einführung* (3rd ed.; Bonn: Bouvier).

Dyserinck, Hugo (2002). 'Von Ethnopsychologie zu Ethnoimagologie. Über Entwicklung und mögliche Endbestimmung eines Schwerpunkts des ehemaligen Aachener Komparatistikprogramms', *Neohelicon,* 29 #1: 57-74.

Eade, J.C. (ed.) (1983). *Romantic Nationalism in Europe* (Canberra: Australian National University).

Ebeling, Frank (1994). *Geopolitik: Karl Haushofer und seine Raumwissenschaft, 1919-1945* (Berlin: Akademie-Verlag).

Edington, Carol (1998). 'Paragons and Patriots: National Identity and the Chivalric Ideal in Late-Medieval Scotland', in *Image and Identity: The Making and Re-making of Scotland Through the Ages,* ed. D. Broun, R.J. Finlay & M. Lynch (Edinburgh: Donald): 69-81.

Edwards, Ruth Dudley (1977). *Patrick Pearse: The Triumph of Failure* (London: Gollancz).

Ehrismann, Otfrid (1975). *Das Nibelungenlied in Deutschland. Studien zur Rezeption des Nibelungenlieds von der Mitte des 18. Jahrhunderts bis zum Ersten Weltkrieg* (München: Fink).

Eijsbouts, W.T. (1993). 'Borders and Democracy: The Schengen Treaties', *Yearbook of European Studies,* 6: 57-70.

Eile, Stanislaw (2000). *Literature and nationalism in partitioned Poland, 1795-1918* (Basingtoke: Macmillan).

Eley, Geoff; Ronald Grigor Suny (eds.) (1996). *Becoming National: A Reader.* (New York / Oxford: Oxford University Press).

Eliot, T.S. (1960 [1920]). 'Tradition and the Individual Talent', in *The Sacred Wood. Essays on Poetry and Criticism* (London: Methuen): 47-59.

Ellis, Peter Berresford (1993). *The Celtic Dawn: A History of Pan Celticism* (London: Constable).

Ellis, Steven (1998a). *Ireland in the Age of the Tudors, 1447-1603* (London: Longman).

Ellis, Steven (1988b). *The Pale and the Far North: Government and Society in Two Early Tudor Borderlands* (Galway: University College Galway).

Emmer, Huibert (1937). *De grenzen van Nederland: Van de Wielingen tot aan de Rijn* (Haarlem: Tjeenk Willink).

Engler, Rudolf (2000). 'Die Accademia della Crusca und die Standardierung des Italienischen', in Auroux *et al,* 1: 815-827.

Eriksen, Thomas Hylland (2002). *Ethnicity and Nationalism* (2nd ed.; London: Pluto).

Espagne, Michel (1990). 'La référence allemande dans la fondation d'une philologie française', in *Philologiques I: Contribution à l'histoire des disciplines littéraires en France et en Allemagne au XIXe siècle,* ed. M. Espagne & M. Werner (Paris: Maison des sciences de l'homme): 135-158.

Espagne, Michel; Michael Werner (eds.) (1994). *Philologiques III: Qu'est-ce qu'une littérature nationale? Approches pour une théorie interculturelle du champ littéraire* (Paris: Maison des sciences de l'homme).

Eyffinger, Arthur (2006). 'Den Haag: Het Vredespaleis', in Bank & Mathijsen, 514-525.

Faensen, Johannes (1980). *Die albanische Nationalbewegung* (Berlin / Wiesbaden: Osteuropa-Institut an der Freien Universität Berlin / Harassowitz).

Feldbæk, Ole (ed.) (1991-92). *Dansk identitetshistorie* (4 vols; København: C.A. Reitzel).

Fermigier, André (1997). 'Mérimée et l'inspection des monuments historiques', in Nora, 1: 1599-1614.

Fewster, Derek (2006). 'Images of Ancient Greatness: Nationalism and Popular Visions of Early Finnish history before 1945' (doctoral thesis, Helsinki: University of Helsinki).

Field, Geoffrey G. (1981). *Evangelist of Race. The Germanic Vision of Houston Stewart Chamberlain* (New York: Columbia University Press).

Fink, Zera S. (1962). *The Classical Republicans: An Essay in the Recovery of a Pattern of Thought in Seventeenth-Century England* (2nd ed.; Evanston, IL: Northwestern University).

Fishman, Joshua (1973). *Language and Nationalism* (Rowley, MA: Newbury House).

Fitzpatrick, Martin (1987). 'Reflections on a Footnote: Richard Price and Love of Country', *Enlightenment and Dissent*, 6: 42-58.

Flacke, Monika (ed.) (1998). *Mythen der Nationen: Ein europäisches Panorama* (München & Berlin: Koehler & Amelang).

Fleury, Antoine (ed.) (1998). *Le Plan Briand d'Union fédérale européenne: Perspectives nationales et transnationales, avec documents: Actes du Colloque international tenu à Genève du 19 au 21 septembre 1991* (Bern: Lang).

Fodor, István; Claude Hagège (eds.) (1983-1994). *Language Reform: History and Future* (6 vols; Hamburg: Buske).

Foster, Roy (1997-2003). *W.B. Yeats: A Life* (2 vols; Oxford: Clarendon Press).

Foucart, Bruno (1997). 'Viollet-le-Duc et la restauration', in Nora, 1: 1615-1643.

François, Etienne; Hagen Schulze (eds.) (2001). *Deutsche Erinnerungsorte* (3 vols; München: Beck).

Fredericq, Paul (1906). *Schets eener Geschiedenis der Vlaamsche Beweging* (3 vols; Gent: Vuylsteke).

Friedman, John Block (1981). *The Monstrous Races in Medieval Art and Thought* (Cambridge, MA: Harvard University Press).

Friemel, Berthold (1990). 'Zu Jacob Grimms «Silva de romances viejos»', *Brüder Grimm Gedenken*, 9: 51-88.

Fritzsche, Peter (2004). *Stranded in the Present: Modern Time and the Melancholy of History* (Cambridge, MA: Harvard University Press).

Frühwald, Norbert (1983). 'Der Regierungsrat Joseph von Eichendorff', in *Joseph von Eichendorff 1788-1857. Leben, Werk, Wirkung. Eine Ausstellung der Stiftung Haus Oberschlesien und des Landschaftverbandes Rheinland, Rheinisches Museumamt Abtei Brauweiler, in Zusammenarbeit mit der Eichendorff-Gesellschaft* (Köln; Dülmen: Rheinland; Laumann): 25-47.

Fürbeth, Frank; Pierre Krügel; Ernst E. Metzner; Olaf Müller (eds.) (1999). *Zur Geschichte und Problematik der Nationalphilologien in Europa. 150 Jahre Erste Germanistenversammlung in Frankfurt am Main (1846-1996)* (Tübingen: Niemeyer).

Geary, Patrick J. (2002). *The Myth of Nations: The Medieval Origins of Europe* (Princeton, NJ: Princeton University Press).

Gellner, Ernest (1983). *Nations and Nationalisms* (Oxford: Blackwell).

Genette, Gérard (1969). 'Vraisemblance et motivation', in *Figures II. Essais* (Paris: Seuil): 71-100.

Genicot, L. (1970). 'Ligne et zone: La frontière des principautés médiévales', *Bulletin de l'Académie Royale de Belgique, Classe des Lettres*, 5e série 56.

Giesen, Bernhard (ed.) (1991). *Nationale und kulturelle Identität. Studien zur Entwicklung des kollektiven Bewußtseins in der Neuzeit, 1* (Frankfurt: Suhrkamp).

Gillis, John R. (ed.) (1994). *Commemorations: The Politics of National Identity* (Princeton, NJ: Princeton University Press).

Giraldus Cambrensis (1978). *Expugnatio Hibernica. The Conquest of Ireland* (ed./trl A.B. Scott & F.X. Martin; Dublin: Royal Irish Academy).

Giraldus Cambrensis (1982). *The History and Topography of Ireland* (ed./trl. J.J. O'Meara; Harmondsworth: Penguin).

Gobbers, Walter (1990). 'Consciences *Leeuw van Vlaenderen* als historische roman en nationaal epos: een genrestudie in Europees perspectief', in *Vlaamse literatuur van de negentiende eeuw. Dertien verkenningen*, ed. A. Deprez & W. Gobbers (Utrecht: HES): 45-69.

Goodwin, Albert (1979). *The Friends of Liberty. The English Democratic Movement in the Age of the French Revolution* (London: Hutchinson).

Gould, Stephen Jay (1981). *The Mismeasure of Man* (New York: Norton).

Greverus, Ina-Maria (1972). *Der territoriale Mensch: Ein literaturanthropologischer Versuch zum Heimatphänomen* (Frankfurt: Athenäum).

Greverus, Ina-Maria; Erika Haindl (eds.) (1983). *Versuche, der Zivilisation zu entkommen* (München: Beck).

Grewe, Uwe (1982). *Einigkeit und Recht und Freiheit: Kleine Geschichte des Deutschlandliedes* (Hamburg: Staats- und Wirtschaftspolitische Gesellschaft).

Grimm, Jacob (1834). *Reinhart Fuchs* (Berlin: Reimer).

Grimm, Jacob (1864-1890). *Kleinere Schriften* (8 vols; Berlin / Gütersloh: Dümmler / Bertelsmann).

Grimm, Jacob (1880 [1848]). *Geschichte der deutschen Sprache* (4th ed.; Leipzig: Weidmann).

Guenée, Bernard (1997). 'Des limites féodales aux frontières politiques', in Nora, 1: 1103-1124.

Guiomar, Jean-Yves (1997). 'Le «Barzaz-Breiz» de Théodore Hersart de la Villemarqué', in Nora, 3: 3479-3514.

Gusdorf, Georges (1993 [1984-85]). *Le romantisme* (2 vols; Paris: Payot).

Haas, J.A.K. (1978). *De verdeling van de Landen van Overmaas, 1644-1662: Territoriale desintegratie van een betwist grensgebied* (Assen: Van Gorcum).

Habermas, Jürgen (1990 [1962]). *Strukturwandel der Öffentlichkeit* (Frankfurt: Suhrkamp).

Habermas, Jürgen (1992). 'Citizenship and National Identity: Some Reflections on the Future of Europe', *Praxis International*, 12: 1-19.

Habermas, Jürgen (1998). *Die postnationale Konstellation* (Frankfurt: Suhrkamp).

Habermas, Jürgen (2001). 'Why Europe Needs a Constitution', *New Left Review*, 11: 5-26.

Hacker, Rupert (ed.) (2000). *Beiträge zur Geschichte der Bayerischen Staatsbibliothek* (München: Saur).

Hafner, Stanislaus (1957). 'August Heinrich Hoffmann von Fallersleben und Bartholomäus Kopitar', *Die Welt der Slaven*, 2: 183-200.

von der Hagen, Friedrich Heinrich (1824 [1807]). *Der Nibelungen Lied, erneuet und erklärt* (2nd ed.; Frankfurt: Varrentrapp).

Hägerstrand, Torsten (1967). *Innovation diffusion as a spatial process* (Chicago: University of Chicago Press).

Haitsma Mulier, E.O.G. (1974). 'Tacitus in de zestiende en zeventiende eeuw', *Lampas*, 7: 407-417.

Hall, John A. (ed.) (1998). *The state of the nation. Ernest Gellner and the theory of nationalism* (Cambridge: Cambridge University Press).

Halliday, F.E. (1957). *The Cult of Shakespeare* (London: Duckworth).

van der Ham, Gijs (2006). 'Amsterdam: het Rijksmuseum. Een gebouw voor het nationaal geheugen', in Bank & Mathijsen, 424-437.

Hamm, Josef (1987). 'Randbemerkungen zur Entstehung und Entwicklung der serbokroatischen Schriftsprache', in *Sprachen und Nationen im Balkanraum. Die historischen Bedingungen der Entstehung der heutigen Nationalsprachen*, ed. C. Hannick (Wien: Böhlau), 56: 65-76.

Hampe, Karl (1936). *Wilhelm I., Kaiserfrage und Kölner Dom* (Stuttgart: Kohlhammer).

Hanak, Harry (1988). 'Czech Historians and the End of Austria-Hungary', in Deletant & Hanak, 70-86.

Hansen, Wilhelm (1976). *Nationaldenkmäler und Nationalfeste im 19. Jahrhundert* (Lüneburg: Niederdeutscher Verband für Volks- und Altertumskunde).

Hanske, Horst; Jorg Traeger (1992). *Walhalla. Ruhmestempel an der Donau* (Regensburg: Bernhard Bosse).

Hardenberg, H.; F. Nuyens (1946). *Inventaris der archieven van het Arondissement Maastricht en van het Departement van de Nedermaas* ('s-Gravenhage: Ministerie van OKW).

Harley, J.B.; David Woodward (eds.) (1987). *History of Cartography* (Chicago: University of Chicago Press).

Harris, Ian (1994). *The Mind of John Locke: A Study of Political Theory in its Intellectual Setting* (Cambridge: Cambridge University Press).

Hartmann, Peter Claus (2001). *Kulturgeschichte des Heiligen Römischen Reiches 1648 bis 1806: Verfassung, Religion und Kultur* (Wien: Böhlau-Wissenschaftliche Buchgesellschaft).

Hartmann, Silvia (1999). *Fraktur oder Antiqua. Der Schriftstreit von 1881 bis 1941* (Frankfurt: Peter Lang).

Haselsteiner, Horst (ed.) (2000). *The Prague Slav Congress 1848: Slavic Identities* (Boulder, CO: East European Monographs).

Hass-Zumkehr, Ulrike (1995). *Daniel Sanders. Aufgeklärte Germanistik im 19. Jahrhundert* (Berlin: De Gruyter).

Hassig, Debra (1995). *Medieval Bestiaries: Text, Image, Ideology* (Cambridge: Cambridge University Press).

Hayman, John G. (1971). 'Notions of National Characters in the Eighteenth Century', *Huntington Library Quarterly*, 35: 1-17.

Heeringa, Wilbert Jan (2004). 'Measuring Dialect Pronunciation Differences using Levenshtein Distance' (doctoral thesis, Groningen: Rijksuniversiteit Groningen).

van der Heijden, Laurens (2004). 'De schaduw van de Jezuïet. Een pathologie van de publieke opinie tijdens de schoolstrijd van 1841-1848' (doctoral thesis, Amsterdam: Universiteit van Amsterdam).

Helleiner, Eric (2003). *The Making of National Money. Territorial Currencies in Historical Perspective* (Ithaca, NY: Cornell University Press).

Herder, Johann Gottfried (1982). *Werke* (ed. Regine Otto,; 5 vols; Berlin: Aufbau).

Hering, Gunnar (1987). 'Die Auseinandersetzungen über die neugriechische Schriftsprache', in *Sprachen und Nationen im Balkanraum. Die historischen Bedingungen der Entstehung der heutigen Nationalsprachen*, ed. C. Hannick (Wien: Böhlau), 56: 125-194.

Herzfeld, M. (1986 [1982]). *Ours Once More: Folklore, Ideology, and the Making of Modern Greece* (New York: Pella).

Hettling, Manfred; Paul Nolte (eds.) (1993). *Bürgerliche Feste: Symbolische Formen politischen Handelns im 19. Jahrhundert* (Göttingen: Vandenhoeck & Ruprecht).

Hettling, Manfred (ed.) (2003). *Volksgeschichten im Europa der Zwischenkriegszeit* (Göttingen: Vandenhoeck & Ruprecht).

Hettne, Björn; Sverker Sörlin; Uffe Østergård (1998). *Den globala nationalismen* (Stockholm: SNS).

Hirsch, Francine (2005). *Empire of Nations: Ethnographic Knowledge and the Making of the Soviet Union* (Ithaca, NY: Cornell University Press).

Hobsbawm, Eric J. (1990). *Nations and Nationalism since 1780: Programme, Myth, Reality* (Cambridge: Cambridge University Press).

Hobsbawm, Eric J.; Terence Ranger (eds.) (1983). *The Invention of Tradition* (Cambridge: Cambridge University Press).

Hoffmann, Richard C. (1983). 'Outsiders by Birth and Blood: Racist Ideologies and Realities Around the Periphery of Medieval European Culture', *Studies in Medieval and Renaissance History*, 6: 3-34.

Höfig, Willi (1973). *Der deutsche Heimatfilm 1947-1960* (Stuttgart: Ferdinand Enke).

Hoppenbrouwers, Peter (2006). 'Such Stuff as Peoples are Made on: Ethnogenesis and the Construction of Nationhood in Medieval Europe', *Medieval History Journal*, 9: 195-242.

Horsman, Reginald (1981). *Race and Manifest Destiny: The Origins of American Racial Anglo-Saxonism* (Cambridge, MA: Harvard University Press).

Hroch, Miroslav (1968). *Die Vorkämpfer der nationalen Bewegung bei den kleinen Völkern Europas. Eine vergleichende Analyse zur gesellschaftlichen Schichtung der patriotischen Gruppen* (Praha: Universita Karlova).

Hroch, Miroslav (1985). *Social Preconditions of National Revival in Europe: A Comparative Analysis of the Social Composition of Patriotic Groups among the Smaller European Nations* (Cambridge: Cambridge University Press).

Hroch, Miroslav (1996). *In the National Interest* (Prague: Charles University).

von Humboldt, Wilhelm (1973). *Schriften zur Sprache* (ed. M. Böhler; Stuttgart: Reclam).

von Humboldt, Wilhelm (1994). *Über die Sprache. Reden vor der Akademie* (ed. Jürgen Trabant; Tübingen: Francke).

Hume, David (1964 [1882]). *The Philosophical Works* (ed. Th. H. Green & Th.H. Grose; 4 vols; Aalen: Scientia).

Hutchinson, John (1987). *The Dynamics of Cultural Nationalism: The Gaelic Revival and the Creation of the Irish Nation State* (London: Allen & Unwin).

Hyde, Douglas (1994 [1892]). *The Necessity for De-Anglicising Ireland* (ed. J. Leerssen; Leiden: Academic Press).

Isnenghi, Mario (ed.) (1996-1997). *I luoghi della memoria* (3 vols; Roma / Bari: Laterza).

Iuvenalis, D. Iunius (2004). *Juvenal and Persius* (ed. Jeffrey Henderson; Cambridge, MA: Harvard University Press).

Jackson, Donald (1973). 'The Irish Language and Tudor Government', *Eire-Ireland,* 8 #1: 21-28.

Jaeger, Stephen, C. (1985). 'The Language of Courtesy: Latin Terminology, Vernacular Counterparts', in *The Origins of Courtliness. Civilizing Trends and the Formation of Courtly Ideals* (Philadelphia: University of Pennsylvania Press): 127-175.

Janota, Johannes (ed.) (1980). *Eine Wissenschaft etabliert sich, 1810-1870* (Tübingen: Niemeyer).

Janssen de Limpens, K.J.Th. (1977). *Rechtsbronnen van het Hertogdom Limburg en de Landen van Overmaze* (Bussum: Kemink & zn.).

Jauß, Hans Robert (1999). 'Ichselbt und der Andere: Bermerkungen aus hermeneutischer Sicht' and 'Probleme des Verstehens: Das privilegierte Du und der kontingente Andere', in *Probleme des Verstehens. Ausgewählte Aufsätze* (Stuttgart: Philipp Reclam): 122-135, 136-187.

Jelavich, Barbara (1983). *History of the Balkans: Eighteenth and Nineteenth Centuries* (Cambridge: Cambridge University Press).

Jolles, Mathys (1936). *Das deutsche Nationalbewußtsein im Zeitalter Napoleons* (Frankfurt: Klostermann).

Jones, Mark Ellis (1998). '«An Invidious Attempt to Accelerate the Extinction of our Language»: The Abolition of the Court of Great Sessions and the Welsh Language', *Welsh History Review / Cylchgrawn Hanes Cymru,* 19 #2: 226-264.

de Jong, Ad (1994). 'Volkskunde im Freien. Musealisierung und Nationalisierung des Landlebens 1850-1920', *Ethnologia Europaea: Journal of European Ethnology,* 24: 139-148.

de Jong, Ad (2001). *De dirigenten van de herinnering. Musealisering en nationalisering van de volkscultuur in Nederland, 1815-1940* (Nijmegen: SUN).

Jordan, Stephan (1999). *Geschichtstheorie in der ersten Hälfte des 19. Jahrhunderts. Die Schwellenzeit zwischen Pragmatismus und Klassischem Historismus* (Frankfurt: Campus).

Jourdan, Annie (1997). *Les monuments de la Révolution, 1770-1804: Une histoire de représentation* (Paris: Flammarion).

Jourdan, Annie (2004). *La Révolution, une exception française?* (Paris: Flammarion).

Juaristi, Jon (1998). *El linaje de Aitor* (2nd ed.; Madrid: Taurus).

Juaristi, Jon (2000). *El bosque originario. Genealogías míticas de los pueblos de Europa* (Madrid: Taurus).

Kahn, Charles H. (1979). *The Art and Thought of Heraclitus: An Edition of the Fragments with a Translation and Commentary* (Cambridge: Cambridge University Press).

Kalmar, Ivan (1987). 'The *Völkerpsychologie* of Lazarus and Steinthal and the Modern Concept of Culture', *Journal of the History of Ideas,* 48: 671-690.

Karuth, Marianne (ed.) (1967). *Kultur und Zivilisation* (München: Hueber).

Kedourie, Elie (1960). *Nationalism* (New York: Praeger).

Kee, Robert (1972). *The Green Flag: A History of Irish Nationalism* (London: Weidenfeld & Nicolson).

Keen, Sam (1986). *Faces of the Enemy. Reflections on the Hostile Imagination* (San Francisco: Harper & Row).

Kelley, Donald R. (1973). *François Hotman: A Revolutionary's Ordeal* (Princeton, NJ: Princeton University Press).

Kemiläinen, Aira (1971). *«L'affaire d'Avignon» (1789-1791) from the Viewpoint of Nationalism* (Helsinki: Suomalainen Tiedeakatemia).

Kemiläinen, Aira (1997). 'Fiction and Reality in Writing of National History in Finland from the 19th Century On', in Řezník & Sleváková, 29-52.

Kemiläinen, Aira (1998). *Finns in the Shadow of the Aryans: Race Theories and Racism* (Helsinki: SHS).

Kirby, David (1995). *The Baltic World 1772-1993: Europe's Northern Periphery in an Age of Change* (London: Longman).

Klein, Adolf (1980). *Der Dom zu Köln. Die bewegte Geschichte seiner Vollendung* (Köln: Wienand).

Kleist, Heinrich (1975). *Sämtliche Werke* (2 vols; Stuttgart: Parkland).

Kliger, Samuel (1952). *The Goths in England: A Study in Seventeenth and Eighteenth Century Thought* (Cambridge, MA: Harvard University Press).

Klimó, Árpád von (2004). 'Volksgeschichte in Ungarn (1939-1945). Chancen Schwierigkeiten und Folgen eines «deutschen» Projekts', in *Historische West- und Ostforschung in Zentraleuropa zwischen dem Ersten und dem Zweiten Weltkrieg – Verflechtung und Vergleich*, ed. M. Middell & U. Sommer (Leipzig: Akademische Verlagsanstalt): 151-178.

Klinge, Matti (1980). '«Let Us be Finns»: The Birth of Finland's National Culture', in Mitchison, 67-75.

Klinge, Matti (1993). 'Finland: From Napoleonic Legacy to Nordic Co-operation', in *The National Question in Europe in Historical Context*, ed. M. Teich & R. Porter (Cambridge: Cambridge University Press): 317-331.

Kluckhohn, Paul (1961 [1942]). *Das Ideengut der deutschen Romantik* (4th. ed.; Tübingen: Max Niemeyer).

Knapp, Heinrich (1990). *Das Schloß Marienburg in Preussen. Quellen und Materialien zur Baugeschichte seit 1456* (Lüneburg: Nordostdeutsches Kulturwerk).

Knippenberg, Hans; Jan Markusse (eds.) (1999). *Nationalising and Denationalising European Border Regions, 1800-2000. Views from Geography and History* (Dordrecht: Kluwer).

Knippenberg, Hans; Ben de Pater (1988). *De eenwording van Nederland* (Nijmegen: SUN).

Kochs, Theodor (1967). 'Nationale Idee und nationalistisches Denken im Grimmschen Wörterbuch', in *Nationalismus in Germanistik und Dichtung. Dokumentation des Germanistentages in München vom 17. bis 22. Oktober 1966*, ed. B. von Wiese & R. Henß (Berlin: Schmidt): 273-284.

Kohn, Hans (1946). *The Idea of Nationalism: A Study in its Origins and Background* (New York: Macmillan).

Kohn, Hans (1960). *Pan-Slavism, its History and Ideology* (New York: Vintage).

Kohn, Hans (1967). *Prelude to Nation-States: The French and German Experience, 1789-1815* (Princeton, NJ: Van Nostrand).

Kokare, Elsa (1985). 'Die Relevanz von Barons' «Latvju Dainas» in der Vergangenheit und für die Zukunft', in Loit, 507-513.

Konstantinou, Evangelos (ed.) (1992). *Europäischer Philhellenismus: Die europäische philhellenische Literatur bis zur 1. Hälfte des 19. Jahrhunderts* (Frankfurt: Peter Lang).

Koselleck, Reinhart (1979). *Vergangene Zukunft. Zur Semantik geschichtlicher Zeiten* (Frankfurt: Suhrkamp).

Koselleck, Reinhart (1992). 'Volk, Nation, Nationalismus, Masse', in *Geschichtliche Grundbegriffe. Historisches Lexikon zur politisch-sozialen Sprache in Deutschland*, ed. O. Brunner, W. Conze & R. Koselleck (7 vols; Stuttgart: Klett-Cotta), 7: 141-431.

Kramer, Johannes (1983-94). 'Language Planning in Italy', in *Language Reform: History and Future*, ed. I. Fodor & C. Hagège (6 vols; Hamburg: Buske), 2: 301-316.

Krapauskas, Virgil (2000). *Nationalism and Historiography: The Case of Nineteenth-Century Lithuanian Historicism* (New York: Columbia University Press).

Krügel, Rudolf (1914). *Der Begrif des Volksgeistes in Ernst Moritz Arndts Geschichtsanschauung* (Langensalza: Beyer).

Kuehnemund, Richard (1953). *Arminius, or the Rise of a National Symbol in Literature* (Chapel Hill, NC: University of North Carolina).

Küttler, Wolfgang; Jörn Rüsen; Ernst Schulin (eds.) (1997). *Geschichtsdiskurs. Band 3. Die Epoche der Historisierung* (Frankfurt: Fischer Wissenschaft).

La Mesnardière, Jules de (1972 [1642]). *La poëtique* (facs. repr.; Genève: Slatkine).

van Laar, Hans (1986). 'Tweespalt in 's-Gravenvoeren. Een politiek-cultureel antropologische studie van een Belgisch dorp' (MA thesis, Amsterdam: Universiteit van Amsterdam, Antropologisch-sociologisch Centrum).

Labrie, Arnold (1994). '«Kultur» and «Zivilisation» in Germany during the Nineteenth Century', *Yearbook of European Studies* 7: 95-120.

Lacouture, Jean (1984-86). *De Gaulle* (3 vols; Paris: Seuil).

Lajosi, Krisztina (2005). 'National Opera and Nineteenth-Century Nation-Building in East-Central Europe', *Neohelicon*, 32 #1: 51-70.

Landau, Jacob M. (1981). *Pan-Turkism in Turkey: A Study of Irredentism* (London: Hurst).

Lange, Fritz (ed.) (1954). *Neithart von Gneisenau. Schriften von und über Gneisenau* (Berlin: Rütten & Loening).

Lawrence, Paul (2005). *Nationalism: History and Theory* (London: Pearson).

Lawrynenko, Jurij (1962). 'Ševcenko and his «Kobzar» in the Intellectual and Political History of a Century', in *Taras Ševcenko 1814-1861: A Symposium*, ed. V. Mijakovs'kyj & G.Y. Shevelov (The Hague: Mouton): 153-258.

Le Goff, Jacques (1988). *The Medieval Imagination* (trl. A. Goldhammer; Chicago: University of Chicago Press).

Ledeen, Michael Arthur (1977). *The First Duce: D'Annunzio at Fiume* (Baltimore, MD: Johns Hopkins University Press).

Leeb, I. Leonard (1973). *The Ideological Origins of the Batavian Revolution: History and Politics in the Dutch Republic, 1747-1800* (Den Haag: Martinus Nijhoff).

Leerssen, Joep (1987). 'Montesquieu's Corresponding Images: Cultural and Sexual Alterity in Pseudo-Oriental Letters', *Comparative Criticism*, 9: 135-154.

Leerssen, Joep (1988). 'Anglo-Irish Patriotism and its European Context: Notes Towards a Reassessment', *Eighteenth-Century Ireland*, 3: 7-24.

Leerssen, Joep (1989). 'Outer and Inner Others: The Auto-Image of French Identity from Mme de Staël to Eugène Sue', *Yearbook of European Studies*, 2: 35-52.

Leerssen, Joep (1991). 'Mimesis and Stereotype', *Yearbook of European Studies*, 4: 165-176.

Leerssen, Joep (1993a). 'Culturele identiteit en nationale beeldvorming', in *De onmacht van het grote. Cultuur in Europa*, ed. J.C.H. Blom, J. Leerssen & P. de Rooy (Amsterdam: Amsterdam University Press): 7-20.

Leerssen, Joep (1993b). 'Europe as a Set of Borders', *Yearbook of European Studies*, 6: 1-14.

Leerssen, Joep (1994). *The «Contention of the Bards» (Iomarbhágh na bhFileadh) and its Place in Irish Political and Literary History* (London: Irish Texts Society).

Leerssen, Joep (1995). 'Wildness, Wilderness, and Ireland: Medieval and Early-Modern Patterns in the Demarcation of Civility', *Journal of the History of Ideas*, 56: 25-39.

Leerssen, Joep (1996a). 'Celticism', in *Celticism*, ed. T. Brown (Amsterdam: Rodopi), 8: 1-20.

Leerssen, Joep (1996b [1986]). *Mere Irish and Fíor-Ghael. Studies in the Idea of Irish Nationality, its Development and Literary Expression Prior to the Nineteenth Century* (2nd ed.; Cork: Cork University Press).

Leerssen, Joep (1996c). *Remembrance and Imagination: Patterns in the Historical and Literary Representation of Ireland in the Nineteenth Century* (Cork: Cork University Press).

Leerssen, Joep (1998). 'Lavaters Physiognomik: Versuch einer Kontextualisierung', in Agazzi & Beller, 15-27.

Leerssen, Joep (1999). 'Law and Border (How and Where we Draw the Line)', *Irish Review*, 24: 1-8.

Leerssen, Joep (2000). 'The Rhetoric of National Character: A Programmatic Survey', *Poetics Today*, 21 #2: 267-292.

Leerssen, Joep (2002a). *Hidden Ireland, Public Sphere* (Galway: Arlen House / Centre for Irish Studies).

Leerssen, Joep (2002b). 'Primitive Orality and Archaic Heroism: The Romantic Conception of Epic', in *Romantična Pesnitev. Ob 200. Obletni Rojstva Franceta Prešerna. Mednarodni Simpozij Obdobja - Metode in Zvrsti, Ljubljana, 4.-6. December 2000*, ed. M. Juvan (Ljubljana: Universa v Ljubljani), 19-32.

Leerssen, Joep (2002c). 'Progress and Nostalgia in Modernity', in *Other Modernisms in an Age of Globalization*, ed. D. Kadir & D. Löbbermann (Heidelberg: Winter): 27-34.

Leerssen, Joep (2004a). 'Literary Historicism: Romanticism, Philologists, and the Presence of the Past', *Modern Language Quarterly*, 65 #2: 221-243.

Leerssen, Joep (2004b). 'Ossian and the Rise of Literary Historicism', in *The Reception of Ossian in Europe*, ed. H. Gaskill (London: Continuum): 109-125.

Leerssen, Joep (2006a). *De bronnen van het vaderland: Taal, literatuur en de afbakening van Nederland, 1806-1890* (Nijmegen: Vantilt).

Leerssen, Joep (2006b). 'Historisme en historicisme', *De negentiende eeuw*, 30: 110-117.

Leerssen, Joep (2006c). 'Nationalism and the Cultivation of Culture', *Nations and Nationalism*, 12 #4: 559-578.

Lefmann, Salomon (1870). *August Schleicher. Skizze* (Leipzig: Teubner).

Lehmann, Hartmut (1983). 'Martin Luther as a National Hero in the Nineteenth Century', in Eade, 181-202.

Lennon, Colm (1994). *Sixteenth-Century Ireland: The Incomplete Conquest* (Dublin: Gill & Macmillan).

Lessing, Gotthold Ephraim (1988). *Werke* (ed. Karl Balser; 5 vols; Berlin: Aufbau).

Leupen, Piet (1998). *Keizer in zijn eigen rijk: De geboorte van de nationale staat* (Amsterdam: Wereldbibliotheek).

Lévi-Strauss, Claude (1963). *Structural Anthropology* (trl. C.J.B. Grundfest; New York: Basic).

Lindheim, Ralph; Georges S.N. Luckyj (eds.) (1996). *Towards an Intellectual History of the Ukraine: An Anthology of Ukrainian Thought from 1710 to 1995* (Toronto: University of Toronto Press).

Locke, John (1960). *Two Treatises of Government* (ed. P. Laslett; Cambridge: Cambridge University Press).

Loit, Aleksander (ed.) (1985). *National Movements in the Baltic Countries During the Nineteenth Century* (Uppsala: Almqvist & Wiksell).

Loock, Hans-Dietrich (1969). 'Zur «großgermanischen Politik» des Dritten Reiches', *Vierteljahrshefte für Zeitgeschichte*, 8: 37-63.

López de Abiada, José Manuel (2004). 'Teoría y práctica de los estudios imagológicos: hacia un estado de la cuestión', in *Imágenes de España en culturas y literaturas europeas (siglos XVI-XVII)*, ed. J.M. López de Abiada & A. López Bernasocchi (Madrid: Verbum): 13-62.

Lord, Albert B. (1963). 'Nationalism and the Muses in the Balkan Slavic Literature in the Modern Period', in *The Balkans in Transition: Essays on the Development of Balkan Life and Politics since the Eighteenth Century*, ed. C. Jelavich & B. Jelavich (Berkeley: University of California Press): 258-296.

Lord, George (ed.) (1975). *An Anthology of Poems on Affairs of State* (New Haven: Yale University Press).

Lovejoy, Arthur O.; G. Boas (1935). *Primitivism and Related Ideas in Antiquity* (Baltimore, MD: Johns Hopkins University Press).

Lučić, Radovan (ed.) (2002). *Lexicography and Language Policy in South-Slavic Languages after 1989* (München: Sagner).

Lukan, Walter (ed.) (1995). *Bartholomäus (Jernej) Kopitar. Neue Studien und Materialien anläßlich seines 150. Todestages* (Wien: Böhlau).

Lukan, Walter (2000). *Bartholomäus Kopitar (1780-1844) und die europäische Wissenschaft im Spiegel seiner Privatbibliothek. Jernej Kopitar in evropska znanost v zrcalu njegove zasebne knjiznice* (Ljubljana: Narodna in universitetna knjiznica).

MacDonagh, Oliver (1983). *States of Mind: A Study of Anglo-Irish Conflict 1780-1980* (London: George Allen & Unwin).

MacDonagh, Oliver (1991). *O'Connell. The Life of Daniel O'Connell, 1775-1847* (London: Weidenfeld & Nicolson).

MacDougall, Hugh A. (1982). *Racial Myth in English History: Trojans, Teutons, and Anglo-Saxons* (Hanover, NH: University Press of New England).

Magocsi, Paul Robert (1995). *Historical Atlas of East Central Europe* (Seattle: University of Washington Press).

Malettke, Klaus (ed.) (1992). *175 Jahre Wartburgfest* (Heidelberg: Winter).

Mandle, W. F. (1987). *The Gaelic Athletic Association and Irish Nationalist Politics* (London: Helm).

Marek, K. (1968). *Identity and Continuity of States in Public International Law* (2nd. ed.; Genève: Droz).

Marienstras, Richard (1969). *Le proche et le lointain: Sur Shakespeare, le drame élisabéthain et l'idéologie anglaise aux XVIe et XVIIe siècles* (Paris: Minuit).

Markusse, Jan (1996). *Zuid-Tirol: De pacificatie van een multi-etnische regio* (Utrecht: Koninklijk Nederlands Aardrijkskundig Genootschap).

Martin, Lawrence (1924). *The Treaties of Peace, 1919-1923* (2 vols; New York: Carnegie Endowment for International Peace).

Mason, Peter (1990). *The Deconstruction of America: Representations of the Other* (London: Routledge).

Mazón, Patricia (2000). 'Germania Triumphant: The Niederwald National Monument and the Liberal Moment in Imperial Germany', *German History,* 18 #2: 163-192.

McCormack, W.J. (1985). 'The Question of Celticism', in *Ascendancy and Tradition in Anglo-Irish Literary History from 1789 to 1939* (Oxford: Clarendon Press): 219-238.

McCormack, W.J. (2005). *Blood Kindred: W.B. Yeats, the Life, the Death, the Politics* (London: Pimlico).

McDonnel, Myles (2007). *Virtus and the Roman republic* (Cambridge: Cambridge University Press).

McMenamin, Iain (1997). '«Self-choosing» and «right-acting» in the Nationalism of Giuseppe Mazzini', *History of European Ideas,* 23 #5/6: 221-234.

Meehan, Michael (1975). *Liberty and Poetics in Eighteenth-Century England* (London: Croom Helm).

Merchiers, Ingrid (2005). 'Cultural Nationalism in the South Slav Habsburg Lands in the Early Nineteenth Century: The Scholarly Network of Jernej Kopitar (1780-1844)' (doctoral thesis, Gent: Universiteit Gent, Faculteit Letteren en Wijsbegeerte).

Mérimée, Prosper (1971). *Notes de voyages* (ed. Pierre-Auzas; Paris: Hachette).

Michel, Bernard (1995). *Nations et nationalismes en Europe centrale* (Paris: Aubier).

Mijakovs'kyj, Volodymyr (1962). 'Ševcenko in the Brotherhood of Saints Cyril and Methodius', in *Taras Ševcenko 1814-1861: A Symposium,* ed. V. Mijakovs'kyj & G.Y. Shevelov (The Hague: Mouton): 9-36.

Milojkovic-Djuric, Jelena (1994). *Panslavism and National Identity in Russia and in the Balkans, 1830-1880: Images of the Self and Others* (New York: Columbia University Press).

Mitchison, Rosalind (ed.) (1980). *The Roots of Nationalism: Studies in Northern Europe* (Edinburgh: John Donald).

Momigliano, Arnaldo (1955). 'Ancient History and the Antiquarian', in *Contributo Alla Storia Degli Studi Classici* (Roma: Edizioni de Storia e Letteratura): 67-106.

Montesquieu, Charles Louis de Sécondat (1964). *Oeuvres complètes* (ed. Daniel Oster; Paris: Seuil).

Moretti, Franco (1998). *Atlas of the European Novel, 1800-1900* (London: Verso).

Morgan, Janet (1986). 'The Meanings of *Vraisemblance* in French Classical Theory', *Modern Language Review*, 81: 293-304.

Moritsch, Andreas (2000). *Der Prager Slavenkongress 1848* (Wien: Böhlau).

Mörke, Olaf (1996). 'Bataver, Eidgenossen und Goten: Gründungs- und Begründungsmythen in den Niederlanden, der Schweiz, und Schweden in der frühen Neuzeit', in *Mythos und Nation. Studien zur Entwicklung des kollektiven Bewußtseins in der Neuzeit, 3*, ed. H. Berding (Frankfurt: Suhrkamp): 104-132.

Mosse, George L. (1975). *The Nationalization of the Masses: Political Symbolism and Mass Movements in Germany from the Napoleonic Wars Through the Third Reich* (New York: Fertig).

Mossner, Ernest Campbell (1980). *The life of David Hume.* (2nd ed.; Oxford: Clarendon).

Mout, M.E.H.N. (1996). '«Vader van de natie»: František Palacký (1798-1872)', in *Historici in de politiek*, ed. M.P. Bossenbroek, M.E.H.N. Mout & C. Musterd (Leiden: Centrum voor Moderne Geschiedenis): 55-76.

Murphy, David Thomas (1997). *The Heroic Earth: Geopolitical Thought in Weimar Germany, 1918-1933* (Kent, OH: Kent State University Press).

Netzer, Katinka (2006). *Wissenschaft aus nationaler Sehnsucht: Verhandlungen der Germanisten 1846 und 1847.* (Heidelberg: Winter).

NEVB (1998). *Nieuwe encyclopedie van de Vlaamse beweging* (3 vols; Tielt: Lannoo).

Nève, P.L. (1972). *Het Rijkskamergerecht en de Nederlanden* (Assen: Van Gorcum).

Nichols, Stephen G. (1996). 'Modernism and the Politics of Medieval Studies', in *Medievalism and the Modernist Temper*, ed. R.H. Bloch & S.G. Nichols (Baltimore: Johns Hopkins University Press): 25-56.

Nipperdey, Thomas (1968). 'Nationalidee und Nationaldenkmal in Deutschland im 19. Jahrhundert', *Historische Zeitschrift*, 206: 529-585.

Nipperdey, Thomas (1986). 'Der Kölner Dom als Nationaldenkmal', in *Nachdenken über die deutsche Geschichte* (München: Beck): 156-171.

Noe, Alfred (ed.) (1994). *Der Philhellenismus in der westeuropäischen Literatur 1780-1830* (Amsterdam: Rodopi).

Nora, Pierre (ed.) (1997 [1984-1992]). *Les lieux de mémoire* (Quarto ed.; 3 vols; Paris: Gallimard).

Nordman, Daniel (1997). 'Des limites d'Etat aux frontières nationales', in Nora, 1: 1125-1146.

Ó Glaisne, Risteárd (1991). *Dúbhglas de h-Íde (1860-1949) 1: Ceannródaí Cultúrtha (1860-1910)* (Baile Átha Cliath [Dublin]: Conradh na Gaeilge).

Oberkrone, Willi (1993). *Volksgeschichte. Methodische Innovation und völkische Ideologisierung in der deutschen Geschichtswissenschaft, 1918-1945* (Göttingen: Vandenhoeck & Ruprecht).

Ogonovsky-Steffens, Judith (1999). *La peinture monumentale d'histoire dans les édifices civils de Belgique (1830-1914)* (Brussel: Académie Royale de Belgique).

Orton, Lawrence D. (1978). *The Prague Slav Congress of 1848* (Boulder: East European Quarterly).

Oudin, Bernard (1987). *Aristide Briand – La paix: Une idée neuve en Europe* (Paris: Laffont).

Ozouf, Mona (1997). 'Le Panthéon', in Nora, 1: 155-178.

Pabst, Klaus (2003). 'Die «Historikerschlacht» um den Rhein', in *Historische Debatten und Kontroversen im 19. und 20. Jahrhundert* (Stuttgart: Franz Steiner Verlag): 70-79.

Palmer, R.R. (1959). *The Age of the Democratic Revolution: A Political History of Europe and America, 1760-1800* (2 vols; Princeton, NJ: Princeton University Press).

Panofsky, Erwin (1930). 'Das erste Blatt aus dem «Libro» Giorgio Vasaris: Eine Studie über die Beurteiling der Gotik in der Italienischen Renaissance', *Städel-Jahrbuch*, 6: 25-72.

Parker, Joanne (2007). *'England's darling': The Victorian cult of Alfred the Great* (Manchester: Manchester University Press).

Paternu, Boris (1993). *France Prešeren: Ein slowenischer Dichter, 1800-1849* (trl. K.D. Olof; München: Slavica-Kovac).

Pearse, Pádraic H. (n.d.). *Political Writings and Speeches* (Dublin: Phoenix).

Pick, Daniel (1989). *Faces of Degeneration: A European Disorder, c.1848-c.1918* (Cambridge: Cambridge University Press).

Pinkard, Terry (2000). *Hegel: A Biography* (Cambridge: Cambridge University Press).

Pisanty, Valentina (2006). *La difesa della razza: Antologia 1938-1943* (Milano: Bompiani).

Pogačnik, Jože (1978). *Bartholomäus Kopitar: Leben und Werk* (München: Trofenik).

Pointon, Marcia (1998). 'Money and Nationalism', in *Imagining Nations*, ed. G. Cubitt (Manchester: Manchester University Press): 229-254.

von Polenz, Peter (2000). 'Die Sprachgesellschaften und die Entstehung eines literarischen Standards in Deutschland', in Auroux *et al*, 1: 827-841.

Poliakov, Léon (1987). *Le mythe aryen: Essai sur les sources du racisme et des nationalismes* (new ed.; Bruxelles: Complexe).

Pomian, Krzysztof (1997). 'Francs et Gaulois', in Nora, 2: 2245-2300.

Poole, Ross (1999). *Nation and Identity* (London: Routledge).

Post, G. (1953). 'Two Notes on Nationalism in the Middle Ages', *Traditio, 9*: 281-320.

Poutignat, Philippe; Jocelyne Streiff-Fenart (1999). *Théories de l'ethnicité* (2d ed.; Paris: PUF).

Praz, Mario (1930). *La carne, la morte e il diavolo nella letteratura romantica* (Milano).

Prebble, John (2000 [1988]). *The King's Jaunt: George IV in Scotland, August 1822.* (Edinburgh: Birlinn).

Pumpurs, Andrejs (1988 [1888]). *Lāčplēsis (Bear-Slayer), the Latvian People's Hero: A National Epic* (trl. R.L. Krievina; Riga: Writers' Union of the Latvian SSR).

Pundt, Alfred G. (1935). *Arndt and the Nationalist Awakening in Germany* (New York: Columbia University Press).

Räthzel, Nora (1997). *Gegenbilder. Nationale Identität durch Konstruktion des Anderen* (Opladen: Leske & Budrich).

Rambo, Elizabeth L. (1994). *Colonial Ireland in Medieval English Literature* (Selingsgrove, NJ: Susquehanna University Press).

Rawson, Elizabeth (1969). *The Spartan Tradition in European Thought* (Oxford: Clarendon Press).

Rearick, Charles (1974). *Beyond the Enlightenment: Historians and Folklore in Nineteenth-Century France* (Bloomington, IN: Indiana University Press).

Reisert, Joseph R. (2003). *Jean-Jacques Rousseau: A Friend of Virtue* (Ithaca, NY: Cornell University Press).

Reiter, Norbert (ed.) (1983). *Nationalbewegungen auf dem Balkan* (Wiesbaden: Harassowitz).

Renan, Ernest (1948). *Oeuvres complètes* (ed. Henriette Psichari; 2 vols; Paris: Calmann-Lévy).

Renan, Ernest (1994 [1882]). *Qu'est-ce qu'une nation?* (ed. J. Leerssen; Leiden: Academic Press).

Revel, Jacques (1997). 'La région', in Nora, 2: 2907-2936.

Reynolds, Beatrice (1931). *Proponents of Limited Monarchy in Sixteenth Century France: Francis Hotman and Jean Bodin* (New York: Columbia University Press).

Reynolds, Leighton Durham (ed.) (1983). *Texts and Transmission: A Survey of the Latin Classics* (Oxford: Clarendon).

Reynolds, Leighton Durham; Nigel Guy Wilson (1991 [1968]). *Scribes and Scholars: A Guide to the Transmission of Greek and Latin Literature* (3rd ed.; Oxford: Clarendon).

Reynolds, Susan (1983). 'Medieval Origines: Gentium and the Community of the Realm', *History, 68*: 375-390.

Reynolds, Susan (1984). *Kingdoms and Communities in Western Europe* (Oxford: Clarendon Press).

Řezník, Miloš; Ivana Sleváková (eds.) (1997). *Nations, Identities, Historical Consciousness. Volume Dedicated to Prof. Miroslav Hroch.* (Prague: Faculty of Philosophy, Charles University).

Ridoux, Charles (2001). *Évolution des études médiévales en France de 1860 à 1914* (Paris: Champion).

Rigney, Ann (1990). *The Rhetoric of Historical Representation: Three Narrative Histories of the French Revolution* (Cambridge: Cambridge University Press).

Rigney, Ann (2001). *Imperfect Histories: The Elusive Past and the Legacy of Romantic Historicism* (Ithaca, NY: Cornell University Press).

Rigney, Ann (2004). 'Portable Monuments: Literature, Cultural Memory, and the Case of Jeanie Deans', *Poetics Today*, 25 #2: 361-396.

Ringmacher, Manfred (2001). 'Die Klassifizierung der Sprachen in der Mitte des neunzehnten Jahrhunderts' and 'Sprachtypologie und Ethnologie in Europa am Ende des 19. Jahrhunderts', in Auroux et al., 2: 1427-1436, 1436-1443.

Rioux, Jean-Pierre; Jean-François Sirinelli (eds.) (1997). *Pour une histoire culturelle* (Paris: Seuil).

Robbins, Caroline (1959). *The Eighteenth-Century Commonwealthman: Studies in the Transmission, Development and Circumstance of English Liberal Thought from the Restoration of Charles II until the War of the Thirteen Colonies* (Cambridge, MA: Harvard University Press).

Robert, Cyprien (1860). *Le Panlatinisme. Confédération Gallo-Latine et Celto-Gauloise. Contre-Testament de Pierre le Grand et Contre-Panslavisme* (Paris: Passard).

Roberts, Gwyneth Tyson (1998). *The Language of the Blue Books: The Perfect Instrument of Empire* (Cardiff: University of Wales Press).

Romani, Roberto (1998). 'All Montesquieu's Sons: The Place of «esprit général», «caractère national», and «moeurs» in French Political Philosophy, 1748-1789', *Studies on Voltaire and the Eighteenth Century*, 362: 189-235.

Roobol, W.H. (1998). 'Notities over de «natiestaat»: Het woord, het begrip en het ding', *Theoretische geschiedenis*, 25 #2/3: 370-381.

Rosenthal, Michael (1986). *The Character Factory. Baden-Powell's Boy Scouts and the Imperatives of Empire* (London: Collins).

Rössing, J.H. (1898). *De Gouden Koets: Huldeblijk aan H.M. Koningin Wilhelmina van het Amsterdamsche volk* (Amsterdam: De Wit).

Rousseau, Jean (2001). 'La genèse de la grammaire comparée' and 'La classification des langues au début du XIXe siècle', in Auroux *et al*, 2: 1197-1210, 1414-1426.

Rubulis, Aleksis (1970). *Baltic Literature: A Survey of Finnish, Estonian, Latvian, and Lithuanian Literature* (Notre Dame, IN: University of Notre Dame Press).

Rüegg, Walter (ed.) (2004). *A History of the University in Europe 3: Universities in the Nineteenth and Early Twentieth Centuries (1800-1945)* (Cambridge: Cambridge University Press).

Ryan, Desmond (1939). *The Sword of Light: From the Four Masters to Douglas Hyde, 1636-1938* (London: Barker).

de Ryckel, A. (1980). 'Les fiefs du comté de Dalhem', *Bulletin de la Société d'art et d'histoire du diocèse de Liège*, 17: 271-384.

Sampimon, Janette (2006). *Becoming Bulgarian: The Articulation of Bulgarian Identity in the Nineteenth Century in its International Context: An Intellectual History* (Amsterdam: Pegasus).

Samson, Jim (2002). 'Nations and Nationalism', in *The Cambridge History of Nineteenth-Century Music*, ed. J. Samson (Cambridge: Cambridge University Press): 568-600.

Samuel, Raphael (ed.) (1989). *Patriotism: The Making and Unmaking of British National Identity* (3 vols; London: Routledge).

Samuel, Raphael (1994-98). *Theatres of Memory* (2 vols; London: Verso).

Saunders, Corinne (1993). *The Forest of Medieval Romance: Avernus, Broceliande, Arven* (Woodbridge: Boydell).

Savage, H.L. (1933). 'Hunting in the Middle Ages', *Speculum*, 8: 30-41.

Scaliger, J.C. (1964 [1561]). *Poetices libri septem* (facs. repr.; Stuttgart - Bad Canstatt: Frommann).

Schäfer, Karlheinz; Josef Schawe (1971). *Ernst Moritz Arndt: Ein bibliographisches Handbuch 1769-1969* (Bonn: Röhrscheid).

Scherer, Wilhelm (1985 [1885]). *Jacob Grimm* (ed. Ludwig Erich Schmitt; Hildesheim: Olms).

Schieffelin, Bambi B.; Kathryn A. Woolard; Paul Kroskrity (eds.) (1998). *Language Ideologies: Practice and Theory* (New York: Oxford University Press).

Schiller, Friedrich (1970). *Vom Pathetischen und Erhabenen. Ausgewählte Schriften zur Dramentheorie* (ed. Klaus L. Berghahn; Stuttgart: Philipp Reclam).

Schilling, René (2000). 'Körner Superstar', *Die Zeit,* 16 November.

Schlegel, Friedrich (1988 [1815]). 'Geschichte der alten und neuen Literatur. Vorlesungen, gehalten zu Wien im Jahre 1812', in *Kritische Schriften und Fragmente: Studienausgabe*, ed. E. Behler & H. Eichner (6 vols; Paderborn: Schöningh), 4: 1-234.

Schmidt, Harald (1994). 'Fremde Heimat. Die deutsche Provinzreise zwischen Spätaufklärung und nationaler Romantik und das Problem der kulturellen Variation: Friedrich Nicolai, Kaspar Riesbeck und Ernst Moritz Arndt', in *Nationales Bewußtsein und kollektive Identität. Studien zur Entwicklung des kollektiven Bewußtseins in der Neuzeit, 2*, ed. H. Berding (Frankfurt: Suhrkamp): 394-442.

Schmidt, Thomas (2000). 'Deutsche National-Philologie oder Neuphilologie in Deutschland? Internationalität und Interdisziplinarität in der Frühgeschichte der Germanistik', in *Internationalität nationaler Literaturen. Beiträge zum ersten Symposion des Göttinger Sonderforschungsbereich 529*, ed. U. Schöning (Göttingen: Wallstein): 311-340.

Schmölders, Claudia (1995). *Das Vorurteil im Leibe. Eine Einführung in die Physiognomik* (Berlin: Akademie-Verlag).

Schmölders, Claudia (1998). 'Der Charakter des Pferdes. Zur Physiognomik der Veterinäre um 1800', in Agazzi & Beller, 403-422.

Schöffer, I. (1975). 'The Batavian Myth during the Sixteenth and Seventeenth Centuries', in *Britain and The Netherlands*, ed. J.S. Bromley & E.H. Kossmann (The Hague: Nijhoff), 5: 78-101.

Schoof, Wilhelm (ed.) (1953). *Briefe der Brüder Grimm an Savigny* (Berlin: Erich Schmidt).

Schoof, Wilhelm (1960). *Jacob Grimm. Aus seinem Leben* (Bonn: Dümmler).

Scurla, Herbert (1984). *Wilhelm v. Humboldt: Reformator, Wissenschaftler, Philosoph* (München: Heyne).

Scurla, Herbert (1985). *Die Brüder Grimm: Ein Lebensbild* (Berlin: Verlag der Nation).

Scurr, Ruth (2006). *Fatal Purity: Robespierre and the French Revolution* (New York: Metropolitan).

von See, Klaus (1994). *Barbar Germane Arier. Die Suche nach der Identität der Deutschen* (Heidelberg: Winter).

von See, Klaus (1999). 'Jacob Grimm und die Göttinger Protestation von 1837', in Fürbeth *et al,* 277-286.

Seidel, Ch.; L.J. Pongratz (1971). 'Charakter', in *Historisches Wörterbuch der Philosophie*, ed. J. Ritter (12 vols; Darmstadt / Basel: Wissenschaftliche Buchgesellschaft / Schwabe), 2: 984-992.

Seitz, Gabriele (1984). *Die Brüder Grimm: Leben, Werk, Zeit* (München: Winkler).

Shackleton, Robert (1962). 'The Evolution of Montesquieu's Theory of Climate', *Revue internationale de philosophie,* 33-34: 317-329.

Sherwood, Peter (1996). '«A Nation May be Said to Live in its Language»: Some Socio-Historical Perspectives on Attitudes to Hungarian', in *The Literature of Nationalism: Essays on East European Identity*, ed. R.B. Pynsent (London / University of London: Macmillan / School of Slavonic and East European Studies): 27-39.

Short, David (1996). 'The Use and Abuse of the Language Argument in Mid-Nineteenth Century «Czechoslovakism»: An Appraisal of a Propaganda Milestone', in *The Literature of Nationalism: Essays on East European Identity*, ed. R.B. Pynsent (London / University of London: Macmillan / School of Slavonic and East European Studies): 40-65.

van der Sijs, Nicoline (ed.) (1999). *Taaltrots. Purisme in een veertigtal talen* (Amsterdam/ Antwerpen: Contact).

Simanowski, Roberto (1998). 'Einleitung: Zum Problem kultureller Grenzziehung', in *Kulturelle Grenzziehungen im Spiegel der Literaturen: Nationalismus, Regionalismus, Fundamentalismus*, ed. H. Turk, B. Schultze & R. Simanowski (Göttingen: Wallstein): 8-60.

Simons, Ludo (1980). *Van Duinkerke tot Königsberg. Geschiedenis van de Aldietsche Beweging* (Nijmegen / Brugge: Gottmer / Orion).

Skendi, Stavro (1967). *The Albanian National Awakening, 1878-1912* (Princeton, NJ: Princeton University Press).

Smeed, John W. (1985). *The Theophrastan «Character»: The History of a Literary Genre* (Oxford: Clarendon Press).

Smith, Anthony D. (1971). *Theories of Nationalism* (New York: Harper & Row).

Smith, Anthony D. (1986). *The Ethnic Origin of Nations* (Oxford: Blackwell).

Smith, Anthony D. (1991). *National Identity* (Harmondsworth: Penguin).

Smith, Anthony D. (1998). *Nationalism and Modernism: A Critical Survey of Recent Theories of Nations and Nationalism* (London: Routledge).

Smith, Michael Llewellyn (1998). *Ionian Vision: Greece in Asia Minor, 1919-1922* (London: Hurst).

Sørensen, Bengt Algot (1999). 'Die Anfänge der deutschen Germanistik – aus nordischer Sicht', in Fürbeth *et al*, 169-180.

Spencer, T. (1986). *Fair Greece, Sad Relic: Literary Philhellenism from Shakespeare to Byron* (Athens: Harvey).

Sperber, Dan (1990). 'The Epidemiology of Beliefs', in *The Social Psychological Study of Widespread Beliefs*, ed. C. Fraser & G. Gaskell (Oxford: Clarendon Press): 25-44.

Sperber, Dan (1996). *La contagion des idées* (Paris: Odile Jacob).

Štaif, Jiří (1997). 'František Palacký a česká historická paměť (jubileum r. 1898)', in Řezník & Sleváková, 229-250.

Stanzel, Franz K. (1974a). 'Der literarische Aspekt unserer Vorstellungen vom Charakter fremder Völker', *Anzeiger der phil. hist. Klasse der Österreichischen Akademie der Wissenschaften*, III: 63-82.

Stanzel, Franz K. (1974b). 'Schemata und Klischees der Völkerbeschreibung in David Hume's Essay «Of National Characters»', in *Studien zur englischen und amerikanischen Literatur (Festschrift for Helmut Papajewski)*, ed. P.G. Buchloh (Neumünster: Wachholtz): 363-383.

Stanzel, Franz K. (1987). 'Das Nationalitätenschema in der Literatur und seine Entstehung zu Beginn der Neuzeit', in *Erstarrtes Denken. Studien zu Klischee, Stereotyp und Vorurteil in englischsprachiger Literatur*, ed. G. Blaicher (Tübingen: Narr): 84-96.

Stanzel, Franz K. (1997). *Europäer. Ein imagologischer Essay* (Heidelberg: Carl Winter).

Stanzel, Franz K.; Ingomar Weiler; Waldemar Zacharasiewicz (eds.) (1999). *Europäischer Völkerspiegel. Imagologisch-ethnographische Studien zu den Völkertafeln des frühen 18. Jahrhunderts* (Heidelberg: Carl Winter).

Statutes (1786). *The Statutes at Large Passed in the Parliaments held in Ireland* (13 vols; Dublin).

Stepan, Nancy (1982). *The Idea of Race in Science: Great Britain, 1800-1860* (London / Oxford: Macmillan / St. Anthony's College).

Stephens, Anthony (1983). 'Kleist's Mythicisation of the Napoleonic Era', in Eade, 165-180.

Stocking, George W. (1987). *Victorian Anthropology* (New York: Free Press).

Storost, Jürgen (1988). 'Jacob Grimm und die Schleswig-Holstein-Frage. Zu den Kontroversen von 1850', *Brüder Grimm Gedenken*, 8: 64-80.

Strodthof, Werner (1976). *Stefan George: Zivilisationskritik und Eskapismus* (Bonn: Bouvier).

Suny, Ronald Grigor; Michael D. Kennedy (1999). *Intellectuals and the Articulation of the Nation* (Ann Arbor, MI: University of Michigan Press).

Sweet, Rosemary (2004). *Antiquaries: The Discovery of the Past in Eighteenth-Century Britain* (London: Hambledon & London).

Swiggers, Pierre; Piet Desmet (1996). 'L'élaboration de la linguistique comparative: Comparaison et typologie des langues jusqu'au début du XIXe siècle', in *Sprachtheorien der Neuzeit II*, ed. P. Schmitter (Tübingen: Narr): 122-177.

Swiggers, Pierre; Piet Desmet (2000). 'Histoire et épistémologie du comparatisme linguistique', in *Le comparatisme dans les sciences de l'homme*, ed. G. Jucquois & C. Vielle (Paris / Louvain-la-Neuve: De Boeck): 157-208.

Tacitus, P. Cornelius (1970). *Agricola, Germania, Dialogus* (ed./trl. M. Hutton & R.M. Ogilvie; Cambridge, MA: Harvard University Press).

Taruskin, Richard (2005). *The Oxford History of Western Music, 3: The Nineteenth Century* (Oxford: Oxford University Press).

Teich, Mikuláš; Roy Porter (eds.) (1993). *The National Question in Europe in Historical Context* (Cambridge: Cambridge University Press).

Teunissen, Harry; John Steegh (2003). *Balkan in kaart: Vijf eeuwen strijd om identiteit* (Leiden: Universiteitsbibliotheek Leiden).

Theleweit, Klaus (1980). *Männerphantasien* (2 vols; Reinbek: Rowohlt).

Thiesse, Anne-Marie (1999). *La création des identités nationales: Europe XVIIIe-XXe siècle* (Paris: Seuil).

Thomas, Keith (1984). *Man and the Natural World: Changing Attitudes in England 1500-1800* (Harmondsworth: Penguin).

Thurville-Petre, Torlac (1996). *England the Nation: Language, Literature, and National Identity, 1290-1340* (Oxford: Clarendon).

Tillion, Germaine (1966). *Le harem et les cousins* (Paris: Seuil).

Tilmans, Karin (1993). 'Aeneas, Bato and Civilis, the Forefathers of the Dutch: The Origin of the Batavian Tradition in Dutch Humanistic Historiography', in *Renaissance Culture in Context: Theory and Practice*, ed. J.R. Brink & W.F. Gentrup (Cambridge: Scolar Press): 121-135.

Todorova, Maria (1997). *Imagining the Balkans* (Oxford: Oxford University Press).

Tollebeek, Jo (1995). 'La Bataille des Eperons d'Or', in *Les grands mythes de l'histoire de Belgique, de Flandre et de Wallonie*, ed. A. Morelli (Bruxelles: Vie ouvrière): 205-218.

Tollebeek, Jo; Tom Verschaffel (1999). 'Het pantheon. De geschiedenis tot weinigen herleid', in *Mise-en-scène. Keizer Karel en de verbeelding van de negentiende eeuw*, ed. R. Hoozee, J. Tollebeek & T. Verschaffel (Antwerpen & Gent: Mercatorfonds & Museum voor schone kunsten Gent): 46-57.

Tollebeek, Jo; Tom Verschaffel (2000). '«A profitable company»: Het pantheon als historisch genre in het negentiende-eeuwse België', *Bijdragen en mededelingen tot de geschiedenis der Nederlanden*, 115 #2: 223-243.

Tollebeek, Jo; Tom Verschaffel (2004). 'Group Portraits with National Heroes: The Pantheon as an Historical Genre in Nineteenth-Century Belgium', *National Identities*, 6 #2: 91-106.

Tolstoy, Leo (1957). *War and Peace* (trl. R. Edmonds; 2 vols; Harmondsworth: Penguin).

Touchard, Jean (1968). *La gloire de Béranger* (2 vols; Paris: Colin).

Treaty (1947). *The Treaty of Versailles and After: Annotations of the Text of the Treaty* (Washington, D.C.: United States Government Printing Office).

Troost, Wout (2005). *William III, the Stadholder-King: A Political Biography* (Aldershot: Ashgate).

Trousson, Raymond (2003). *Jean-Jacques Rousseau* (Paris: Tallandier).

Unverfehrt, Gerd (1981). 'Arminius als nationale Leitfigur. Anmerkungen zu Entstehung und Wandel eines Reichssymbols', in *Kunstverwaltung, Bau und Denkmalpolitik*, ed. E. Mai & S. Waetzold (Berlin: Mann): 315-340.

Unwin, T.; V. Hewitt (2001). 'Banknotes and National Identity in Central and Eastern Europe', *Political Geography*, 20: 1005-1028.

Valensi, Lucette (2000). 'Traumatic Events and Historical Consciousness: Who is in Charge?', in *Historians and Social Values*, ed. J. Leerssen & A. Rigney (Amsterdam: Amsterdam University Press): 185-195.

Van Delft, Louis (1993). *Littérature et anthropologie: Caractère et nature humaine à l'âge classique* (Paris: Presses universitaires de France).

Van Delft, Louis (1996). 'Caractère et style', *Romanistische Zeitschrift für Literaturgeschichte*, 20 #1/2: 48-63.

Van der Linden (1930). 'Histoire de notre nom national', *Bulletin de la classe des lettres et des sciences morales et politiques (Académie Royale de Belgique)*, 5e série 16: 160-174.

Van Houtte, Hubert (1898). *Les Kerels de Flandre. Contribution à l'étude des origines ethniques de la Flandre* (Louvain: Peeters).

Van Houtte, Hubert (1934). 'Le baron Joseph Kervyn de Lettenhove (1817-1891)', in *La Commission Royale d'Histoire, 1834-1934: Livre jubilaire composé à l'occasion du centième anniversaire de sa fondation* (Bruxelles: Académie Royale de Belgique): 169-180.

Van Tieghem, Paul (1969 [1948]). *Le romantisme dans la littérature européenne* (2nd ed.; Paris: Michel).

Venturi, Franco (1971). *Utopia and Reform in the Enlightenment* (Cambridge: Cambridge University Press).

Verhandlungen (1847). *Verhandlungen der Germanisten zu Frankfurt am Main, am 24., 25. und 26. September 1846.* (Frankfurt: Sauerländer).

Verhandlungen (1848). *Verhandlungen der Germanisten zu Lübeck, am 27., 28. und 30. September 1847.* (Lübeck: Boldemann).

Verkooren, Alphons (ed.) (1916-1961). *Inventaire des chartes et cartulaires des duchés de Brabant et de Limbourg et des pays d'Outre-Meuse* (12 vols; Bruxelles: Hayez).

Verschaffel, Tom (1999). 'Aanschouwelijke Middeleeuwen. Historische optochten en vaderlandse drama's in het negentiende-eeuwse België', *Theoretische geschiedenis*, 26 #2: 129-148.

Verschoor, Andries David (1928). *Die ältere deutsche Romantik und die Nationalidee* (Amsterdam: H. J. Paris).

Viallaneix, Paul; Jean Ehrard (eds.) (1982). *Nos ancêtres les Gaulois. Actes du colloque international de Clermont-Ferrand* (Clermont-Ferrand: Faculté des Lettres et Sciences humaines de l'Université de Clermont-Ferrand II).

Viķe-Freiberga, Vaira (1985). 'Andrejs Pumpurs's *Lāčplēsis* («Bearslayer»): Latvian National Epic or Romantic Literary Creation?', in Loit, 523-536.

Virol, Michèle (2003). *Vauban: De la gloire du roi au service de l'état* (Seyssel: Champ Vallon).

Viroli, Maurizio (1995). *For Love of Country: An Essay on Patriotism and Nationalism* (Oxford: Clarendon Press).

Vlnas, Vit; Zdeněk Hojda (1998). 'Tschechien: «Gönnt einem jeden die Wahrheit»', in Flacke, 502-527.

Vocabolario (1863-1923). *Vocabolario degli Accademici della Crusca.* (5th ed.; 11 vols; Firenze: Tipografia Galileiana).

Vovelle, Michel (1997). '«La Marseillaise»', in Nora, 1: 107-152.

Wachtel, Andrew B. (1998). *Making a Nation, Breaking a Nation: Literature and Cultural Politics in Yugoslavia* (Stanford, CA: Stanford UP).

van der Wal, Mieke (1983). 'Krijgsheer of staatsman? De oprichtingsgeschiedenis van de twee standbeelden voor Willem de Zwijger in Den Haag', *Nederlandsch kunsthistorisch jaarboek*, 34: 39-72.

Walder, Ernst (ed.) (1948). *Das Ende des alten Reiches: Der Reichsdeputationshauptschluss von 1803 und die Rheinbundakte von 1806 nebst zugehörigen Aktenstücken* (Bern: Lang).

Walicki, Andrzej (1994). *Philosophy and Romantic Nationalism: The Case of Poland* (new ed.; Notre Dame, IN: University of Notre Dame Press).

Warner, Marina (1985). *Monuments and Maidens: The Allegory of the Female Form* (London: Weidenfeld & Nicolson).

Weber, Eugene (1976). *Peasants into Frenchmen: The Modernization of Rural France, 1870-1914* (Stanford, CA.: Stanford University Press).

Wes, M.A. (1980). 'Tussen Hermann en Hitler', in *Verslagen verleden. Over geschiedenis en oudheid* (Amsterdam: Wetenschappelijke uitgeverij): 124-231.

Wetzel, Christoph (ed.) (1983). *Brüder Grimm* (Salzburg: Andreas).

White, Harry; Michael Murphy (eds.) (2001). *Musical Constructions of Nationalism: Essays on the History and Ideology of European Musical Culture 1800-1945* (Cork: Cork University Press).

White, Hayden (1978). *Tropics of Discourse* (Baltimore, MD: Johns Hopkins University Press).

Wigard, Franz (ed.) (1848-50). *Stenographischer Bericht über die Verhandlungen der Deutschen Constituirenden Nationalversammlung zu Frankfurt am Main* (9 vols; Frankfurt: Sauerländer).

Willemyns, Roland (1994). 'Taalpolitiek in de Bourgondische tijd', *Verslagen en mededelingen van de Koninklijke Academie voor Nederlandse Taal- en Letterkunde*, 2 #3: 162-177.

Williams, Glanmor (1980). 'Wales: The Cultural Bases of Nineteenth and Twentieth Century Nationalism', in Mitchison, 119-129.

Williams, Gwyn A. (1985). *When was Wales? A History of the Welsh* (London: Penguin).

Williams, N.J.A. (ed.) (1981). *Pairlement Chloinne Tomáis* (Dublin: Dublin Institute for Advanced Studies).

Williams, Raymond (1973). *The Country and the City* (London: Chatto and Windus).

Wils, Lode (1994). *Vlaanderen, België, Groot-Nederland. Mythe en geschiedenis* (Leuven: Davidsfonds).

Wilson, Duncan (1970). *The Life and Times of Vuk Stefanović Karadžić, 1787-1864: Literacy, Literature and National Independence in Serbia* (Oxford: Clarendon Press).

Winock, Michel (1982). *Nationalisme, antisémitisme et fascisme en France* (Paris: Seuil).

Winter, Jay (1995). *Sites of Memory, Sites of Mourning. The Great War in European Cultural History* (Cambridge: Cambridge University Press).

von Wintzingerode-Knorr, Karl-Wilhelm (1999). 'Hoffmann von Fallersleben. Ein Leben im 19. Jahrhundert', in Behr et al., 11-33.

Wiseman, Nicholas (1866 [1835]). *Twelve Lectures on the Connexion Between Science and Revealed Religion, Delivered in Rome* (new ed.; Dublin).

Wolf, Louis B. (1968). *Louis XIV* (New York: Norton).

Wolff, Larry (1994). *Inventing Eastern Europe: The Map of Civilization on the Mind of the Enlightenment* (Stanford, CA: Stanford University Press).

Wolff, Larry (2001). *Venice and the Slavs. The Discovery of Dalmatia in the Age of Enlightenment* (Stanford, CA: Stanford University Press).

Woodward, David (1987). *Art and Cartography* (Chicago: University of Chicago Press).

Woolf, Stuart (ed.) (1996). *Nationalism in Europe, 1815 to the Present. A Reader* (London: Routledge).

van der Woud, Auke (1990). *De Bataafse hut: Verschuivingen in het beeld van de geschiedenis (1750-1850)* (Amsterdam: Meulenhoff).

Wyss, Ulrich (1979). *Die wilde Philologie: Jacob Grimm und der Historismus* (München: Beck).

Yamamoto, Dorothy (2000). *The Boundaries of the Human in Medieval English Literature* (Oxford: Oxford University Press).

Young, Charles R. (1979). *The Royal Forests of Medieval England* (Leicester: Leicester University Press).

Zacek, Joseph Frederick (1970). *Palacký. The Historian as Scholar and Nationalist* (The Hague: Mouton).

Zach, Wolfgang (1987). 'Das Stereotyp als literarische Norm. Zum dominanten Denkmodell des Klassizismus', in *Erstarrtes Denken. Studien zu Klischee, Stereotyp und Vorurteil in englischsprachiger Literatur*, ed. G. Blaicher (Tübingen: Narr): 97-113.

Zacharasiewicz, Waldemar (1977). *Die Klimatheorie in der englischen Literatur und Literaturkritik von der Mitte des 16. bis zum frühen 18. Jahrhundert* (Wien: Braumüller).

Zaitsev, Pavlo (1988). *Taras Shevchenko: A Life* (trl. G.S.N. Luckyj; Toronto: Toronto University Press).

Ziegerhofer-Prettenthaler, Anita (2004). *Botschafter Europas: Richard Nikolaus Coudenhove-Kalergi und die Paneuropa-Bewegung in den zwanziger und dreißiger Jahren* (Wien: Böhlau).

Zientara, Benedykt (1986). 'Populus, Gens, Natio: Einige Probleme aus dem Bereich der etnischen Terminologie des frühen Mittelalters', in *Nationalismus in vorindustrieller Zeit*, ed. O. Dann (München: Oldenbourg): 11-20.

Zink, Jochen (1982). 'Zur Vollendung des Kölner und Speyerer Doms. Mittelalterrezeption und frühe deutsche Denkmalpflege', in *Mittelalter-Rezeption. Gesammelte Vorträge des Salzburger Symposions*, ed. J. Kühnel, H.-D. Mück, U. Müller & U. Müller (3 vols; Göppingen: Kümmerle), 2: 169-194.

Ziolkowski (1990). *German Romanticism and its Institutions* (Princeton, NJ: Princeton University Press).

Index

Deken, Agatha 97
Delacroix, Eugène 132-133, 214-215
democracy 25, 51, 69, 71, 74-76, 89, 91-92, 132, 147-149, 173, 233, 235
Deutsches Wörterbuch 156, 179, 182, 200
dialects 54, 131, 138-139, 142, 148, 151, 154, 157, 168, 175, 178-181, 184, 195, 200, 208, 255-258, 260-264
diaspora, diaspora nationalism 163n., 174, 256
Dickens, Charles 61, 193
dictionaries 167, 200-201
Diderot, Denis 69
D'Indy, Vincent 192n.
Dix, Otto 232
Dobrovský, Josef 154
Dominian, Leon 220, 222
Down's Syndrome 212
Dreyfus, Alfred 213
Droste-Hülshoff, Annette von 194
Dryden, John 76
Du Bartas, Guillaume 65
dynasticism 37-39, 45, 71-73, 80, 84, 89, 106, 127-129, 133, 135, 142, 145-146, 187-188, 248
Dyserinck, Hugo 11, 16, 112, 268

Eça de Queirós, José Maria 216
education 13, 20, 63, 89, 139-140, 142, 145, 164, 167-168, 194, 239, 248-249
eisteddfod 157
Elias, Norbert 31n.
Eliot, George (Mary Ann Evans) 194
Eliot T.S. 194
Elizabeth I, queen 45, 47, 97, 237
Elizabeth II, queen 237
encyclopedia 55, 62, 70
Enlightenment 20-22, 66-67, 69-72, 75-76, 80, 82, 98-100, 110-112, 114, 138-140, 143, 160, 162, 227, 236, 245
Enlightenment Patriotism 22, 114, 162
enosis 174, 230
Entartung 207, 212, 216
epic 65, 78, 124-125, 168-169, 198-199, 202
essentialism 64, 210
Estates General 45, 84, 187
ETA 238
États généraux 87-89
ethnic nationalism 113, 170, 204, 231, 233-234, 242
ethnicity 13-14, 16-17, 64, 160-161, 165, 167, 207, 214, 220, 223, 229, 234, 251, 262

ethnotypes 11, 17, 20-21, 35, 40, 51, 56, 101, 154
eugenics 213-214
Euroscepticism 242-243
excursionistas 217
exoticism 25, 28, 30, 93, 101, 111, 196

Fallersleben *see* Hoffmann von Fallersleben
Fanon, Frantz 237
fascism 91, 148, 157, 173, 215, 217, 233-234, 245-246
Fauriel, Claude 197
Fawlty Towers 61
Feijoo, Benito Jerónimo 64
Fichte, Johann Gottlieb 107, 109, 113-114, 117-119, 122, 152, 211, 214, 216
filiki eteria 131-132
flags 187,187n.
folk, folklore, folksongs, folk- and fairytales 74, 97, 99-101, 119, 122, 130, 160, 169, 192-195, 197-198, 200n., 204, 239
forest 27-28, 31-33, 39, 42-43, 115
Fortuyn, Pim 246n.
Foucault, Michel 56
'Fourteen Points' 220-223, 227
Francis II, emperor 106
Franco, Francesco 91, 235n., 238-239, 245
Frank, Anne 246n.
Frankfurt Parliament 84, 109, 147-150, 155, 177, 179, 182-183
Franks 49-50, 146, 179, 184, 204, 207, 229
Frederick II, king 95
Freud, Sigmund 31n.
frontiers 52-54, 70, 151, 170, 173-176, 220-222, 228, 236-237, 266 *and see* borders

Galilei, Galileo 36
Galton, Sir Francis 213n.
Gandhi, Mohandas K. (Mahatma) 160, 237
Garašanin, Ilija 156, 174
Garibaldi, Giuseppe 151-153, 173, 236n.
Gaul, Gauls 26, 36-37, 39, 46, 49-51, 204, 207, 229, 256
Geist 108-110, 112
Gellner, Ernest 13-15, 163, 175, 265, 268
Gemeinschaft see community
Genette, Gérard 94
Geneva 45, 49, 66, 82, 84-86
geopolitics 52, 106, 151, 156, 170, 173, 220, 230
George IV, king 134-135, 186

Plato 109
playhouses *see* theatre
Pliny (C. Plinius Caecilius Secundius) 29-30
poetics 57-58, 60-61, 66, 111
polygenism *see* monogenism/polygenism
Pope, Alexander 186
Popović, Jovan Serija 202
popular sovereignty 22, 82-86, 89, 135, 137, 140, 218
Powell, Enoch 244, 244n.
Powell, Michael 194, 238
Prešeren, France 198
Pressburger, Emeric 194, 238
Price, Richard 79 and n.
Prichard, James Cowles 207, 211
primitivism 36-37, 39, 43, 49-51, 66, 75, 81
printing 36, 42, 54-55, 162
Protocols of the Elders of Zion 213
public opinion 88, 94, 96, 135, 161-163, 178, 182, 185, 213
public spaces 94, 127, 142, 162, 169, 188-190
public sphere 93, 96, 140, 161-162, 166-167, 203, 219, 246, 248-249, 262
Pugin, Nicholas 189
Pumpurs, Andrejs 198
Pushkin, Alexander 111n., 125, 192n., 203

race 16-17, 80, 154, 155, 196-197, 204, 207-213, 215-217, 220, 222, 228-231, 237, 261
Racine, Jean 95
Rakovski, Georgi 237
Rangavis, Alexandros 125
Ranke, Leopold von 124
Rapin, René 94
Rask, Rasmus 180-182, 184, 260
Reagan, Ronald 242n.
Rechtsstaat 74
regionalism 136, 138, 158, 239-241
Reinaert 199
Reitz, Edgar 194
religion 37, 42, 44-45, 49, 59, 63-64, 66, 68, 83, 118, 140n., 142-143, 160, 175-176, 206, 219, 229, 234, 237, 245, 247, 249-250, 259
Remarque, Erich Maria 232
Rembrandt van Rijn 47, 192
Renan, Ernest 158, 227-231, 233-234, 249
Rhine 37, 42-43, 47, 49, 53, 56, 72-74, 105, 107-108, 114-115, 141, 157, 178, 189-190
Richardson, Samuel 81, 97
Richelieu, Louis de 52
risorgimento 145, 153, 173, 200

rituals 74, 127, 186, 195, 250
Robespierre, Maximilien 84, 90-91, 250
Rodenbach, Albrecht 206n.
Rohmer, Sax 217
Rolls Series 199
Romanticism 20-22, 72, 82, 97, 99, 100-101, 105, 107, 109-114, 116-118, 121, 126, 128-130, 133-135, 140, 145-153, 155-156, 159, 161, 165, 168, 187-188, 193, 195, 197-198, 201-204, 218, 220, 222, 232, 237-238, 263
Rome 36-37, 39, 42-44, 47, 49-51, 74-75, 85, 152-153, 186, 233, 239, 250, 258, 262
Roobol, W.H. 16, 232n.
Rost van Tonningen, Florentine 245
Rousseau, Jean-Jacques 51, 66, 68, 71, 78, 81-86, 88-92, 101, 110n., 113, 119, 125, 135, 152, 170, 230, 248
Runeberg, Johan Ludvig 117, 168
rustic novel 193

Sacher-Masoch, Leopold von 216
Sade, Donatien Alphonse François de 81
Šafárik, Pavol 155
Saint-Just, Louis Léon Antoine de 90
Salazar, António 235n.
Sand, George 193
Sands, Bobby 157
Sartre, Jean-Paul 238
Savigny, Friedrich Carl von 122-123
Saxons 48-50, 146, 156, 176, 179, 184, 205-207, 229
Scaliger, Julius Caesar 56-57
Schelling, Friedrich Wilhelm Joseph 109
Schiller, Friedrich 96-97, 109, 202, 272-273
Schlegel, August Wilhelm 122
Schlegel, Friedrich 107, 114-115, 118-119, 121-122, 260
Schleicher, August 208, 208n.
Schleiermacher, Friedrich 114, 118
Schneckenburger, Max 178, 187
Schottelius, Justus Georg 182n.
Schubert, Franz 99
Scott, Sir Walter 49, 111n., 124-125, 127, 134-135, 153-154, 186, 197, 199, 202-203, 205-206, 262
sculpture *see* monuments
secularization 120
self-image 16-17, 40, 45, 51, 112, 161-162, 167, 195, 197
Seneca (L. Annaeus Seneca) 31
Senghor, Léopold Sédar 237

sentimental comedy 81, 94-95, 97
Shaftesbury, Anthony Ashley Cooper, lord
    76, 94
Shakespeare, William 60, 95, 110, 122, 198,
    202
Shelley, Mary Wollstonecraft 202
Shelley, Percy Bysshe 110, 111n., 130
Shevchenko, Taras 117
Sibelius, Jean 192
Sienkiewicz, Henryk 203n.
Sieyès, Emmanuel 86-88, 105, 113, 138, 204
Slavic Congress 155
Smetana, Bedřich 192, 192n.
Smith, A.D. 13-17, 268
Sneedorf, Jens Schielderup 140
sociability, societies 20, 66, 69, 76-77, 99,
    130-131, 158n., 161-162, 166-167, 169, 200,
    217
Sokol 217
Solinus, C. Iulius 29
Solomós, Dionysos 117
Solon 75
sources, source editions 39, 124, 143, 197-199,
    202
south see north/south
Southey, Robert 111n.
sovereignty 248 and see popular sovereignty
Spalatin, Georg 42
Sparta 75, 91-92, 273
Spectator 94n.
Spengler, Oswald 216
Sperber, Dan 19, 269
sports 91, 108, 217
St. Denis 127, 134, 187
Staatsnation see Kulturnation
Stalin (Iosif Vissarionovich Dzugashvili) 91
Stanford, Charles Villiers 192n.
statues see monuments
Stein, Karl vom 108
Steinthal, Heymann 210, 210n.
stereotypes 17, 56, 58, 62, 65-67, 70, 110, 112,
    209-210
Stevenson, Robert Louis 212, 216
Strasbourg 53, 72n., 74, 150, 178, 189, 228-
    229, 239
style 61n.
Sue, Eugène 204-205, 213
Sukarno 237n.
Suttner, Bertha von 231
Swedberg, Jesper 140
Swift, Jonathan 76

Swift, Graham 194
Sydney, Algernon 84

Tacitus, P. Cornelius 38-39, 41, 43, 47-51, 71,
    74-75, 83, 114, 121, 217
Taine, Hippolyte 228-229
taxonomy 55-56, 64, 70, 180, 259
Tchaikovsky, Pyotr Ilyich 192n.
Tegnér, Esaias 124
Tell, Wilhelm 75, 97, 153, 202
temperament 57, 60, 65, 234
Teutonic Order 28, 127
Thatcher, Margaret 239
theatre 73, 94, 96-97, 162, 202-203
Theophrastos 60, 93n.
Thierry, Amédée and/or Augustin 204, 206
Thiesse, Anne-Marie 19
Third Reich 207, 213
tiers état 86, 88-89, 204
Tito, Josip Broz 237n., 242
Toland, John 75n.
Tollens, Hendrik 188
Tolstoy, Lev Nikolaevich 194, 197, 203-204,
    231
Tönnies, Ferdinand 193
totalitarianism 90-92, 170, 214, 223, 227, 233-
    234, 236, 245
Turnverein 108, 217

Uhland, Ludwig 147
Unamuno, Miguel de 237

Van Duyse, Prudens 263
Vartabed, Komitas 192
Varus, P. Quinctilius 42
Vasa, Gustav 75, 202
Vasari, Giorgio 38n.
Vauban, Sébastien de 52-53, 72
Vaughan Williams, Ralph 192-193
Velestinlis, Rigas 237
Venelin, Yurii 166
Venice 45, 66, 85, 105, 153, 173
Venturi, Franco 75-76
Vercingetorix 39
Verdi, Giuseppe 153, 173, 192n.
Verfassungspatriotismus 249
Verlooy, Jan-Baptist 140n.
Versailles 74, 88, 95, 150, 152, 219, 223-234,
    227, 232
vertical see horizontal/vertical
vice 26, 31, 40, 64, 93-94